The Spectral Army of Souther Fell:

The Story of a Story

Stephen Matthews

BOOKCASE

George Smith's map of the Caudebec Fells as it appeared in The Gentlemen's Magazine *in 1747. Detail showing the area around Souther Fell.*

First edition 2011

ISBN 978 1904 147 55 8
Bookcase, 19 Castle Street, Carlisle, CA3 8SY
01228 544560 bookcasecarlisle@aol.com
Printed by CPI Antony Rowe

Preface

The Spectral Army of Souther Fell is a story I've half-known since childhood. Two years ago, driving beneath the fell with some friends, I realised I did not really know it at all.

Since then I've followed a trail that has led me through neglected byways of history, literature, science, parapsychology, folk-lore and much more besides.

The story of the Spectral Army acquired a life of its own after the sightings during the years before the Jacobite Rebellion. Within a hundred years, it had been translated into many languages and travelled all round the globe. It attracted the attention of some of the greatest writers of all time: William Wordsworth, Samuel Taylor Coleridge and Sir Walter Scott and of others such as James Hogg and Allan Cunningham who deserve to be more widely read. It also proved irresistible to some far lesser poets and novelists who found that such a story lent itself to patriotic verse and risque stories. Leading thinkers such as Harriet Martineau and Sir David Brewster found it worthy of their attention and charlatans found that such a well attested tale served their purpose.

The story itself originated with a most interesting man, George Smith of Wigton, who has been unjustly neglected in the history of the Lake Counties. He had much to say about the Lakes before anyone else and he played an adventurous part during the Jacobite revolution.

Following the story through the years, I find that, in observing the details by the way, I have written several partial histories. There is the unfolding tale of how people came to appreciate the scenery of the Lakes. There is the way in which people thought, especially about the supernatural, changed over two centuries. There is the story of the '45 Rebellion and especially the siege of Carlisle and there are the lives of some extra-ordinary people.

Above everything, there is the landscape itself: Souther Fell, Blencathra, Carrock and Ullswater seen through the eyes of many different people.

All-in-all, it has proved a rich and fascinating trail.

I have quoted many writers at length, partly because their work is not readily obtainable and partly for the pleasure and period interest of the writing itself.

The name, Souther Fell, is found in various forms: Southerfell, Souter Fell and Souterfell, as well as Soutrafell and Soutra Fell, which, I suspect, are coinages by Allan Cunningham.

The photograph of Souther Fell on the front cover is by Delores Claire Storr. (www.deloresstorr.com)

Contents

Chapter One: Chinese Whispers 7
Chapter Two: The Original Accounts 18
Chapter Three: George Smith and James Clarke 37
Chapter Four: The Jacobites 58
Chapter Five: Ann Radcliffe and Britton & Brayley 89
Chapter Six: Coleridge and the Wordsworths 103
Chapter Seven: Sir Walter Scott 130
Chapter Eight: David Brewster and the Scientists 144
Chapter Nine: James Hogg 166
Chapter Ten: Allan Cunningham 192
Chapter Eleven: John Charles Bristow 220
Chapter Twelve: White, Gresley and Soane 231
Chapter Thirteen: Harriet Martineau 252
Chapter Fourteen: Conclusion 282
Notes 303
Bibliography 312
Index 314

George Smith's map of the Caudebec Fells as it appeared in The Gentlemen's Magazine *in 1747.*
Detail showing the upper Caldew valley

Chapter One:

Chinese Whispers

Let us begin with the words of Harriet Martineau. She was a woman of great reputation and authority, a political journalist of the first order, a bold anti-slavery campaigner and an acute observer of society, a woman and an atheist, forceful, moral, radical, rational and stone-deaf; the acquaintance of everyone from William Wordsworth to John Stuart Mill, a woman who had settled in Ambleside in 1842 when she was 42 years old, and built her home there, a woman who championed the Lakes and, with admirable energy, researched and wrote the most influential of Victorian guidebooks to the English Lakes. Her "true presentation of the land we love" was published in 1855. Even she seemed torn between superiority and delight when she came to tell the story of the spectral army of Souther Fell:

"Souther Fell, over which we have just passed, is the very home of superstition and romance. This Souther or Soutra Fell, is the mountain on which ghosts appeared in myriads, at intervals during ten years of the last century; presenting the same appearances to twenty-six chosen witnesses and to all the inhabitants of all the cottages within view of the mountain; and for the space of two hours and a half at one time – the spectral show being closed by darkness! The mountain – be it remembered is full of precipices, which defy all marching of bodies of men; and the north and west sides present a sheer perpendicular of 900 feet. On Midsummer eve, 1735, a farm servant of Mr. Lancaster's, half a mile from the mountain, saw the eastern side of its summit covered with troops, which pursued their march for about an hour. They came, in distinct bodies, from an eminence on the north end, and disappeared in a niche at the summit. When the poor fellow told his tale, he was insulted on all hands; as original observers usually are when they see anything wonderful. Two years after – also on a midsummer eve, - Mr. Lancaster saw some men there, apparently following their horses, as if they had returned from hunting. He thought nothing of this; but he happened to look up again ten minutes after, and saw the figures, now mounted, and followed by an interminable array of troops, five abreast, marching from the eminence and over the cleft as before. All the family saw this, and the manoeuvres of the force, as each company was kept in order by a mounted officer, who galloped this way and that. As the shades of twilight came on, the discipline appeared to relax and the troops intermingled, and rode at unequal paces, till all was lost in darkness. Now, of course, all the Lancasters were insulted, as their servants had been: but their justification was not long delayed. On the midsummer eve of the fearful 1745, twenty-six persons, expressly summoned by the family, saw all that had been seen, and more. Carriages were now interspersed with the troops; and everybody knew that no carriages ever had been, or could be, on the summit of Souther Fell. The multitude was beyond imagination; for the troops filled a space of half a mile, and marched quickly until night hid them, - still marching. There was nothing vaporous or indistinct about the appearance of these spectres. So real did they seem, that some of the people went up the next morning to look for the hoof marks of the horses; and awful was it for them to find not one footprint on heather or grass. The witnesses attested the whole story on oath before a magistrate; and fearful were the expectations held by the whole country side about the coming events of the Scotch rebellion. It now came out that two others had seen something of the sort in the interval, viz., in 1743, but had concealed it, to escape the insults to which their neighbours were subjected. Mr. Wren of Wilton Hall, and his farm servant, saw, one summer evening, a man and a dog on the mountain, pursuing some horses along a place so steep that a horse by any possibility could keep a footing on it. Their speed was prodigious, and their disappearance at the south end of the fell so rapid, that Mr. Wren and the servant went up the next morning, to find the body of the man, who must have been killed. Of man, horse or dog, they found not a trace: and they came down and held their tongues. When they did speak, they fared not much better for having twenty-six sworn comrades in their disgrace. As for the explanation, - the Editor of the 'Lonsdale Magazine' declared (Vol. II. p.313) that it was discovered that on that midsummer eve of 1745, the rebels were 'exercising on the western coast of Scotland, whose movements had been reflected by some transparent vapour, similar to the Fata Morgana'. This is not much in the way of explanation: but it is, as far as we know, all that can be had at present. These facts, however, brought out a good many more; as the spectral march of the same kind seen in Leicestershire, in 1107: and the tradition of the tramp of armies over Helvellyn, on the eve of the battle of Marston Moor. And now the tourist may proceed, - looking for ghosts, if he pleases, on Souther Fell."[1]

Harriet Martineau, with her credentials, sceptical, rational, a sociologist and historian of rare distinction, must be one of the most reliable of all reporters. But she was dealing with a ghost story and she was keen to encourage people to come to her beloved Lakes and that throwaway phrase at the end about "looking for ghosts" may suggest that she was not quite as serious or credulous as she might appear. She was retailing a story that was over a century old at the time and one that had gone through so many revisions and retellings and redactions that we can reasonably claim that it had come to have a life of its own.

Stories, especially ghost stories, are like living creatures, they grow and change and mutate. A word is altered, a detail lost, a plot summarised, atmosphere or character is added, a little local colour here or there, a slight fudging of the facts and the story, that was once the careful telling of a real, if perhaps imagined, experience, is transformed.

The story of the spectral army of Souther Fell has suffered more than most from this process of Chinese whispers in the two hundred and fifty years of its telling and retelling. The sightings appear to have caused something of a sensation. The first account we have was written in 1747, two years after the last sighting, by a gentleman who had purposely ventured into the remote lands hidden beneath Saddleback. He talked of it as an event with which his readers were already well acquainted: "It was on this fell that the astonishing phaenomenon appeared to exhibit itself, which in 1735, 1737, and 1745, made so much noise in the north, that I went on purpose to examine the spectators, who asserted the fact, and continue in their assertion very positively to this day."

This gentleman, George Smith, published his account in *The Gentleman's Magazine* in 1747. The only other account we have that took its evidence directly from the original witnesses was written forty years later by James Clarke and published in his *A Survey of the Lakes* in 1787.

Together, these two very different accounts laid the foundations of a ghost story that has been felt to be among the best authenticated and most convincing that we have. It is a story that still excites the imagination.

The most recent account I have read comes from a book about the parish of Mungrisedale. Colin Smith has written a useful guide to *Mungrisdale Heritage Trails* and his view, apparently quoting from earlier sources, gives us a taste of how people in the area might be aware of this remarkable story: "On midsummer evening in 1735 a servant in the employ of William Lancaster of Blake Hills Farm related seeing an army 'marching five abreast for a solid hour', along the ridge of Souther Fell which forms the backcloth to the farm. He was belittled for his tale. On Midsummer's Day 1745, ten years after the first appearance of the army, 'twenty-six persons, expressly summoned by the family, saw all that had been seen before and more. Carriages were now interspersed with troops'. The witnesses attested the whole story on oath before a magistrate. Later in 1743, Mr. Wren, of Wilton Hill, and his farm servant saw 'a man and his dog on Souther fell pursuing some horses along a place so steep that a horse could hardly, by any possibility, keep a footing on it. They 'held their tongue' until much later."[2]

Tony Walker, in *The Ghostly Guide to the Lake District*, published ten years ago, was summarily dismissive: "The last shoulder of the mountain to your left is called Souther Fell. On Midsummer's Eve in 1735, two farm workers saw a ghost army marching, rank after rank, for over an hour over this fell. In 1745 many people saw the army again - also on Midsummer's Eve. As far as I know it hasn't been seen since."[3]

Gerald Findler in two books written within a few years of each other offered two divergent accounts. In 1967, in *Legends of the Lake Counties* he reported as follows: "In 1774, a certain Daniel Strickland was out walking on Souter Fell on Midsummer's day, and was startled by what he saw. There in front of him was a troop of horsemen, dressed in uniforms with which he was not acquainted, all mounted on fine looking horses. He was even more surprised when the horsemen rode up a slope far too steep for any horse to ascend. He reported this unusual spectacle to the villagers nearby, and it was discovered that similar incidents had been recorded in 1734 and 1745. The latter instance may have been a mirage, a reflection of the Jacobite troops who were manoeuvering some distance to the north."[4]

When Gerald Findler returned to this "best authenticated" story in 1975, in a book titled *Ghosts of the Lake Counties*, he had changed the dates, developed detail, added a certain amount of local alcoholic colour, and offered some speculative explanation: "The best authenticated ghost story of all time is told, not of a solitary ghost or a large phantom dog or a mysterious coach being drawn by four fiery horses - no, none of these weird sights - but that of a full army of marching ghosts. In 1735 on Souter Fell near Saddleback, two farmworkers were astonished when they saw in the distance an army of men marching five abreast for a solid hour, each rank in turn disappearing over a sheer precipice. Very much afraid, after the phantom army had disappeared, they rushed away to tell of what they had seen. Their friends thought the two men had just had a little drop too much to drink because it was a very hot Midsummer's Eve.

"But three years later the Souter Fell Army was seen again, not by the same two men but by thirty or more people. One man actually timed the first appearance of the soldiers until the final disappearance - and it took two hours. In the year 1745, ten years after the first appearance of the ghost army, hundreds of people witnessed this strange sight on Midsummer's Eve. So certain were some of the people present that they walked to the place where the army had passed to look for footprints but they found none.

"It has been suggested that this was a 'Brocken' spectre, formed of actual marching men on the clouds, but where was the real army at the time? Why would the same army be seen at various intervals of years if it was a reflection? And why was such a spectre only seen on a Midsummer's Eve if it was a reflection of a live army?"[5]

A. H. Griffin, climber and *Guardian* correspondent and one of the finest of all writers on the Lake District, had little time for the detail of the story and introduced his own extraneous details: "But the phantom army of Souther Fell, the eastern outlier of Blencathra, was never really explained, although it was said to have been seen three times - in 1735, 1737 and 1745. A large army, they said - troops, horses and gun carriages - moving across the fell, but no foot-prints or hoof marks were ever found. First a farm servant saw it, then the farmer's whole family and then, in 1745, so they say, most of the population of Threlkeld and district. Each time on Midsummer Eve. On the last occasion there was said to be a Jacobite army on manoeuvres somewhere in the south of Scotland and the explanation offered was that, in some strange way, the reflection had been thrown on to Souther Fell. But this was far from a satisfactory story and the whole business remains a fascinating mystery."[6]

In all these accounts the tale is confused. Dates and sightings and detail are treated with careless abandon. Yet, Gerald Findler was a man with considerable knowledge of local folklore. For many years he was editor of *John Peel Jottings*, a curious little magazine that was published monthly by Redmaynes, the Cumberland Tailors in Wigton, who specialized in producing quality suits for local farmers. He was also an entertainer, who had performed in over a thousand troop shows making lightning cartoons, tearing paper and doing magic tricks.

Alfred Wainwright, somewhat grumpily, included Souther Fell in *Book Five* of *A Pictorial Guide to the Lakeland Fells*, which covered the Northern Fells.[7] In 1961, he was seven years into his massive task of meticulously drawing and writing a detailed account of every every footpath on every fell in the Lake District and he had found the low rounded slopes of Souther Fell less than sympathetic. It was "of little merit as a climb and of unattractive appearance". He did, however, empathize with the remarkable Glenderamackin "which encircles its base almost completely like a great moat, with the narrow Mousthwaite col serving as a drawbridge". The river starts as a "trickle from a marsh below the col" and "soon gathers strength and aims purposefully for a gap in the hills to the south, eager to be away from its desolate place of birth and join other waters in a tranquil and pleasant passage through Lakeland". The young river is turned east "and then a greater disappointment – Souther Fell thrusts across the route". Having been turned east and south, "Hope revives . . . and almost encircling Souther Fell, a sudden and glorious view of Lakeland opens up to the west, the way thereto at last being clear, and lying through sylvan meadows and rocky gorges and woodlands and great lakes". Souther Fell, it seems, was to be blamed for frustrating the Glenderamackin's infant aspirations.

Wainwright had actually enjoyed the solitude of the Northern Fells, "a place of no false notes in this peaceful symphony, no discords, no harshness", and he provided his own eulogy of the local people: "I must mention the grand people of the little communities around the base of these fells . . . Sturdily independent, here are folk, unspoiled by 'tourism', whose roots go deep in their own soil. Ever alert for sights and sounds on the fellsides or in the valley fields, their work is their life. It is a pleasure to be in their company, an honour to be in their confidence."

With such faith in the observation of the native inhabitants, it is not surprising that the down-to-earth AW offered a very positive account, in neat but cramped calligraphy, of "The Spectral Army of Souther Fell":

"This is no legend.

"This is the solemn truth, as attested on oath before a magistrate by 26 sober and respected witnesses. These good people assembled on the evening before Midsummer day 1745 at a place of vantage in the valley to the east to test incredulous reports that soldiers and horsemen had been seen marching across the top of Souter Fell (Soutra Fell was probably the name in those days). They saw them all right: an unbroken line of quickly moving troops, horses and carriages extending over the full length of the top of Souter, continuously appearing at one end and vanishing at the other – and passing unhesitatingly over steep places that horses and carriages could not possibly negotiate, as the bewildered observers well knew. The procession went on until darkness concealed the marching army. Next morning the skyline was deserted, and a visit to the summit was made by a party of local worthies fearful that the expected invasion from over the border had started (this was the year of the '45 Rebellion). There was not a trace of the previous night's visitors. Not a footprint, not a hoofmark, not a wheel rut in the grass. Nothing.

"There was no doubting the evidence of so many witnesses, and yet it was equally certain that the marching army had no substance. Scientists and students of the supernatural had no solution to offer. The only explanation ever given was of some kind of a mirage had been seen, probably a vaporous reflection of Prince Charlie's rebels, who (it was discovered on enquiry) had that very evening been exercising on the west coast of Scotland . . . This beats radar."

To complete his account, Wainwright squeezed in a picture of Souther Fell, outlined with a single bumpy line, surmounted by a dense pack of short vertical lines looking more like bristles on a rough-hewn chin than a marching army.

Three twentieth century accounts avoided Chinese whispers by the simple expedient of quoting the original account by George Smith at length. Ex-editor of *The West Cumberland Times*, Frank Carruthers, writing in *Lore of the Lake Country* was disdainful of Smith's apparently ridiculous exaggerations. He justified himself, quite reasonably, by quoting from Smith's account: "Smith, not averse to creating a wrong impression among readers who were unlikely to check on his findings, was on form: . . . in the neighbourhood of Mosedale he found 'villages in the narrow bottoms that feel no more benefit from the solar rays for two months, about the winter solstice, than the old Cimmerians, or the Laplanders who inhabit the North cape of Norway'."

Carruthers referred to Clarke's account, but failed to take it seriously and did not note the disparities between Smith's and Clarke's versions of the same events obtained from, possibly, the same witnesses. "It was forty years after the army's last march that Clarke came along, and added little to the original account except to give the name of Mr. Lancaster's servant, who first observed the phenomenon, as Daniel Stricket, whom Clarke found living under Skiddaw and had come on in the world to the extent that he was now an auctioneer, which, the cynic might say, was a happy choice of career for a man who could sell a ghost army to an entire community."

Frank Carruthers noted that Clarke's account extended the length of the last vision to two and a half hours, "which was an advance on the 'above an hour' which Lancaster had recorded". He was also ambiguous about his witnesses' statements saying that "Clarke obtained from those who said they had seen the ghost army an attestation stating: 'We, whose names are hereto subscribed, declare the above account to be true, and that we saw the phenomenon as here related. As witness our hands this 21st day of July, 1785.' " He speculated that, "The date of the declaration suggests that Clarke had probably been in the district on Midsummer Day that year in the hope of seeing the ghost army for himself, and not having seen it - probably having expressed some doubt about it - goaded the local inhabitants into making and signing their attestation".[8]

The most thorough modern version of the matter was by J. A. Brooks and appeared in his book *Ghosts and Legends of the Lake District*, in 1988. "This is the most famous of all the ghost stories of the Lake District," he claimed and he printed Smith's version as it is found in William Hutchinson's *History of the County of Cumberland*. The earlier version he mistakenly credited to the second volume of *The Lonsdale Magazine* of 1749, (which did not appear until 1819) rather than *The Gentleman's Magazine* of 1747. He then repeated the idea that the vision was of "a rebel army exercising on the western coast of Scotland at this time whose movements were reflected 'by some fine transparent vapour similar to the Fata Morgana'".[9]

Brooks followed Carruthers in not being able to resist a dig at the poor farm servant, Daniel Stricket, who had risen in the world sufficiently to become an auctioneer: "The cynical might say that anyone in this line of business must be able to exaggerate anything." He also confused James Clarke with a Rev. C.C. Clarke who, we are told, included *The Ghost Army* in his book *One Hundred Wonders of the World*. A Rev. C.C. Clarke did publish a book, in 1818, called *The Hundred Wonders of the World And of the three Kingdoms of Nature, described according to the best and latest authorities and illustrated by engravings*, which was a compendium of scientific papers presented for a popular audience, but it made no mention of the ghostly army of Souther Fell.

Brooks was similarly ambiguous in having all surviving witnesses of the event "sign an affidavit". Like Carruthers he speculatively dramatized the little scene between his supposedly clerical Clarke and his witnesses: "Perhaps the sensation seeking clergyman bullied the locals into signing, pointing out that they could hardly dilute their account at this time, forty years on, when the Ghost Army was already a legend".

Brooks discussed the matter of spectral armies further and cited instances of their appearance being recorded by authors as diverse as the medieval Walter Mapp and the mountaineer F. S. Smythe. Mapp described "this company of Herlethingi last espied in the Marches of Hereford and

Wales in the first year of King Henry II, tramping along at high noon with carts and beasts of burden, with pack saddles and provender baskets, with birds and dogs and a mixed multitude of men and women". He also mentioned other phantom armies seen after the Battle of Culloden, after Marston Moor (on Helvellyn) and the well-known apparition of the Civil War battle of Edgehill to shepherds on a Christmas Eve after the battle. This sighting was said to have been investigated by a commission at the command of King Charles and they subsequently reported that they had seen the army and been able to identify individuals who were known to have been killed.

By far the most intelligent account of the spectral army was given by Norman Nicholson in *The Lakers*, a book which has been such an important pioneer in the discussion of the appreciation of the Lakeland landscape. His view of the legend put it neatly in its historical context. The story of the spectral army of Souther Fell gained currency at just that time when the rational temper of an educated elite was discovering and being entertained by the different and the exotic. The Highlands of Scotland and the tales of Ossian, the legends of Ireland and the imagination of the Middle Ages were an almost necessary tensor to the easy order of the enlightened mind. Nicholson put the matter succinctly: "Here is a tale which contained much the travellers were seeking. To begin with, though it had the tone, the timbre, of a medieval romance, it was set in a near-present, the mid-eighteenth century, and because it was founded on evidence at no more than secondhand, it seemed almost contemporary, almost subject to verification, belonging among curiosities rather than folklore. There were good, reliable sounding names like that of William Lancaster to witness for the event, and even that of Daniel Sticket who - and this should dispose of any further doubt - was an auctioneer.

"It is not likely that any of the tourists really believed the story, but it had just the apparently objective, quasi-scientific sound which made it plausible in that quasi-scientific age. There was a queer suggestion of a mirage, perhaps a time-mirage by which the people of Souter Fell had been able to see an event that had not taken place. Again the fact that the last recorded appearances were in 1745 linked them with the Rebellion, and therefore with Scotland and the wild Highlanders and all the romantic lawlessness which Hanoverian England could now afford to regard with condescending pleasure. But these figures were prophetic of much more than the invasion of the Young Pretender. They were prophetic of new explorings of the imagination, of the re-appearance of half-forgotten symbols, of movements in and out of consciousness on strange unturnpiked regions of the human mind. Some of that exploring was to take place among these very hills, and the mist in which these phantoms precipitated and dissolved like a sediment was soon to surge and simmer through *Christabel* and *The White Doe of Rylstone*, to mingle with the opium fumes of De Quincey's dreams, and to ascend like prayers to the adolescent saints who dropped roses into the delirium of the aged John Ruskin."[10] He then quoted the central paragraphs of George Smith's account as it is found in Hutchinson.

You will notice that even Norman Nicholson could not resist having a dig at the auctioneer. However, Nicholson's perceptive and suggestive picture of the legend in its own time, why it caught the imagination of contemporaries and succeeding generations and how it was treated by the writers and scientists of the early nineteenth century, is very much the theme of this book.

The spectral army of Souther Fell is not simply one of the best and most convincing of ghost stories. It became a touchstone for the values of the Romantic era. It intrigued poets and novelists for the succeeding hundred years and was a stimulus to scientific speculation.

First, however, it will be necessary to look carefully at the original accounts of the legend on which all the later speculation was based.

Chapter Two:

The Original Accounts

The first extant account we have of the sighting of the spectral army on Souther Fell is in *The Gentleman's Magazine* for November, 1747. The article, *A Journey to the Caudebec Fells with a Map and Description of the Same*[1] was listed as both the "Natural History of the Cumberland Fells, strange sight there" and as "Cumberland mountains described – Plants and mines there – Strange phenomenon on them" and the accompanying copper-plate map was described as "A view of a desolate and mountainous part of Cumberland". It was published more than two years after the last event of which it gave an account. No author was cited, but William Hutchinson, when he reprinted the article in 1795, identified it as the work of one of the magazine's regular correspondents, a Mr. George Smith of Wigton.

Smith talked of going with the express intention of making first-hand inquiries into "the astonishing phaenomenon" that had so excited the public's imagination: "It was on this fell that the astonishing phaenomenon appeared to exhibit itself, which in 1735, 1737, and 1745, made so much noise in the north, that I went on purpose to examine the spectators, who asserted the fact, and continue in their assertion very positively to this day." There is a degree of scepticism in his tone. Smith was a man with a scientific background, keen to provide an accurate record for his educated and literate readers of events that had taken place in some of the most remote and benighted regions of the country. His account reads as follows:

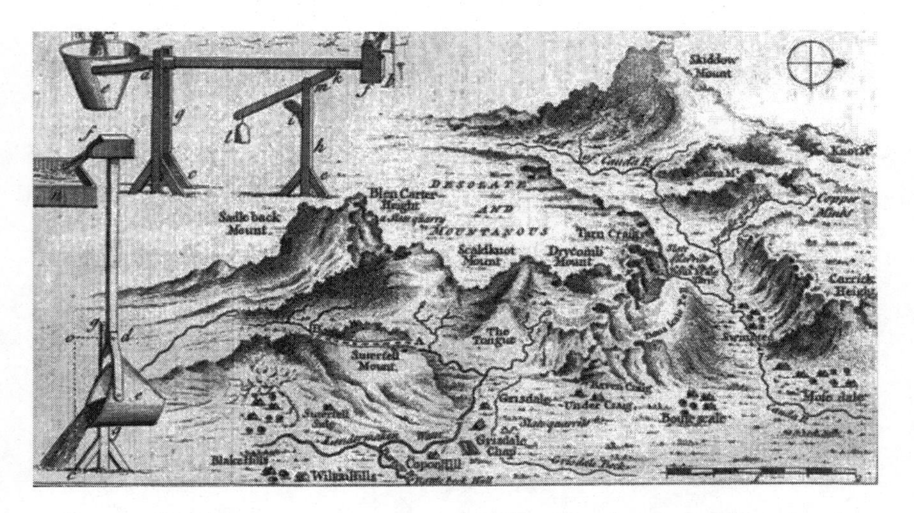

George Smith's map as it appeared in The Gentleman's Magazine *in 1747. The diagrams on the left illustrate a device for raising water.*

"Souter-fell is a distinguished mountain of itself, encompassed quite round with a turbinated trough, through which Lender-maken is conveyed. The west and the north sides are barricadoed with rocks; the east is more plain, but withal steep, and seemingly 900 yards in height; but every where of difficult access. It was on this fell that the astonishing phaenomenon appeared to exhibit itself, which in 1735, 1737, and 1745, made so much noise in the north, that I went on purpose to examine the spectators, who asserted the fact, and continue in their assertion very positively to this day.

"On Midsummer eve, 1735, William Lancaster's servant related, that he saw the east side of Souter-fell, towards the top, covered with a regular marching army for above an hour together; he said they consisted of distinct bodies of troops, which appeared to proceed from an eminence in the north end, and marched over a niche in the top (marked A and B in the place) but, as no other person in the neighbourhood had seen the like, he was discredited and laughed at. Two years after, on Midsummer eve also, betwixt the hours of eight and nine, William Lancaster himself imagined that several gentlemen were following their horses at a distance, as if they had been hunting, and taking them for such, he paid no regard

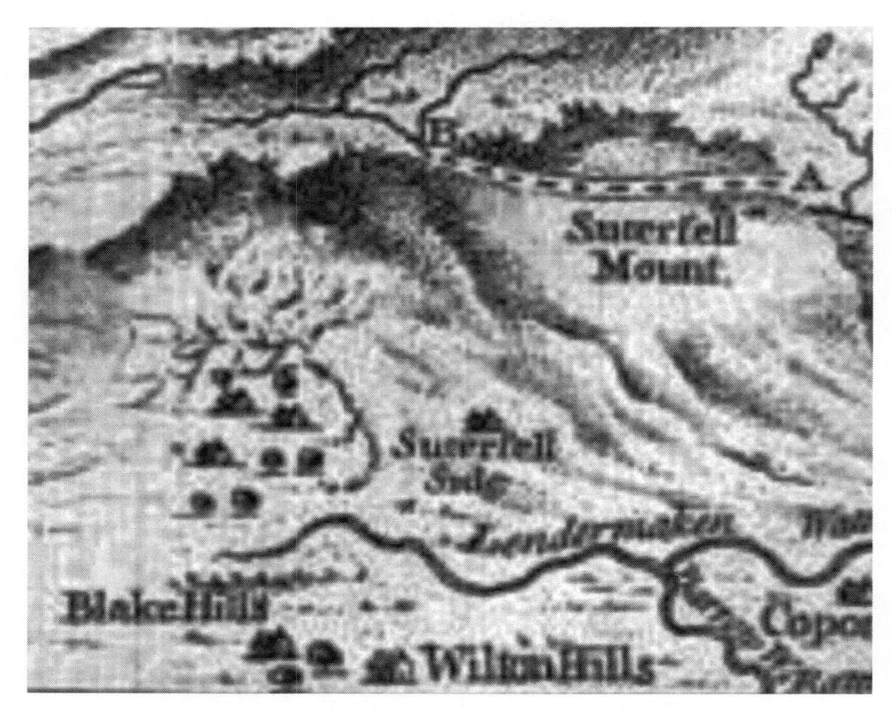

Detail of George Smith's map showing the route taken by the army from A to B. .

to it, till about ten minutes after, again turning his head towards the place, they appeared to be mounted, and a vast army following, five in rank, crowding over at the same place where the servant said he had saw them two years before. He then called his family, who all agreed in the same opinion; and, what was most extraordinary, he frequently observed that some of the five would quit rank, and seem to stand in a fronting posture, as if he was observing and regulating the order of their march, or taking account of their numbers, and, after some time, appeared to return full gallop to the station he had left, which they never failed to do as often as they quitted their lines; and the figure that did so was generally one of the middlemost men in the rank. As it grew later, they seemed more regardless of discipline, and rather had the appearance of people riding from a market, than an army; though they continued crowding on, and marching off, so long as they had light to see them.

"This phaenomenon was no more seen till the Midsummer eve which preceded the rebellion, when they were determined to call more families to be witness of this sight, and accordingly went to Wilton-hill and Souter-fell side, till they convened about 26 persons, who all affirm they then saw the same appearance, but not conducted with the usual regularity as the preceding ones, having the likeness of carriages interspersed; however, it did appear to be less real; for some of the company were so affected with it, as, in the morning, to climb the mountain, through an idle expectation of finding horse shoes after so numerous an army; but saw not the vestige or print of a foot."

It is important to appreciate exactly what Smith reported that the servant, William Lancaster and, possibly, other "spectators" had described to him. According to this account there were three sightings.

The first sighting took place on Midsummer Eve, 1735. It happened, as did the second sighting, between the hours of eight and nine, that is about the time when the sun would appear to set over Souter Fell to someone living in one of the farms close to the east side and in the shadow of the fell. The sighting was made by one person, William Lancaster's servant, who is not named. He is reported as having claimed to have seen "a regular army" proceeding from an eminence in the north end of the eastern side of Souter Fell and marching through a niche in the top of the fell. The accompanying map is very precise about the points where the troops appeared and disappeared. Point A, on the north-west of the fell, is above a fairly steep side, though not what we would today describe as a precipice. Point B, if the troops departed down to the west towards the valley of the Glenderamakin, is a less steep incline. The troops would have marched across a distance of some three-quarters of a mile. Smith gave no detail as to the appearance of the troops. However, he did describe them as "a regular marching army" that "consisted of distinct bodies of troops". They were watched for about an hour. The servant's account was not accepted as credible by the local people to whom he reported his sighting and there is no mention of any attempt being made to find any physical corroboration of the sighting.

The second sighting took place exactly two years later, between eight and nine on Midsummer's Eve, 1737. The initial sighting was made by William Lancaster himself, a property owner and the person who had received a report of the first sighting from his servant. His first response was to casually interpret a distant view as representing something familiar, several gentlemen following their horses home as if they had been hunting. It seems there was nothing unusual in seeing horses on the top of the fell and, one assumes, in men riding them there. Ten minutes later Lancaster looked again and felt he discerned the scene more precisely. There seems to be little visual correspondence between this view and the one Lancaster claimed to have seen ten minutes earlier. The gentlemen/soldiers were now mounted and they were followed by a vast army clearly discerned, even from a distance, as being five in rank. Lancaster's farm at Blakehills is at least a full mile from the summit of Souther Fell, which, at 1680 feet, is two hundred or so feet lower than Smith's estimate of 900 yards. They would have been at such a distance for any detail to be barely determined especially against the light of the setting sun. However, it was observed that a soldier from the middle of the rank would move aside from the march as though to regulate it and then gallop forward to rejoin his fellows. The precision of the detail is surprising and, perhaps, correspondingly convincing. The gradual dissipation of the troops' discipline as they were reduced, despite their "crowding on and marching off", "to the appearance of people riding from market", does not accord with the accustomed behaviour of an army. Again it was a circumstantial detail that may be convincing or may suggest some specific prompting of the imagination. Lancaster, after making his solitary observation, called on his family who "confirm his opinion" as to what he claims to be seeing. As in 1735, there appears to have been no attempt made to find physical evidence of the troop movement.

The third sighting took place eight years later. It was again on Midsummer's eve, but no time is referred to. There is a sense that Lancaster and his family have been waiting for a re-occurrence in order to call witnesses to confirm their sighting. The families from Wilton Hill and Souter-fell Side, both about half a mile away across the fields, were "convened" at, one supposes, Blakehills, where all 26 of them saw the same appearances pass before them on the side of Souther Fell. The army was not described with the precision of the earlier two sightings. We are told that "the likeness of carriages" and that the whole image "did appear to be less real". The tensions and contradictions in the final clause of Smith's description indicate both the conviction of the witnesses and something of Smith's superior scepticism. They were sufficiently convinced of what they had seen to climb the mountain in the expectation of finding physical evidence, but their hope is "an idle expectation". There is an essential contradiction in the "expectation of physical evidence" since the size and detail of the sighting at the distance of a mile must have excluded the possibility of the army being real, and yet these farming people, who knew the area well and must have been used to scrutinising the hills for sheep or people, acted as though it was.

The editor of *The Gentleman's Magazine* added a footnote to Smith's account: "To this relation we may add that in the spring of the year 1707, early in a serene still morning, was observed by two persons, one of the name of Churchill, who were walking from one village to another in Leicestershire, a like appearance of an army marching along, till going behind a great hill, it disappeared – The forms of pikes and carbines were distinguishable, the march was not entirely in our direction, but was at the first like the function of two armies, and the meeting of generals."

There is much more to say about the circumstances of Smith's report, his character and his own opinions of what he had heard. However, there is one other report on the aerial army of Souther Fell which is equally important.

James Clarke's *A Survey of the Lakes*[2] was published in 1787 and was based on evidence he had gathered in 1785, that is forty years after the last of the events described. He offers a similar account of the events, but with a number of significant disparities:

"Opposite the nine-mile post, on the right hand, is Southerfell; rather smoother than its neighbours, and remarkable for an extraordinary phaenomenon, which perhaps can scarcely be paralleled by history, or reconciled to probability; such, however, is the evidence we have of it that I cannot help relating it, and then my readers must judge for themselves. I shall give it nearly in the words of Mr. Lancaster of Blackhills, from whom I had the account, and whose veracity, even were it not supported by many concurrent testimonies, I could fully rely upon. The story is as follows:

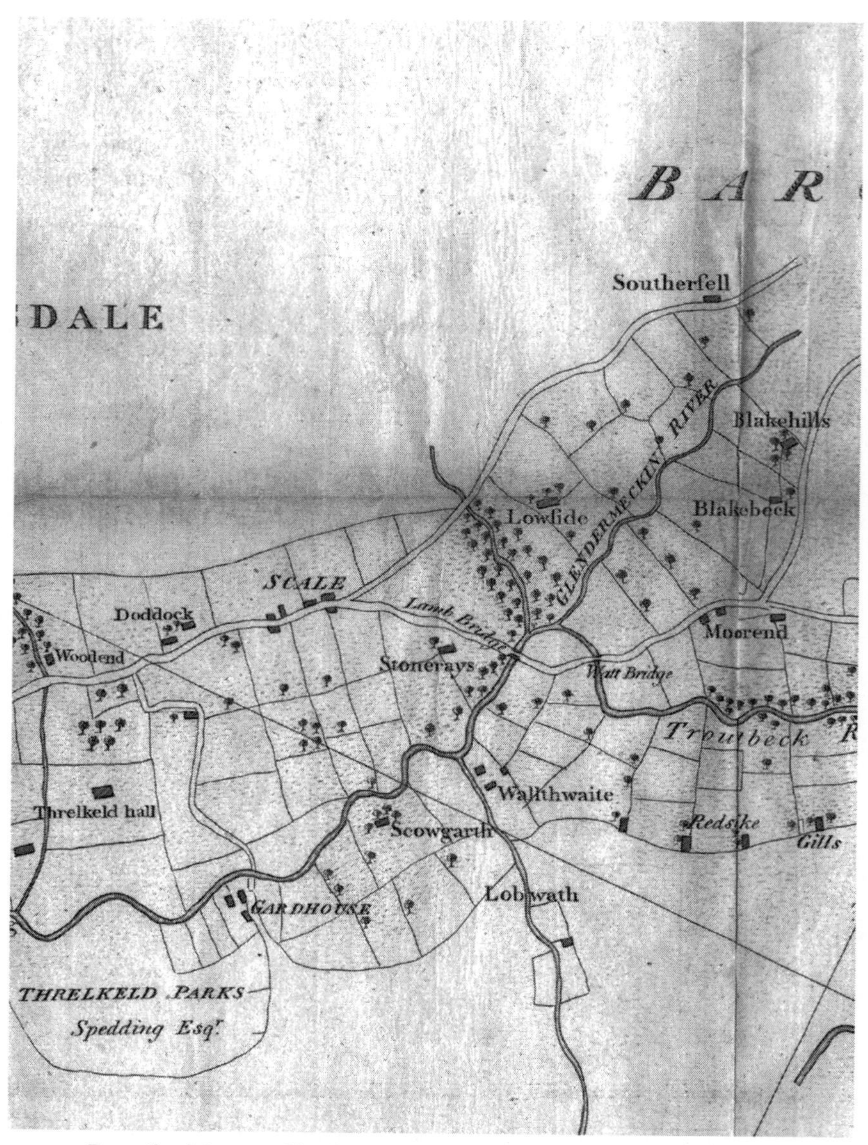

Detail of James Clarke's map. Blakehills is to the top right. Wiltonhill is not marked, and there is no indication of Souther Fell even though it dominates this section of the map.

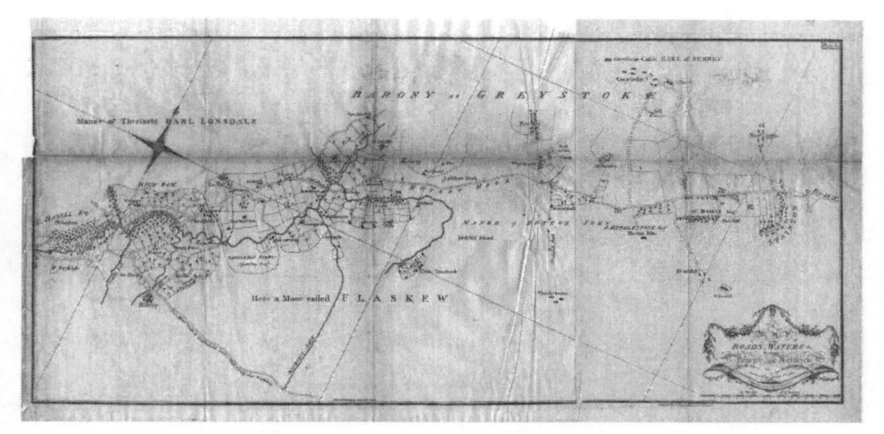

A Map of the Roads, Waters &c. Between Penrith and Keswick
as it appears in Clarke's Survey. *The map is 86.7 x 41.1cms. Souther Fell (un-named) is to the left of centre.*

"'On the 23rd June 1744, his father's servant, Daniel Stricket, (who now lives under Skiddaw, and is an auctioneer,) about half past seven in the evening was walking a mile above the house. Looking round him, he saw a troop of men on horseback riding on Southerfell-side, (a place so steep that an horse can scarcely travel on it at all,) in pretty close ranks, and at a brisk walk. Stricket looked earnestly at them some time before he durst venture to acquaint anyone with what he saw, as he had the year before made himself ridiculous by a visionary story, which I beg leave here also to relate: He was at that time servant to John Wren of Wilton-hill, the next house to Blakehills, and sitting one evening after supper at the door along with his master, they saw a man with a dog pursuing some horses along Southerfell-side; and they seemed to run at an amazing pace till they got out of sight at the low end of the fell. This made them resolve to go next morning to the place to pick up the shoes which they thought these horses must have lost in galloping at such a furious rate; they expected likewise to see prodigious grazes from the feet of these horses on the steep side of the mountain. And to find the man lying dead, as they were sure he ran so fast that he must kill himself. Accordingly they went, but, to their great surprise, found not a shoe, nor even a single vestige of a horse having been there, much less did they find the man lying dead as they expected. This story they sometime concealed; at length, however, they ventured to tell it, and were (as might be expected) heartily laughed at. Stricket, conscious of his former ridiculous error, observed these aerial troops some time before he ventured to mention what he saw: at length, fully satisfied that what he saw was real, he went into the house and told Mr. Lancaster he had something curious to shew him, Mr. Lancaster asked what it was, adding, 'I suppose some bonfire,' (for it was then, and still is a custom, for the shepherds, on the evening before St John's day, to light bonfires, and vie with each other in having the largest.) Stricket told him, if he would walk with him to the end of the house he would shew him what it was. They then went together, and before Stricket spoke or pointed to the place, Mr. Lancaster himself discovered the phaenomenon, and said to Stricket, 'Is that what thou hast to shew me?' 'Yes, Master,' replied Stricket: 'Do you think you see as I do?' They found they did see alike, so they went and alarmed the family, who all came, and all saw this strange phaenomenon.

"These visionary horsemen seemed to come from the lowest part of Souther-Fell, and became visible first at a place called KNOTT; they then moved in regular troops along the side of the Fell, till they came opposite Blake-hills, when they went over the mountain: thus they described a curvilinear path upon the side of the Fell, and both their first and last appearance were bounded by the top of the mountain.

"Frequently the last, or last but one, in a troop, (always either the one or the other,) would leave his place, gallop to the front, and then take the same pace with the rest, a regular, swift walk: these changes happened to every troop, (for many troops appeared,) and oftener than once or twice, yet not at all times alike. The spectators saw, all alike, the same changes, and at the same time as they discovered, by asking each other questions as any change took place. Nor was this wonderful phaenomenon seen at Blake-hills only, it was seen by every person in every cottage within the distance of a mile; neither was it confined to a momentary view, for from the time that Stricket first observed it, the appearance must have lasted at least two hours and an half, viz. from half past seven, till the night coming on prevented the farther view, nor yet was the distance such as could impose rude resemblances on the eyes of credulity. Blake-hills lay not half a mile from the place where this astonishing appearance seemed to be, and many other places where it was likewise seen are still nearer.

"Desirous of giving my readers every possible satisfaction, I procured the following attestation, signed by Mr. Lancaster and Stricket:

'We whose names are hereunto subscribed, declare the above account to be true and that we saw the phaenomena as here related. As witness our hands this 21st day of July 1785.'

William Lancaster.
Daniel Stricket."

Clarke's account identified two sightings, only one of which was of the army, which occurred in 1743 and on Midsummer's eve, 1744. He made no mention of the sightings reported by Smith on Midsummer's eve in 1735 and 1737 and 1745.

Clarke's informant was William Lancaster. There was a William Lancaster living at Blakehills in 1785. He died three years later, in 1788, when he was about 78 years old. If this is the William Lancaster referred to he would have been 25 in 1735, 34 in 1744 and 75 in 1785 when he would have been recounting the exciting happenings of forty years ago to a no-doubt enthusiastic educated interlocutor. Lancaster's father and grandfather had also lived at Blake-hills.[3]

Clarke's first sighting was made by Daniel Stricket and John Wren in, I assume, 1743. We are told only that "he had the year before made himself ridiculous by a visionary story". Although Daniel Stricket is identified as the servant of William Lancaster's father, he is not necessarily the same servant referred to in Smith's account. In 1743 Stricket is servant to John Wren in the neighbouring farm, Wilton-hill. He was later servant to Mr. Lancaster, the father of Clarke's informant, and may also have been his servant at an earlier date. (It is also possible that the William Lancaster in Smith's account may have been the father of Clarke's informant.)

The first sighting in 1743 was made by two observers, master and servant, sitting together. It occurred in the evening after supper although no specific time is given. The sighting was of a man and a dog running after some horses along Southerfell-side. What drew the attention of Wren and Stricket was the "amazing pace" at which the man and dog were pursuing the horses. Their amazement led them to expect to find the man lying dead from his exertions and the following day they investigated the side of the fell where he made his disappearance and found no trace of man or horses. They did not tell their story for some time for fear of being laughed at. There is an inherent contradiction again here as the man and dog were seen from a distance that would make them barely discernable and yet the witnesses are so convinced of the reality of what they have seen that they go to look for evidence.

The second sighting took place at 7.30 on Midsummer eve, 1744. Stricket talks of being "a mile above the house" and was viewing the Fell from a different position which may not have been any closer to or further away from the fell. He "looked earnestly" at the troop of soldiers who were riding at a brisk walking pace along Southerfell-side. His consciousness of "his former ridiculous error" makes him particularly careful in ascertaining the "reality" of what he was seeing before going the mile to the house to have his master confirm what he had seen without any prompting from himself. Having agreed on what they had seen, they sought confirmation from other members of the family and claimed that "it was seen by every person in every cottage within the distance of a mile".

The description of the troop movements is similar to that in Smith's account. The route they follow is "a curvilinear path upon the side of the Fell". Smith is very precise in saying that the troops proceeded "from an eminence in the north end, and marched over a niche in the top" and he marks this very clearly on his map with an indication of the southward direction of the march from A to B. Clarke is equally precise indicating that the troops became visible at a place called Knott and disappeared opposite Blake-hills. *The Place Names of Cumberland* identifies Clarke's Knott with the southern end of Southerfell which the OS map names as Knotts. (possible Brunte Knott on the 6" map.) They disappeared in the same place as Smith's troops but, if Knotts is the place referred to, they had arrived at that point from the south. The troops manoeuvred in a similar, but not an identical fashion. It is just possible that Knott refers to the hill two miles to the north-west which might have been used as a line of direction. In which case the army would have appeared at the same place on Souther Fell as in Smith's report and marched south. Like Smith's report, Clarke's is meticulous in detailing their precise movements and seems to see it as a corroboration of the shared vision.

The credibility of the sighting is reinforced by the number of people from the cottages of the area who concurred in the detail of the sighting, the extent of the sighting lasting for over two hours and the fact that many witnesses were closer than half a mile to "where this astonishing appearance seemed to be".

The final corroboration is provided by the signed declaration made by William Lancaster and Daniel Stricket. Daniel Stricket was no longer living in the area. On Clarke's own account he had become an auctioneer and was living some ten miles away in Bassenthwaite. His social rise from servant to auctioneer would have merited Clarke's respect. They may well have met him at Blake Hills by prior arrangement.

If all sightings are to be credited, then we have five sightings in all, in 1735, 1737, 1743, 1744 and 1745. The 1735 appearance was seen by one servant alone; 1737 was observed by William Lancaster and his family; 1743 was of a man and a horse and was seen by Mr. Wren and his servant, Daniel Stricket, 1744 was seen by Stricket and Lancaster and all the people in the neighbourhood and the 1745 appearance was witnessed by 26 people.

Only two people, Daniel Stricket and William Lancaster, actually signed an "attestation" although others were said to have corroborated the sighting. The "attestation" does not appear to have any legal force. There is nothing to indicate it was signed before magistrates. 'Attestation' is an ambiguous term. In the eighteenth century it had a popular usage but the term seems to have become more formal and legal over the years and a nineteenth century usage might well have been taken to imply a sworn statement made before magistrates.

Both Smith and Clarke provided some analysis of their reports. George Smith cited William Lancaster as providing reasons for the unreality of the beings he had seen: "William Lancaster, indeed, told me, that he never concluded they were real beings, because of the impracticability of a march over the precipices, where they seemed to come on; that the night was extremely serene; that horse and man, upon strict looking at, appeared to be one thing, rather than two distinct ones; that they were nothing like any clouds or vapours which he had ever perceived elsewhere; that their number was incredible, for they filled lengthways near half a mile, and continued so in a swift march for above an hour, and much longer, he thinks, if night had kept off."

The reasoning seems to be that of a man who was not over-readily credulous. The serenity of the night, I assume, refers to the clarity of vision. The dismissal of clouds or vapours suggests a willingness to look for a rational explanation. The other details are very matter-of-fact distinctions about a vision that was perceived to be supernatural. It is the route that the troops take and their numbers that make them seem unreal. The southern and eastern sides of Souther Fell are grassy slopes, steep, though easily walked and certainly not precipitous. The western and northern sides allow a ready but not orderly ascent or descent on foot or on a sure-footed horse. The fell is distinguished by the flatness of the summit ridge which would readily accommodate martial manoeuvres should anyone choose to do so. The numbers talked of, whilst probably very large by eighteenth century standards, are not incredible. A body of mounted troops that extended over half a mile when marching in formation five-a breast might be composed of between a thousand and two thousand soldiers. However, if they were passing continuously for an hour, as Smith reported, that would represent a column of soldiers four miles in length, that is five to eight thousand soldiers. If the procession was seen throughout a period of two and a half hours, as in Clarke's version, the number of soldiers would be proportionately greater and we would be thinking of an incredibly large army of twelve to fifteen thousand men. The only detail that suggested something supernatural was that "horse and man, upon strict looking at, appeared to be one thing, rather than two distinct ones". This point was not mentioned anywhere else. It is also reminiscent of the centaurs of classical mythology, an image that would spring readily to Smith's mind.

Smith trod a cautious path in presenting this account of incredible happenings witnessed by country folk to his educated readers. He felt that the story was fantastic, but he was sufficiently convinced with the testimony of his witnesses that the matter required explanation: "The story has so much the air of romance, that it seemed fitter for Amadis de Gaul, or Glenville's System of Witches, than the repository of the learned; but, as the country was full of it, I was only giving a version from the original relation of a people that could have no end in imposing on their fellow creatures, and are of good repute in the place where they live.

"It is my real opinion, that they apprehended they saw such appearances; but how an undulating ambient meteor could affect the optics of many people, is difficult to say. No doubt fancy will extend to miraculous heights in persons disposed to indulge it; and whether there might not be a concurrence of that to assist the vapour, I will not dispute, because three difficulties seem to occur worthy of solution:

1st, Why a lambent agitated meteor should appear to stop at certain intervals, and return with augmented velocity to re-assume the forsaken place.

2d, Why it should, for a long time, preserve so regular a system, as to appear still five in a line.

3d, Why one particular evening in the year only exhibited the unusual meteor for three times, at so long intervals.

"As these are at present beyond my philosophy to explain, it may be an amusement to such as will give themselves the trouble of enquiry, having neither added nor diminished to the accounts given me, Those who treat it as a mere illusion, or a deceptio visus, should assign reasons for so large a fascination in above 20 persons; probably one, indeed, might serve to aggrandize the fancy of others; but I should think they could not be so universally deceived, without some flamina of the likeness exhibited on the mountain from a meteor, or some unknown cause."

Those initial dismissive references to Amadis of Gaul and Glenville on Witches are revealing of Smith's sceptical temper. Amadis of Gaul was the representative author whom Cervantes charged with addling Don Quixote's brain. *Don Quixote* was hugely popular at the time. Charles Jarvis's translation appeared in 1742 and Tobias Smollett's in 1755. Henry Fielding had written a burlesque ballad opera called *Don Quixote in England* in 1734, and his novel, *Joseph Andrews* from 1742, was subtitled as "written in the manner of Cervantes". Amadis of Gaul was a touchstone for romantic fantasy. Glenville, that is Joseph Glanvil, (1636-1680) is more interesting. He had been Chaplain in Ordinary to Charles II and was concerned that questioning the existence of spirits and witches was the first step on the road to atheism. His *Sadducimus Triumphatus, Or, A full and plain EVIDENCE concerning Witches and Apparitions in Two Parts, The First Treating of their Possibility, Whereunto is added, The true and genuine NOTION, and consistent EXPLICATION of the Nature of a Spirit, for the more full Confirmation of the Possibility of their Existence* was published in 1688. Glanvill was a Fellow of the Royal Society and his arguments still merited serious consideration seventy years after their first publication: "If the Notion of a Spirit be absurd, as is pretended, that of a God and a Soul distinct from Matter, and immortal, are likewise Absurdities; and then, that the World was jumbled into this elegant and orderly Fabrick by Chance; and that our Souls are only Parts of Matter that came together, we know not whence, nor how, and shall again shortly be dissolv'd into those loose Atoms that compound them; that all our Conceptions are but the Thrusting of one Part of Matter against another and the Ideas of our Minds meer blind and casual Motions."[4] The existence of ghosts was not only a popular superstition, but a necessary foundation of theology. If ghosts did not exist the whole order of theology was undermined and the world was without physical, spiritual or moral order. A world created by chance was an absurdity. "These, and a Thousand more, the grossest Impossibilities and Absurdities will be sad Certainties and Demonstrations." Glanvil felt that if he conceded the non-existence of "witches and apparitions" the sacred truths themselves would be laid open to question. His argument is worth quoting at length as it demonstrates not only the sincerity of his belief, but also the complexity and ingenuity of his argument and stands in contrast to the very different mode of thought that proto-scientists like George Smith adopted during the succeeding century. "And yet, sadly, tho' it would be granted them, that a Substance immaterial is as much a Contradiction, as they can fancy; yet why should they not believe, that the Air, and all the Regions above us, may have their invisible intellectual Agents of Nature, like unto our Souls, be that what it will, and some of them, at least, as much degenerate as the vilest and most mischievous among Men? This Hypothesis will be enough to secure the Possibility of Witches and Apparitions. And that all the upper Stories of the Universe are furnished with Inhabitants, 'tis infinitely reasonable to conclude from the Analogy of Nature since we see there is nothing so contemptible and vile in the World we reside in, but hath its living Creatures that dwell upon it; the Earth, the Water, the inferior Air, the Bodies of Animals, the Flesh, the Skin, the Entrails, the Leaves, the Roots, the Stalks of Vegetables; yea, and all Kind of Minerals in the subterraneous Regions. I say, all these have their proper Inhabitants: yea, I suppose, this Rule may hold in all distinct Kinds of Bodies in the World, That they have their peculiar Animals. The Certainty of which, I believe, the Improvement of microscopical Observations will discover. From whence I infer, That since this little Spot is so thickly peopled in every Atom of it, 'tis Weakness to think, that all the vast Spaces above, and Hollows under Ground, are desert and uninhabited. And if both the superior and lower Continents of the Universe have their Inhabitants also, 'tis exceedingly improbable, arguing from the same Analogy, that they are all of the meer sensible Nature, but that they are, at least, some of the rational and intellectual Orders. Which supposed, there is good foundation for the Belief of Witches and Apparitions, tho' the Notion of a Spirit should prove as absurd and unphilosophical as I judge the Denial of it."

This argument was not that of an extremist, but that of a man keenly involved in the intellectual debates of his time and aware of the latest scientific developments such as "the improvement of microscopical observations". Such a view was increasingly challenged over the coming century. The book came to be seen as a repository of ghost and witch stories, a subversion of its original deep and serious intent. George Smith might cite it as a vade-mecum of absurdities, but it still posed the key proposition that to question or deny the existence of ghosts was to question or deny the existence of the Holy Ghost and the existence of God himself. A hundred fifty years later Walter Scott and Sir David Brewster still found it necessary to avoid offending Christian belief.

If we return to Smith's conjecturing on the spectral army, he seems to be suggesting that the people concerned have witnessed some meteorological phenomenon, that is literally a meteor, some unusual display of light, some flamina, which had then been developed by their community imagination into a unified vision. He was very specific in the term he employed. A "lambent ambient meteor" suggests that the meteor filled the surrounding air with a moving, literally a flame-like, light.

Two contemporary descriptions of a meteor that were read to the Royal Society in 1752 indicate something of what Smith's conception of a meteor might have been and why he should describe something that could have been interpreted as an army marching for an hour as a "lambent ambient meteor". Mr. Wm. Smith of Peterborough wrote of "that beautiful phænomenon, that appeared this last summer at this place, and the neighbouring villages": "On Sunday the 22 of July last about 20 minutes before 9, as near as I can remember, in the evening, as I came from Werrington, two miles north-west of this place, I saw to the left of me (as did two others then in company with me) and seemingly about the height of the sun when about two hours high, a ball of light, bigger than a star of the first magnitude to our appearance; the colour like that of a rocket, when thrown, and in its full glory. It drew a tail of light, to our view about 3 feet and a half long, which was broadest and brightest next the ball, and grew taper in form, and languid in colour, to its termination. Its course was about north-west to south-west. It moved in a direct line horizontally, and its motion thro' the air was little swifter than the passage of a duck, hawk, or pigeon, in their flight.

"We had the view of it for about three fourths of a minute but, being in the road near the north end of Walton, and under the trees, lost sight of it sooner than I desired.

"Several people coming from Peterborough, and on the south side of the town coming from Fletton, saw the same, and give the same account of it as I have above done.

I heard it was seen at Bourn, which is north-west 12 miles off us, in the same manner. It must consequently be at a great height from us (tho' it did not seem to be so) by reason people in Borough-Fen, which lies north-east of the place where I was when I saw it, saw the same on the same hand I did, and its form and course in the same manner."

A Mr. William Arderon F.R.S., along with thousands of others in Norwich, had seen the same meteor: "Its direction, he says, was, as near as he could guess, from north to south, moving with great velocity. When due east of him, its altitude was about 30 degrees at which time the great distinctness of its figure made him imagine it was not above two or three miles from him. The splendour and beauty of its nucleus, particularly the fore part thereof, surpassed, he says, all the fires he ever saw, being of a bright silver colour: its tail was of the colour of a burning coal, tho' something fainter. Its head, or nucleus, appeared to him, under an angle of somewhat more than two degrees, and its tail of about 2 1 degrees,

"He lost sight of it in a cloud, not above 20 degrees above the southern part of the horizon, into the middle of which it enter'd: but a friend of his, being about 4 miles more southward, saw it again, after it came out of this cloud, till it enter'd into another.

"The excessive hot weather in the preceding part of the month of July, especially on Wednesday the 11th day thereof, which is supposed to have been the hottest day we have had for many years in England, may perhaps account, in some measure, for the generation of this fiery meteor."[5]

The understanding of meteors was little developed at the time. Both observers described the meteor as being within a few miles and moving slowly, and. one could even suggest a size of three and a half feet. They found this appearance hard to reconcile with the meteor's appearance in distant places. Smith himself had participated in a series of letters to *The Gentleman's Magazine* which discussed the appearance of a comet that had been observed from various places throughout the north and thereby they determined that it must be high in the sky.

George Smith was puzzled that the Souther Fell phenomenon, which, if it were a meteorological phenomenon, would be unpredictable and variable, had returned on a regular basis to the same place. If it had been a vapour, it seemed odd that its appearance should have been so consistent as to maintain a convincing appearance of troops marching five abreast over an extended period of time. Again, if it had been a meteor, then it seemed very strange that it should appear on the same night of the year at such widely separated annual intervals.

However, he was uneasy with such a ready dismissal of the sightings by the local people. The fact that over twenty people shared the same interpretation of what they had seen and spoke with such conviction suggested something beyond mere fancy. George Smith arrived at no ready explanation, but seemed perplexed, neither believing it could be an apparition, nor being able to explain it adequately as a "meteorological" phenomenon. He wanted to explain the description of the army as "a mere illusion, a deceptio visus" as others had done, but found it hard to do so in face of the number of witnesses and the unanimity of their opinion.

Clarke admitted to a similar perplexity. His romantic temper led him to exempt its primitive origin and to see the appearances as a visionary product of the tumult of the times. "Thus have I given the best account I can procure of this wonderful appearance; let others determine what it was. This country, like every other where cultivation has been lately introduced, abounds in the aniles fabulae of fairies, ghosts, and apparitions; but these are never even fabled to have been seen by more than one or two persons at a time, and the view is always said to be momentary. Speed tells of something indeed similar to this as preceding a dreadful intestine war. Can something of this kind have given rise to Ossian's grand and awful mythology? or finally, Is there any impiety in supposing, as this happened before that rebellion which was intended to subvert the liberty, the law, and the religion of England; that though immediate prophecies have ceased, these visionary beings might be directed to warn mankind of approaching tumults? In short, it is difficult to say what it was, or what it was not."

James Clarke's attempt at an explanation is suggestive rather than analytic. He thought it might be the superstition of a community that had yet to feel the full benefits of agricultural improvement and the modern ways that would come with it. This area beneath Southerfell might have been considered backward even to a near neighbour from Penrith. However, he felt that the number of witnesses and the duration of the event – he spoke of more than two hours compared to Smith's one – entitled it to special consideration. His use of the phrase "anniles fabulae" or old wives' tales is unusual and probably pretentious. It was a Latin tag, from Quintillian, that seems to have had very little currency even in the eighteenth century. I cannot identify the reference to Speed, but assume it is to John Speed who wrote a *Historie of Great Britaine*, to accompany his atlas of county maps, *The Theatre of the Empire of Great Britaine*, which was published in 1611. The rhetorical question about "Ossian's grand and awful mythology" feels like a general invocation of a work that was enjoying an enormous popularity rather than a specific reference, but indicates the way the story caught the mood of the time. The interesting phrase is that one asking, "Is there any impiety in supposing?" as it implies that either Clarke was not quite the enlightened man he presented himself as being, still clinging to his anniles fabulae, or else that he was being something of a charlatan invoking an earlier mythology of omens and prophecies decked in the jingoistic garb of liberty, law and religion.

George Smith had ridiculed the fantastic elements likening them to Amadis of Gaul and Glanvil, but he had tried to be explicit about the perplexities the phenomenon seemed to present. James Clarke, in the spirit of his age, had romanticised the story, relishing its colour and drama and seeking to make it appear even more remarkable.

Chapter Three:

George Smith and James Clarke

Such evidence as we have for the sighting of the spectral army relies on the published reports of George Smith and James Clarke. Their accounts differ, even contradict each other, in significant details. Are we to believe either or both of them? Were they careful and painstaking in their investigations, assessments and reporting, or were they men intent on a good story, looking for exciting copy that would sell their work and guarantee a sensational response?

The first encounter with George Smith's work might lead one to distrust the author. He seems to be readily credulous, to be easily impressed and to ridiculously exaggerate both his observations and his feelings. The opening paragraph of *A Journey to Caudebec Fells with a Map and Description of the Same*[i] suggests an author who is not to be trusted: "One curiosity is apt to excite another: after visiting Cross-fells, my inclination led me to examine those of Caldbeck, that later detachment of the British Alps, which overspreads a great part of Cumberland, distinguished by insuperable precipices and towering peaks, and exhibiting landscapes of a quite different and more romantic air than any part of the general ridge, and of a nearer affinity to the Switzerland Alps. My intention in this journey was to visit the WAD-MINES, the peculiar product of these mountains, and no where else discovered on the globe; but as they are kept close shut-up, and the weather was extremely unfavourable, I deferred that examination to a more proper time, and contented myself with the varieties in the neighbourhood of Mosedale;

here I found villages in the narrow bottoms, that feel no more benefit from the solar rays, for two months, about the winter solstice, than the old Cimmerians, or the Laplanders, who inhabit about the north cape of Norway.

"Swinsted on Caldew is a strong instance that the property of the arctic circle is not confined to those unhappy regions which lie within twenty-three degrees of the pole, especially with regard to solar light."

F. J. Carruthers was ready to scoff at Smith: "Smith, not averse to creating a wrong impression among readers who were unlikely to check on his findings, was on form."[2] Carruthers sensed that Smith was exaggerating for effect and it is easy to share his view when we read phrases such as "insuperable precipices and towering peaks" and "of a nearer affinity to the Switzerland Alps" and when he makes a claim that even the benighted inhabitants of Mosedale would dispute.

However, Smith was a serious traveller, a conscientious pioneer in exploring the extremes of the country. That visit he mentioned to Cross Fell was undertaken on Midsummer's day to verify the persistence of snow on the summit throughout the year.[3] Smith's account is careful and observant. His attitude is that of the scientific observer. We know little of his life, but we do know that for a time, "He lived with and assisted Dr Desagulier in his philosophical experiments".[4] Jean Theophilius Desagulier was a distinguished natural philosopher. He had been Isaac Newton's assistant and was himself awarded the Copley Medal, the Royal Society's highest honour, for his work on electricity. He is credited with developing the planetarium. Smith would have worked closely alongside him and must have shared much of the scientific outlook of this man who was some seventeen years his senior.

George Smith's enthusiasm for enlightenment is clearly demonstrated in his articles in *The Gentleman's Magazine*. Of the hundred or so pieces he may have written over a period of either twenty or twenty-five years starting in 1735, a dozen or so are on matters astronomical and there may be up to forty three on meteorological topics including, between 1756 and 1759, a series of regular reports on his observations of the weather in Wigton;[5] sixteen articles treat of antiquarian subjects ranging from finds at Old Carlisle and Roman remains at Netherby to speculations about Long Meg. A number of articles describe Smith's travels in

Cumberland. Not only did he venture up Cross Fell and, later, to the Wad Mines in Honister, but he surveyed the Cumbrian coast and explored the Border hills as far as Christianbury Crags. In addition he wrote several commendable poems and contributed translations from Latin and Greek.

The Gentleman's Magazine, founded by Edward Cave in 1731, was a powerfully influential magazine with a circulation of some 6000 among the comparatively small educated elite of Hanoverian England. Many monthly issues contained Doctor Johnson's fictitious *Debates of the Senate of Magna Lilliputia*, which satirically reported the proceedings of a censored parliament, as well as a monthly record of events and articles by varied contributors on everything and anything from Greek poetry to the latest speculations in science, mathematics and technology. In the forty-eight crammed double-columned pages of the same November issue of 1747 as Smith's article on the Caudebec Fells and the phaenomenon of Souther Fell was not exceptional. There was an extract from a biography of Edmund Halley, a discussion of the French Wars, the King's speech and addresses, explanations of a cheap engine for raising water and of "a machine for saving fewel", extracts in English of Dr. Mead's Latin treatise on the Small-pox, a proposal for Milton as a school-book, a report on the "Carnality of a Methodist teacher" and one on "making incombustible cloth". Added to these were the regular selection of poetry – odes to Hope and on the King's birthday, A lady's Farewell to London, and verses on such diverse subjects as the character of the Lord Chancellor and the success of Dr Henry's nervous medicine – and the *Historical Chronicle* which told of smugglers breaking prison, Sussex people seizing a wreck and petrify'd rarities being discovered.

A Journey to the Caudebec Fells concludes with a paragraph indicative of Smith's intellectual assurance and self-confidence and his sense that he was playing a leading role in the mapping of the country: "I shall reserve my further observations in my surveys of the several parts of England for those intended new maps. Those which have of late appeared are entirely old things, and are not worth looking on; for tho' you mention but eleven parks omitted in that of Berks, I can confirm there are no less than fourteen; and in their map of Bucks, I could not imagine that a noble duke's seat so near London and the present road to the shire town should be omitted: so that I need not wonder at their losing credit

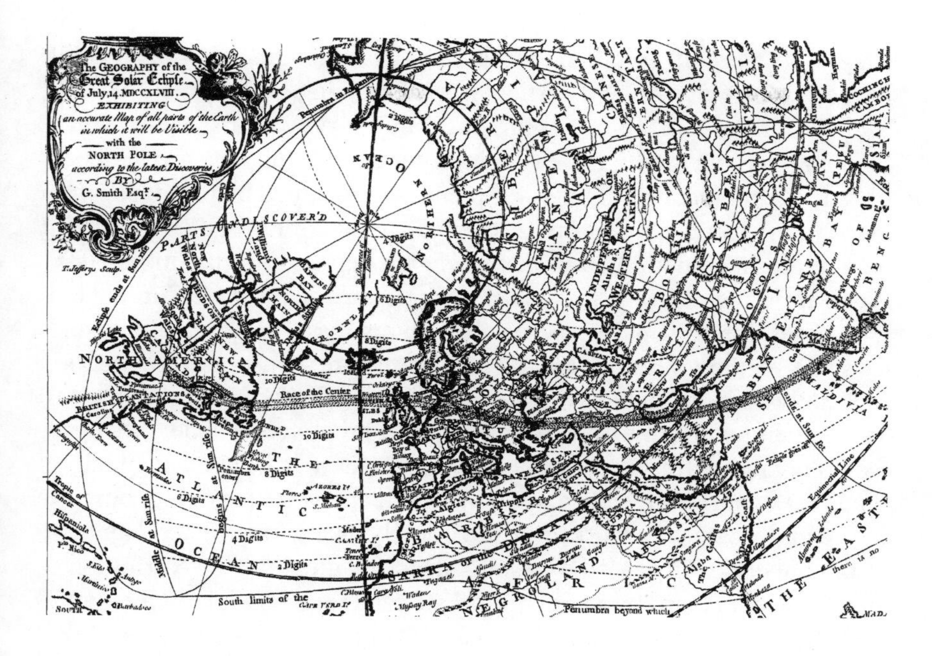

Detail of George Smith's map from his book on Eclipses.

every day."[6]

George Smith published two independent works. In 1744 there appeared a 46 page book on comets which was comprehensively entitled: "A treatise of comets, containing I. An explication of all the various appearances of the late comet, both in its own Trajectory and the Firmament of the Fixt Stars, to its setting in the Sun-beams: Illustrated with a plan of the Earth's and Comet's Orbits II. The history of comets from the earliest Accounts of those kind of Planets, to the present Time; wherein the sentiments of the Antient and Modern Philosophers are occasionally display'd. With remarks on the Intentional End of Comets, and the Nature and Design of Saturn's Ring. III. The distance, velocity, size, solidity, and other properties of those bodies consider'd; and the wonderful Phaenomena of their Tails and Atmospheres accounted for. Illustrated also by a Copper-Plate". Four years later he published a work, which in its nineteen brief pages reviewed the history of eclipses and sought to predict future eclipses: "A Dissertation on the General Properties of Eclipses; and particularly the ensuing Eclipse of 1748".

Smith was an able cartographer and surveyor in an age when mapping was becoming increasingly accurate. His map of the Caldbeck Fells is a combination of landscape picture and detailed map and his other maps in the *Gentleman's Magazine* have a similar drawing-cum-sketch-map appearance with the same extravagant depiction of the mountains. Aside from the diagram "of a cheap engine for raising water" in the top left corner, Smith's map represents the rivers reasonably accurately and to scale, although their twists and turns are somewhat overdone, especially in the mountains. His way of showing the mountains is unusual and, hugely exaggerating their heights and precipices, renders them as fearsome and dramatic. Blencathra and Skiddaw, with their distinctive shapes are not recognisible and Souther Fell appears excessively bumpy.

Smith may have worked professionally as a cartographer. His map of the Sauceries in Carlisle was produced for the Duke of Norfolk and there are extant maps by Smith of Carlisle castle and possibly of the Battle of Clifton, as well as the very fine map of Carlisle produced for the Duke of Cumberland which is discussed in the next chapter. He was probably commissioned to draw an accurate map of the Cumberland coast after the Jacobite Rebellion.

He was a thoroughly learned man of his day: a polymath with a questioning, observing, scientific bent; an antiquarian, astronomer, meteorologist, surveyor, cartographer, topographer and poet.

We can gather something of the quality of the man from the brief but strongly opinionated biography of Smith that appeared in *Biographia Cumbriensis* which was appended to Hutchinson's *History of Cumberland*. The work's author was the remarkable and distinguished Jonathan Boucher, preacher, loyalist and one-time friend of George Washington. His short biography of George Smith is as follows: "George Smith, Esq., was a native of Scotland; a man of genius and learning; but of an assuming air, irritable temper, and suspicious principles as to religion. After being some time an assistant in some seminary of learning, in or near London, he lived with and assisted Dr. Desagulier in his philosophical experiments. Marrying soon after, he engaged in an academy in Wakefield, afterwards lived near Brampton; and finally settled at Wigton, where he lived on a small annuity, but from what source it was derived was never known. He instructed several persons in that neighbourhood in Mathematics and philosophy, and was a great contributor to *The Gentleman's Magazine*. Both he and his wife died at Wigton. He had the merit of exciting, in that neighbourhood, a very general attention to literature; and the demerit of promoting a spirit of suspicion and infidelity. He had a daughter, Mrs. Sarah Smith, who, for some time, was a preacher among the Quakers."[7]

Boucher was born the son of a publican in Blencogo, a small farming community about four miles from Wigton, in 1738. He attended Joseph Blaine's School in Wigton and may have emigrated to America at the age of sixteen. However, he took up a post at St Bees School in west Cumberland in 1756. Smith's articles for *The Gentleman's Magazine* were sent from Wigton from 1747 onwards. It is more than possible that the young Boucher knew George Smith personally and may well have been one of those "several persons in that neighbourhood" that Smith instructed in mathematics and philosophy. This would readily account for his awareness of his irritable temper. Smith certainly appears to have distinguished himself in the small community by his superior air as well as his learning. The remarks about "suspicious principles as to religion" and "the demerit of promoting a spirit of suspicion and infidelity", as well as, perhaps, the marked reference to his daughter being "a preacher among the Quakers", suggest that Smith (at least in the eyes of Boucher, who was an orthodox and committed Anglican) was of an independent mind. His spiritual and scientific disposition suggests that he was not the sort of person to believe in ghosts and spectres.

A later biographical note in John Nichol's *Illustrations of the Literary History of the Eighteenth Century* elucidates Boucher's remark about the source of Smith's annuity. Nichol is able to comprise the last ten or thirty years of Smith's financial and literary life in one sentence: "Having impaired his fortune by literary pursuits, he retired to Wigtown,(sic) on an annuity settled on him by his elder brother, a Turkey merchant; and prosecuted the antiquities of the County of Cumberland till his death in 1773."[8]

That date for Smith's death is almost certainly wrong. The burial register at Wigton refers to a George Smith being buried on 3 Sept 1755[9] and a letter in *The Gentleman's Magazine* written by T. Thomlinson, from Wigton on July 16, 1756, speaks of "the late George Smith".[10] There is no evidence of him "prosecuting the antiquities of the County of Cumberland" after 1755 and the articles in the *Gentleman's Magazine* that are attributed to him after that date – monthly statistical reports on the weather in Wigton - are done so on no authority except their continuity.

George Smith's independence of mind and spirit is best demonstrated by his extraordinary behaviour at the time when Bonnie Prince Charlie's army passed through Carlisle in 1745. Smith was arraigned before the magistrates at the restoration of Hanoverian power when the Jacobites were expelled from Carlisle. The accusation brought against him, by two of his neighbours at Boothby, was that he visited the rebels when they occupied Naworth Castle and showed them a map of England. Smith's deposition to the magistrates claimed that he was seeking to garner information of the rebels' intentions: "Saith he having heard that some of the Rebels were at Naward Castle and having occasion for a map to examine went to Naward Castle with aforesaid map of England with an intent to introduce himself to the Rebels and thereby to be enabled to penetrate into the discussions of the Rebells as to their March and to gather such Informations from them as might be of Service to the Government." The case does not seem to have been brought to court. The whole issue is discussed more fully in the following chapter.

When Smith talked of the small dwelling of Swinsted being "a strong instance that the property of the arctic circle is not confined to those unhappy regions which lie within twenty-three degrees of the pole, especially with regard to the solar light," he is speaking as a natural philosopher who knew the northern counties well, was a keen observer of the weather, and was well aware that this narrow elevated valley cruelly exposed to the east winds in winter, suffered from extremely low temperatures.

His further observations are less questionably astute, noting the quality of the rocks, soil and vegetation: "These mountains differ not only in figure, but are very dissimilar in property to the main body, being dry smooth, and more agreeably verdant, where precipices occur not. The rocks upon which they are built, being of a fossile, absorbent nature, serving to imbibe the descending rains, which are thrown off from the more compact strata of the general ridge, and take broken and uneven courses through the loose and spungy texture of the outward covering, forming sometime morasses, but more frequently rotten bogs, and sinuous mires of difficult passage. No such disagreeable objects interrupt the traveller here; if he guards against the precipices, he has no other danger to encounter.

"The most common plants I observed, are, Adianthum nigrum officinarum (of Ray) black maiden hair

Lujola, acetosa silvestris, wood or mountain sorrel

Museus squammosus montanus repens, sabinae folio

Museus clavatus janiperinis foliis reflexis, clavis singularibus sine pedeculis. Several mosses of the capsulated kind.

Brush moss.

Rorella longifolia perennis, and other sun-dews.

The shrubs rising from the lattices of the rocks, are dwarf birch, dwarf mountain ash, of so untractable genius that no soil will meliorate it.

Fraxinus sylvestris, ornus montana, wild mountain ash with red fruit. I do not remember to have seen this tree in the south, nearer than Derbyshire; it differs both in size and leaf from the service tree, of which species it is, according to the botanists; and is a very beautiful one when the fruit is ripe: the superstitious use it against witchcraft.

The only bird peculiar to these rocks is the raven."

George Smith's geological analysis is even more impressive than his botanical. Here is an intelligent and well informed man, using a specialized, technical vocabulary to make astute and rational observations of the world about him.

"It is a received Cumberland proverb, that the mountains of Caldbeck are worth all England besides; but it has never yet been verified by experience; and if we may be allowed to conjecture from the nature of the stones found in the rivulets and quarries, it will be difficult to say when they will. Most of their lapilli are a fluor of the stalactite kind, or a sparry talc resembling white flint, variegated with hexagonal crystalline spars, whose points will cut glass like the adamant; but immediately lose that property, from their fragil quality. Others are impregnated with the marcasite of lead, but so blended with an arsenical sulphur, that they evaporate in the process of separation; and others are of the copperas kind: all of them contained such heterogeneal qualities in their composition, as never to yield a proper gratification for their trial. Their quarries also only abound with a fissile bluish slate, useful for the covering of their houses, but very remote from the metalline nature: indeed, in Brandlegill beck, and the northern descents, copper has been formerly dug, but the mines are long since worn out; hereabouts the lapis calaminaris is also found."

Another facet of Smith's intellectual character is revealed by his sceptical but investigative attitude towards the reports of the country people. He is prepared to listen to accounts of the unusual and exceptional in a fair-minded, ig not gullible, way.

"Under mount Skiddaw is the head of the river Caldew; it issues through a narrow trough, and takes its winding course with great rapidity to Mosedale, where it turns northward for Carlisle. Near two miles above that village (Mosedale) it receives a small rivulet from Bouscale tarn, a lake near a mile in circumference, on the side of a high mountain, so strangely surrounded by an amphitheatrical ridge of quarry rocks, that it is excluded the benefit of the sun for at least three months of the winter; but this is not its only singularity. Several of the most reliable inhabitants thereabouts affirming, that they frequently see the stars in it at mid-day; but in order to discover that phaenomenon, the firmament must be perfectly clear, the air stable, and the water unagitated. These circumstances not occurring at the time I was there, deprived me of the pleasure of that sight, and of recommending it to the naturalists upon my own occular evidence, which I regret the want of, as I question if the like has been any where else observed. The spectator must be situated at least 200 yards above the lake, and as much below the summit of the semi-ambient ridge; and, as there are other high mountains, which, in their position, may break and deaden the solar rays, I can only give an implicit credit to the power of their agency, till I am convinced of their effects, and am qualified to send it better recommended to the public.

"At Grisdale the water turns both ways; so that, in a sudden however, you may, with your foot only, send the rain-water either to Carlisle or Cockermouth, by the channels of the Caldew or the Lender-maken. This last springs under Saddleback, a Parnassian eminence, with two prominent peaks, the most northerly is called Blencarter, a surprisingly high precipice of the quarry kind."

George Smith is a man of the Enlightenment, observing, identifying, cataloguing, mapping the wild and unknown in order to control it. The flora, the fauna, the geology and geomorphology, the meteorology and the agriculture are all objects of his enquiry. The strange and the extreme are encompassed by being identified with the "familiar" world of Greece and Rome. The land is contained, is made to conform with his cultivated, cultural map. However, one wonders whether the simple Cumberland peasants, those "most reliable inhabitants", did not find some amusement in pulling his leg when they told him that they frequently saw the stars in Bowscale Tarn at mid-day.

After such a careful account of the country with a judicious assessment of its curiosities and an enlightened respect for the understanding of the inhabitants and their lore, it is surprising, but not out of character, that such a rational, learned man as George Smith was ready to give half of his report on this unfrequented area to a sensational story. The story itself may have been sensational. It may have "made so much noise in the north". Smith's approach was not sensational. He was a sceptical, questioning reporter, who neither believed his witnesses nor dismissed their accounts as out of hand. He found that "the people that could have no end in imposing on their fellow creatures, and are of good repute in the place where they live".

He was clearly perplexed as to how to explain the phenomenon. His own scientific inclinations led him to an explanation of "a lambent agitated meteor" and his previous writings would have lent this view considerable weight. Meteors and other aerial phenomenon were little understood at the time. The idea that the sighting was prompted by the motions of a bright meteor crossing across the front of Souther Fell is a reasonable speculation founded on the understanding of the day.

However, even though he sought to explain away the spectral army, he was not as readily dismissive of the observations of the country people as other previous commentators must have been. They were prepared to explain the phenomenon away as "a mere illusion, or a deceptio visus". Smith argued that there must have been an original cause for so many people to be "universally deceived".

James Clarke was, unlike Smith, a native of the country, very much a man of the local community. He was born in Cumberland, at High Head, Watermillock, above the Cumberland shore of Ullswater. The house is not identified on his map of Ullswater, although there is a small dwelling called Clarke Gate, a field or so to the north west of the hamlet of Longthwaite in the parish.

His partisanship is reflected in the way he promoted Watermillock in the *Survey*. Tourists were urged to send word ahead to prepare the fishermen for their visit and given advance notice of the, I assume, advantageous terms on which the fish might be purchased. He even talked of his own angling achievements there: "I one day caught, in this manner, between Powley and the small island, twenty-nine trouts." His knowledge of fish and fishing practices in Ullswater was considerable and indicates he was both an enthusiastic angler and cook: "I shall not here enlarge upon the cookery of our fish; I only add, their flavour is far the finest when dressed as soon as taken, and is still improved by the plain manner of dressing; I mean roasting them, (wrapped up in wet paper) among wood ashes: the reader may laugh if he pleases at my cookery, but if he will try it he will find it far exceed his expectations."

He believed, "We may, without hesitation, give (Ullswater) the first place among the Lakes . . . We find neither the rugged horrors of Derwent Water, nor the cultivated scenes of Winandermere." His praise of Watermillock itself, whilst paying due deference to the lord of the manor, was nothing short of ecstatic: "The next remarkable place is the village of Water-Millock, the seat and manor of John Robinson, Esq.; . . . and is one of the most beautiful situations our island affords. It is completely sheltered from every inclement blast by mountains and groves, and every window in the house presents you with a beautiful landscape, each varied from another both in objects and stile. On one side is the lake; on another a beautiful and cultivated scene composed of water, wood and hills; on another, high, rugged, and broken rocks, interspersed with here and there a green shrub; and on the other is a beautiful view of the lake, including the rugged and varied hills on the opposite side, together with Helvellin and its craggy inferiors." He recounted, in his customary folksy manner, a "whimsical" anecdote as the origin of "the appellation of the wicked of Water-millock" which "sticks to the inhabitants of that place till this day".

And he spoke with some feeling of the people of Watermillock being deprived of their ancient privileges by an unscrupulous attorney: "in consequence thereof the tenants of Water-Millock lost their undoubted rights". In 1759 he was witness to an enthusiastic hunt which remedied the consequences of a dispute when the bailiff refused to contain the vermin. With boyish accuracy he tells us that: "the sum-total of vermin destroyed, were fifteen foxes, seven badgers, twelve wild cats, and nine martens, (called here, by way of distinction, Clean Marts) besides a prodigious number of foul-marts, eagles, ravens, gleads, &c."

James Clarke was also peculiarly proud of his local town. Penrith was the home of good people and offered a warm welcome for the stranger, the tourist and the traveller. His *Survey*, eccentric and idiosyncratic as it is, was aimed at the tourist. And, as landlord of two of the principal inns, the White Swan and the Griffin, he had a vested interest in Penrith proving a welcoming and convivial place.

He may have purchased the tenancy of the White Swan in the early part of 1777. Its previous landlord, Mr. William Nelson, "a Gentleman universally esteemed and much regretted by a numerous acquaintance" had died and his widow, Mrs Mary Nelson, advertised for a tenant on 18th February of that year. While not the principal coaching inn on a main stop on one of the major routes north, the White Swan was a hostelry of some importance. The notice in *The Carlisle Chronicle and Whitehaven Intelligencer* described the White Swan as: "The large and commodious premises, well situate, in every Respect, for Travellers has one very large and commodious Dining Room, fronting the Main Street; two very good Parlours and two small ones; a very good Kitchen with Stoves in it; a Hall; three very good and dry Cellars and Pantries; ten very good Bed Chambers, with Fire Places in them; three Stables, with standing in them for fourteen Horses, and Hay Lofts over them; a Granary and Servants Room; a good Brewhouse, and other Conveniences, and a Garden near the same; a large Yard, into which a Carriage may enter and turn, and a good Pump therein; and Parts of two Pews in the Parish Church . . . The Excise Office is kept there, and this Inn has been well known to, and frequented by, several Gentlemen, Tradesmen, and Travellers, for a number of Years . . . The whole of the Premises are in very great Repair." More probably he acquired the White Swan in 1783 at the same time as he became proprietor of the Griffin Inn, a lesser establishment on the Cornmarket.

His *Survey* was ready to extol the virtues of Penrith and in particular, praise the exertions of the town's publicans: "Those, likewise, whom a taste for natural beauties impels to visit the Lakes, always consider Penrith as a kind of home in these solitary regions; and the consequence is natural, all the inns here seem to vie with each other in attention, and strain every sinew in making the country as agreeable as possible."

Penrith was also in a state of enviable economic and social health: "Though an inland town, there are some very considerable manufactories of checks which are daily increasing; two common breweries in good employ; two hair merchants, who, (limited as their business may seem,) are both men of property; and a tannery, where some business is done. Yet as these employ but a small part of the inhabitants, perhaps the manners of no place are more strongly or generally stamped with the marks of ease and peace. Few are rich, but as few miserably poor. Whoever wishes to enjoy a social glass, is seldom at a loss for a companion. A regular Card-Assembly, during the Winter; and small, though agreeable private parties all the year round, furnish the fair sex with ample amusement; whilst two well-frequented bowling greens afford, during the fine weather, exercise and amusement to such of the males as have no better employment. During the races and assizes, a more gay and agreeable place cannot be imagined. The more than usual bustle of those times rousing the inhabitants out of that placid dream of existence they at other times enjoy, and animating them to a degree of real mirth and festivity rarely met with in more pompous scenes.

"But why not here, as well as any where else, should I pay tribute, due to the general manners of the country? They deserve it. Every reputable farmer in the neighbourhood prides himself on the goodness of his ale, and is never so happy as when his friends have as much of it as they can carry home. The gentlemen are remarkable for affability and hospitality. True it is, that, like trees which grow single, every little irregularity has ample room to expand and shew itself; but, at the same time, all is pure nature, undisguised by art."

During his time as an inn-keeper, James Clarke continued to style himself as a land surveyor. He is described as "James Clarke, Land-

Surveyor" on the title-page of his book. One imagines he must have continued with this skilled work which brought him into close contact with the land-owning and professional classes. *The Survey* has a verbose and grandiloquent dedication,: "To His Royal Highness Henry Frederick, Duke of Cumberland and Strathern, earl of Dublin, Ranger of Windsor Park, Admiral of the Blue Squadron, Knight of the Most Noble Order of the Garter, Grand Master, &c. &c. &c. The Right Honourable Thomas Howard, Earl of Effingham, Lord Howard, Acting Grand master; The Grand Wardens, Past and Present Grand Officers of the Grand Lodge of England, and Brethren of the most Ancient Society of Free and Accepted Masons: This Book is Humbly Dedicated by Their Most Obedient Brother and Servant, James Clarke." Only by being a fellow mason might Clarke offer fraternal greetings to a younger brother of George III and some of the most eminent aristocrats in the country. The masonic dedication would have helped to promote sales of what must have been a very risky venture. *A Survey of the Lakes of Cumberland, Westmorland, and Lancashire: together with an Account, Historical, Topographical and Descriptive, of the Adjacent Country. To which is added, A Sketch of the Border Laws and Customs* was "Printed for the Author, and sold by him at Penrith, Cumberland; also by J. Robson, and J. Faulder, New Bond Street; P.W. Fares, No. 3 Piccadilly; the Engraver, S.J. Neale, 352, Strand, London. I. Bull and J. Marshall, Bath; Rose and Drury, Lincoln; Todd, Stonegate, York, Ware and Son, Whitehaven; C. Elliot, Edinburgh, and most other Booksellers in the Kingdom".

Clarke may well have paid for the book himself. Other contemporary books were printed for (and financed by) the booksellers. The book was certainly an expensive production. There were 194 folio pages and ten very large fold-out maps. The map of the "Southern Part of the Lake Windermere and its Environs" is over a metre wide, measuring 490 x 1042 millimetres. Eight of the maps were published six years prior to the book's publication in 1781. The engraver was Samuel J. Neele. In the 1780s he charged Thomas Jefferson £28 for an engraved map of Virginia that was smaller than Clarke's maps.

In 1798, a London bookseller, William Clarke of 38 New Bond Street, was selling Clarke's *Survey* "in one large Volume, Folio, Price One Guinea. – The same, with Twenty Views, elegantly bound", was available for the enormous sum of six pounds. William Clarke had a similar set of sixteen views "elegantly bound with West's Guide" at a quarter of the price. There was also a special offer of the maps in a form that should have proved useful to the ever-growing number of tourists: "Plans of the Lakes of Cumberland, Westmorland &c. With an accurate Survey of the Roads leading to them from Penrith, Keswick &c. and forming a complete Guide for those who make the Tour of the Lakes. By James Clarke, Land Surveyor. In a portable Quarto Volume. Price 12s. in boards". The same publisher was also promoting the two volume Quarto edition of Hutchinson's *History of Cumberland* at two pounds ten shillings and a considerably smaller duodecimo volume of ballads by Robert Anderson of Carlisle for three shillings and sixpence. Another bookseller in a far lengthier catalogue that was issued in 1791 and 1796 priced the *Survey* at two pounds five shillings, making it one of the most expensive single volumes listed. An authoritative catalogue lists the first edition of 1787 at £2 5s. and the second in 1790 at less than half that price at one guinea.

The *Survey* was the product of James Clarke's years in the 1760s and 1770s being "profitably employed by landowners in the Penrith, Derwentwater area". The rapid growth of commerce and the building of the turnpike roads created a demand for more detailed and accurate maps. In 1759 the Royal Society for the Encouragement of the Arts had offered a prize of £100 for accurate county maps at a scale of one inch to the mile. Thomas Donald's map was one such map tailored to meet the requirements of his 96 mostly aristocratic and land-owning subscribers. It covered the county of Cumberland accurately depicting the physical features, (although the mountains lacked detail) the major roads including those recently turn-piked with their gates, towns and villages and significant rural houses and farms (named) as well as selected antiquities and such industrial establishments as mills and mines.

Clarke's maps, some at six inches to the mile, were on a larger scale. They did not attempt to cover the whole county and showed little of the mountains. Otherwise, they displayed all the features of Donald's map together with field boundaries and individual trees. In the area to the east of Souther Fell, Donald showed the road that runs along the base of the fell but not the one that runs north to the east of Blakehills. Clarke named more farms, indicated the properties of the principle land-owners, and showed the boundaries of the enclosed fields. His maps also showed spot depths in the lakes.

Donald's map was republished by Hodkinson in 1783 at both an inch and a half inch to the mile and a section of the map showing the "Environs of Keswick" was issued in 1789 to meet the needs of the tourist trade.

Clarke's rival, Peter Crosthwaite, refused to sell his maps in his museum of curiosities at Keswick "as he considered them inaccurate and misleading". Crosthwaite's Seven Maps of the Lakes were surveyed between 1783 and 1794. His copy of Clarke's *Survey* is in Barrow Library. There are some eighteen hand-written notes in the margins. They usually find fault with Clarke on points of accuracy, and otherwise defend Father West and Thomas Gray against Clarke's sneering remarks and accuse him of "throwing dirt" at "sublime authors". Clarke is said to be "barbarous" and his book "ignorant", "monstrous" and "unsaleable". Crosthwaite's maps were more accurate than Clarke's and more pictorial, but they did not describe such detail as field boundaries and farms which were found on Clarke's maps.

Clarke had great respect for his origins: "Few possess more native genius, or more intrinsic worth and honesty: among the most unpolished of them are men of very considerable learning; I mean men who are tolerable proficient of the classics, and who are more than tolerable mathematicians; even among the poor artificers, such as tailors and shoemakers, may be found some tolerable poets." However, he had little respect for the more gentlemanly romantic tourists who proceeded him: "Passing along the road to Threlkeld, take a view of that rugged and stupendous mountain SADDLEBACK, a mountain which is itself a fund of curiosities: How Mr Gray passed it without notice I cannot say; but, if I may be allowed to conjecture, it was in the same manner as he actually visited several other scenes of awful grandeur, blindfolded! Let us however consider, that Mr Gray was not a mountaineer: - His tender, melancholy, and delicate muse, delighted to sport in sunny vales; or to recline under the shade of the spreading oak, listening to the warbling of the feathered choir over his head, or the tinkling of the stream that ran purling at his feet."

Clarke's personality and his social background caused him to write a book that was different in its approach to the other topographical works of its day. He was an intelligent, but probably largely self-educated, egocentric man who delighted in the curiosity and idiosyncrasies of his own county and, knowing a good story when he saw one, was as ready as any public house raconteur to shape it according to his listener's pleasure. His emotional and mental map of the Lakes was very different from that of his fellow surveyor George Smith and his book was markedly different in intent and content from those of his predecessors. The most popular of these was Thomas West's *Guide to the Lakes*, which had been published nine years previously. This was, first and foremost, an aesthetic guide to the proper appreciation of the scenery of the Lakes, going so far as to designate precise "stations" from which the tourist might obtain the most picturesque view of the mountains and the lakes. James Clarke's *Survey* "is deliberately an everyman's guide, and counters the effeteness of West with bawdy jokes, miniscule and random histories of people and places and precise maps of roads: Clarke was, after all, a land-surveyor and not a painter or sketcher".[11]

Knowing little as we do about James Clarke's life, we do have a brief, but graphic description of his death on 1st July, 1799. *The European Magazine and London Review* printed a notice in its *Monthly Obituary* for July and August to the effect that: "He went into a little public house called the Blue Bell about three miles from Sutton Coldfield and five from Lichfield. When there he called for a pint of ale and a pipe, which having lighted, he was seized with a fit of coughing, fell on his face and expired immediately".[12] The same notice had first appeared in *The Cumberland Pacquet* for 4th July. The coroner's jury astutely concluded that James Clarke's death had been "by the visitation of God". He was probably buried in Lichfield.

However, there is a possibility that Clarke put about this story of his death in order to escape his creditors.[13] The most intriguing of Peter Crosthwaite's marginalia gloatingly suggested that Clarke had been imprisoned for debt: "The author seems to have been hardened; and blind to future good; for after having sneared at the fame of all the Divine Philosophers who wrote on the Lakes before Him; his great work is unsaleable; and Himself cast into Carlisle jail by his Engraving, where he has continued and it is said likely to continue."[14] Crosthwaite was angry with Clarke for mocking Thomas Gray who had supposedly been so terrified at the sight of Skiddaw that he had had the blinds of his carriage drawn. If this was true, and the enormous cost of publishing the *Survey* and its apparently slow sales make it a possibility, it was probable that James Clarke saw the inside of Carlisle Jail in the late 1780s or early 1790s.

Some ten years after Clarke's reported death, on 28th February, 1809, *The Cumberland Pacquet* reported that the Penrith surveyor offered for sale the entire property and copyright of his *Descriptive Survey of the Lakes of Cumberland and Westmorland*". The prospective purchasers were requested to enquire of Mr Clarke, care of "Ann Bell, Printer, Penrith".[15]

Clarke's *Survey of the Lakes* received luke-warm reviews from the London press. They praised the pretentiously grandiloquent introduction on Border History and the Debateable lands which was the work of the poet Isaac Ritson. Ritson who was born in Eamont Bridge in 1761, being "decripit and lame" displayed a rare genius at Dr Blain's school in Appleby before becoming himself a schoolmaster in Carlisle and Penrith and then a medical student in Edinburgh and London. His poetry received high praise and he was regarded as something of a natural genius. He died in London in 1789.[16] However the reviewers had little taste for Clarke's own exaggerated and folksy anecdotes.

The Monthly Review, or, Literary Journal of 1789, commended the book but carped at its high price, noting that the *Survey* "will, probably, afford entertainment and instruction to those who can attain the purchase. Mr. Clarke writes like a man of capacity, observation, and learning; and though his performance cannot, in point of style, rank with those of considerable elegance and taste, yet it is plain and expressive". The reviewer sensed that it was "the work of a man who had acquired scientific knowledge, rather by dint of application, and the aids of native genius".

A certain Tobias Smollett, not the novelist of the rumbustious and picaresque adventures of such as Humphrey Clinker and Peregrine Pickle, was patronising in his praise and reflects something of the superiority felt by the London educated classes towards the remote reaches of Cumberland: "Clarke's *Survey* is a very valuable one: it is entirely the result of observation, and adds considerably to our topographical knowledge of this curious and romantic country. The 'Account' of which the volume in other respects consists, is, in the author's language, historical, topographical, and descriptive. It is difficult to define its nature, or point out its merits with precision. Mr. Clarke seems to be a man of a strong, sound understanding; to have spent his life in this country; to have examined repeatedly its different parts, and the historical relations connected with them. In this remote spot, however (the Land of Faerie, the retreat of the suspected Arthur, of Robin Hood and his followers), the imagination some times seems to vanquish the reason, and a few narratives, particularly of the aerial horsemen, &c. resemble too much the superstitions of the nursery, to command our assent."[17]

James Clarke had known the country about Penrith as man and boy and he would have been thoroughly acquainted, especially as a publican and a surveyor, with the stories and folklore of the area. However, even with this knowledge his work displays a tendency to self-promotion and exaggeration. He had every reason, including the exceptional financial risk he was taking, to make his work as arresting as possible and he had a good eye for a popular anecdote and the clinching journalistic detail. George Smith was writing for his peers whereas Clarke was writing for a tourist audience that he did not always fully respect. James Clarke's interviewing of Lancaster and especially Strickett, since he was no longer at Blake Hills, and his obtaining their signatures in attestation of the story has something of the opportunistic about it. Those two signatures gave his account an added credibility and it was Clarke's version of events rather than the more nearly contemporaneous account by Smith that was to be the preferred version in most of the later discussion of the story of the spectral army.

Chapter Four:

The Jacobites

The final sighting of the army took place on St John's Eve, 1745, that is on Wednesday, the 23rd June, Midsummer Eve. Strictly speaking the 24th June in 1745 was not the day of the summer solstice. Great Britain chose to retain the Julian Calendar with its slight accumulated discrepancy. Consequently, when the Gregorian Calendar was belatedly adopted in 1752, there was a public outcry at the apparent loss of eleven days. The astronomical solstice had been eleven days earlier on the 13th of June, 1745, old style.

We might reasonably assume that the account we have from George Smith is his own direct transcription and rendering of William Lancaster's words. Smith presents Lancaster's words in what appears a semi-verbatim form not employing direct speech but appearing to offer some indication of the informant's specific words.

William Lancaster, was a young man, probably in his twenties, in 1735. He is unlikely to have had any experience of armies – the Rebellion of 1715 occurred when he was in his infancy and the nation itself had been sufficiently at peace in the intervening years for there to have been no significant military activity in an area as remote as Souther Fell.

Nevertheless, the account of the army displays a degree of military knowledge. We are told of "a regular marching army", marching five abreast which suggests some awareness of proper formations and discipline. (It would be exceptional for the columns to be five abreast as marching columns were usually in even numbers to permit them to split into two equal columns.) Similarly, we have very specific detailing of procedures en route: "He frequently observed that some of the five would quit rank, and seem to stand in a fronting posture, as if he was observing and regulating the order of their march, or taking account of their numbers, and, after some time, appeared to return full gallop to the station he had left, which they never failed to do as often as they quitted their lines; and the figure that did so was generally one of the middlemost men in the rank."

Such regulation would have been shown by the Duke of Cumberland's army. They were a well-disciplined and established force. They had experienced the rigours of the War of the Austrian Succession and had been involved in the Battle of Fontenoy, on 11th May, a few weeks before the apparition. Good marching order was essential for an army if it wished to proceed securely and at speed through enemy territory.

The army that had gathered around Charles Edward Stuart was composed of irregular: clansmen from the Highlands. They would have been regarded as among the least civilized and least disciplined fighters in Europe. Through the charismatic force of Bonnie Prince Charlie's personality and the suppressed resentment of half a century, they accepted military direction, but, despite their terrifying success, they never acquired the discipline to march in the tight and regular formation of the spectral army.

It was more than a full month after the last apparition on Souther Fell, that Charles Edward Stuart embarked on his epic but doomed venture. He landed on Eriskay on 23rd July, 1745, with seven companions and then proceeded to gather the clans about him as they marched south towards their victory over General Sir John Cope at Prestonpans on 21st September. News of his taking Edinburgh and his defeat of the Hanoverian army may have spread like wildfire throughout the country, but these events took place after the appearance of the spectral army on Souther Fell.

On 21st October, a month after the battle of Prestonpans, George Smith, from his home in Boothby near Brampton, was writing to *The Gentleman's Magazine* with an analysis of the relative strengths of regular and irregular forces.[1] His essay was a judicious attempt to explain the defeat of the British army by a "mob" of "madmen". "When, therefore, in the case of regular troops engaging with mobs, the former are defeated, some reasons ought to be assigned, which, in my opinion, are chiefly reducible to the following: Superiority of numbers, misconduct of officers, particularly the general, surprize, temerity, cowardice, difference of weapons, and confusion. . . .

"In the late affair of Gladsmuir (Prestonpans) most of the troops had never been in action; wherefore to the reasons being named, cowardice and surprise ought to be join'd, tho' the last seems to be the greatest part of the charge."

Such a reasoned perspective on what was a dangerously threatening army reflected the complacency of the citizens of Carlisle in the face of imminent danger. The Highlanders were uncivilized and Carlisle was, after centuries as a military city overseeing an unruly border, enjoying a period of peace and increasing prosperity.

In a further letter to *The Gentleman's Magazine* Smith tells of the city's bemused lack of preparation: "So many idle rumours of the march of the rebels into England, had been spread previous to the fact, that to flatter our indolence we presumed it to be impossible, and therefore took no measure to prevent it; we cloistred up the light horse and militia of both counties within the walls of Carlisle, and left the country to shift for itself; our nobility, except Lord Lonsdale, did nothing, even those whose fortunes depended greatly on the route of the rebels, raised not a single man in the cause."[2]

Six days after Smith had written his magisterially detached letter on the better management of the troops, he was faced with the reality of actual fighting. "By letters from Scotland on Tuesday, Nov. 5, we began to understand that the long projected expedition was now undertaken, and our frontiers quite open and unguarded; the garrison at Carlisle were under no apprehensions, judging they would march past them as in the rebellion of 1715. We secreted our most valuable effects, and sent the ladies eastward from these miscreants, of whom we had most terrible representations, determined to abide them ourselves."[3]

Smith was writing with the benefit of hindsight – the published letter is undated but appeared in the May issue of *The Gentleman's Magazine* – and there was, perhaps, a note of looking to excuse his compatriots' lack of preparation, but Carlisle was cruelly exposed and vulnerable: "On

Thursday the easternmost column had gained Stangarth side on the English border, and we suspected their intention was to proceed through the wastes of Beucastle for Brampton, being the properest place to subsist so numerous a corps; but that night we learn'd that they had turned to the right for Longtown, which gave us hopes they would continue their march for Row-cliff and pass the river Eden there, the dryness of the season having reduc'd that stream to a tolerable fording in several places below Carlisle.

"On Friday the middlemost column joined them, and on Saturday their hussars advanced to Stanwix bank, to take a view of the city, on which the 8 gun battery at B (see map) fir'd from the castle and they disappear'd. On Sunday they invested the city on all sides, having pass'd Eden at several fords below. The marq. of Tullibardin was driven with his corps from Shaddon-gate by the four gun battery at D, and those on the north under the Duke of Perth remained in the village of Stanwix, where some houses received considerable damage from the continued fire of the eight gun battery.

"The troops on the south side under the pretender's son were in like manner repuls'd by the citadel and the turret guns. Being in want of materials for a siege a resolution was that night taken to remove to Brampton, and the quartermasters accordingly came into the place about midnight."

At this point, when everyone around must have been in a state of apprehension, if not terror, George Smith acted in a way that was either exceptionally foolish or remarkably courageous. Smith chose to visit the rebel general in his headquarters and provide him with a map of the undefended country that lay before them. He described what took place: "On Monday the 11th the prince's lifeguards, as they were called, came to Naworth Castle the earl of Carlisle's seat, and I went to see them, they behaved in general with much complaisance and were well-dress'd, good-looking men: they were very solicitous to see a good map of England, and I carry'd them one on Tuesday morning, to try if I could penetrate their intentions: but these were inscrutable: only I observed they made great enquiry about Wales, and after about other places, artfully to disguise their aim; which however I am apt to think they scarce knew themselves."

Smith's explanation of his potentially treasonous behaviour – "to try if I could penetrate their intentions" – seems naïve in the extreme and his visit had potentially serious repercussions.

Three of his neighbours, who may not have felt at ease with this urbane, intellectual Scotsman of uncertain temper living in their small community, reported him to the authorities.[4] On 17th July, 1746, two months after Smith's letter appeared in *The Gentleman's Magazine*, depositions were taken from witnesses under oath in open sessions at a court convened in Carlisle in the case of "The King against Smith". Thomas Scot, a gardener who lived in Boothby, offered some hearsay evidence of Smith's traitorous inclinations: "About two years ago (Smith) said that His Majesty King George ruined this nation with the keeping of misses, and that one of them was another man's wife and six thousand pounds a year settled upon her more than she had before, paid out of the Excise." More pertinently, he claimed that "Smith was frequently amongst the Rebels and assisted them in getting quarters". The remarks about "misses" may not have shown a proper respect for the sovereign, but King George was a notorious womanizer. There was a degree of truth in this latter statement as Smith, in his article, wrote of "Betwixt that and the 16th, I had some of their hussars, an audacious, insolent, lying rabble, and on Saturday the 16th six of the officers of the McPhersons, who were by far the civilest of their foot, and paid for what they had in genteel manner enough", which suggests that Smith had Jacobite troops billeted on him. The Young Pretender was seeking to win hearts and minds by the observation of civilized standards.

A second informant, Thomas Wasdale, who was of a higher standing and also literate – Thomas Scot affirmed his deposition with his mark – clearly indicated that Smith was of a treasonous disposition: "This informant saith that about a fortnight before the Rebels came to Brampton Mr George Smith of Boothby in the said county came to the Informant at his fulling mill at Tenterbank aforesaid with a letter in his hand and told the informant that he had received a letter from the pretender's own hand and began to read it but the mill and water making so much noise this informant was not capable to distinguish what he so read but looking over the said Smith's shoulder the informant saw the said letter signed T. Graham. Saith on his asking him if it was from the pretender's self, Smith answered it was from his own hand and that every Gentleman in the county had one of the same on which the Informant asked him for what reason to which said Smith made answer - our Business is to Inquire in the neighbourhood who will joyn the rebels and who wd not - and on Informants asking to see the said letter Smith answered t'was no matter - Informant shd see it another time."

The final witness, William Tennent of Boothby, was also able to sign the testimony he made before the magistrates Aglionby and Hudleston. His testimony was specific and to the point: "This informant upon oath said that on Martinmas - Tuesday now last past about eight in the morning just as he was going to Narward castle fro his house at Bothby aforesaid in order to assist the servants of Lord Carlisle, a number of the Rebels then being there Mr George Smith of Bothby aforesaid came into this Informants house and understanding this informant was going to Naward castle on the occasion aforesaid he the said Smith said to this Informant I will go with you and carry along with me the mapp of England to show said Rebels the roads which will cause them to befriend the houses of Bothby. Saith when he came to Naward Castle the rebels desired the said Smith to leave the said mapp which he did till the evening when said Smith returned again to Naward Castle and had the said mapp returned him."

Smith was required to answer the accusations against him on the same day. His response was brief: "This examinand absolutely denies that he ever spoke any treasonable or disrespectful words of His Majesty or Government - saith he never had any letter from the pretender or declared he had any - admits he had a written paper signed for C Regent which paper was afterwards published in the Newcastle Journal which he rec'd inclosed from Mr Graham of Carlisle and which he admitted he showed to Thomas Wasdale and several other persons in the neighbourhood. Saith the aforesaid paper so produced purported to be a letter or Address from the loyal City of Glasgow . . . Saith he having heard that some of the Rebels were at Naward Castle and having occasion for a map the examinand went to Naward Castle with aforesaid map of England with an Intent to introduce himself to the Rebels and thereby to be enabled to penetrate into the discussions of the Rebells as to their March and to gather such Informations from them as might be of Service to the

Government."

Smith's plea seems to have been accepted as there is no further record of any proceedings being taken against him. We are, however, left with the difficulty of explaining Smith's extraordinary behaviour. He might have been hedging his bets as to the war's outcome and been seeking to curry favour with the rebels, but his social position would suggest that he would have been wise to continue quietly with his everyday life and not draw attention to himself. If he was genuinely seeking information in order to help the king, as a private citizen he would have found it difficult to make that information known in the right quarters. Thirdly, it is possible that Smith was acting under general or specific instructions from the authorities. The eccentricities of his behaviour corresponded with the irascibility of his character.

George Smith's account of the rebels around Carlisle continues, describing the undisciplined behaviour of the rebels, which was far different from the orderly marching of the regular army across Souther Fell: "The same morning capt. Hamilton, quarter master general of the foot, came to Naworth, demanding billets for 6000 men: the guards look'd very blank at the proposal, and began to secure their portables and I soon found what a nest of thieves we were going to have.

"About noon several hundreds of a wretched, ill-looking, shabby crew pass'd by armed with targets, broad swords, muskets, &c. and seemed very angry if no deference was paid to their flag: that afternoon and all the next day they spent in shooting sheep, geese, &c. and robbing on the highway: tho' their chiefs express'd great dissatisfaction at their proceedings, yet they dar'd not restrain them for fear of putting them out of humour. Betwixt that and the 16th, I had some of their hussars, an audacious, insolent, lying rabble, and on Saturday the 16th six of the officers of the McPhersons, who were by far the civilest of their foot, and paid for what they had in genteel manner enough: it was not my business to expose their extravagant chimeras, but I found they were kept extremely ignorant of our affairs, by the artifice of their superiors. Some of them had their sons in his majesty's army, but were made to believe that all our regular forces were detained by the French in Flanders, and they already possess'd London in their elevated imaginations without drawing a sword.

“The fate of Carlisle you must have heard from other hands, we are yet in doubt whether that ignominious surrender was caused by cowardice or treachery, or both; I think it most probable that it was lost thro’ a presumption that it would never be attack’d, and for want of regular discipline among the men. The map exhibits that pretend’d battery which contributed to this false step, to which I refer you. The pretender’s son was proclaimed at the cross, the keys of the city being carry’d to him at Brampton by the mayor and attendants; it should seem a necessary question how the keys of a garrison town, the custody of which was always till then committed to the governor, nominal or residential, came to be delivered into the mayor’s hands for such a use at such a time.

“During the pretended siege the garrison had a lad kill’d on the citadel by a musket shot, and one by the accidental firing of a piece on the walls, which was all their loss, slain or wounded. What the rebels lost is not to be ascertained, a person of distinction was report’d to be slain near Harraby, and bury’d with great solemnity at Wetheral; a principal engineer was seen to fall by a shot from the citadel at the head of their pretended battery: doubtless they lost more, but I am apt to believe, not many, because they kept too great a distance, and could not be discover’d because of a very thick and uncommon mist which continued all the time; so that the garrison may be said to have fir’d in the dark, directing their guns only by the sound of their pipes or voices. Their own reports were not at all to be credited, some of them pretending that the cannon balls had hit them without hurting them, credit judaeus Apella.”

Some two weeks of the marauding army were enough for the people of Brampton and they sought to flee. Smith himself claimed, thereby demonstrating his loyalty, to have gone to Haltwhistle in order to join General Wade and his troops who had been thwarted by the weather in their march from Newcastle.

“On Tuesday the 19th, about 100 horse more came to Brampton from Scotland, and the greatest part of the inhabitants of the country, tir’d out with finding subsistence for such a voracious crew, fled. I went to Haltwesel, hearing that General Wade’s army was in full march for our relief, determining to join him, but the day following that rout was countermanded, on hearing that the rebels were proceeding southward. Such was the position of our affairs, from the 5th to the 20th November; a long period of uneasiness and expence in carrying off and bringing back effects."

It is worth printing George Smith's account in full. It is not strictly relevant to our theme, but it is, as would be expected of the man, a spirited, opinionated account and gives a fair picture of the times and the levels of perturbation prevailing among the Cumberland population.

"I must do the rebels the justice to say, that they never used so much as a single woman in the whole country with the least indecency, notwithstanding the crimes of that nature laid to their charge: 'Tis said their prince had given strict orders to the contrary, and declared that every officer should suffer as the criminal for the actions of that nature committed by any of the ruffians under him: whether true or not I cannot say.

"All the time they lay in this neighbourhood they were marching and counter-marching constantly, the better to conceal their numbers, which were reported to be 22000, but were only about one third of that number.

"From the time the rebels left this neighbourhood, every day brought different accounts of them, which were all reported with so many improbable circumstances that they gained no credit. We too plainly perceiv'd that they had many well-wishers, who industriously conceal'd whatever might be to their prejudice, and exaggerated every circumstance in their favour. Sometimes it was reported that they were defeated, and presently afterwards that they were within a day's march of London, and that the mob had taken arms to support them: Everything began to be in confusion, for those who had nothing to lose were ready to break down the partition wall that separated properties; what contributed greatly to our uneasiness was that we could gain no intelligence that could be rely'd upon; the intercourse between Newcastle and Carlisle, being in a manner suspended after that city fell into the enemies hands. It was not long before several of the inhabitants of that and neighbouring places, exasperated against the tyranny of the Highland government, began to rouze themselves, necessity inspiring them with courage; associations were formed to regain their liberty, and a scheme laid to storm the castle and destroy the rebel garrison; chimerical as this project may appear, it terrify'd the governor into an artful invitation of the mayor and the aldermen to an entertainment within his precincts; which they accepted for fear of giving offence, and were immediately secur'd, tho' soon after released, on parole that they would encourage no such attempt for the future; others were confined on suspicion and every village in the neighourhood of the city search'd for arms or ammunition by the rebels, who nevertheless were continually deserting as apprehensive of surprise. The governor neglected nothing to keep them in spirits, sometimes flattering them with expectations from Scotland, at other times from France, and when all this wou'd not do, he fir'd the guns round the batteries for joy of a pretended victory, got I know not where. I do assure you their joy, ill-grounded as it was, gave all real well-wishers to their country sufficient uneasiness, especially as no certain intelligence could be obtained.

"In the mean time frequent skirmishes happen'd betwixt the citizens and the rebels, in all of which the townsmen had the better, and made several prisoners, whom they sent to distant goals, whilst the governor, to prevent a general defection, seiz'd the fathers of the offenders, as if punishing them would atone for the fault of their sons. He likewise attempted several methods to remove the odium which his party lay under, sometime by fair words, and at other times by menaces, and locking up the gates, all of which proved ineffectual; so that the whole extent of his government seem'd to be in a state of hostility and confusion."

While the rebels maintained an uneasy hold on Carlisle, the main body of Jacobite troops had made a rapid march south to Derby. With his commanders apprehensive of proceeding and marching the 125 miles or so to London, Bonnie Prince Charlie accepted the need to retreat at a moment when he might have ventured and seized the kingdom. The rebels turned northwards on 6th December.

"Affairs were in this situation 'till about the middle of December, when the governor being appriz'd of the retreat of his partisans, seiz'd on the market, and fixed his own price on the commodities, ransacking the country people, and under pretence of searching for letters, and impressing beds for the use of his garrison from the inhabitants.

"The rebels all this time were making forc'd marches to regain Scotland before his royal highness. The dread of the return of the mob of exasperated ruffians, disappointed of their grand project, and in want of all things, threw us into a general consternation: Penrith beacon was fir'd as a signal of distress, and the whole country flock'd southward to its relief. A party of about 120 rebels, which had been driven from Kendal before the rest came up, were intercepted in their flight and pursued into Orton craigs; but they regain'd their main body, tho' with great difficulty, and after a very close pursuit, one only being taken

"As there were no officers among them and the people were very ill-arm'd, 'twas judg'd extremely imprudent to hazard an action, especially as the distance of the duke's army could not certainly be known; so they separated to guard the avenues leading to their respective habitations, and left Penrith to shift for itself."

George Smith does not mention the battle of Clifton in his account and seems to have been in Carlisle at the time on the 18th December. However, there is a detailed plan of the skirmish, which is almost certainly in Smith's hand. The battle, notable as the last on English soil, was a successful rearguard action fought out in a matter of minutes beneath a fleeting wintry moon between perhaps a thousand Jacobites led by Lord George Murray and an advance guard of some 500 dragoons. The dismounted dragoons in their heavy riding boots advanced in the dark across the quaggy ground against strategically positioned rebels. The clansmen's charge on the shout of "Claymore" left forty dragoons dead or wounded, but only twelve Jacobites were killed. Murray had secured his retreat towards Scotland and Cumberland stayed in Clifton overnight.[5]

"On Wednesday, Dec 18, about midnight, by an express from his royal highness, we were summon'd to give all the assistance possible, by endeavouring to intercept the rebels, or any part of them, before they regain'd Carlisle. But they kept in so compact a body that we thought the attempt impractible, especially considering the difference of weapons and numbers; so they reached the city on Thursday night and Friday morning, excepting a few inconsiderable stragglers, who were secur'd.

"Had it not been for the surrender of Carlisle, where they had now a comfortable retreat, and necessary supplies, they must have been extremely embarrass'd, as the rains had now render'd the river Eden unfordable; but on the news of the duke's marching from Penrith, they abandoned the city, and left the old governor, with about 400 Highlanders and the English auxilaries, to garrison the castle, with a view to retard the pursuit, having suffer'd incredible fatigues in the course of their flight from Derby; in which, had not a halt, of near 30 hours, been happily order'd to the king's troops, on the false notion of an invasion in Sussex, they would have been infallibly destroy'd. They forded Esk near Longtoun, but lost some men by the rapidity of the current, seem'd to be in great uneasiness at Graitna, and vented repeated menaces against England for it; disloyalty and backwardness in so just a cause, threatening a return after being join'd by the forces which were then in Scotland for the service. As the principal topic of the rebel conversation, while they prepared to attack Carlisle, was on the beauties of their prince, the valour of their men, the tyranny of the present government, the justness of their cause, and their disregard of death; so now they were always boasting their skill and capacity in making an unparallel'd retreat, and their great prudence in timing it, so as to prevent their being inclos'd between two fires."

Within two days of the Duke of Cumberland reaching Carlisle, Smith had approached him and presented him with a carefully prepared plan of the city and its defences and a proposition for the placing of his artillery that was both topographically and militarily well informed.

"His royal highness arrived before Carlisle on Saturday the 21st, and honour'd Blackhall by taking up his lodgings there; at the farmhouse in which the pretender's son was quarter'd in his march round the city. His royal highness sent notice privately to the well-affected citizens to withdraw with their effects, and on Sunday Carlisle was again invested on all sides. On Monday, I sent his royal highness a plan of the city and castle of Carlisle, of which this is a copy, with my humble opinion where the batteries might be commodiously rais'd, to distress the town least, and the enemy most, by firing on the west curtain from Primrose Bank, and endeavouring to break down the arch over the sally-port door, which was accordingly approv'd of, and put in execution."

Smith's plan, as it appeared in *The Gentleman's Magazine*[6] is a highly professional, polished piece of work. It has an elegant cartouche and a romanticised view of "The West Prospect of Carlisle Castle", with closely nurturing rounded hills – the real hills are far smaller and much further away - and proud, though damaged castle walls and an enormous pennant flying from the tower. However, it does show precisely where

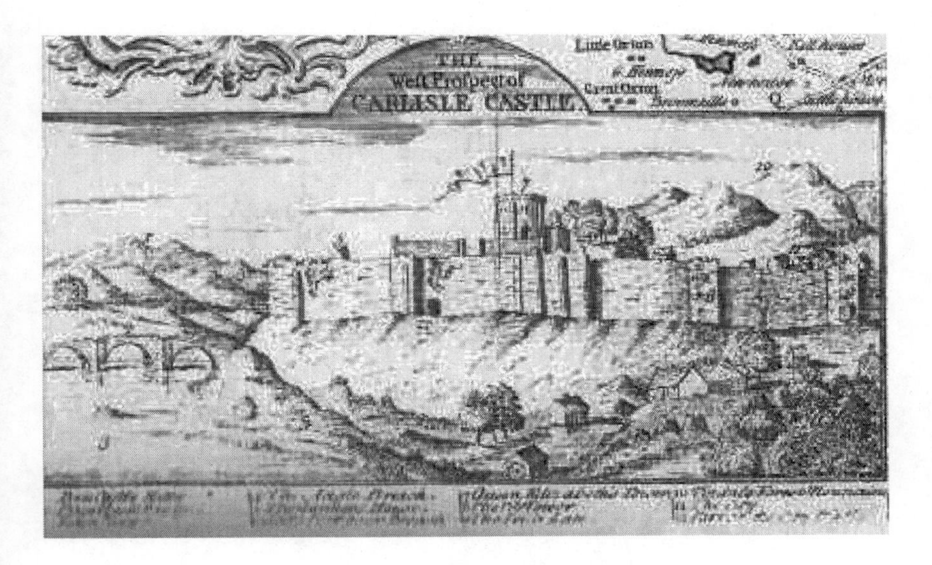

The West Prospect of Carlisle Castle
Vignette from George Smith's map of Carlisle

the guns should be targeted to maximum advantage. Lord George Murray, some seven weeks earlier, had found it difficult to place his inadequate siege guns "so as not to be annoyed from the cannon and the small arms of the town".[7] The four hundred men under the command of Colonel Francis Towneley were better prepared for the defence of the castle than the citizen militia that preceded them. They had all their guns together with ten brass cannon that the main army had left behind and they had strengthened the weakened and damaged walls and created ramparts with earth and sandbags and fixed iron spikes on the gates.[8]

The Duke of Cumberland may not have welcomed Smith's advice. He had been bloodied at the Battle of Fontenoy eight months earlier and, with an eye that had assessed the innovative complexities of continental castles, he was not one to be challenged by the outmoded and dilapidated walls of Carlisle. He declared that the castle was "'an old hen-coop' which he would speedily bring down about their ears, when he should have got artillery".[9] Mounsey described his actions: "He immediately dispatched orders to Whitehaven to procure cannon from the merchants there, and

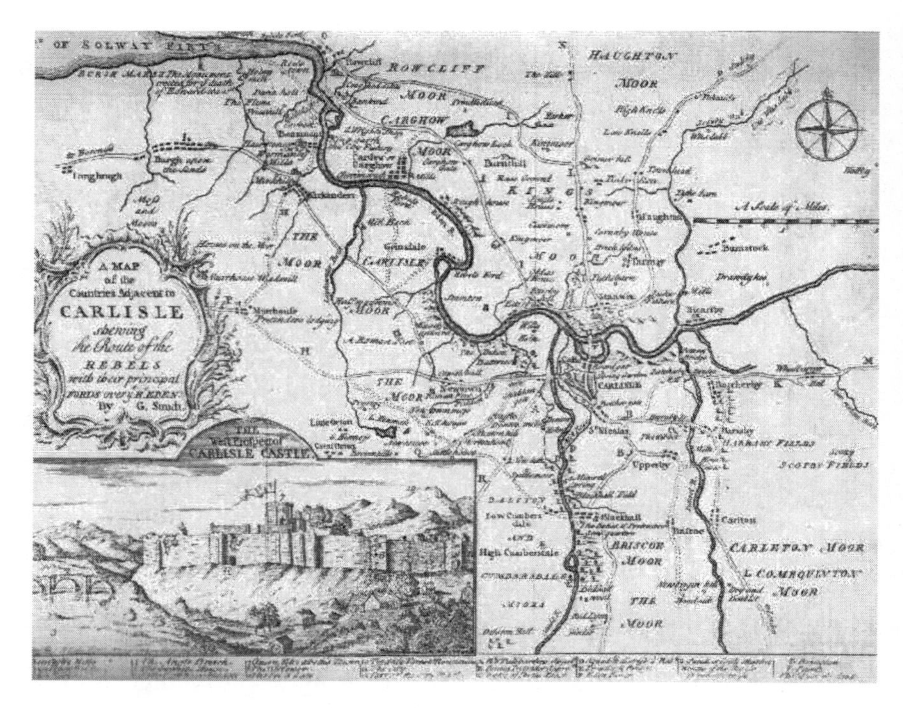

A Map of the Countries adjacent to Carlisle shewing the Route of the Rebels *by George Smith.*

surveyed the high grounds over against the Castle for the purpose of raising batteries against it. On the range of Primrose Bank, opposite to the western face of the Castle wall, where the Canal basin and the yards now are,[10] he marked out the site of two batteries; and whilst engaged in doing that he was fired on from the Castle, and narrowly escaped the shot, which passed between him and the engineer . . . The garrison fired incessantly from the Castle, but were not able to impede the progress of the works; their gunnery was not, from all accounts effective."[11]

Smith gave a blow by blow account of these proceedings, ensuring that the reader understood the dispositions fully by making constant reference to his map and drawing: "As the army had left their trenching tools behind to facilitate the pursuit, the country were summon'd in with theirs, who with great alacrity flock'd to the place, and cast up the ditch at L, notwithstanding the fire from the garrison, which hurt not a single man, there being an advanc'd guard of soldiers to inform the trenchers at every flash. On Thursday the 26th his royal highness went round to visit the works on the North side near Stanwix, and some friends of the rebels having driven a flock of sheep on the Swifts, the garrison, under favour of some cannon placed on Eden bridge, made a sally, and brought several head into the castle; flour was also furnish'd them from time to time, notwithstanding the prohibition, which obliged his royal highness to cut the aqueducts that drove the mills, to disappoint their supplies; the rebels burnt a barn and a house near English gate the same day. On Friday, six eighteen pounders which arrived from Whitehaven were brought from Rowcliff, and planted on the batteries, in order to begin to play on Saturday at day-break, which they accordingly did, 3 against the single battery at C, and the other 3 against the 4 gun battery at D. 'Tis to be noted that as the parapet of the castle wall was extremely low, and the gunners on that account greatly expos'd, the inhabitants had rais'd an artificial bulwark of wet turf to a considerable thickness, with proper embrasures for cannon, before the first march of the rebels out of Scotland, a work sufficient to drown the shot of any pieces which the enemy cou'd bring along with them, the road they came. But these were presently thrown down by the repeated shocks of the eighteen pounders, and the rebels, expos'd to too brisk a fire, abandon'd the battery at D by noon, the army continuing to batter in breach all that afternoon and the next day, besides the cohorns which were thrown from the ditch, at the end of Priestbeck bridge, as exhibited in the map, and which greatly incommoded the garrison. The wall by Sunday night began to totter, three more cannon arriving they were erected on a new battery at H, somewhat nearer, to play on the angle C; the other 5 were to batter in breach (one of the six having burst). At the sight of this new battery the governor hung out a flag of truce, before any breach was effected, subsequent to which were the conditions publish'd in the Gazette, to which I refer."

George Smith's map clearly shows the location of the batteries on rising ground to the west of the Poddon Beck. A large scale map drawn after the siege, and titled "Plan of the Attack on the Castle of Carlisle Taken by, HIS ROYAL HIGHNES the DUKE of CUMBERLAND.39 debr 1745"[12], shows the placement of the two batteries and the castle's defences in far greater detail. This, and two further maps, showing the damage to the walls and proposals for refashioning the castle and city's defences in the manner of those at Berwick may also be by George Smith.[13]

Over the rest of the decade the various proposals for repairing and strengthening the castle – some had an ambition that extended far beyond the military needs and the financial capability of the government – are indicative of the continuing unease over the security of the North.

Within a few weeks of being brought before the magistrates, George Smith was undertaking a *Survey of the Coast of Cumberland.* In the manuscript copy kept in Carlisle Library[14], he began: "As my orders were to commence at the mouth of the River Eden" and, at the end he stated, "At Southfield point, the Lancashire Survey terminating gave me the opportunity of doing the same, and I return'd agreeable to my intentions that night to Raven-glass." His final commendation of his work is: "This is an accurate account of the Coasts of Cumberland taken by an actual survey, according to my orders, the maps will exhibit this description more properly to which I all along refer. My observations were as many as the hurry of time wou'd admitt off, six weeks being short enough for so extensive a survey, which I compleated in one."

When the survey was published some sixteen months later in the January, 1748, issue of *The Gentleman's Magazine*, it was headed: *Extract of a Letter giving an Account of a Survey of the North West Coast of England, in August 1746, at our Expence*. And Smith introduced the article by bewailing the "want of correct maps" because the English had failed to adopt a standard meridian. It is probable that George Smith had been commissioned by an anxious government to produce a map of England's most exposed coast with the utmost urgency.

In the interim between making the survey and its appearance in the magazine, George Smith published three articles all of which may have arisen from a concern, personal or official, for his country's security. *A Dissertation on the Roman Wall,*[15] in July, 1746, was prompted by the thought that, "In the present situation of affairs, a plan of the method antiently practis'd by the vigilant Romans for securing the isthmus of Britain, with some remarks on it, will not I believe be unacceptable to the public." Smith would have had "6 or 7000 regular forces plac'd in the line of the wall, from Hexham to Brampton" and would thereby "have effectually prevented the incursion of the rebels into England".

His journey to Cross Fell was made on 19th August and published almost immediately in the August issue of *The Gentleman's Magazine*. He justified the journey by claiming, "The following account of Cross-fell, will entertain such of your readers whose genius inclines them to the description of romantic scenes. A mountain that is generally ten months bury'd in snow, and eleven in clouds, cannot fail of exciting the attention and curiosity of a traveller."[16] His account is concerned with the geology and botany of "these almost impervious wastes" and he had no observation to make on Alston, where he picked up a guide. However, it was Alston that may have drawn him to this isolated part of the Pennines. The area had long been an important area for the mining of lead and other non-ferrous metals and was enjoying a boom in the mid-eighteenth century.[17]. The lead mines had once been in the possession of the Derwentwater family. They were confiscated by the crown in 1716 because of the role played by James, Earl of Derwentwater in the Jacobite Rebellion of 1715. They had been granted by the crown, in 1734, to the Royal Hospital for Seamen, at Greenwich. In troubled times there might be good cause to make an assessment of this radical community that controlled one of the country's principal resources.

In introducing his journey to the Caldbeck fells, itself an area of mineralogical importance, George Smith declared that: "My intention in this journey was to visit the Wadd-mines, the peculiar product of these mountains, and no-where else discovered on the globe, but as they are kept close shut up, and the weather was extremely unfavourable, I deferred that examination to a more proper time."[18] Two months later, Smith explained his decision more fully: "I am very glad that such remarks as I have been able to make, are so agreeable to your readers. – For their satisfaction, I must inform you, that wadd mines in the Cumberland dialect signifies the black-lead mines, being synonymous terms. Their cause and nature has employ'd the great Bp Nicholson in two manuscript letters, whose opinion with my own, I intended to transmit to you; but as I could not have the opportunity of seeing them myself, I defer publication till a better opportunity. We are positive the whole world affords not another, nor does it appear that the Romans ever knew of this.

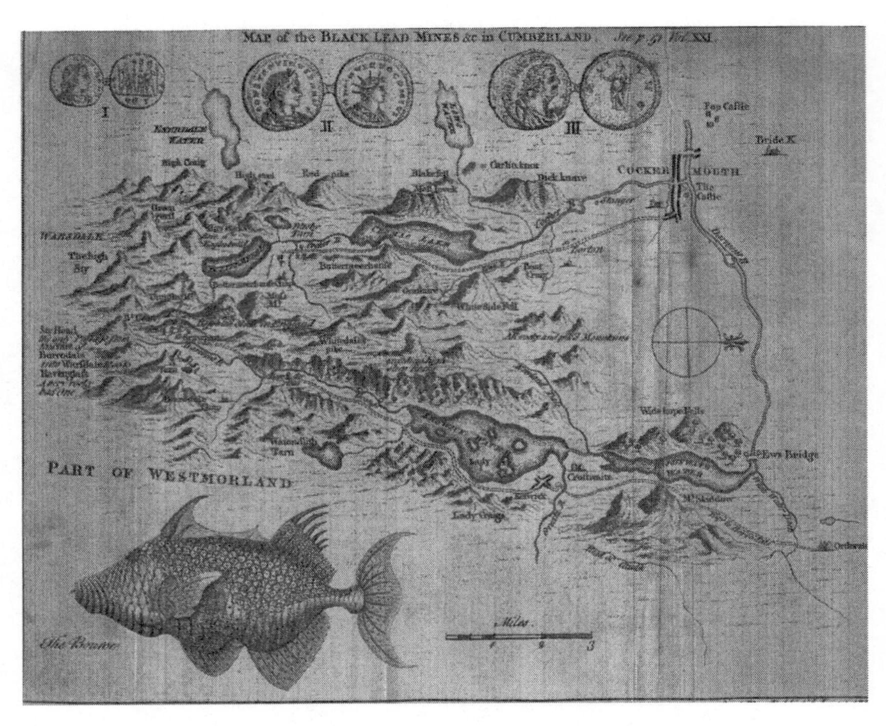

George Smith's map of his journey to the Wadd mines as it appeared in The Gentleman's Magazine

It was accidently discover'd by a tree blown up by the roots in a tempest, - The produce has nothing common with lead but the name, not being fusible in any fire. The mines are seldom opened, except a great demand require it; tho' notwithstanding the vigilance of the owners, it may be procured from the smugglers thereabouts; it sells at 6s.6d per lb. generally. – The inclemency of the weather, and rocks of so formidable ascent, prevented my intention to see them." Smith finally went to the wadd mines three years later in August 1749 after an armed attack on the mine steward's house in 1749 with the explicit aim of stealing graphite[19]. and published his account in the January issue of *The Gentleman's Magazine* in 1751[20] Writing seventy years later, Jonathan Otley summed up the situation and gave some idea of the strategic importance of this isolated and secretive mine: "To prevent the depredations of intruders, it has sometimes been necessary to keep a strong guard upon the place; and for its better protection, an Act of Parliament was passed 25th Geo. 2d. cap. 10th, by which an unlawful entering of any mine, or wadhole of wad, or black-cawke, commonly called black-lead, or unlawfully taking, or carrying away any wad, &c. therefrom, as also the buying, or receiving the same, knowing it to be unlawfully taken, is made felony. In the preamble of this Act, it is stated to be 'necessary for divers useful purposes, and more particularly in the casting of bomb-shells, round shot, and cannon balls."[21]

It is not unreasonable to suggest that George Smith was not quite the innocent and curious traveller. His curiosity may have been political in times of acute political crisis. His actions in Carlisle prove his interest, his maps suggest that he may have been in official employment and his survey of the coast may have been instigated by the government. It is equally possible that he was asked to act as the eyes and ears of the authorities and to examine any possible cause for concern. The reports on the apparitions of Souther Fell in an area which owed allegiance to their landlord, the Duke of Norfolk, who was head of one of the leading Catholic families in the country, must have alarmed the government and raised concern about their effect on public morale. A spectral army that may have appeared almost as a harbinger of Bonnie Prince Charlie was a potential rallying cry for disaffected radicals. Smith may have been sent to investigate such a dangerous story and re-present the matter in a more acceptable public form.

Is it credible that against the glare of the setting sun, at a distance of almost a mile, an uninformed servant and a young farmer would have eyes sharp enough to discern a regular army? "And, what was most extraordinary, he frequently observed that some of the five would quit rank, and seem to stand in a fronting posture, as if he was observing and regulating the order of their march, or taking account of their numbers, and, after some time, appeared to return full gallop to the station he had left, which they never failed to do as often as they quitted their lines; and the figure that did so was generally one of the middlemost men in the rank. As it grew later, they seemed more regardless of discipline, and rather had the appearance of people riding from a market, than an army; though they continued crowding on, and marching off, so long as they had light to see them." The spectral army that was reported to the wider world was not a mythical army or a Roman army, or an anonymous army or least of all the semi-savage "mob of madmen" united under the cause of Bonnie Prince Charlie. The regular spectral army marching five abreast was the Hanoverian army of the Duke of Cumberland, Butcher Cumberland, marching towards Culloden and the final assertion of a brutal peace on a United Kingdom.

The most remarkable aspect of Smith's analysis of the 'phaenomenon' is that he makes no mention of the recent rebellion. The Jacobite army had twice passed within ten miles of the area within six months following the sighting, and the passage of Cumberland's pursuing army must have been bruited throughout the countryside. The people around Penrith had shown no inclination towards the Jacobites. "This was also one of the most loyal areas in the whole country. The men of Penrith had formed themselves into a company late in October, declaring their support for George II. Although they prudently laid low when the rebel army marched through their town on its way south, they had successfully beaten off a party of marauders from the garrison at Carlisle which had attempted to ransack Lowther Hall. They also stopped the duke of Perth, who had been sent ahead by the Young Pretender to make contact with is supporters in Scotland."[22] Lord Elcho saw no reason to question the loyalty of the people of Carlisle and Cumberland: "All the people of both the town and the County show'd a great dislike to the Prince's cause."[23] Nevertheless, it must have been a cause of concern to a nervous government, that in the more remote areas of a remote county that continued to have some traditional sympathy for the Derwentwater family, there were rumours of an army marching across the fells.

Smith's analysis, if we imagine that he was acting on behalf of the government and seeking to quell a dangerously unsettling rumour, was subtle. He rubbished the information without rubbishing the informants: "They had no end in imposing on their fellow creatures, and are of good repute in the place where they live." But the story itself was utterly fantastical: "The story has so much the air of romance, that it seemed fitter for Amadis de Gaul, or Glenville's System of Witches." He was clear as to a possible scientific explanation but left the matter unresolved. Three difficulties presented themselves, the irregular motion of the meteor; the regular system of its appearance; and its reappearance on the same day of the year. He also suggested that "fancy" had an important part to play in the whole apparition. Most significantly, if he did shape the contents of the story, the army that was seen marching across Souther Fell was recognisably the Hanoverian Army of the Duke of Cumberland. It was not the Jacobite army of Highlanders led by Charles Edward Stuart.

Nothing in George Smith's account suggests fear, apprehension or amazement on the part of the witnesses. Their response has been neutralized. Smith may simply be providing an objective account. On the other hand, as a political agent sent to calm a disturbing rumour, he may have found it necessary to remove all emotional colouring from the story.

Phantom armies have long been associated with times of civil and military unrest and it is not improbable that the witnesses or the reporter may have had their apprehension informed by earlier understandings. Lancaster and Stricket may have been aware of folk traditions and Biblical accounts and Smith, with his wide reading, would certainly have been aware of images of phantom armies or armies in the sky in classical and modern literature as well as instances in recent English history.

The most famous sighting of phantom armies was after the first major battle of the Civil War, the bloody but inconclusive battle of Edgehill in Worcestershire, which was fought on Sunday 23rd October, 1642. Like the spectral army of Souther Fell the apparition was seen several times by an increasing number of people, was apparently sworn on oath and was described in very precise detail. However, in the instance of Edgehill, the apparition was of a conflict, inspired fear and the witnesses felt that it was a sign from God. Two pamphlets recorded the apparitions which were seen by shepherds some two months after the battle, during Christmas, 1642. *A Great Wonder in Heaven, shewing the late Apparitions and Prodigious Noyses of War and Battels, seen on Edge-Hill, neere Keinton in Northamptonshire. Certified under the Hands of WILLIAM WOOD, Esquire, and Justice for the Peace in the said Countie, SAMUEL MARSHALL, Preacher of GODS Word in Keinton, and other Persons of Qualitie* was a mere seven page pamphlet. It had been printed in London and was rushed out to appear within less than a month of the sighting, being "Printed for Thomas Jackson, Jan. 23, Anno Dona.

1642."[24] Its version of events given in highly charged language is as follows: "But to our purpose. Edge-Hill, in the very confines of Warwick shire, neere unto Keynton in Northamptonshire, a place, as appeares by the sequele, destined for civill warres and battells; as where King John fought a battell with his Barons, and where, in defence of the Kiugdomes lawes and libertie, was fought a bloody conflict between his Majesties and the Parliaments forces; at this Edge-Hill, in the very place where the battell was strucken, have since, and doth appeare, strange and portentuous Apparitions of two jarring and contrary Armies, as I shall in order deliver, it being certified by the men of most credit in those parts, as William Wood, Esquire, Samuel Marshall, Minister, and others, on Saturday, which was in Christmas time, as if the Saviour of the world, who died to redeem mankinde, had beene angry that so much Christian blood was there spilt, and so had permitted these infernall Armies to appeare where the corporeall Armies had shed so much blood; between twelve and one of the clock in the morning was heard by some sheepherds, and other countrey-men, and travellers, first the sound of drummes afar off, and the noyse of soulders, as it were, giving out their last groanes; at which they were much amazed, and amazed stood still, till it seemed, by the neerenesse of the noyse, to approach them; at which too much affrighted, they sought to withdraw as fast as possibly they could; but then, on the sudden, whilest they were in these cogitations, appeared in the ayre the same incorporeall souldiers that made those clamours, and immediately, with Ensignes display'd, Drummes beating, Musquets going off, Cannons discharged, Horses neyghing, which also to these men were visible, the alarum or entrance to this game of death was strucke up, one Army, which gave the first charge, having the Kings colours, and the other the Parliaments, in their head or front of the battells, and so pell mell to it they went; the battell that appeared to the Kings forces seeming at first to have the best, but afterwards to be put into apparent rout; but till two or three in the morning in equall scale continued this dreadful fight, the clattering of Armes, noyse of Cannons, cries of souldiers, so amazing and terrifying the poore men, that they could not believe they were mortall, or give credit to their eares and eyes; runne away they durst not, for feare of being made a prey to these infernall souldiers, and so they, with much feare and affright, stayed to behold the successe of the businesse, which at last suited to this effect: after some three houres fight, that Army which carryed the Kings colours withdrew, or rather appeared to flie; the other remaining. as it were, masters of the field, stayed a good space triumphing, and expressing all the signes of joy and conquest, and then, with all their Drummes, Trumpets, Ordnance, and Souldiers, vanished; the poore men glad they were gone, that had so long staid them there against their wils, made with all haste to Keinton, and there knocking up Mr. Wood, a Justice of Peace, who called up his neighbour, Mr. Marshall, the Minister, they gave them an account of the whole passage, and averred it upon their oaths to be true. At which affirmation of theirs, being much amazed, they should hardly have given credit to it, but would have conjectured the men to have been either mad or drunk, had they not knowne some of them to have been of approved integritie: and so, suspending their judgments till the next night about the same houre, they, with the same men, and all the substantiall Inhabitants of that and the neighbouring parishes, drew thither; where, about halfe an houre after their arrivall, on Sunday, being Christmas night, appeared in the same tumultuous warlike manner, the same two adverse Armies, fighting with as much spite and spleen as formerly: and so departed the Gentlemen and all the spectatours, much terrified with these visions of horrour, withdrew themselves to their houses, beseeching God to defend them from those hellish and prodigious enemies. The next night they appeared not, nor all that week, so that the dwellers thereabout were in good hope they had for ever departed; but on the ensuing Saturday night, in the same place, and at the same houre, they were again seene with far greater tumult, fighting in the manner afore-mentioned for foure houres, or verie neere, and then vanished, appearing againe on Sunday night, and performing the same actions of hostilitie and bloudshed; so that both Mr. Wood and others, whose faith, it should seeme, was not strong enough to carrie them out against these delusions, forsook their habitations thereabout, and retired themselves to other more secure dwellings; but Mr. Marshall stayed, and some other; and so successively the next Saturday and Sunday the same tumults and prodigious sights and actions were put in the state and condition they were formerly. The rumour whereof comming to his Majestie at Oxford, he immediately dispatched thither Colonell Lewis Kirke, Captaine Dudley, Captaine Wainman, and three other Gentlemen of credit, to take the full view and notice of the said businesse, who, first hearing the true attestation and relation of Mr. Marshall and others, staid there till Saturday night following, wherein they heard and saw the fore-mentioned prodigies, and so on Sunday, distinctly knowing divers of the apparitions or incorporeall substances by their faces, as that of Sir Edmund Varney, and others that were there slaine; of which upon oath they made testimony to his Majestie. What this does portend God only knoweth, and time perhaps will discover; but doubtlessly it is a signe of his wrath against this Land, for these civill wars, which He in his good time finish, and send a sudden peace between his Majestie and Parliament. FINIS."

A second pamphlet, with equal self-dramatization, proclaimed its contents through its title: *The New yeares wonder: Being a most cernaine* [sic] *and true relation of the disturbed inhabitants of Kenton, and other neighbouring villages neere unto Edge-Hil, where the great battaile betwixt the kings army, and the Parliaments forces was fought. In which plea is heard & seene fearfull and strange apparitions of spirits as sounds of drums, trumpets, with the discharging of canons muskies, carbines pettronels, to the terrour and amazement, of all the fearfull hearers and behoulders. Certified under the hands of William Wood, Esquier, and Iustice for the peace in the said countie, Samuel Marshall, preacher of Gods word in Keynton, and other persons of qualitie.*[25] It was published by an eye-witness, one "Robert Ellit, lodger neere the old Rose in Thames street" and differed in several significant details. A first sighting was made by herdsmen on 1st January. On the night of 4/5th January, the people of Kineton heard "dolful and hydious groanes of dying men". Some dared to look out and saw "armed horsemen riding one againe the other". The night after throughout the district an immense battle was seen with "the foot against the foot and horse against the horse . . . and Ordinance playing on against the other as plainely visible. This battle vanished "in the twinkling of an eye" at daybreak. Marshall told the king who "presently sent to Edge-Hill Colonell Lewis Kirke, Captaine Dudly, Captaine Winman, and three other gentleman of worth who heard of this sad fearful and hisious fight . . . and then departed wondrous fearfull amaized and affrighted, & saw divers to their appearance that were there slaine as Sir Edward Varney, with divers others". Almost thirty thousand troops had fought at Edge Hill and there had been carnage on a terrifying scale. The events of that awful day and its consequences, pastoral fields strewn with the dead and dying, with the bodies of fellow Englishmen, must have deeply tormented the villagers of Kineton, and been a cause of fear and foreboding throughout the country. The nation was in turmoil. Our authors saw the hand of the Almighty in the phantom armies: it was "as if the Saviour of the world, who died to redeem mankinde, had beene angry that so much Christian blood was there spilt, and so had permitted these infernall Armies to appeare where the corporeall Armies had shed so much blood".

There is no record of either William Wood, who was said to be a Justice of the Peace, nor of a clergyman called Samuel Marshall.[26] The various officers are recorded among the lists of serving officers, but there is no mention of a commission reporting to the king. However, rumours of apparitions were current at the time, although none corresponded closely with the colourful accounts given in the pamphlets. A Newsbook for 17th-24th January 1643 noted that "The Letters from Banburie say, that the Cavaliers in the Castle there are frighted at the sight of a great man that walks in a surplice, and that about Edge-hill and Keinton, there are men seen walking with one legge, and but one arme, and passing to and fro in the night."[27] A lawyer of Lincoln's Inn Fields, a certain John Greene, wrote in his diary on the 19th January, days before either pamphlet was published: "There are now divers reports of strange sights seen, and strange noises heard at Edgehill where our last battle was fought; in the place wher the Kings army stood terrible outcries; Where the Parliaments music and singing Psalms".[28]

If there was any substance to the events described in the pamphlets, the stories would have deeply affected a credulous population at a time of great unrest. *A Great Wonder* emphatically says: "as if the Saviour of the world, who died to redeem mankinde, had beene angry that so much Christian blood was there spilt, and so had permitted these infernall Armies to appeare where the corporeall Armies had shed so much blood;" and *The New yeares wonder* condemns "evel councelares which are about the king!" These were strongly partisan accounts determined to play a part in the fierce political and religious debates of the time.

The phantom battle of Edgehill was the most vivid of the phantom battles of the Civil War. Two warlike apparitions were described in a far more fantastical pamphlet published in 1659: *The five strange wonders, in the north and west of England: as they were communicated to divers honourable members of Parliament, from several countrey gentlemen and ministers; concerning the strange and prodigious flying in the air of a black coffin betwixt Leicester and Nottingham, ... , with a flaming arrow, and a bloody sword, casting forth streams of fire, ... with a conjecturation thereupon, what these dreadful signs from heaven, may denote and signifie to the people on earth this present summer. Likewise, the great and wonderful warlike prodigies, ... between two fiery or flaming pillars. And the three monstrous creatures found in three eggs, ... Together with the opening of the skie in a fearful manner over Standish town five miles from Gloucester, and the appearing of a terrible fiery shaking sword from the heavens ... . Attested by an eye-witness, and entred upon record, in the Original Mirrour, or Looking Glass: and for more general satisfaction, presented to the view of the three nations of England, Scotland, and Ireland.* We are told that "the two Pillars represent his Highness and the Parliament, and the Northern Army the Forces of this Common wealth, vanquishing their Enemy, and maugre the Designs of all Forreign and Popish Confederates. Who need not in the least be feared, if the mutual closings and claspings of redintegrate affections and endearments be insisted upon between the Supream Authority and People, and each member of this Common-wealth, to return to his duty and proper station, and firmly to unite together, for the recovery of our long lost Liberties, and dear-eam'd Priviledges."[29]

Such accounts were the common currency of a superstitious population in a time of unrest. But, at the end of the seventeenth century they were also the subject of serious theological debate. The supposed images appearing in the skies were seen as portents and signs from God and to reduce them to purely physical phenomena was to deny the deity's presence in the world. Such prodigies were readily the subject of political and religious controversy with various parties choosing to interpret the signs that God had placed in the skies as auguries and assurances and justifications and vindications.

A case very much in point, and one that demonstrates the developing theological and philosophical debate on aerial phenomena, was the remarkable and brilliant display of northern lights, the aurora borealis, seen on 6th March, 1716. It occurred within a few weeks of the execution of some of the leaders of the Jacobite rebellion in 1715 and within two years of the disputed accession of Georg Ludwig of Hanover as George I. Edmund Halley, thrilled to witness the first London appearance of the aurora since it had been observed by Camden and Stow a hundred and seventy four years earlier, presented a lengthy and precise description of the spectacle to the members of the Royal Society: "Whilst we stood astonished at this surprizing Sight, and expecting what was further to come, the Northern End of the upper Lamina by degrees bent downwards, and at length closed with the End of the other that was under it, so as to shut up on the Northside an intermediate Space, which still continued open to the East. Not long after this, in the said included Space, we saw a great Number of small Columns or whitish Streaks to appear suddenly, erect to the Horizon, and reaching from the one Lamina to the other which instantly disappearing were too quick for the Eye, so that we could not judge whether they arose from the Under or fell from the Upper, but by their sudden Alterations they made such an Appearance, as might well be taken to resemble the Conflicts of Men in Battle."

Others expressed a genuine wonder and amazement. Mary, Countess Cowper, married to the Lord Keeper of the Great Seal and herself a Lady of the Bedchamber in the new Hanoverian Court, wrote in her diary: "An extraordinary light in the sky, . . . First appeared a black cloud, from whence smoke and light issued forth at once on every side, and then the cloud opened, and there was a great body of pale fire, that rolled up and down, and sent forth all sorts of colours like the rainbow on every side; but this did not last above two or three minutes. After that it was like pale elementary fire issuing out on all sides of the horizon, but most especially at the north and north-west, where it fixed at last. The motion of it was extremely swift and rapid, like clouds in their swiftest rack. Sometimes it discontinued for a while, at other times it was but as streaks of light in the sky, but moving always with great swiftness. About one o'clock this phenomenon was so strong, that the whole face of the heavens was entirely covered with it, moving as swiftly as before, but extremely low. It lasted till past four, but decreased till it was quite gone. At one, the light was so great that I could, out of my window, see people walk across

Lincoln's Inn Fields, though there was no moon."

However, she reported how such a prodigious aerial display was instantly interpreted by the various political factions: "Both parties turned it on their enemies. The Whigs said it was God's judgment on the horrid rebellion, and the Tories said that it came for the Whigs taking off the two lords that were executed." But it also caused consternation and alarm: "I could hardly make my chairmen come home with me, they were so frightened, and I was forced to let my glass down, and preach to them as I went along, to comfort them. I'm sure anybody that had overheard the dialogue would have laughed heartily. All the people were drawn out into the streets, which were so full one could hardly pass, and all frighted to death."

Rumours abounded and extraordinary accounts of the appearance of the lights were published the following day: "March 7. The town full of lies of what was seen in the air last night. Papers printed and sold that two armies were seen to fight in the air, that two men with flaming swords were seen to fight over Lincom's-inn-fields. The mob that went to Mr. Linet's burial last night said they saw two men in the sky fight without heads."[30]

The "two lords who were executed" were James Radclyffe, Lord Derwentwater, the one who owned the mines at Alston, and Lord Kenmure. Both had been captured in the fighting at Preston, when the Jacobite army was defeated by government troops. The twenty-six year old Radclyffe, illegitimately descended from Charles II, had been brought up with the exiled Stuarts in the Court of St Germain, and had only returned to his family estates at Dilston Hall six years before. Nevertheless, he was very popular with his tenants both in Northumberland and Cumberland. His Cumberland properties extended along the shores of Derwentwater, and included Lord's Island and the manor of Castlerigg.

The near coincidence of Radclyffe's execution on 27th February and the extraordinary aurora borealis on 6th March led to a popular association of the two events and the people in the North of England came to refer to the northern lights as Lord Derwentwater's Lights. In 1847 when the sun-spot cycle was at its height and brilliant auroras were being seen all over England, one commentator elaborated the story of the tragic lord beloved of the peasantry: "The impression made by Lord Derwentwater's fate, was deep and painful in proportion as his early promise had been great, and the apparent cruelty of his execution led to his being esteemed in the light of a martyr; handkerchiefs steeped in his blood were preserved as sacred relics; and when the mansion house was demolished amid the regrets of the neighbourhood, there was great difficulty in obtaining hands to assist in a work of destruction which was considered almost sacrilegious. The ignorant peasantry too were not slow to receive the superstitious stories that were propagated, and often has the wandering rustic beside the winter's hearth listened to the fearful tale—of how the spouts of Dilston Hall ran blood; and the very corn which was in the act of being ground, came from the mill tinged with a sanguine hue on the day the Earl was beheaded. The Aurora Borealis was observed to flash with unwonted brilliancy on that fatal night—an omen, it was said, of heaven's wrath; and to this day many of the country people know that meteor only by the name of 'Lord Derwentwater's lights'."[31]

James Radclyffe was the subject of ballads found throughout the North of England and Scotland,[32] which, like the story of the spectral army, were developed and extended by both James Hogg in his *Jacobite Songs* of 1821 and Allan Cunningham in 1825. Hogg, for example, says specifically: "The *aurora borealis,* which appeared remarkably vivid on the night of the unfortunate earl's execution, is still known in the north by the name of *Lord Derwentwater's Lights*".[33]

Edmund Halley, viewing the skies dispassionately, may have seen images of battle, others may have seen signs and prodigies, and the northern peasantry may have felt that the heavens sympathized at the execution of Lord Derwentwater, for it was a time when natural philosophy and what we now see as Newtonianism was disentangling itself from theology even as the peasantry continued to retain their primitive beliefs. William Whiston, a natural philosopher and theologian and a man whom George Smith would probably have known when he was Desagulier's assistant, observed the aurora and commented that what "the unthinking, affrighted, or superstitious call Armies, Spears and Battel in the Air, which yet to a sober and judicious Person they did no way properly resemble". He sought to explain how the hand of God was present in such phenomena, but, at the same time, they were not to be read as signs or portents: "On which account, in a sober Sense, all the Phenomena of the World are deriv'd from a Supernatural and Divine Power. But then, till God's particular Meaning be discovered to us, this will not enable us to foretel future Events from them. I am indeed under a peculiar Temptation my self to Wish and Suppose that this and the like unusual Appearances, may be Prognosticks and Fore-warnings of the Coming of those Great Concussions and Mutations which I expect soon in the World, to the Depression of Antichristianism, and the Revival of true Christianity in its stead. But this notwithstanding, I shall keep to Truth and Evidence; and till I see apparent Marks of a Supernatural Intention herein, shall not pretend to interpret the Secrets of Divine Providence in favour of any Opinions, I have entertain'd on other Foundations."

The army that William Lancaster, Daniel Stricket and their neighbours saw on Souther Fell at a time of national tension, may have appeared to be on or near solid ground and not in the heavens, but no-one at the time, neither the peasants nor their educated interlocutor, chose to see it as a sign, omen, prodigy or premonition.

They may, however, have been predisposed to interpret whatever aerial phenomena they actually observed as taking the form of an army. There were precedents with which all might have been familiar. In the *Apocrypha* there is a passage that, according to Erasmus Darwin, may represent the reaction of "an ignorant and alarmed people"[34] to the aurora borealis, when the appearance of an aerial army is seen as a precedent of destruction: "And then it happened, that through all the city, for the space almost of forty days, there were seen horsemen running in the air, in cloth of gold, and armed with lances, like a band of soldiers, And troops of horsemen in array, encountering and running one against another, with shaking of shields, and multitude of pikes, and drawing of swords, *and* casting of darts, and glittering of golden ornaments, and harness of all sorts. Wherefore every man prayed that that apparition might turn to good."[35]

A similar vision, a close parallel to the Souther Fell story, is found in *Book V* of *The Antiquities of the Jews* by Flavius Josephus. The translation, by William Whiston who commented so judiciously on the 1716 aurora, was one of the most popular of all eighteenth and nineteenth century books and might well have been among the half dozen books to be found in a farmer's household. "Besides these, a few days after that feast, on the one and twentieth day of the month Artemisius, a certain prodigious and incredible phenomenon appeared; I suppose the account of it would seem to be a fable, were it not related by those that saw it, and were not the events that followed it of so considerable a nature as to deserve such signals: for, before sun-setting, chariots and troops of soldiers in their armour were seen running about among the clouds, and surrounding of cities."[36]

Shakespeare, in *Julius Caesar*, drawing on Plutarch, had Calpurnia seek to stop Caesar going forth to the Capitol by urging the prodigious events that had occurred:

> Fierce fiery warriors fought upon the clouds,
> In ranks, and squadrons, and right form of war,
> Which drizzled blood upon the Capitol:
> The noise of battle hurtled in the air;
> Horses did neigh, and dying men did groan;
> And ghosts did shriek and squeal about the streets.[37]

The same imagery was available to John Milton, who was himself closely involved in the politics of the Civil War, when he described the Devil's armies on the plains of hell in *Paradise Lost*:

> As when to warn proud cities war appears
> Waged in the troubled sky, and armies rush
> To battle in the clouds, before each van
> Prick forth the airy knights, and couch their spears
> Till thickest legions close; with feats of arms
> From either end of heav'n the welkin burns."[38]

In 1747, two years after the last appearance on Souther fell, but before the publication of George Smith's article, James Thomson, in his last poem, *The Castle of Indolence,* which enjoyed enormous popularity throughout the next fifty years, had written of a solitary shepherd in the far Hebrides imagining vast assemblies in the sky as the sun was setting:

> As when a Shepherd of the *Hebrid-Isles'*,
> Plac'd far amid the melancholy Main ,
> (Whether it be lone Fancy him beguiles;
> Or that aerial Beings sometimes deign
> To stand, embodied, to our Senses plain)

Sees on the naked Hill, or Valley low,
The whilst in Ocean *Phœbus* dips his Wain,
A vast Assembly moving to and fro:
Then all at once in Air dissolves the wondrous Show.[39]

The origins of the spectral army that marched across Souther Fell were complex. The army did not come out of the blue.

Chapter Five:

Ann Radcliffe and Britton & Brayley

The accounts of the phantom army by George Smith and James Clarke are the only two that have survived from the eighteenth century, even though the story seems to have been widely known. It certainly had some currency in the popular press, although I have been able to find just one reference to it in eighteenth century newspapers and books.

On Saturday 29th December, 1764, the *London Evening Post*, among the crowded notices on its front page, carried a classified advert for "THE WONDERFUL MAGAZINE, or Marvellous CHRONICLE", a sixpenny magazine that was making the fourth appearance of its short life. It promised that "among other curious articles" it would contain: "A new History of Free masonry, from its first Grand Master the Devil, to the present Time. The Wonder of the Scold cured, a Tale by Jack Lovesun. Account of the great Eater of Kent, who devoured eighty four Rabbits at a meal. The dancing Elephant. The grateful Lion. Strange Discovery of Murder. The dancing Lake. The Salamander Man. The Bearded Infant. The enchanted Tower. The Fountain of Bones. Wonders of Marburg. The Pope's dreadful Curse. A lost Ring strangely found. A Cook boiled in Smithfield. Long Abstinence. Strange Phenomenon of Souter Fell. Remarkable Storms. Preferment gained by a Blunder. Account of a Pike swallowing a Mare, &c."[1] *The Wonderful Magazine* was "Printed for J. Cooke, at Shakespear's Head in Paternoster Row; and sold by all other Booksellers and News Carriers", but, unfortunately, despite telling the stories of the gargantuan eater from Kent and the devilish freemasons and the boiled cook it failed to print the promised story of the "Strange Phenomenon of Souter Fell".

Whether the story was found elsewhere or not, twenty years after the event it was well enough known nationally to be recognized by the enthusiastic consumers of fantastic tales. The strange phenomenon of Souter Fell was certainly in circulation.

The story may well have acquired a degree of respectability as Clarke's account became better known. *The Arminian Magazine*, which with its strong Wesleyan emphasis on salvation, was not a vehicle for frivolous or sensationalist literature, published Clarke's account verbatim in its May issue in 1795.

In *The Lakers: A Comic Opera* Miss Veronica Beccabunga proclaims: "I design to work up the story of the Visionary Horsemen on Souther-Fell-side into a ballad in imitation of the German." Unfortunately Sir Charles Portinscale immediately changes the subject. Pointing to the scene before him, he says, "This, madam, is the celebrated lake of Keswick, or Derwent-water; and the place where we now are, Crow Park, Mr West's second station. It was formerly a glade of ancient oaks, but the wasting hand of avarice has spoiled it of its beauties."[2] The ever-rapturous Beccabunga forgets her literary designs as she reaches for her pencil to note down every detail as Sir Charles describes the "spacious amphitheatre of picturesque mountains" that lay before them. The author of *The Lakers*, James Plumptre, responding to the offer of a friend of the Deputy Manager of Covent Garden whereby he hoped "to put a few hundred pounds into his pocket . . . for a few weeks trouble", had been ambitious for a certain Mrs Mattocks to play the part of Miss Beccabunga. His manuscript was returned and the author decided the work "was better adapted to the closet rather than the stage". And so this rather heavy-handed satire on the picturesque and other fashionable fads was published in book form in 1798.

Clearly, the "visionary horsemen" were known and recognized by advanced society and the story was felt to have Romantic elements. It seems strange that one of the most romantic novelists of all time, the young and retiring Ann Radcliffe, made no mention of the Souther Fell army when she toured the Lakes in 1795. She had made a fortune from the success of such novels as *The Romance of the Forest* and *The*

Mysteries of Udolpho. Sir Walter Scott later saluted her as "the founder of the class or school" of Gothic writing and she was celebrated for evoking a sense of sublime terror in her readers through suggestions of supernatural agencies which were then reduced to rational explanations. A disappointed Coleridge commented that, "The interest is completely dissolved when once the adventure is finished, and the reader, when he is got to the end of the work, looks about in vain for the spell which had bound him strongly to it."[3] Her heightened depictions of dark and densely forested mountain scenery were imagined from the paintings of Salvator Rosa, Gaspard Dughet and Claude Lorrain. The thirty-year-old Ann Radcliffe would have been expected to have a natural and literary affinity with the Lakes.

In 1795 Radcliffe and her lawyer husband had set out on the Grand Tour through Switzerland to Italy, but they had been forced to turn back by political difficulties after visiting Holland and parts of Germany. Frustrated in their intention of seeing mountain scenery, they headed for the Lakes and Ann's first experience of real mountains. They travelled through Kendal and over Shap. Ann was much taken with the Duke of Norfolk's castle and grounds at Greystoke, but as she turned towards Blencathra her nervous sensibility seemed to apprehend a mysterious otherness in the atmosphere: "The Graystock road, which we took for the first five or six miles (from Penrith) is uninteresting, and offers nothing worthy of attention, before the approach to the castle, the seat of the Duke of Norfolk. The appearance of this from the road is good; a gray building, with gothic towers, seated in a valley among lawns and woods, that stretch, with great pomp of shade, to gently-rising hills. Behind these, Saddleback, huge, gray and barren, rises with all its ridgy lines; a grand and simple background, giving exquisite effect: to the dark woods below. Such is the height of the mountain, that, though eight or ten miles off, it appeared, as we approached the castle, almost to impend over it. Southward from Saddleback, a multitude of pointed summits crowd the horizon; and it is most interesting, after leaving Graystock, to observe their changing attitudes, as you advance, and the gradual disclosure of their larger features. Perhaps a sudden display of the sublimest scenery, however full, imparts less emotion, than a gradually increasing view of it; when expectation takes the highest tone, and imagination finishes the sketch.

About two miles beyond Graystock, the moorlands commence, and, as far as simple greatness constitutes sublimity, this was, indeed, a sublime prospect; less so only than that from Shapfell itself, where the mountains are not so varied in their forms and are plainer in their grandeur. We were on a vast plain, if plain that may be called, which swells into long undulations, surrounded by an amphitheatre of heathy mountains, that seem to have been shook by some grand convulsion of the earth, and tumbled around in all shapes. Not a tree, a hedge, and seldom even a stone wall, broke the grandeur of their lines; what was not heath was only rock and gray crags; and a shepherd's hut, or his flocks, browsing on the steep sides of the fells, or in the narrow vallies, that opened distantly, was all that diversified the vast scene. Saddleback spread his skirts westward along the plain, and then reared himself in terrible and lonely majesty. In the long perspective beyond, were the crowding points of the fells round Keswick, Borrowdale, and the vales of St. John and Leyberthwaite, stretching away to those near Grasmere. The weather was in solemn harmony with the scenery; long shadows swept over the hills, followed by gleaming lights. Tempestuous gulls alone broke the silence. Now and then, the sun's rays made a singular appearance; pouring, from under clouds, between the tops of fells into some deep vale at a distance, as into a focus.

"This is the very region, which the wild fancy of a poet, like Shakespeare, would people with witches, and shew them at their incantations, calling spirits from the clouds, and spectres from the earth.

"On the now lonely plains of this vast amphitheatre, the Romans had two camps, and their Eagle spread its wings over a scene worthy of its own soarings. The lines of these encampments may still be traced on that part of the plain, called Hutton Moor, to the north of the high road; and over its whole extent towards Keswick a Roman way has been discovered. Funereal urns have also been dug up here, and an altar of Roman form, but with the inscription obliterated.

"Nearer Saddleback, we perceived crags and heath mingled on its precipices, and its base broken into a little world of mountains, green with cultivation. White farms, each with its grove to shelter it from the descending gusts, corn and pastures of the brightest verdure enlivened the skirts of the mountain all round, climbing towards the dark heath and crags, or spreading downwards into the vale of Threlkeld, where the slender Lowther shews his shining stream.

"Leaving Hutton Moor, the road soon began to ascend the skirts of Saddleback, and passed between green hillocks, where cattle appeared most elegantly in the mountain scene, under the crags, or sipping at the clear stream, that gushed from the rocks, and wound to the Vale below. Such crystal rivulets crossed our way continually, as we rose upon the side of Saddleback, which towers abruptly on the right, and, on the left, sinks as suddenly into the vale of Threlkeld, with precipices sometimes little less than tremendous. This mountain is the northern boundary of the vale in its whole length to Keswick, the points of whose fells close the perspective. Rocky heights guard it to the south. The valley between is green, without wood, and, with much that is grand, has little beautiful, till near its conclusion; where, more fertile and still more wild, it divides into three narrower vallies, two of which disclose scenes of such sublime severity as even our long view of Saddleback had not prepared us to expect.

"The first of these is the vale of St. John, a narrow, cultivated spot, lying in the bosom of tremendous rocks, that impend over it in masses of gray crag, and often resemble the ruins of castles. These rocks are overlooked by still more awful mountains, that fall in abrupt lines, and close up the vista, except where they also are commanded by the vast top of Helvellyn. On every side, are images of desolation and stupendous greatness, closing upon a narrow line of pastoral richness; a picture of verdant beauty, seen through a frame of rock work. It is between the cliffs of Threlkeld-fell and the purple ridge of Nadale-fell, that this vale seems to repose in its most silent and perfect peace. No village and scarcely a cottage disturbs its retirement. The flocks, that feed at the feet of the cliffs, and the steps of a shepherd, 'in this office of his mountain watch', are all, that haunt the 'dark sequestered nook'."[4]

It is as though the landscape of her novels has come alive. The castles and the forests rising to the threatening hills, the precipitous rocks and the desert mountains of the paintings by Gaspard Dughet and Salvator Rosa that were her mental habitation are present before her eyes. Greystoke Castle, the classical seventeenth century building extended and renovated six years earlier "in a fanciful, castellated style, including a pair of seven-sided towers",[5] meets her aesthetic approval, "gothic" "grey" and framed by the gentle, aristocratic landscape – "the pomp of shade". "Saddleback, huge, gray and barren" provides the sublime effect, the "exquisite" contrast. She approaches as an artist, drawing a pre-determined emotional charge from the landscape that is shaped by her imagination. She faces a dramatic prospect, an amphitheatre where the elements of a Burkean sublime aesthetic are assembled to play their parts. It is a place of terror, of "grandeur", of "some grand convulsion of the earth". At Greystoke man had dominated the landscape. Here there is only "the shepherd's hut, or his flocks" to diversify "the vast scene". She is constructing her painting. "Diversified" is an artist's thought and even the alternative offered between a shepherd's hut or his browsing flocks is not describing what is before the eyes, but shaping it according to a pre-conceived aesthetic. Saddleback "in terrible and lonely majesty" becomes a hero in a Shakespearean tragedy, a landscape worthy of the great events of history, of "the soarings" of the Roman eagle. "The long perspective", "the crowding points", the wild "solemn harmony" and the concept borrowed from optics of "the suns rays . . . pouring . . . as into a focus" are shaping the landscape before her eyes into the generalised, fallaciously pathetic landscape of her novels.

Ann Radcliffe had discovered her ideal landscape, a country displaying, personifying both beauty and terror. "Crystal rivulets" contrast with "precipices sometimes little less than tremendous" and two valleys "disclose scenes of such sublime severity". The Vale of St. John excited Mrs Radcliffe as it later excited Walter Scott. Before her eyes, she saw the perfectly framed picture of the sublime and the beautiful: "On every side, are images of desolation and stupendous greatness, closing upon a narrow line of pastoral richness; a picture of verdant beauty, seen through a frame of rock work."

It was rumoured that Ann Radcliffe suffered from depression in 1797 and she may have had bouts of madness in her later years. She published nothing after *The Italian* in 1797 and the remaining twenty-six years of her life were spent in seclusion from society. It is tempting to see the impending rocks and the sheltered vale as a simulacrum of her own mental condition. Whatever the situation, and despite her sensitivity to the landscape and her poetic apprehension of the supernatural, even her invocation of "spirits from the clouds, and spectres from the earth", she failed to mention the spectral army of Souther Fell. However, that detailed and extended description – the white farms may well have housed our witnesses – show us how one of the most influential of Romantic writers coloured the landscape for the eyes of others.

The story of the spectral army was firmly re-established in the public mind by the publication of Volume III of *The Beauties of England and Wales, or, Delineations, topographical* by John Britton and Edward Wedlake Brayley, in 1802. Volume III was dedicated to delineating Cornwall, Cumberland and Derbyshire.

This vast and ambitious work, which eventually covered the whole country in twenty nine volumes, caught the spirit of the age. The understanding of the country's history had become more detailed, comprehensive and accurate, although, apart from the work of a few individuals, it was very far from meeting modern standards of scholarship. In Hanoverian England, men such as William Stukeley on a national scale and John Horsley, for example, on the Roman Wall, and, on a smaller scale, George Smith on antiquities in Cumberland, had contributed to a picture of the country's history that corresponded to its increasing commercial and political power in the world. The later county histories that were written mostly towards the end of the eighteenth century were, like William Hutchinson's comprehensive work, vast vade-mecums of anything and everything that had been written, but they served to cultivate a sense of place among the gentry and better-off classes as they themselves became more involved in the life of the nation. They were, however, expensive books published in very small numbers and bought by the wealthy few. Britton and Brayley caught the wave of popular pride in the country during the French Revolution and the Napoleonic Wars when tourists turned away from the continent to explore their own country. Their volumes were cheap and they were widely read. The price of each volume was a mere two shillings and sixpence, just a seventeenth of the two guineas that Clarke hoped to receive for his expensive production. *The Beauties* sold in their thousands whereas their predecessors had sold in their hundreds.

The epigraph to the third volume is significantly patriotic: """In whatever Light we regard the BRITISH ISLANDS, whether as the Cradle of Liberty, the Mother of Arts and Sciences, the Nurse of Manufactures, the Mistress of the Sea; or whether we contemplate their genial Soil, their mild Climate, their various natural and artificial Curiosities; we shall find no equal Extent of Territory on the Face of the Globe of more Importance, or containing more Attractions, even in the Estimation of those who cannot be biassed by native Partiality." Britton and Brayley constructed a composite picture of the country fit to match this proud claim. Their view of the land is a hodge-podge of the sentiment of their times and recent past, an amalgam of the sublime, the picturesque, the gothic, the romantic, the topographical and the antiquarian.

Britton and Brayley had read Hutchinson. They borrowed from the book extensively throughout their account of the county. Their redaction of the Souther Fell story shows an awareness of Smith's version referring to Bouscale Tarn and unashamedly using such terms as "amphitheatrical" and "barricadoed".

However, although they acknowledged that "particulars are related somewhat differently", they opted to summarise James Clarke's more recent account because he "procured the attestations of two of the persons to whom the phenomena were first visible".[6]

Their account is one of the few extended anecdotes in the delineation of Cumberland and the only one that included a long discussion of material that is not directly related to the county. They had a sharp eye for what would interest their wider readership. The story of the spectral army of Souther Fell given a new speculative twist by Britton and Brayley was to prove very influential. Here is their account as they published it in 1802.

"To the north and east of Skiddaw, there is a continuation of several hills of less importance, which are principally covered with heath, of uninteresting forms, and terminated in the open cultivated part of the county. The most remarkable are Caldbeck-fells, Carrock-fells, Bouscale-fell, and Souter-fell. On Bouscale-fell is a spacious sheet of water, so inclosed by an amphitheatrical ridge of craggy rocks, that the rays of the sun never reach its surface for four months in the winter season.

"Souter-fell is nearly 900 yards high, barricadoed on the north and west sides with precipitous rocks, but somewhat more open on the east, and easier of access. On this mountain occurred the extraordinary phenomena, that, towards the middle of the past century, excited so much conversation and alarm. We mean the visionary appearances of armed men, and other figures; the causes of which have never yet received a satisfactory solution; though, from the circumstances hereafter mentioned, there seems reason to believe, that they are not entirely inexplicable. The particulars are related somewhat differently; but as Mr. Clarke procured the attestations of two of the persons to whom the phenomena were first visible, to the account inserted in his Survey of the Lakes, we shall relate the circumstances from that authority.

"By the attested relation, it seems, that the first time any of these visionary phenomena were observed, was on a summer's evening in the year 1743. As Daniel Stricket, then servant to John Wren, of Wilton-hall the next house to Blakehills, (These places are about half a mile from Souter-fell.) was sitting at the door with his master, they saw the figure of a man with a dog, pursuing some horses along Souter-fell side, a place so steep that a horse can scarcely travel on it at all. They appeared to run at an amazing pace, till they got out of sight at the lower end of the fell. The next morning Stricket and his master ascended the steep side of the mountain, in full expectation that they should find the man lying dead: as they were persuaded that the swiftness with which he ran must have killed him; and imagined likewise, that they should pick up some of the shoes, which they thought the horses must have lost in galloping at such a furious rate. They, however, were disappointed; for there appeared not the least vestiges of either man or horses; not so much as the mark of a horse's hoof upon the turf. Astonishment, and a degree of fear, perhaps, for some time, induced them to conceal the circumstances; but they at length disclosed them; and, as might be expected, were only laughed at for their credulity.

"The following year, 1744, on the 23d of June, as the same Daniel Stricket, who at that time lived with Mr. William Lancaster's father, of Blakehills, was walking a little above the house, about half past seven in the evening, he saw a troop of horsemen riding on Souter-fell side, in pretty close ranks, and at a brisk pace. Mindful of the ridicule which had been excited against him the preceding year, he continued to observe them in silence for some time; but being at last convinced that the appearance was real, he went into the house, and informed Mr. Lancaster, that he had something curious to show him. They went out together; but, before Stricket had either spoken or pointed to the place, his master's son had himself discovered the aerial troopers; and when conscious that the same appearances were visible to both, they informed the family, and the phenomena were alike seen by all.

"These visionary horsemen seemed to come from the lowest part of Souter-fell, and became visible at a place called Knott; they then moved in regular troops along the side of the fell, till they became opposite to Blakehills, when they went over the mountain: thus they described a kind of curvilineal path; and both their first and last appearances were bounded by the top of the mountain."

"The pace at which these shadowy forms proceeded, was a regular swift walk; and the whole time of the continuance of their appearance was upwards of two hours: but further observation was then precluded by the approach of darkness.

"Many troops were seen, in succession; and frequently the last; or last but one, in a troop, would quit his position, gallop to the front, and then observe the same pace with the others. The same changes were visible to all the spectators; and the view of the phenomena was not confined to Blakehills only, "but was seen by every person at every cottage within the distance of a mile." Such are the particulars of this singular relation, as given by Mr. Clarke. The attestation is signed by Lancaster and Stricket, and dated the 21st of July, 1785. The number of persons who witnessed the march of these aerial travellers seems to have been twenty-six."

Britton and Brayley have slightly condensed Clarke's account, leaving aside the process by which the witnesses constantly confirm each others findings. They introduced William Lancaster's son as the first to agree with Stricket's description and make no mention of Clarke's parenthetical comment about bonfires lit by the shepherds on St John's eve. As with Smith and Clarke, they are concerned to note the precise manoeuvring of the officers about the marching column. The figure of twenty-six witnesses was taken from Smith's account.

In a footnote Britton and Brayley add: "It should be remarked, that the time when these appearances were observed, was the eve of the rebellion, when some troops of horsemen might be privately exercising" that sought to explain the phenomenon as an optical illusion, but then dismissed the idea, saying that it seemed improbable that so many people could be deluded at the same time. They then went on to explain the idea of what we understand as an optical illusion through a detailed discussion of the Brocken spectre.

"These phenomena have by some been considered as a mere deceptio visus; but to us it appears in the highest degree improbable, that so many spectators should experience the same kind of illusion, and at exactly the same period. We should rather attribute the appearances to particular states of the atmosphere, and suppose them to be the shadows of realities, the airy resemblances of scenes actually passing in a distant part of the country, and, by some singular operation of natural causes, thus expressively imaged on the acclivity of the mountains." Ideas of the deceptio visus, the phrase used by Smith to denote an optical illusion, had been keenly discussed throughout the eighteenth century and there were many popular accounts of places being seen from impossible distances. A recent report on the Broken spectre had been widely commented on and, oddly, for a description of the topography of Cumberland, Britton and Brayley chose to transcribe the following accounttranslated from the *Gottingisches Journal der Naturwissenschaften Vol 1 part III* at great length: "We shall illustrate our opinion by some particulars relating to the Spectre of the Broken, an aerial figure that is sometimes seen among the Harz mountains in Hanover." The Brocken spectre was a new and spectacular phenomenon for English readers. *The Philosophical magazine: a journal of theoretical, experimental and applied physics*, had described it in 1798 and *The Sporting Magazine; or Monthly Calendar of the Transactions of the Turf, the Chace, and every other Diversion interesting to the Man of Pleasure, Enterprize and Spirit* must have decided that it offered congenial copy for they published an article on *The Surprizing Spectre of the Broken Mountain* in their issue for October, 1799.

Brritton and Brayley's version was as follows:"'Having ascended the Broken,' observes M. Haue, from whose diary this account is transcribed, 'for the thirtieth time, I was at length so fortunate as to have the pleasure of seeing this phenomenon. The sun rose about four o'clock, and the atmosphere being quite serene towards the east, his rays could pass without any obstruction over the Heinrichshohe: In the southwest, however, towards Achtermannshohe, a brisk west wind carried before it thin transparent vapours. About a quarter past four I looked round, to see whether the atmosphere would permit me to have a free prospect to the south-west, when I observed, at a very great distance, towards Achtermannshohe, a human figure of a monstrous size! A violent gust of wind having almost carried away my hat, I clapped my hand to it, by moving my arm towards my head, and the colossal figure did the same.

" 'The pleasure which I felt at this discovery can hardly be described; for I had already walked many a weary step in the hopes of seeing this shadowy image, without being able to gratify my curiosity. I immediately made another movement, by bending my body, and the colossal figure before me repeated it. I was desirous of doing the same thing once more, but my colossus had vanished. I remained in the same position, waiting to see whether it would return, and in a few minutes it again made its appearance on the Achtermannshoho. I paid my respects to it a second time, and it did the same by me. I then called the landlord of the Broken, (the neighbouring inn,) and having both taken the same position which I had taken alone, we looked towards the Achtermannshohe, but saw nothing. We had not, however, stood long, when two such colossal figures were formed over the above eminence, which repeated their compliments by bending their bodies as we did, after which they vanished. We retained our position, kept our eyes fixed on the same spot, and in a little time the two figures again stood before us, and were joined by a third. Every movement that we made these figures imitated; but with this difference, that the phenomenon was sometimes weak and faint, sometimes strong and well defined.' "

The editors may have included M. Haue's experience to prove that even when it came to "natural curiosities" Britain was best, but, having illustrated this loosely analogous phenomenon, and applied it with speculative contrivance, Britton and Brayley felt they had made a convincing case: "This curious detail concerning the imitative powers of the Spectre of the Broken, demonstrates that the actions of human beings are sometimes pictured on the clouds; and when all the circumstances of the phenomena on Souter-fell are considered, it seems highly probable, that some thin vapours must have been hovering round its summit at the time when the appearances were observed. It is also probable, that these vapours must have been impressed with the shadowy forms that seemed to 'imitate humanity,' by a particular operation of the sun's rays, united with some singular, but unknown refractive combinations, that were then taking place in the atmosphere."

Britton and Brayley's explanation is not of a mirage where the image of a distant army would have been refracted so as to appear on Souther Fell, but the more complicated one, prompted by the idea of the Brocken, of a refracted image itself being projected onto the vapours above Souther Fell in the same way as the shadow of M. Haue desperately grabbing his hat had been projected onto the clouds that clung to Achtermannshohe.

With the idea of the Brocken Spectre still shaping their thoughts, they continued with their description of the mountains, quoting Ann Radcliffe in passing: "Saddle-back rears its vast head on the western side of Souter-fell, which, in fact, is only an appendage to this more stupendous mountain. It obtained its name from its shape resembling a saddle, when seen from several different points of view. Its base, to use the expression of a popular writer, is broken into a "little world of mountains, green with cultivation:" its north-western skirts unite with the declivities of Skiddaw; but its southern face is furrowed by several hideous chasms; and its summit is in many parts frightful and desolate. It appears to have been in a volcanic state; and a lake on the upper part of the mountain, called Threlkeld-tarn, whose bed is apparently the solid rock, is supposed, from the lava and burnt stones found in its neighbourhood, to have been the crater. This cavity is of several acres in extent, and said to be so deeply situated in the bosom of the rocks, that the sun never shines upon it: its waters appear black, but smooth as glass. The views from the summit are exceedingly extensive; but those immediately under the eye, on the mountain itself, so tremendous and appalling, that few persons have sufficient resolution to experience the emotions which those awful scenes inspire, and they are therefore but seldom visited. One of the points of the summit juts out between two horrid gulphs, that seem to be more than 800 feet deep, having their sides craggy and barren, and their bottoms paved with broken rocks, of various hideous forms and dimensions. The height of this mountain, as taken by

Mr. Donald, is 3324 feet: that of Skiddaw, as ascertained by the same gentleman, 3270."

The mountain rears its vast head; it is anthropomorphic; the awful scenes inspire emotions "that few persons have sufficient resolution to experience"; even the word "broken" is used twice in the short passage. The powerful image of the Brocken spectre possessed their imaginations and had been strongly linked with that of the spectral army. Both had a high intensity of imaginative resonance and both seemed capable of rational explanation.

Britton and Brayley's curiosity had been aroused by the story. They sought an explanation in quasi-scientific terms that is suggestive but really lacks any clarity or precision. They did not question the credibility of the witnesses or the reporter. The numbers involved and the signed attestation, for them, were assurances of truth and they were left to explain the phenomenon in physical terms.

They were excited by the imaginative romance inherent in the story, the possibility that a spectral army was so convincingly seen marching repeatedly across the impossible fell and yet they wanted the story reduced to a rational explanation.

This tension between the romantic, the poetic, the imaginative and the scientific and rational was part of the temper of the age. Ann Radcliffe had excited the reader's imagination with her romantic mysteries and then, explaining them away, she had returned him to the real world. Science might try to explain the mystery of things, but there was always a yearning for a "but yet", for a more powerfully experienced imagined world beyond the rational.

Chapter Six:

Coleridge and the Wordsworths

In 1798, four years before Britton and Brayley published the Cumberland volume in *The Beauties* series, Samuel Taylor Coleridge had transcribed the same passage by M. Haue into his notebooks, when he was staying in Gottinggen. He also included the account by M. Jordan, which Britton and Brayley referred to in a footnote. In addition, he copied out the account by John Haygarth of a spectre that he had seen in North Wales. Here, it was the glory, the brilliant prismatic anti-corona that surrounded the head of the projected individual rather than the spectre itself, which had aroused the interest. "Vide Description of a Glory, by John Haygarth, Manchester Trans. Vol.3. p.463. On thirteenth February, 1780, as I was returning to Chester, and ascending at Rhealt, the mountain which forms the eastern boundary of the Vale of Clwyd, - in the road above me, I was struck with the peculiar appearance of a very white shining cloud, that lay remarkably close to the ground. The sun was nearly setting but shone extremely bright. I walked up to the cloud, and my shadow was projected into it; the head of my shadow was surrounded at some distance by a circle of various colours whose centre appeared to near the situation of the eye, and whose circumference extended to the Shoulders. The circle was complete except where the shadow of my body intercepted it – it exhibited the most vivid colours, red being outermost – all the colours seemed in the same order and proportion that the rainbow presents to our view – the beautiful colours of hoarfrost on snow in sunshine – red, green and blue – in various angles"[1]

Coleridge was then aged twenty six and had been married for three years with a young baby son. A short time later he visited the Brocken hoping to see the spectre. In a letter home, on 17th May, 1799, to his wife, Sara, where he seems to be questioning his own imaginative abilities and the nature of the mind and perception, he described his experiences: "My last letter concluded with the Oder Teich, from thence we entered a second wood, and now the snow met us in large masses, and we walked for two miles knee-deep in it, with an inexpressible fatigue, till we came to the mount called Little Brocken: - here even the firs deserted us, or only now and then a patch of them, wind-shorn, no higher than one's knee, matted and cowering to the ground, like our thorn bushes on the highest sea-hills. The soil was plashy and boggy; we descended, and came to the foot of the Great Brocken without a river - the highest mountain in all the north of Germany, and the seat of innumerable superstitions. On the 1st of May all the witches dance here at midnight, and those who go may see their own ghosts walking up and down with a little billet on the back, giving the names of those who had wished them there: for, "I wish you on the top of the Brocken," is a common curse throughout the whole empire. Well, we ascended, the soil boggy, and at last reached the height, which is 573 toises above the level of the sea. (3,743 ft) We visited the Blocksterg, a sort of bowling-green, inclosed by huge stones, something like those at Stonehenge, and this is the witches' ball-room - thence proceeded to the house on the hill, where we dined - and now we descended. My toe was shockingly swollen, and my feet bladdered, and my whole frame seemed to be going to pieces with fatigue."

The letter referred to the witches' ballroom where Goethe had set Faust's encounter on Walpurgisnacht, but did not mention the spectre even though Coleridge must have been in a state of some expectation. In fact he seems more concerned about his "bladdered" feet. There is a poignancy in some lines from a poem that he wrote in the hotel album that night:

Holy remembrances of child, or friend,
Or gentle maid, our first and early love,

Coleridge had been away from home on his lively German tour where, in contrast to William and Dorothy Wordsworth, though equally impecunious, he made friends readily and seemed to have had few thoughts for the wife and son he had left behind. When he wrote these lines, his first-born son, was already dead, but the news had been kept from him by the meddling of a friend who was over-solicitous for his intellectual development.

Although Coleridge did not see the Brocken spectre at the time the image and concept of the Brocken was important to him in determining his philosophy of the imagination. If previously he had held a view that the mind, as Locke and David Hartley had seen it, was a tabula rasa that was developed through the experience of the senses, the image of the Brocken spectre, in correspondence with German idealist philosophy, offered the idea that, in the same way as a man's image might be shadowed on the clouds, so the imagination might not be just the product of sensory experience, but the creation of man and nature working together. This understanding grew to be central to Coleridge's thinking and in a poem, that may have been written in Malta in 1802, but was possibly written as late as 1826, *Constancy to an Ideal Object*, he seems to resolve his despair at the passive nature of the imagination by apprehending, in the image of the Brocken spectre, that the imagination is truly active.

> And art thou nothing? Such thou art, as when
> The woodman winding westward up the glen
> At wintry dawn, where o'er the sheep-track's maze
> The viewless snow-mist weaves a glist'ning haze,
> Sees fall before him, gliding without tread,
> An image with a glory round its head;
> The enamoured rustic worships its fair hues,
> Nor knows he makes the shadow he pursues!

That pastoral version of the Brocken spectre, innocent and beneficent, had matured in Coleridge's mind to be a representation of the animating nature of the imagination. Without it the poet is as desolate as the Ancient Mariner; with it he creates and pursues a glorious and sustaining illusion. In a footnote Coleridge describes the spectre as "a phenomenon the author has himself experienced", although Coleridge did not observe the Brocken on either of his two trips to the Hartz Mountains and he makes no reference to this experience elsewhere. De Quincey, when he wrote an essay on the Brocken spectre in 1850 confirmed this in a note, in which he also acutely observed that Coleridge got to the

Brocken from when the sun was already too high in the sky:" He also seemed to suggest that Coleredge distinguished the phenomenon which he actually saw from the Brocken spectre: "Afterwards in England . . .he saw a much rarer phenomenon", This is the phenomenon with the glory around the head, which he described in the lines in *Constancy to an Ideal Object.*[2]

Whenever it was that Coleridge experienced the Brocken spectre, it was important to him and stayed with him. In his *Lectures on Literature* he recalled the experience with vivid power in order to explain the workings of the reader's imagination. He was distinguishing the response of Shakespearean readers "who, without affecting to understand or criticize, merely feel and are the recipients of the poet's power", from those who "read with feeling and understanding". "The reader often feels that some ideal trait of our own is caught, or some nerve has been touched of which we were not before aware, and it is proved that it has been touched by the vibration that we feel, a sort of thrilling, which tells us that we know ourselves the better for it. In the plays of Shakespeare every man sees himself without knowing that he sees himself, as in the phenomena of nature, in the mist of the mountain, a traveler beholds his own figure, but the glory round the head distinguishes it from a mere vulgar copy; or as a man traversing the Brocken in the north of Germany at sunrise, when the glorious beams are shot askance the mountain; he sees before him a figure of gigantic proportions and of such elevated dignity, that he only knows it to be himself by the similarity of action – or as the Fata Morgana at Messina in which all forms at determined distances are presented in an invisible mist, draped in all the colours of prismatic imagination, and with magic harmony uniting them and producing a beautiful whole in the mind of the Spectator."[3]

Coleridge was searching for the right image for that feeling of the poet's power. He moved between three recollections. First was that phenomenon of nature he may have undergone himself in the mist of the mountains and which may draw on Haygarth's account. where he saw himself, but "the glory round the head" made it into a special, a particular image. Secondly, he distinguished the experience as recalled from the descriptions he'd noted by M. Haue and M. Jordan, where the person knew himself only by the correspondence of his actions. And then, thirdly, in a totally different image, but one often associated with similar optical phenomena, he saw the reader apprehending a magical coherence just as someone might when he saw the Fata Morgana at Messina which magically magnified and elevated the distant shore above the waters of the strait.

The Brocken spectre and the glory, those aspects of the same phenomenon that were seen as antithetical by Coleridge, supplied him with another sharp clarification in a mercurial footnote in *Aids to Reflection*. He is arguing for the necessity for the student to learn precise scholarly language, and not to reject it because it is difficult. He compares this to the way people react when they encounter genius. "As many as are not delighted by it are disturbed, perplexed, irritated. The beholder either recognizes it as a projected form of his own being, that moves before him with a glory round its head, or recoils from it as from a spectre."

Thomas de Quincey found in the Brocken spectre a complex and subtle image that allowed him to reflect on his own inner darkness. Drawing on a scientific explanation of the phenomenon by David Brewster in 1831 and on Coleridge's accounts, de Quincey playfully apprehended and teased the imagined phenomenon – he'd never actually seen the spectre. He concluded that "the apparition is but a reflex of yourself; and, in uttering your secret feelings to *him,* you make this phantom the dark symbolic mirror for reflection to the daylight what else must be hidden for ever.

"Such a relation does the Dark Interpreter, whom, immediately the reader will learn to know as an intruder into my dreams, bear to my own mind. He is originally a mere reflex of my inner nature. But as the apparition of the Brocken sometimes is disturbed by storms or by driving showers, so as to dissemble his real origin, in like manner the Interpreter sometimes swerves out of my orbit, and mixes a little with alien natures. I do not always know him in these cases as my own parhelion. What he says, generally is but that which I have said in daylight, and in meditation deep enough to sculpture itself on my heart. But sometimes, as his face alters, his words alter; and they do not always seem such as I have used, or could use. No man can account for all things that occur in dreams. Generally I believe this — that he is a faithful representative of myself;

but he also is at times subject to the action of the god *Phantasm,* who rules in dreams."[4]

Science, in the process of explaining the phenomenon, had nullified the supernatural. De Quincey renders it spiritual, psychological, a mirror to his deepest self. Imagining the "solitary apparition", knowing and fearing that he has "lived so many ages with foul Pagan sorcerers", gesturing so that it, evasively in the hail and the rain, repeats the sign of the cross, plucks an anemone, the sorcerer's flower, and kneeling at the altar stone, de Quincey seeks absolution and would have the apparition do so too: "Father, which art in heaven, this lovely anemone, that once glorified the worship of fear, has travelled back into thy fold; . . . The darkness is gone; the cruelty is gone which the darkness bred; . . . And lo! I thy servant, with this dark phantom, whom for one hour on this thy festival of Pentecost, I make *my* servant, render thee united worship in this thy recovered temple." When the phantom responds as he veils his head, de Quincey finds a sympathy with his deepest grief. It is "as if he also had a human heart, and that he also, in childhood, having suffered an affliction which was ineffable, wished by these mute symbols to breathe a sigh towards heaven in memory of that affliction, and by way of record, though many a year after, that it was indeed unutterable by words."

William and Dorothy Wordsworth had travelled to Germany with Coleridge, but they went to live in a small town called Goslar in the Hartz region. They had intended to stay with a German family and thereby learn the language, but they failed to find the appropriate accommodation and endured a bitterly cold winter in a miserable apartment and had very little opportunity to talk to any German people.

On 27th February, 1799, Dorothy wrote to Coleridge: "I ought to have said that before this we had a view of the Brocken, the Mont Blanc of the Hartz forest, and the glory of all this part of Germany. I cannot speak of its height compared with any of our British mountains, but from the point from which we saw it, it had nothing impressive in its appearance. The day continued chearing and delightful, and we walked through a country presenting forest views of hill and valley, one of which a deep valley with a village built of wood scattered in the bottom was very interesting. We lingered under the shades of the trees and did not arrive at Osterode till four o'clock in the afternoon."

The sight of the Brocken seems of little special significance, apart, perhaps, from that unconscious use of the word "glory", and Dorothy's concerns are with the scenery and the unusual village built of wood.

On 14th or 21st December, Dorothy (and William) wrote to Coleridge of their stay in Goslar after Coleridge had left to continue his walking tour of Germany. The letter was ordinary enough in its everyday concerns. Dorothy complained about the post's unreliability: "It is Friday evening. This letter cannot go till tomorrow. I wonder when it will reach you. One of yours was Eleven days upon the road". Her plea –"You will write by the first post" – perhaps suggests something of their sense of isolation. In the same letter as this mundane matter were transcripts of poetry that William had just written, poetry that, in part, may have been prompted by their alienation in a foreign community and their longing for home. Coleridge, with his accustomed enthusiasm, had written of skating in Ratzeburg. Dorothy urged him to come to the North of England and enjoy the skating there and she transcribed "a description of William's boyish pleasures" when,

> In the frosty season . . .
> All shod with steel
> We hissed along the polished ice, in games
> Confederate [5]

In the same letter Dorothy also transcribed the first version of the episode when Wordsworth as a boy had stolen a boat and rowed across Ullswater:

> A rocky steep uprose
> Above the cavern of the willow tree
> And now, as fitted one who proudly rowed
> With his best skill, I fixed a steady view
> Upon the top of that same shaggy ridge,
> The bound of the horizon; for behind
> Was nothing, but the stars and the grey sky.
> She was an elfin pinnace: twenty times
> I dipped my oars into the silent lake,
> And as I rose upon the stroke, my boat

> Went heaving through the water, like a swan.
> When from behind the rocky steep, till then
> The bound of the horizon, a huge cliff,
> As if with voluntary power instinct,
> Upreared its head: I struck & struck again,
> And growing still in stature, the huge cliff
> Rose up between me & the stars, & still
> With measured motion like a living thing,
> Strode after me. . . .
> But huge & mighty forms that do not live
> Like living men moved slowly through my mind
> By day, and were the trouble of my dreams."

Wordsworth was recalling an incident from his childhood when the forms of nature appeared to act like a moral agency. The physics of the incident are made "unpoetically" clear. Coleridge, at a later date when he was at Ullswater, spent some time drawing diagrams to explain the incident. The further the "elfin pinnace" moved away from the nearby mountain the more the mountain that lay behind was revealed. The elementary optical explanation is in sharp contrast to the impact of the image on the mind and conscience. The mountain that "upreared its head" is a projection of the viewer's imagination. The parallel is there with the Brocken spectre, the giant figure that is readily explained as the viewer's own body projected on the clouds ahead. The image, which so excited Coleridge and must have been part of Wordsworth's imaginative background as he endured that cold winter in Goslar, has been transformed into "huge & mighty forms . . . moved slowly through my mind."

Wordsworth was interested in optical phenomena. In advocating the Lakes to the tourist who might have been tempted abroad, he claimed that: "One of the aesthetic advantages that the English Lakes afforded over those of Switzerland was the greater quality of their mirror-like surfaces. The water of the English Lakes, on the contrary, being of a crystalline clearness, the reflections of the surrounding hills are frequently so lively, that it is scarcely possible to distinguish the point where the real object terminates, and its unsubstantial duplicate begins."[6]

That "crystalline clearness" had produced some very lucid effects, but Wordsworth was always ready to rationalize the appearance that had been bodied forth. He found that the imagination's seductive illusion was explicable as a creation of nature. In his *Guide to the Lakes* he described two optical illusions of great clarity that had made a strong impression on him many years earlier: "Walking by the side of Ullswater upon a calm September morning, I saw, deep within the bosom of the lake, a magnificent Castle, with towers and battlements; nothing could be more distinct than the whole edifice; - after gazing with delight upon it for some time, as upon a work of enchantment, I could not but regret that my previous knowledge of the place enabled me to account for the appearance. It was in fact the reflexion of a pleasure-house called Lyulph's Tower - the towers and battlements magnified and so much changed in shape as not to be immediately recognized. In the meanwhile, the pleasure-house itself was altogether hidden from my view by a body of vapour stretching over it and along the hill-side on which it stands, but not so as to have intercepted its communication with the lake; and hence this novel and most impressive object, which if I had been a stranger to the spot, would, from its being inexplicable, have long detained the mind in a state of pleasing astonishment."

The detail and precision of Wordsworth's explanation demonstrates how, though enchanted by the imaginative possibilities of his vision, he retained the scientific rationalism of his age and education, keen to explain the phenomenon almost diagrammatically in optical terms. That determined explanation is in opposition to an enthusiasm for the "pleasing astonishment" that the imagination, if it were not otherwise informed, might have supplied. He further went on to reject the romantic fantasy of the illusion in a way that suggested a sense of the superiority of contemporary understandings of nature over those of previous ages: "An appearance of this kind, acting upon the credulity of early ages, may have given birth to the stories of subaqueous palaces, gardens, and pleasure-grounds — the brilliant ornaments of Romance."

It might have been something of the very same promptings of romantic fancy which caused Wordsworth to write *The Somnambulist*, first published in 1833. This "mournful tale" of Sir Eglamore, a medieval knight, and his love, Emma, is set in the very location he had earlier dismissed as the source of an illusion.

List, ye who pass by Lyulph's Tower

At eve, how softly then
Doth Aira-Force, that torrent hoarse,
Speak from the woody glen!

Lyulph's Tower had been built by the Duke of Norfolk whose fine castle at Greystoke had so impressed Anne Radcliffe. Wordsworth explained how the poem had started: "While we were making an excursion together in this part of the Lake district we heard that Mr Glover the Artist, while lodging at Lyulph's tower, had been disturbed by a loud shriek & upon rising he learnt that it had come from a young woman in the house who was in the habit of walking in her sleep: in that state she had gone down stairs & while attempting to open the outer door, either from some difficulty, or the effect of the cold upon her feet, had uttered the cry which alarmed him. It seemed to us all that this might serve as a hint for a poem, & the story here told was constructed & soon after put into verse by me as it now stands."[7]

Sir Eglamore returned unannounced after many months pursuing noble deeds to discover Emma sleep-walking on the treacherous rocks above Aira Force. She called on the waterfall in her sleep:

"Roar on, and bring him with thy call;
"I heard, and so may He!"

Soul-shattered was the Knight, nor knew
If Emma's Ghost it were,
Or boding Shade, or if the Maid
Her very self stood there.
He touched; what followed who shall tell?
The soft touch snapped the thread
Of slumber - shrieking back she fell,
And the Stream whirled her down the dell
Along its foaming bed.

In plunged the Knight! - when on firm ground
The rescued Maiden lay,
Her eyes grew bright with blissful light,
Confusion passed away;
She heard, ere to the throne of grace

Her faithful Spirit flew,
His voice beheld his speaking face;
And, dying, from his own embrace,
She felt that he was true."

That vision of a watery Lyulph's Tower, prompted by the real report of Glover's somnambulist, had, after many years, provided the setting for a poem set out in all the trappings of medieval romance. However, the spectral possibilities, Sir Eglamore's speculation that Emma is a ghost, are misleading. One touch from the hand of Sir Eglamour and the other world of romance becomes the tragic reality of her falling into the torrent. She dies at the very moment of his embrace when she knows the truth of his love, but the presence of her memory has sanctified the waters. The ghostly has been suggested as a possibility and then been dismissed and explained as an interesting scientific phenomenon.

The second instance of an optical illusion Wordsworth described underlines the idea that our imaginative fancies are at the prompting of nature. Wordsworth, in contrast to Coleridge, was being essentially Lockean insisting that the source of all imagination lies in sensation. "With this inverted scene," he continued, after describing the vision of Lyulph's Tower, "I will couple a much more extraordinary phenomenon, which may shew how other elegant fancies may have had their origin, less in invention than in the actual processes of Nature.

"About eleven o'clock on the forenoon of a winter's day, coming suddenly, in company of a friend, into view of the Lake of Grasmere, we were alarmed by the sight of a newly-created Island; the transitory thought of the moment was, that it had been produced by an earthquake or some other convulsion of nature. Recovering from the alarm, which was greater than the reader can possibly sympathize with, but which was shared to its full extent by my companion, we proceeded to examine the object before us. The elevation of this new island exceeded considerably that of the old one, its neighbour; it was likewise larger in circumference, comprehending a space of about five acres; its surface rocky, speckled with snow, and sprinkled over with birch-trees; it was divided towards the south from the other island by a narrow frith, and in like manner from the northern shore of the lake: on the east and west it was separated from the shore by a much larger space of smooth water.

"Marvellous was the illusion! Comparing the new with the old Island, the surface of which is soft, green, and unvaried, I do not scruple to say that, as an object of sight, it was much the more distinct. 'How little faith,' we exclaimed, 'is due to one sense, unless its evidence be confirmed by some of its fellows? What Stranger could possibly be persuaded that this, which we know to be an unsubstantial mockery, is really so; and that there exists only a single Island on this beautiful Lake?' At length the appearance underwent a gradual transmutation; it lost its prominence and passed into a glimmering and dim inversion, and then totally disappeared; - leaving behind it a clear open area of ice of the same dimensions. We now perceived that this bed of ice, which was thinly suffused with water, had produced the illusion, by reflecting and refracting (as persons skilled in optics would no doubt easily explain) a rocky and woody section of the opposite mountain named Silver How."[8]

In his very earliest writings the young William Wordsworth had relished the possibilities of an imagination inspired by Gothic romance. When he was fourteen in Hawkshead School he was drawn to the possibility of ghosts. We only have fragmentary lines from 'The Vale of Esthwaite', a hugely ambitious poem that he projected and may even have completed. Here, in "a long poem running upon my own adventures and the scenery of the country in which I was brought up"[9], he responded to the gothic literature of the time, seeking out his own ghostly touchstones in local legend and landscape. The loss of his mother and father and his separation from Dorothy may have inclined him naturally towards the melancholic mode that was then fashionable. He imagined himself the sacrificial victim of an ancient priesthood:

> And hark, the ringing harp I hear
> And lo, her druid sons appear.
> Why roull on me your glaring eyes?
> Why fix on me for sacrifice?[10]

Even though he excused it as a dream, his imagination sensed ghostly presences:

> So oft in castle moated round
> In black damp dungeon underground
> Strange forms are seen that white and tall
> Stand straight against the cold black wall"[11]

An extended fantasy of a ghostly encounter is well stocked with all the usual images of gothic horror, but it drew its detail from the landscape:

> The daemons of the storm in crouds
> Glar'd through the partings of the Clouds
> While Satan calling them around
> He trod the hills with thundering sound.[12]

The Vale of Esthwaite manuscript is made up of notes and of jottings, of a long poem seen in the very process of composition. There are extended sections of verse, some broken or with gaps for words or alternative words, and there are short groups of lines and odd phrases and there are brief fragments of prose. One of these fragments is, in the light of Wordsworth's later writings, suggestive in part of the spectral army.

"Nay since the hour when in my infant bed with closed eyes I saw perpetually [?] a rising before me the face of live horses link'd to [?of lions] have the forms of fear been dear to me the half form'd visions or the long processions of solemn terror been dear."[13]

It is possible that Wordsworth wrote this prose fragment in 1787, when he was seventeen and when he may have had sight of Clarke's *Survey*. The most recent edition suggests that "The Survey may have been early enough to influence Wordsworth's account . . . though Clarke's account does not share the nightmarish quality of those visions."[14] It is equally possible that the young Wordsworth may have been aware of the spectral army of Souther Fell, if not of Clarke's *Survey*, long before its publication. Clarke interviewed his witnesses in 1785 and he probably knew of the story before then. He had owned the substantial Swan Inn and the Griffin Inn, both of which were within a short distance of William Cookson's draper's shop in Penrith Marketplace. William Wordsworth had spent many, frequently unhappy, months, even before his mother died in 1778, staying with his grandparents and, after the death of his father in 1781, the rooms in Penrith, became his home during the holidays from school. Clarke and the Cooksons must have known each other, moving, as they did, in the same social circles in a town as small as Penrith and Clarke's visit to Blake Hills must have been the talk of the town. It is also probable that the story of the spectral army of Souther Fell had been part of the local folklore ever since the mid-century. Wordsworth's father probably knew the story. As the Earl of Lowther's land agent he was friendly with William Calvert, and Calvert's sons, William and Raisley, were Wordsworth's contemporaries and friends in the school at Hawkshead. William had nursed the dying nineteen-year old Raisley and there is a memorial plaque to him in Mungrisedale Church. William Calvert was agent to Lord Norfolk of Greystoke Castle and had close connections with Mungrisedale. It is probable that Wordsworth had been familiar through oral sources with the story throughout his childhood and Clarke's account, whether known before or after publication, would have offered colour and detail, if not credibility.

That haunting idea of "the long processions of solemn terror" found in the prose fragment, and that may have been the nucleus of an idea intended for *The Vale of Esthwaite*, became elaborated in one of Wordsworth's first published poems, *An Evening Walk*, into an extended and specific reference to the Souther Fell story.

Wordsworth had been working on the poem for several years, in many ways re-working the materials of *The Vale of Esthwaite*. The poem was addressed to a young lady, whom, fifty years later, he identified as his sister Dorothy. She had been living with an uncle in a rectory some fifty miles from Cambridge and although he did visit her, the poem feels as though he is revealing the land he loves to Dorothy who has been an exile from the Lakes since the death of their father.

An Evening Walk is an imaginary walk around the places he knew: "the plan of it has not been confined to a particular walk or an individual place, - a proof (of which I was unconscious at the time) of my unwillingness to submit the poetic spirit to the chains of fact and real circumstance. The country is idealised rather than described in any one of its local aspects." Despite this, it was in *An Evening Walk* that Wordsworth felt that he had found a fresh poetic principle of truthfulness to natural appearances that became the bedrock of his poetry: "There is not an image in it which I have not observed; and now, in my seventy-third year, I recollect the time and place where most of them were noticed. I will confine myself to one instance:

> Waving his hat, the shepherd, from the vale,
> Directs his winding dog the cliffs to scale, -
> The dog, loud barking, 'mid the glittering rocks,
> Hunts, where his master points, the intercepted flocks.

I was an eye-witness of this for the first time while crossing the Pass of Dunmail Raise. Upon second thought, I will mention another image:

And, fronting the bright west, yon oak entwines
Its darkening boughs and leaves, in stronger lines.

This is feebly and imperfectly expressed, but I recollect distinctly the very spot where this first struck me. It was in the way between Hawkshead and Ambleside, and gave me extreme pleasure. The moment was important in my poetical history; for I date from it my consciousness of the infinite variety of natural appearances which had been unnoticed by the poets of any age or country, so far as I was acquainted with them; and I made a resolution to supply, in some degree, the deficiency. I could not have been at that time above fourteen years of age. The description of the swans, that follows, was taken from the daily opportunities I had of observing their habits, not as confined to the gentleman's park, but in a state of nature. There were two pairs of them that divided the lake of Esthwaite and its in-and-out-flowing streams between them, never trespassing a single yard upon each other's separate domain."

It is in between these precise natural descriptions, which he remembered so clearly after fifty years and which he felt to be so crucial to his poetic development, that Wordsworth's inserted a paragraph summarized as "Sunset - Superstition of the Country connected with that moment". This was a much-elaborated version of the story of the spectral army of Souther Fell.

In these secluded vales, if village fame,
Confirmed by silver hairs, belief may claim;
When up the hills, as now, retired the light,
Strange apparitions mocked the shepherd's sight.
The form appears of one that spurs his steed
Midway along the hill with desperate speed;
Unhurt pursues his lengthened flight, while all
Attend, at every stretch, his headlong fall.
Anon, appears a brave, a gorgeous show
Of horsemen-shadows moving to and fro;
At intervals imperial banners stream,
And now the van reflects the solar beam;
The rear through iron brown betrays a sullen gleam.

While silent stands the admiring crowd below,
Silent the visionary warriors go,
Winding in ordered pomp their upward way
Till the last banner of the long array
Has disappeared, and every trace is fled
Of splendour—save the beacon's spiry head
Tipt with eve's latest gleam of burning red.

Wordsworth's description, telescoped into one appearance, was a modified version of Clarke's. A lone horseman, not "a man with a dog pursuing some horses", "spurs his steed . . . with desperate speed". The "regular troops" describing " a curvilinear path" moving at a "swift walk" have become "a gorgeous show". There was an insistent factualness about Clarke's account which Wordsworth both made more specific and romanticised. That precise observation of natural appearances was there in the description of the rays of the setting sun: "the van reflects the solar beam; / The rear through iron brown betrays a sullen gleam", and in the last rays tipping Penrith Beacon on the eastern horizon "with eve's latest gleam of burning red". Wordsworth saw himself there watching the setting sun ("When up the hills, as now, retired the light,") and he peopled the sunset with the shepherd's vision.

Just as he dismissed the apparition of Lyulph's tower as an enchanted castle, Wordsworth rejected the "gorgeous show", "the imperial banners" and "the ordered pomp". They were "horsemen shadows".

Even if Wordsworth seemed to dismiss the sightings of the spectral army as old men's memories at twilight, "Strange apparitions mocked the shepherd's sight", the image was one that may well have impressed him so deeply as to be re-used as an image of the oppressive multitude that crowded the streets of London.

In the much-revised 1850 version of *The Prelude* the image of that mysterious army across the secluded fell was matched with the ceaseless oppressive weight of anonymous passing faces:

How oft, amid those overflowing streets,
Have I gone forward with the crowd, and said
Unto myself, 'The face of every one
That passes by me is a mystery!'
Thus have I looked, nor ceased to look, oppressed

By thoughts of what and whither, when and how,
Until the shapes before my eyes became
A second-sight procession, such as glides
Over still mountains, or appears in dreams;[15]

If the "second-sight procession, such as glides/ Over still mountains" was but the most cursory reference, equating Martin Martin's tales of portentous apparitions in the Hebrides with the spectral army, Wordsworth asis nevertheless suggesting that it was an image that has been a persisting part of his dream landscape.[16]

In the more personal, less formalized, 1805 version of *The Prelude*, the same passage was succeeded by lines that show how the secure familiar world that he knew was threatened by this "second-sight" or "dream" procession. The lines that followed showed that the army on Souther Fell was as alien as the multitude on the streets of London:

And all the ballast of familiar life,
The present, and the past; hope, fear; all stays,
All laws of acting, thinking, speaking man
Went from me, neither knowing me, nor known.[17]

The powerful picture that had fed Wordsworth's imagination, a fantastic vision that had so notoriously disturbed the Cumberland shepherds, men, who in their very lives had that moral ballast that came from a close communion with the natural world, now corresponded to the deep sense of anomie he had felt in the teeming city. Raymond Williams said of this passage: "These important lines are, I believe, the first expression of what has since become a dominant experience of the city. Blake saw a common condition of 'weakness and woe'. Wordsworth saw strangeness, a loss of connection, not at first in social but in perceptual ways: a failure of identity in the crowd of others which worked back to a loss of identity in the self, and then, in these ways, a loss of society itself, its overcoming and replacement by a procession of images: the 'dance of colours, lights and forms', 'face after face' and there are no other laws. No experience has been more central in the subsequent literature of the city."[18]

An earlier fragmentary draft of *The Prelude* filled out this image of the deeply disturbing dream in a flood of images in which aspects of the spectral army are confused amongst many other elements.

when in my bed I lay
Alone in darkness, I have seen the gloom
Peopled with shapes arrayed in hues more bright:
Than flowers or gems, or than the evening sky:
Processions, multitudes in wake or fair
Assembled, puppet shews with trumpet, fife,
Wild beasts, and standards waving in the [field ?}.
These mounting ever in a sloping line
Were followed by the tumult of the shew
Or horses [ ]
These vanishing, appeared another scene –
Hounds and the uproar of the chase, or steeds
That galloped like the wind through standing corn.
Then headless trunks and faces horrible.
Then came a throng of forms all [
Unutterably, horribly arranged
In parallel lines, in feature and in look
All different, yet marvelously akin;
Then files of soldiery with dazzling arms
Still mounting, mounting upwards, each to each
Of all these specters every band and c[lass?]
Succeeding with fantastic difference
And instant, unimaginable change.[19]

The ordered procession "in parallel lines", "files of soldiery with dazzling arms" and that insistent, threatening "mounting upwards" were specific elements that Wordsworth had elaborated from the Souther Fell story and it may well have been that a memory of that visionary army had haunted his childhood dreams.

In the first edition of *An Evening Walk*, a book of a mere twenty-seven pages, Wordsworth added a footnote which identified his source: "See a description of an appearance of this kind In Clark's *Survey of the Lakes*, accompanied by vouchers of its veracity, that may amuse the reader." The superior tone and the complicit humour with the reader at the expense of the witnesses and, probably Clarke, sits oddly with Wordsworth's reverence for:

"Shepherds, dwellers in the valleys, men

Whom I already loved; — not verily
For their own sakes, but for the fields and hills
Where was their occupation and abode.[20]

The people who formed "the admiring crowd below" and the silver-haired shepherd whose sight was "mocked" – Joseph Lancaster was a farmer rather than a shepherd – lived in the same "secluded vales" which had educated Robert Clifford, the shepherd lord in *Song at the Feast of Brougham Castle* written fourteen years later in 1807. During the Wars of the Roses, the young Clifford, seeking refuge, had been brought up by the shepherds in these hills under the guardianship of Sir Lancelot Threlkeld. The poem tells how the harper welcomed his returning lord, hoping that, after his rural education, he would answer the call to arms.

The area between Carrock Fell and Blencathra was, for Wordsworth, the area where the young Clifford,

. .   long compelled in humble walks to go,
Was softened into feeling, soothed, and tamed.
Love had he found in huts where poor Men lie,
His daily Teachers had been Woods and Rills,
The silence that is in the starry sky,
The sleep that is among the lonely hills.

The landscape and the location were evoked very specifically: "Carrock's side"; "Mosedale's Groves"; "Blancathara's rugged Coves" and "the Flowers that Summer brings/ To Glenderamakin's lofty springs". The country where Young Clifford wore his humble garb "with such a noble mien" was a pastoral Eden:

To his side the Fallow-deer
Came and rested without fear;
The Eagle, Lord of land and sea,
Stooped down to pay him fealty;

It was also a place where traditional and supernatural beliefs were confirmed by their presence in this removed, natural world and were equally part of his education:

And both the undying Fish that swim
Through Bowscale-Tarn did wait on him. . . .
He knew the Rocks where Angels haunt
On the mountains visitant;

He hath kenned them taking wing:
And the caves where faeries sing
He hath entered;

"On their tour to Scotland in 1803, William, Dorothy and Coleridge traveled alongside the eastern edge of the fells and "Slept at Mr. Younghusband's publick-house, Hesket Newmarket" on the night of Monday, 15th August. "In the evening," writes Dorothy, "walked to Caldbeck Falls,[21] a delicious spot in which to breathe out a summer's day – limestone rocks, hanging trees, pools, and waterbreaks – caves and caldrons which have been honoured with fairy names, and no doubt continue in the fancy of the neighbourhood to resound with fairy revels."[22] Britton and Brayley, writing at about the same time, described this enchanted place in greater detail: "In the bed of the river Caldew, somewhat more than a quarter of a mile west of Caldbeck is a singular natural curiosity, called the *Howk,* a word seldom used as a substantive, but frequently as a verb; it being the common northern term for *scooping out* or mak*ing a hole.* This is a water-fall in a narrow glen, in which the stream rushes through the narrow arches of a bridge of lime-stone rock, with vast impetuosity, and dashing over irregular masses of other rocks, empties itself into a large bason, where it boils up in foaming eddies. A few feet from this bason is a curious excavation, called the Fairy *Kettle,* about six yards in diameter, and scooped out in nearly the shape of a huge cauldron, with an inside as smooth as if polished by a statuary. Several smaller excavations are near it. Not far distant is a cascade formed between two perpendicular rocks, about eighteen or twenty yards in height; and a *little* to the right of this, is a cavern, called the *Fairy Kirk,* where the roaring of the cataract, heard without being visible, has a pleasing effect."[23]

Wordsworth, acknowledging the romantic spell of the landscape, metaphorically imagined Robert Clifford learning from the faeries. From them he had

. . .been told
By voices how men lived of old.

And he had the power of second sight

Among the heavens his eye can see
Face of thing that is to be;

He also had magic powers, able to "whisper words of might". When he left the shepherd's life to be "restored to the Estates and Honours of his Ancestors" Clifford, like Prospero, renounced his magic powers, "And hath buried deep his Book". Having been reared among these tranquil hills, he would not lead "the flock of War" but, instead,

In him the savage Virtue of the Race,
Revenge, and all ferocious thoughts were dead:
Nor did he change; but kept in lofty place
- The wisdom which adversity had bred.

The countryside where Wordsworth found the image of the alienating terrors of urban life was the same countryside where a lord might be fostered by nature and learn the ways of peace. It was the place where, in one poem, he rejected gothic fantasy, but where, in a later one, he entertained a belief in the beneficence of fairies and angels.

The overnight stop in Hesket Newmarket was the first night out from Keswick for Dorothy, William and Coleridge. They had left Keswick at eleven o'clock, and the journey appears to have been fairly arduous and not without its problems: "The day was very hot; we walked up the hills, and along all the rough road, which made our walking half the day's journey \traveled under the foot of Carrock, a mountain covered with stones on the lower part; above it is very rocky, but sheep pasture there; we saw several where there seemed to be no grass to tempt them. Passed the foot of Grisedale and Mosedale, both pastoral vallies, narrow, and soon terminating in the mountains – green with scattered trees and houses, and each a beautiful stream. At Grisdale our horse backed upon a steep bank where the road was not fenced, just above the pretty mill at the foot of the valley; and we had a second threatening of disaster in crossing a narrow bridge between the two dales; but this was not the fault of man or horse."[24]

Coleridge knew this eastern side of the Skiddaw massif well, as he knew most of the mountains in the Lake District. Three years previously, on 18th August, 1800, he had written to Humphrey Davy describing the pell-mell descent he had made of Carrock Fell. *A Thought Suggested by a View of Saddleback in Cumberland* was probably composed in the same year.

On stern Blencartha's perilous height

The winds are tyrannous and strong;
And flashing forth unsteady light
From stern Blencartha's skiey height,
As loud the torrents throng!
Beneath the moon in gentle weather,
They bind the earth and sky together.
But oh! the sky and all its forms, how quiet!
The things that seek the earth, how full of noise and riot!

Coleridge composed "the versified reflection" as he called it, "while the author was gazing on three parallel forces on a moonlight night, at the foot of the Saddleback Fell". Blencathra has a drama of tyrannous winds and flashing light, so very different from the gentle moon. The first line was an adaptation of the first line of a poem by Isaac Ritson, (1761-1789) the poet from Eamont Bridge who had written the *Introduction* in Clarke's *Survey*. Ritson's poem was published as part of his biography in the first volume of Hutchinson's *History*. Coleridge read widely in Hutchinson, for instance using names he encountered in the *History* in the second part of *Christabel*, which he wrote when he returned to Cumberland in 1799.

At the end of August, 1800, Coleridge was rambling and scrambling in his mad energetic way over the eastern hills of the Skiddaw massif. On August 27th, in staccato jotting prose, almost as though he was notating his passing thoughts, he told of his walk over Saddleback to Isaac Todd's in Mungrisdale. He was covering much the same territory as George Smith did over half a century earlier, but his enthusiasms and interests and observations were very, very different:

"August 27 – Friday evening saw the force of the Sattleback Tarn beck about 40 ft high – for the first 8 or 9 ft it falls perpendicular, water-colour – meets a rock, & rushes down in a steep slope, all foam, till the last two feet when the rock ceases but the water preserves the same colour and inclination as if it were there/ the pool into which it falls is almost a circle, ten yards in diameter with blue slate at the bottom/ a young Mountain ash, with one unripe and never to be ripe cluster is growing athwart it – the fall when perpendicular is a good yard across, when it runs slope, not more than a foot and a half – but in winter and after rain no doubt it fills the whole capacity of its Scoop, & will then be a yard &

a half in breadth/

Something more than a furlong from the Force, not ten yards from the beck, on the hill 8 heaps of moss, ranged thus (diagram of 8 horizontal lines decreasing upwards) each an exact grave, each in the descent somewhat longer than the one higher up, the first 4 feet in length, the lowest 81/2. feet - /You have then an august view of (Cove-Cragg) (a sloping Edge) with a tree on it – a few yards further a small force with a fine mountain ash over it, and a beautiful long smooth bathing pool at its foot – 6 or 7 yards long -/a little further down a third force, uninteresting, but then what a view of that half-moon crag before me, and the inverted crescent on its right hand – ran along & in another half furlong another beck joined my fellow traveller. I looked up it into a magnificent embracement of cliff, an embracement two thirds of an oval/ another tarn! Another tarn! I cried - I ran, and ran, as I approached, psha! Said I - where are my wits – 'tis the same as I before visited & I have been blundering – every moment this conviction increased - & no I saw every minute object of my old friend/ but behold! When I came up there was no Tarn awhile-/ It might be made a whole Tarn by a couple of stout men in a day's time/-/As I approached, I thought that Cove Ban Crag & the adjacencies were mossier/

A far more magnificent embrace than the Tarn – the ascent in its central part more bulged and step-like – the crag that imitated Foul Cragg not so fantastic or terrible, but far far more green ledge-top of its black violey naked Clifflet/"

Coleridge blundered around Scales Tarn and beneath Sharp Edge, noting, feeling, responding to everything, immersing himself, actually losing himself in the landscape. George Smith was far more circumspect. He observed the mountains, at times was impressed, but he didn't delight in the sheer sensual pleasure of their otherness which seems to course through Coleridge's veins.

After coming down from Scales Tarn - it's not clear where he spent the night, but he might well have sought accommodation in Mungrisdale – he climbed Bannerdale across the valley of the Glenderamackin to the west of Souther Fell and then descended to the river in Smith's "turbinated valley".

"On the next morning I was on top of Bannerdale Cliff – an erection of stones is there/

Conical Hill standing belly high over the Hill (Tongue end) which forms the left bank of the beck – the right bank that precipice so steep, so very high – (Southerfell) Now our beck joind again".

That "right bank that precipice so steep, so very high" is the precipitous side of that "eminence in the north end" of Souther Fell where Smith was told that the spectral army had first appeared to William Lancaster's servant in 1735. Coleridge's bracketed note (Southerfell) is probably just a reminder of the fell's name.

"Bannerdale Beck

Bannerdale Crag – but the fine one Cove Crag"[25/26]

When he was in Mungrisdale, Coleridge heard a story about Isaac Ritson, whose poetry prompted his verse on Blencathra. Ritson, who had lived at the nearby How Mill, was a staunch Quaker. The area had been a strong Quaker area from the earliest days. George Fox had stayed at Woodhall near Caldbeck in 1654 and there were three Meeting Houses in the area at Whelpo (1698), Mosedale (1702) and Howbeck (1729). Coleridge briefly recorded the anti-Anglican venture: "Isaak Ritson with Slee & others carried off the Bell of Grisdale Chapel & buried it among some stones in woody Park – They took it down on a ladder, it made a hole in the Earth/ weighed 14 Stone/ hummed the folks & sent them to seek for it in strange places –"[27] The chapel had been rebuilt in 1756 on an ancient site. The dedication to St. Kentigern, popularly known as Mungo, indicates a very early foundation. That rebuilding in the years after the Jacobite Rebellion might have been a response to potential unrest in the district, and Ritson's practical joke suggests that the area persisted in its independent ways.

The next morning, a Saturday, Coleridge left Isaac Todd's at a good hour and headed north on the road along the edge of the fells towards Bowscale and Mosedale:

"Left Isaac Todd's at Grisdale about 8 o'clock, passed along under Raven Crag, not very high, but craggy as need be, then under a part of Bowscale Fells/ and came to Bowscale/ a pretty cluster of 4 houses, with 5 Sycamores in the green yard of the first – still kept over by Bowscale Fell, on my right hand Carrock, dirt-stone, & red brown Heath / at its foot the sweet cluster of Mosedale, each home with its own trees – before me

Slatestone Crag – some houses at Mosedale had Firs, some Ashes, some Sycamores. So I would along still under Bowscale Fells till I came just above Drycombe Beck which runs up in the (diagram of division between slate and stone crag) the syke divides it B. & Slatestone Crag, if division it may be called which a baby might pass – there I stopped to look at Swinside three houses, equidistant, each perhaps a furlong from the other, the middle house hid by Trees, the nearest Mosedale with two trees at its Gavel end (diagram of house, gable end and trees) Mosedale the house other with a fine group of trees – the Caldew flowing between stone walls both by Swinside and Mosedale. this is two houses, Nicholson the proprietor of all lives there -/ the middle is uninhabited – at the bottom of Carrock it has five Scotch firs – the other trees which encompass are Ash & Sycamore/ Two dry gills, torrent-worn, run down the heath-patched rubbish precipice Carrock, and at the house (diagram of shape like a flowing V) the fields on the other side so green till you reach the Caldew – I counted 21 fields in this hamlet in its broadest one long field is its breadth, about 41/2 acres in length is that field whose length forms the breadth of the vale – from the foot of Carrock to the Caldew – the last & small house with 2 trees is only a wintering House for Hogs – i.e. sheep one year old –

I now would along up to the Tarn – the water runs nearly from East to West in something of this form (diagram of oval with various markings) A A A A its shores are a craggy precipice, bulging out where I have put the (diagram of mark) than at the very edge & with floating reflections of Green, hang a few dwarf trees – B. B. its shores rises up into a round hill of gradual ascent, not above 80 strides, for I measured it – lay on its slope, and look at the central part of the Bow (diagram of bow with mark in middle): a fine effect of the crags laying as I did on my face sideways to look at the/ it looked in this way like a strange City where nothing was left but the Churches and Steeples – churches & steeples with green spaces betwixt them – standing at the East and looking down it – you see its outlet the center of an inverted arch, & you look over upon that dreaded clay chasm called Brandel head Gill, on that part of Carrock which ascends from the Skiddaw side –"

Coleridge's visions of Bowscale Tarn are very different from George Smith's doomed attempt to see the stars reflected in the tarn's depths at mid-day. He then climbed up above the tarn and headed south to the col below Blencathra where the Glenderamackin begins its deviant course and where George Smith imagined that, simply by imposing his foot, he might divert the waters to either Carlisle or Cockermouth. He followed the stream as far as the ridge that leads between the southern end of Souther Fell and Blencathra and made his way down to the Penrith-Keswick road.

"Climbed up the highest part, and came out in Bowscale Mungrane, Skiddaw fronting me, Carrock, Westfell, Brandelhead Gill, Cokelakes, Snab, & [?Cawvey] which is part of Caldbeck fells/ Skiddaw ends in Littledaw Crag – on my left the eminences, into which the Grand Island rises up, are Tarn Crag, 7 Scaknot – mounted Scaknot.

Down down & ascended again to the stone-raise on the highest part of Bannerdale Crag – My God! What a thing a Lake would make that place! –Behind me now was Foul Cragg, it is as if it were the step before Bannerdale Crag – a step for Homer's Neptune/ went toward it, faced *my* Tarn the first, descended to the Beck by the Sheepfold in the valley, ascended a small part of Blenkarthur and followed the road almost to Souterfell then wound down, passed a spring cold as ice & not larger than the palm of my hand, & finally came down to the White horse, about 51/2 miles from Keswick."[28]

Coleridge's experience of the fells was too immediate for him to colour his vision with extraneous detail, for him to add stories and folklore and inhabit some-one else's creation. Souther Fell had been before his eyes for the best part of two days – his route had taken him to the west and north of the fell and then back again – but he had had no thoughts of the spectral army.

He had probably been aware of the tale, through Wordsworth and his poetry, through reading Hutchinson and probably Clarke, and possibly through knowing the people of Grisdale. Almost twenty years later, when he was living in Highgate, he made one passing reference to the story among the sporadic jottings in his notebook, which were later assembled for his lectures on literature. In the entry for 5th March, 1818, Coleridge quoted a Latin passage from the *Saxon Chronicles* for the year 1104, which he remembered from a section in the *Miscellanies* where Aubrey was writing about "Ostenta or Portents". He noted: "This is translated by

Aubrey – Four Circles of a White Color were seen to ROLL IN CONJUNCTION around the sun", and then glossed this extraordinary phenomenon by seeing it as, "One of 1000 instances of the manner in which the extraordinary grows by superaccretion into the inexplicable Miraculous." This reminded him of a misreading in Pausanias (in fact, Herodotus) of a word for *pigeons* or *doves* as the word for *women*, which resulted in the story of a miracle: "So Pausanias's story of the miracle during the Oracle – not indeed palaia, but peleaia - not winged old women but really however there did take place a flight of Pigeons." And then, following that note, he simply wrote, with no explanation or conjunction to the previous note: "The march of an army across the breast of Blenkarthur, seen at Threlkeld, near Keswick – on the entrance of the young Pretender-."

The notes for the lecture that grew out of these pages in the notebook make no mention of the spectral army but the lecture dealt, in part, with the relation between the imagination and apparitions. Coleridge began by observing that "The fact really is, as to apparitions, that the terror produces the image instead of the contrary."[29] This is one of the first reflections on the psychology of the apparition on Souther Fell.

Chapter Seven:

Sir Walter Scott

James Clark failed to sell his expensive but small edition of *The Survey of the Lakes*. Britton and Brayley, reprinting his account of the spectral army, probably sold an edition of six thousand copies of the Cumberland volume over a period of years after its publication in 1804.

The sales of Walter Scott's poetry were phenomenal. *The Edinburgh Review*, in 1810, faced with the poem's enormous popularity, excused its audacity in daring to critically assess *The Lady of the Lake*: Mr Scott though living in an age unusually prolific of original poetry, has manifestly outstripped all his competitors in the race of popularity; and stands already upon a height to which no other writer has attained in the memory of any one now alive. We doubt, indeed, whether any English poet ever had so many of his books sold, or so many of his verses read and admired by such a multitude of persons, in so short a time. We are credibly informed, that nearly thirty thousand copies of *The Lay* have been already disposed of in this country; and that the demand for *Marmion*, and the poem now before us, has been still more considerable, - a circulation, we believe, altogether without example, in the case of a bulky work, not addressed to the bigotry of the mere mob, either religious or political."[1]

The Lady of the Lake swept across Europe, inspiring poems, plays, operas – Rossini's *La Donna del Lago* being the most famous – and song settings, Schubert set seven of the songs, including Ellen's tender *Ave Maria*, and both Felix and Fanny Mendelssohn, Glinka and many others responded to the emotional force of the poem. Few poems have evoked such a wide and enthusiastic popular response. Tourists sought out the haunts of Ellen and James Douglas and Rhoderick Ddu and Malcolm Graeme on the shores of Loch Katrine and Landseer's *Stag at Bay* became the emblem of an age.

Our concern is with the footnote to four lines of the five thousand or so that make up the six cantos of the poem that concludes with the pure and beautiful Highland Ellen being given the key to her lover's golden chains.

Brian the hermit is sacrificing a goat to sanctify the bloody burning cross which will be carried from village to village to summon the clans. (The flaming cross as depicted in this poem acquired sinister connotations when it was adopted by the Ku Klux Klan in America.) Brian's mother had conceived him innocently when, among the bones of a deserted battlefield,

> "All night, in this sad glen, the maid
> Sate, shrouded in her mantle's shade"
> She locked the secret of his conception "in her breast
> And died in travail, unconfessed."[2]

The hermit had grown up "with fired brain and nerves o'erstrung,

> And heart with mystic horrors wrung

His melancholy disposition made him a seer and visionary, able to see forms and spirits in the patterns of nature:

> The desert gave him visions wild,
> Such as might suit the Spectre's child.
> Where with black cliffs the torrents toil,
> He watched the wheeling eddies boil,
> Till from their foam, his dazzled eyes
> Beheld the river-daemon rise;
> The mountain-mist took form and limb,
> Of noontide hag, or goblin grim;
> The midnight wind came wild and dread,
> Swelled with the voices of the dead;
> Far on the future battle heath
> The eye beheld the ranks of death;
> Thus the lone seer, from mankind hurled,

Shaped forth a disembodied world.

Brian the Hermit is willingly self-deceived by the suggestive forms of nature. Even in the poetry Scott was providing a physical and psychological explanation for the mystical and supernatural. In his madness, the hermit retains his sense of belonging to his mother's clan and he fears for the safety of Roderick Ddu, the head of that clan, in the forthcoming battle.

One lingering sympathy of mind
Still bound him to the mortal kind;
The only parent he could claim
Of ancient Alpine's lineage came.
Late had he heard, in prophet's dream,
The fatal Ben-Shie's boding scream;
Sounds, too, had come in midnight blast,
Of charging steeds, careering fast
Along Benharrow's shingly side,
Where mortal horseman ne'er might ride;
The thunderbolt had split the pine,—
All augur'd ill to Alpine's line.
He girt his loins, and came to show
The signals of impending woe.[3]

Scott had taken the image of the horsemen riding on an impossible mountain side that was central to the story of Souther Fell and, combining it with a Highland legend, made it part of "the prophet's dream" and transferred it to the sides of Benharrow sloping down into Loch Katrine. The phenomenon, which had been authenticated by eye-witnesses, is now the imaginative dream beheld by a man with second sight. The image has become an aural and not a visual one. It is combined with brief references to legends, all drawn from Scott's extensive knowledge of Highland mythology. He was one of the great folklorists. The image of the "charging steeds" becomes, along with the wailing banshee, a portent of doom.

The long, and poetically unjustified note is on the four lines:

Sounds, too, had come in midnight blast,
Of charging steeds, careering fast
Along Benharrow's shingly side,

Where mortal horseman ne'er might ride;

It runs as follows:

"A presage of the kind alluded to in the text, is still believed to announce death to the ancient Highland family of M'Lean of Lochbuy. The spirit of an ancestor slain in battle is heard to gallop along a stony bank, and then to ride thrice around the family residence, ringing his fairy bridle, and thus intimating the approaching calamity. How easily the eye as well as the ear may be deceived upon such occasions, is evident from the stories of armies in the air, and other spectral phoenomena, (sic) with which history abounds. Such an apparition is said to have been witnessed upon the side of Southerfell mountain, between Penrith and Keswick, upon the 23rd June, 1744, by two persons, William Lancaster of Blakehills, and Daniel Stricket, his servant, whose attestation to the fact, with a full account of the apparition, dated the 21st July, 1785, is printed in Clarke's *Survey of the Lakes*. The apparition consisted of several troops of horse moving in regular order, with a steady rapid motion, making a curved sweep around the fell, and seeming to the spectators to disappear over the ridge of the mountain. Many persons witnessed this phoenomenon, the last, or last but one, of the supposed troop, occasionally leave his rank, and pass, at a gallop, to the front, when he resumed the same steady pace. This curious appearance, making the necessary allowance for imagination, may be perhaps sufficiently accounted for by optical deception.—Survey of the Lakes, p. 25."[4]

Scott had portrayed in Brian the Hermit a figure worthy of Ossian. James MacPherson's supposed translations from the Gaelic, had been greeted with enormous enthusiasm until Dr Johnson, with inadequate justification, denounced him as "a mountebank, a liar, and a fraud" and his poems as "forgeries". However, Ossian remained a favourite on the continent with people as diverse as Goethe, Schubert and Napoleon. His work had done much to change the image of the degraded Highlander after Culloden and its wild imagination had been an antidote to Enlightenment values and had served to usher in Romanticism. Scott's own views on Ossian, which had changed since he was a young man, are indicated by his opinion of Napoleon's continuing enthusiasm for the bard: "He had, therefore, never corrected his taste in the belles lettres, but retained his admiration for Ossian, and other books which had fascinated his early attention. The declamatory tone, redundancy of expression, and exaggerated character, of the poetry ascribed to the Celtic Bard, suit the taste of very young persons; but Napoleon continued to retain his relish for them to the end of his life; and, in some of his proclamations and bulletins, we can trace the hyperbolical and bombastic expressions which pass upon us in youth for the sublime, but are rejected as taste and reason become refined and improved."[5] *The Lady of the Lake* might be said to civilize Ossian, taking the scenery and the culture and the heightened imagination and refining and distancing them. The story of the spectral army, as Norman Nicholson suggested, was Ossianic.

Scott chose to treat the story of a spectral army seriously as poetry and to dismiss it as an "optical illusion" but he did hedge his scientific dismissal with the triple qualifications contained in the phrase "may be perhaps sufficiently accounted". Scott was showing something of the same ambivalence displayed by Wordsworth in respect to optical illusions, an imaginative yearning for their possibility and an everyday rationalism that dismissed them as mere fancy.

Throughout his notes to *The Lady of the Lake* and, often elsewhere, Scott displayed an intellectual tension which was central to his life and to his writings. He was possessed by an imaginative longing for romance, for heroic deeds and grand actions, for the passions and tragedies of an aristocratic or mythical past, but he was also lame and sat at his desk for many hours as a writer and lawyer and was a rational man in a rational society, the son of the Scottish Enlightenment. His poetry and his fiction might celebrate the romance and mythology of the Highlands, but his notes explain the credibility of the apparently fantastic.

Clarke's account of Souther Fell was used uncritically, but with the substantiating detail, to show how such well-known and persuasive accounts of the supernatural were subject to rational explanation. The story of the spectral army had become a touchstone for the scientific explanation of the supposed supernatural.

Four years later, Walter Scott was probably responsible for another appearance of the Souther Fell story, this time in the *Edinburgh Annual Register*. The *Register* was a foolhardy, ambitiously encyclopaedic work that was edited, anonymously, by Scott with the support of its publisher and printer, James Ballantyne. Although Scott had included an annual register in his visionary proposals to Ballantyne as early as 1800, the ambition was reinforced by the heady success of *The Lady of the Lake* and Scott's other poems. Within four years of the first issue in 1808, it was losing a thousand pounds a year and publishing a poor shadow of its promised coverage of world events, literature, science, fine arts, 'useful arts', meteorology and commerce. The *Register* brought ruin to the publishing and printing house of the Ballantyne Brothers and Scott was only able to protect his own reputation by some deft but not very wise financial manoeuvring.

In the *Annual Register* for 1812, published two years late in 1814, among the articles chronicling the events of the year, is the following:

"Leeds. - Extraordinary Phenomena - The following marvellous narrative, communicated by the ghostseers, has produced a good deal of conversation in a part of this county, and may serve to astonish the credulous, amuse the sceptical, and occupy the speculative: -

" 'On Sunday evening, the 28th ultimo, between seven and eight o'clock, A. Jackson, farmer, aged 45 years, and M. Turner, the son of W. Turner, farmer, aged 15 years, while engaged in inspecting their cattle, grazing on Havarah Park, near Ripley, part of the estate of Sir J. Ingleby, Bart. were suddenly surprised by a most extraordinary appearance in the park. Turner, whose attention was first drawn to this spectacle, said, "Look, Anthony, what a quantity of beasts!"—"Beasts!" cried Anthony, "Lord bless us! they are not beasts, they are men!"—By this time the body was in motion, and the spectators discovered that it was an army of soldiers, dressed in a white military uniform, and that in the centre stood a personage of commanding aspect, clothed in scarlet. After performing a number of evolutions, the body began to march in perfect order to the summit of a hill, passing the spectators at a distance of about one hundred yards. No sooner had the first body, which seemed to consist of several hundreds, and extended four deep, over an inclosure of 30 acres attained the hill, than another assemblage of men, far more numerous than the former, dressed in dark-coloured clothes, arose and marched, without any apparent hostility, after the military spectres; at the top of the hill both the parties formed what the spectators called an L, and passing down the opposite side of the hill, disappeared. At this time a volume of smoke, apparently like that vomited by a park of artillery, spread over the plain, and was so impervious, as for nearly two minutes to hide the cattle from the view of Jackson and Turner, who hurried home with all possible expedition: and the effect upon their minds, even at this distance of time, is so strong, that they cannot mention the circumstance without visible emotion.

" 'We have had the curiosity, and an idle curiosity perhaps it was, to collate the accounts of this strange vision, as given by the two spectators, and find them agree in every part, with these exceptions: - the young man says, that as far as he could mark the progress of time, while a scene so novel and alarming was passing before him, he thinks that from the appearance of the first body to the disappearance of the smoke, might be about five minutes; Jackson says, it could not be less than a quarter of an hour, and that during all this time they were making to each other such observations as arose out of the spectacle. The junior spectator says, he observed, amongst the first body, arms glistening in the sun; the senior says it may be so; but that did not strike him, nor can he, in thinking of it since, recall any such appearance to his recollection.

" 'On this strange story we shall only observe, that the ground forming the scene of action is perfectly sound, and not likely to emit any of those exhalations which might arise from a swamp; that the narrators are both persons of character; that those who know them best, believe them most, and that they themselves are unquestionably convinced of the truth of their own narrative; that tradition records a scene somewhat similar, exhibited on Stockton forest, about the breaking out of the present war; and that we shall be glad to receive any satisfactory elucidation of this *Phantasmagoria.'*

"Thus far the *Leeds Mercury* — We do not know whether the following article will be considered as affording any satisfactory elucidation; but it may, perhaps, contribute something to the amusement of our readers:—"[6]

"The following article" is the full account of the Souther Fell phenomenon, taken verbatim from Britton and Brayley, including not only the abridged version of Clarke's account, but also the reprinting of M. Haue's article on the Spectre of the Brocken and the brief speculations by Britton and Brayley as to an explanation. The whole article, including the story from *The Leeds Mercury*, is a piece of cheap copy used by an editor looking to fill his pages, but it does serve to show Scott's continuing awareness of, if not interest in, such phenomena.

The incident in Havarah Park became another case of a spectral army that was often quoted in conjunction with the Souther Fell and Stockton stories. The parallels are clear. First there was a misapprehension, in this case the "beasts", and then the identification and the confirmation as greater and greater details of the troops manoeuvres were apprehended. As with Souther Fell, there was a minimum of two corroborating witnesses to rule out a mental aberration and a cloud of smoke played a part. Even though the sharp eyed journalist detected some minor discrepancies between the witnesses, the credibility of the story is seen to be adequately guaranteed by the good character of the witnesses and their obvious conviction. However, in the case of Havarah park the two men exp[ressed great astonishment and still cannot recall "the circumstance without visible emotion".

In 1815, Scott was amusing himself with the forms of the gothic novel as he pursued the fortunes of Jonathan Oldbuck in *The Antiquary*. That novel, published in 1816, contains Scott's own working of a German folktale, *The Fortunes of Martin Waldeck,* which is set in the Harz mountains. The story is said to have been copied by Isabella Wardour, a self-confessed lover of fairyland, but it is her would-be lover, Lovel, who, "suppressing his emotions", reads it aloud:

'The Fortunes of Martin Waldeck.

'The solitudes of the Harz forest in Germany, but especially the mountains called Blockberg, or rather Brockenberg, are the chosen scene for tales of witches, daemons, and apparitions. The occupation of the inhabitants, who are either miners or foresters, is of a kind that renders them peculiarly prone to superstition, and the natural phenomena which they witness in pursuit of their solitary or subterraneous profession, are often set down by them to the interference of goblins or the power of magic. Among the various legends current in that wild country, there is a favourite one, which supposes the Harz to be haunted by a sort of tutelar daemon, in the shape of a wild man, of huge stature, his head wreathed with oak leaves, and his middle cinctured with the same, bearing in his hand a pine torn up by the roots. It is certain that many persons profess to have seen such a form traversing, with huge strides, in a line parallel to their own course, the opposite ridge of a mountain, when divided from it by a narrow glen; and indeed the fact of the apparition is so generally admitted, that modern scepticism has only found refuge by ascribing it to optical deception.' "[7]

In the collected, annotated edition of his works in 1832, another very necessary money-making venture as Scott, mortally ill, sought honourably to clear his debts, he added a short note on the optics of the situation to dispel any mystery: "Note: The shadow of the person who sees the phantom, being reflected upon a cloud of mist, like the image of a magic lantern upon a white sheet, is supposed to have formed the apparition."[8]

That short, optically-confused note echoed the view he had expressed in his *Letters on Demonology and Witchcraft*. This intriguing book, which is as much the product of Scott's complex intellectual personality as the novels and poetry, is, not surprisingly, often overlooked in the whole body of his writings. Walter Scott had an enormous capacity for work and, despite the urbane sociability which was a mark of life at Abbotsford, he was a man driven by social, even aristocratic, ambition and by a deep sense of honour and financial necessity. He was also driven by his own considerable and individual intellectual interests which fed his creative work. The young lawyer in his twenties was translating German poetry and plays and researching the folklore of his native area. The *Minstrelsy of the Scottish Border* is as important for its extensive notes as it is for its huge contribution to folk poetry and song. His editions of Dryden and Swift were considerable undertakings and the astuteness of his literary reviews places him among the leading critics of his day. His long biography of Napoleon is one of the great biographies in the language and is complementary to the understanding of military affairs displayed in the novels. *Tales of a Grandfather* presents a history of Scotland that has a vitality unmatched by other contemporary accounts. Scott also wrote significantly on religion, politics and, even, economics, being instrumental in enabling Scottish banks to continue to issue legal tender. His personal writings, which include accounts of his travels, his letters and, especially, the moving *Journal,* which he kept during the last seven years of his life, demonstrate the breadth of humanity of a man who, for the succeeding century, was held to have been one of the greatest of all writers in English.

The *Letters on Demonology and Witchcraft* was written after the widowed Sir Walter Scott suffered the first of the strokes that were to result in his death two years later, a month after his sixty-first birthday. His phenomenal memory was somewhat diminished, but his brain was as acute as ever. The work was one that had been in his mind for many years from the days when he was writing the notes to *The Lady of the Lake*. It was one of the most popular volumes in *Murray's Family Library*, an eighty volume series "planned to secure a wide diffusion of good literature in cheap five-shilling volumes". Richard Dorson, the historian of folklore studies, had no doubt about its importance. He described it as "the first sustained treatise in English on supernatural beliefs of gentry and peasantry and promptly joined Brand (Observations on the Popular Antiquities of Great Britain) on the shelf of indispensable reference works for the antiquary interested in occult matters."[9] Contemporary notices thought it would prove the most popular of Murray's little volumes and expected it to acquire a " 'parlour-window' immortality".[10]

Scott, himself, was far more modest in his claims: his "information is only miscellaneous"; he sought to "erect no new system" but "to confine myself to narratives of remarkable cases". The breadth and depth of his lifelong interest and reading gave the work significance.

Walter Scott was a social rather than a devout Christian. He must have been aware that too ready a rational dismissal of the spiritual world laid him open to criticism from those of deeply held religious beliefs. In a carefully worded statement in his introduction, he outlined his own understanding of the divine and the complete separation of the spiritual from the physical world: "The general, or, it may be termed, the universal belief of the inhabitants of the earth, in the existence of spirits separated from the encumbrance and incapacities of the body, is grounded on the consciousness of the divinity that speaks in our bosoms, and demonstrates to all men, except the few who are hardened to the celestial voice, that there is within us a portion of the divine substance, which is not subject to the law of death and dissolution, but which, when the body is no longer fit for its abode, shall seek its own place, as a sentinel dismissed from his post. . . . the conviction that such an indestructible essence exists . . . infer the existence of many millions of spirits, who have not been annihilated, though they have become invisible to mortals who still see, hear, and perceive, only by means of the imperfect organs of humanity. . . The abstract idea of a spirit certainly implies, that it has neither substance, form, shape, voice, or any thing which can render its presence visible or sensible to human faculties." As a folklorist, novelist and sheriff, he had no doubt that the majority of less educated people believed in the supernatural: "But these sceptic doubts of philosophers on the possibility of the appearance of such separated spirits, do not arise till a certain degree of information has dawned upon a country, and even then only reach a very small proportion of reflecting and better informed members of society. To the multitude, the indubitable fact, that so many millions of spirits exist around and even amongst us, seems sufficient to support the belief that they are, in certain instances at least, by some means or other, able to communicate with the world of humanity." And he was also aware of the central role that psychology played in the apprehension of the supernatural: "Ocular testimony to an intercourse betwixt earth and the world beyond it" may well be the product of intense feeling by the bereaved or the guilty, ("the wretched man who has dipped his hand in his fellow-creature's blood") and "such a vision may take place in the course of one of those lively dreams" when "the spectre, though itself purely fanciful, is inserted amidst so many circumstances which he feels must be true beyond the reach of doubt or question. That which is undeniably certain, becomes in a manner a warrant for the reality of the appearance to which doubt would have been otherwise attached."[11]

In an essay on *The Tales of Hoffmann*, having recognised that a belief in Christianity necessitated the existence of a spiritual world, Scott wrote: "The belief in prodigies and supernatural events has gradually declined in proportion to the advancement of human knowledge; and that since the age has become enlightened, the occurrence of tolerably well-attested anecdotes of the supernatural character are so few, as to render it more probable that the witnesses have laboured under some strange and temporary delusion, rather than that the laws of nature have been altered or suspended. At this period of human knowledge, the marvellous is so much identified with fabulous, as to be considered generally as belonging to the same class."[12]

Scott is possessed of a sense of the divine, which, as Glanvil felt, necessitated a belief in the existence of spirits, but, he also considered, unlike Glanvil, that by their very nature spirits cannot be susceptible to human faculties. However, his novelist's awareness of human psychology and the breadth of his sympathies with the "unenlightened" led him to take a serious interest in the folklore of spirits and ghosts. This serious (and aesthetic) interest in the psychology and sociology of ghosts balanced by a philosophical scepticism was very much a mark of the Romantic and Gothic sensibility. As in his novels, there was a high playfulness in Scott's talk of ghosts. When he wrote about them in letters he represented himself as "an initiated Ghost-seer" and "ghost-raiser". He enjoyed telling of how he had slept soundly at an inn in one bed of a double room, while the other bed was occupied by dead men. He did talk of having experienced a feeling of "eeriness" when he had been at Glamis Castle. Glamis Castle had strong literary and historical associations and the heavy, ancient castle and tales of a secret chamber made an impression on a romantic and susceptible young man still in his teens. He also believed that an apparition had appeared before his eyes on one occasion when he was travelling home in the twilight.

In the *Demonology* he rationalised a compelling apparition of Lord Byron that he had seen in a moonlit Abbotsford. He coyly transferred the anecdote to an unidentified third person: "Another illusion of the same nature we have the best reason for vouching as a fact, though, for certain reasons, we do not give the names of the parties. Not long after the death of a late illustrious poet, who had filled, while living, a great station in the eye of the public, a literary friend, to whom the deceased had been well known, was engaged, during the darkening twilight of an autumn evening, in perusing one of the publications which professed to detail the habits and opinions of the distinguished individual who was now no more. As the reader had enjoyed the intimacy of the deceased to a considerable degree, he was deeply interested in the publication, which contains some particulars relating to himself and other friends. A visitor was sitting in the apartment, who was also engaged in reading. Their sitting-room opened into an entrance-hall, rather fantastically fitted up with articles of armour, skins of wild animals, and the like. It was when laying down his book, and passing into this hall, through which the moon was beginning to shine, that the individual of whom I speak, saw, right before him, and in a standing posture, the exact representation of his departed friend, whose recollection had been so strongly brought to his imagination. He stopped for a single moment, so as to notice the wonderful accuracy with which fancy had impressed upon the bodily eye the peculiarities of dress and posture of the illustrious poet. Sensible, however, of the delusion, he felt no sentiment save that of wonder at the extraordinary accuracy of the resemblance, and stepped onwards towards the figure, which resolved itself, as he approached, into the various materials of which it was composed. These were merely a screen, occupied by great-coats, shawls, plaids, and such other articles as usually are found in a country entrance-hall. The spectator returned to the spot from which he had seen the illusion, and endeavoured, with all his power, to recall the image which had been so singularly vivid. But this was beyond his capacity; and the person who had witnessed the apparition, or, more properly, whose excited state had been the means of raising it, had only to return into the apartment, and tell his young friend under what a striking hallucination he had for a moment laboured."[13] He was also fond of quoting an anecdote concerning Coleridge which typifies the sceptical pleasure his generation took in ideas of the supernatural: "This species of deception is so frequent, that one of the greatest poets of the present time answered a lady who asked him if he believed in ghosts, — 'No, madam; I have seen too many myself.' "[14]

The *Demonology* surveys the range of superstition throughout history touching on instances from the Bible and other religions as well as supposedly well-documented cases in law, before briefly discussing instances that, with hindsight, appear to have been cases of readily explained deception: "Other stories of the same kind are numerous and well known. The apparition of the Brocken mountain, after having occasioned great admiration, and some fear, is now ascertained by philosophers to be a gigantic reflection, which makes the traveller's shadow, represented upon the misty clouds, appear a colossal figure of almost immeasurable size. By a similar deception, men have been induced in Westmoreland and other mountainous countries, to imagine they saw troops of horse and armies marching and countermarching, which were in fact only the reflection of horses pasturing upon an opposite height, or of the forms of peaceful travellers."[15]

Scott's comments were vague and generalised. Other sightings of armies had been seen in flatter land – Leicestershire, Cambridgeshire and Warwickshire – and perhaps the Marston Moor armies over Helvellyn, but no account talked of counter-marching. His explanation was so uncritical that he confused the opposed concepts of a shadow and a reflection - a case of passing on the more precise explanations of people more qualified to comment than himself. It is interesting that he did not concern himself with the detail – the spectral army is vaguely suggested to be "the reflection of horses pasturing upon an opposite height, or of the forms of peaceful travellers" and made no attempt to demonstrate the optics of the situation. No commentary had suggested armies on an opposite height and the peaceful travellers may have been a recollection of the stragglers that followed the spectral army.

That slip of the pen imagining the marching armies in Westmoreland rather than Cumberland may have been due to his failing memory. Scott had long been familiar with the Penrith area. He had climbed Helvellyn with Wordsworth and visited Robert Southey in Keswick. The antiquarian Scott had carried off his stone trophies to his garden at Abbotsford from the site of the Roman fort at Old Penrith. The novelist Scott had imagined the young Waverley escaping from the skirmish at Clifton and seeking shelter on a farm by Ullswater and had sympathised with Jeanie Deans as she journeyed along the road from Penrith towards the corpse swinging like a spider from the gibbet at High Harrabee; and the poet Scott had set *The Bridal of Triermain* at the rocky castle in the Vale of St Johns and had the action of the poem sweep across the borderlands to Triermain itself. In a note on the line "The surface of that sable tarn" he uncritically copied the tale of the sunless Bowscale Tarn told seventy years previously by a credulous George Smith and transferred it to the equally cold and solemn waters that lie in the shade of Blencathra: "The small lake called Scales-tarn lies so deeply embosomed in the recesses of the huge mountain called Saddleback, more poetically Glaramara, is of such great depth, and so completely hidden from the sun, that it is said its beams never reach it, and that the reflection of the stars may be seen at mid-day."[16]

Chapter Eight:

Sir David Brewster and the Scientists

The man who would have demonstrated the optics of the spectral army to Sir Walter Scott with precision and clarity was his near neighbour and frequent guest, Sir David Brewster. His book, an almost equally successful volume in *Murray's Family Library*, was actually titled *Letters on Natural Magic Addressed to Sir Walter Scott, Bart.* This "popular account of those prodigies of the material world" was written at Scott's suggestion and Brewster deemed it as "no slight honour if they shall be considered as forming an appropriate supplement to your valuable work".[1]

Brewster had lived at Allerly House two miles further down the Tweed towards Melrose since 1826, and was a frequent dinner guest at Abbotsford. Eleven years younger than Scott, he had been born in Jedburgh in 1781, the son of the school rector. He was ill-disposed for his intended career. James Hogg tells the story in his inimitable fashion: "He got the prizes at the college, and then was licensed: but the first day he mounted the pulpit was his last — for he had then, if he has not still, a nervous something about him that made him swither when he heard his own voice, and saw a congregation eyeing him; so he sticked his discourse, and vowed never to try."[2] By 1808 he had secured a demanding and poorly remunerated post as editor of the projected *Edinburgh Encyclopaedia*. This enabled him to continue with his studies in the sciences and especially optics. Much of his work was "focused" (as the DNB puts it) on the polarisation of light including the discovery of the angle of polarisation now known as the Brewster angle. He calculated the refractive indices of many materials. He invented and refined a sizeable number of scientific and investigative tools including the spectroscope and the polyzonal lens, which gave an intense beam of light and was later used in lighthouses. His most celebrated invention, and least useful, which became a social craze in 1817, was the kaleidoscope. As so often, the enthusiasm with which this novelty was adopted led to moral outrage. One Christian observer defined the toy as "a machine in which, by means of an optical deception, a few pieces of tawdry glass and tinsel acquire apparent symmetry and beauty, adjusting themselves in a ceaseless variety of novel and amusing forms, and leading us to hope that each new change may be still more attractive than the last. Such, Mr. Editor, is also the world."[3] The kaleidoscope had a faulty patent and made its inventor a household name, but little, if any, money.

David Brewster was one of the leading scientists of his day, much respected for his investigative and painstaking research and for the breadth of his knowledge. In his life he published some 299 scientific papers and perhaps a further thousand articles and books. Brewster's biography of Isaac Newton is still felt to be a serviceable and honest piece of work, even though it is biased towards Newton's research in optics. There were, in fact, two distinct biographies, the popular *Life of Newton* published in *Murray's Family Library* in 1831, and the much larger *Memoirs of the life, writings and discoveries of Sir Isaac Newton*, which was published in two volumes in 1855. This work was the first to examine Newton's private papers, including the 650,000 words of notes on the subject of alchemy and the million or so on theology. These subjects figured as largely in Newton's own mind as the mathematics and physics, which cause him to be viewed as one of the greatest of all geniuses. Newton may have held Arian or Socinian views, which disputed the mystical elements of the identity of the Father, Son and Holy Ghost. David Brewster sought to square Newton's questioning of the Trinity and his alchemical enthusiasms with the enlightened rationalist that he revered. His extensive involvement in alchemy when the subject was deemed disreputable may have been prompted by an interest in chemistry, but Brewster felt that, "In so far as Newton's inquiries were limited to the transmutation and multiplication of metals, and even to the discovery of the universal tincture, we may find some apology for his researches; but we cannot understand how a mind of such power, and so nobly occupied with the abstractions of geometry, and the study of the material world, could stoop to be even the copyist of the most contemptible alchemical poetry, and the annotator of a work, the obvious production of a fool and a knave."[4]

In 1810 David Brewster married Juliet Macpherson, the youngest daughter of James Macpherson, the writer/translator of Ossian. Macpherson had never married, but, perhaps in the character of the bard, he had fathered two daughters and three sons whom he treated with generosity. Juliet inherited his estate at Belleville and the five Brewster children adopted the additional surname of Macpherson. Their only daughter Mary, in her biography of her father, told how this moral, clear-thinking, utterly rational man nevertheless held the memory of his romantic and possibly duplicitous father-in-law in high regard. "They never had a moment's doubt as to the complete and entire authenticity of the poems. The originals, they were fully persuaded, had been received by Mr. Macpherson in most cases by oral recitation, and in others from mss. which had been written down two or three centuries before from the old Highland bards, whose predecessors had sung them long before such innovations as pen, ink, and paper were known amongst the Celts."[5]

With Newton and Ossian, and perhaps with Scott, David Brewster found himself steering a difficult course as he sought, in the face of the temptations of mysticism and romance, to explain the world in a rational, scientific manner. It was an intriguing position for one of the foremost of European scientists to be in. The spectral army of Souther Fell was one of many apparently inexplicable phenomena that demanded a scientific and rational explanation.

The Letters on Natural Magic was addressed to "My Dear Sir Walter". Brewster saw this very successful book on popular science as having a religious and political purpose to explain the "dark conspiracy" of an elite who thereby held the superstitious in awe: "The subject of Natural Magic . . . embraces the history of the governments and the superstitions of ancient times, - of the means by which they maintained their influence over the human mind, - of the assistance which they derived from the arts and the sciences, and from a knowledge of the powers and phenomena of nature. . . . The prince, the priest, and the sage, were leagued in a dark conspiracy to deceive and enslave their species;

and man, who refused his submission to a being like himself, became the obedient slave of a spiritual despotism, and willingly bound himself in chains when they seemed to have been forged by the gods." Acoustics, mechanics, hydrostatics, chemistry and optics were the possessions of elite castes and were all employed to apparently magical effect to ensure submission. Such knowledge as the ancients possessed being secret was consequently lost to later generations. He intended to show how the senses of men were deceived either by the conspiracy of their fellows or by the misinterpreting of nature. "The principal phenomena of nature, and the leading combinations of art, which bear the impress of a supernatural character, will pass under our review, and our attention will be particularly called to those singular illusions of sense, by which the most perfect organs either cease to perform their functions, or perform them faithlessly; and where the efforts and the creations of the mind predominate over the direct perceptions of external nature."[6]

In the same way as Scott found it necessary in his introduction to his *Letters on Demonology* to locate himself clearly and non-controversially within the theological thinking of the time, Brewster found it equally necessary to explain that, as a scientist, explaining the supposedly supernatural, he was not questioning the divine within Christianity. He concluded his analysis with an unequivocal profession of faith: "To remain willingly ignorant of these revelations of the Divine Power is a crime next to that of rejecting the revelation of the Divine Will. Knowledge, indeed, is at once the handmaid and the companion of true religion. They mutually adorn and support each other; and beyond the immediate circle of our secular duties, they are the only objects of rational ambition. While the calm deductions of reason regulate the ardour of Christian zeal, the warmth of a holy enthusiasm gives a fixed brightness to the glimmering lights of knowledge."[7]

Brewster's position indicates how difficult it then was to clearly demarcate scientific and theological debate. This difficulty seems to have been a determining factor in there being very little rational discussion of apparitions during the eighteenth century. In 1685, Joseph Glanvil, himself a man of a rational and philosophic bent, had argued strongly that to deny the existence of spirits was to deny the scriptures and later arguments drew on Biblical rather than empirical evidence. Daniel Defoe, the ever curious enquiring journalist and novelist, aroused interest with a story of the apparition of Mrs Veal in 1707 which he claimed to be as strongly attested as James Clarke did with his later report: "This relation is matter of fact, and attended with such circumstances, as may induce any reasonable man to believe it. It was sent by a gentleman, a justice of peace, at Maidstone, in Kent, and a very intelligent person, to his friend in London, as it is here worded." In 1727 Defoe wrote a lengthy book on apparitions which argued for the necessary existence of spirits of angels and devils on Biblical evidence. The title clearly indicates the intention of the work: *An Essay on the History and Reality of Apparitions. Being an Account of what they are, and what they are not. As, also, how we may distinguish between the Apparitions of Good and Evil Spirits, and how we ought to behave to them. With a great variety of surprising and diverting Examples, never published before.* Daniel Defoe did not believe that the dead, being in heaven, returned as ghosts:

By Death transported to th'eternal shore,
Souls so removed re-visit us no more:
Engrossed with joys of a superior kind,
They leave the trifling thoughts of life behind.[8]

And he did consider that many reports of apparitions were false: "the sham apparitions which people put upon themselves are indeed very many; and our hypochondriac people see more devils at noonday than Galilaeus did stars and more by any than really appeared." However, he still argued in his particular way for the existence of spirits: "But this noways impeaches the main proposition, viz. that there are really and truly apparitions of various kinds; and that spirits or angels, call them what we will, inhabitants of the invisible and empty spaces, do visit us here upon many occasions, either for good or evil, as he who made them is pleased to direct."[9]

Dr Johnson's agnostic views on ghosts, which would have accorded with Walter Scott's later position, were perhaps representative of a period some forty years later. In his *Table Talk*, the irrepressible Boswell asked him about apparitions: "A total disbelief of them is adverse to the opinion of the existence of the soul between death and the last day; the question simply is, Whether departed spirits ever have the power of making themselves perceptible to us? A man who thinks he has seen an apparition can only be convinced himself; his authority will not convince another; and his conviction, if rational, must be founded on being told something which cannot be known but by supernatural means."[10]

Attempts to understand the nature of apparitions sought to explain how they could be so convincing to intelligent and educated witnesses. A paper attributed to M. Meyer, Professor of the University of Halle, in 1748, suggested that for an image to be so realistic it must, in some way, appear on the retina. This supposition was the basis of many of the explanations of apparitions that appeared over the next half century or more including those of David Brewster.

John Ferriar was another remarkable man from Jedburgh, A generation older than David Brewster, he was born a son of the manse in 1761. The twenty-five-year-old Ferriar presented an *Essay on Popular Illusions* to the newly-formed Manchester Literary and Philosophical Society. He found it useful, at a time when philosophical mystics such as Lavater in Switzerland could still talk seriously about apparitions and spirits, to survey the literature on demonology and subject it to a clear-headed empiricism, before which it readily unravelled. Everything he considered from vampirism to mesmerism was the consequence of a too active imagination or a too ready gullibility, and was based on unreliable evidence and inadequate reporting. John Ferriar was a practical medical man who worked tirelessly to improve the health of the people crammed into the insanitary and typhoid-ridden slums of Manchester, but, as so many boys educated in the Borders, he was an enthusiast for literature, writing plays and poems and critical works on Sterne and Massinger.

Some twenty years later, one of the earliest attempts to explain convincing apparitions from a physiological point of view was the short *Essay on Apparitions, in which their Appearance is Accounted for by Causes wholly independent of preternatural agency* by John Alderson, M.D. Senior Physician to the Hull General Infirmary. He described five cases in which the subject had been utterly convinced by an apparition and then related the appearance to a physical disorder such as illness or inebriation.

Two years before his death in 1813, Ferriar published a more comprehensive work: *An Essay Towards a Theory of Apparitions*. In a somewhat facetious introduction he promised to relieve fashionable gothic authors of the need to rationalize their devices – the complaint of Scott and Coleridge about Ann Radcliffe – by offering them truer and more remarkable explanations. He was the gentleman author who invited the reader into his warm library: "Take courage, then, good reader, and knock at the portal of my enchanted castle, which will be opened to you, not by a grinning demon, but by a very civil person, in a black velvet cap, with whom you may pass an hour not disagreeably." However congenial he might have been, it was still very necessary for him to be wary of trespassing on religious territory: "Observe, however, that the following treatise is applicable, in its principles, to profane history, and to the delusions of individuals only. If any thing contained in the ensuing pages could be construed into the most indirect reference to theological discussions, the manuscript would have been committed, without mercy, to the flames. What methods may have been employed by Providence, on extraordinary occasions, to communicate with men, I do not presume to investigate."[11]

The investigation he undertook was determinedly physiological: "It is well known, that in certain diseases of the brain, such as delirium and insanity, spectral delusions take place, even during the space of many days. But it has not been generally observed, that a partial affection of the brain may exist, which renders the patient liable to such imaginary impressions, either of sight or sound, without disordering his judgment or memory. From this peculiar condition of the sensorium, I conceive that the best supported stories of apparitions may be completely accounted for."[12]

He also chose to account for the eye being deceived by the persistence of images on the eyeball as might occur after someone has been gazing at bright light. Newton had reported the effects of staring at the sun for a long time and Erasmus Darwin had investigated these "ocular spectra" with what were probably injurious effects to his own eyes. "It is a well-known law of the human oeconomy, that the impressions produced on some of the external senses, especially on the eye, are more durable than the application of the impressing cause. The effect of looking at the sun, in producing the impression of a luminous globe, for some time after the eye has been withdrawn from the object, is familiar to every one."[13] Ferriar took the idea further and included instances of precise recollection as part of this physiological reaction. "In young persons, the effects resulting from this permanence of impression are extremely curious. I remember, that about the age of fourteen, it was a source of great amusement to myself. If I had been viewing any interesting object in the course of the day, such as a romantic ruin, a fine seat, or a review of a body of troops, as soon as evening came on, if I had occasion to go into a dark room, the whole scene was brought before my eyes, with a brilliancy equal to what it had possessed in day-light, and remained visible, for several minutes. I have no doubt that dismal and frightful images have been presented, in the same manner to young persons, after scenes of domestic affliction, or public horror."[14]

Ferriar developed the idea of apparitions being a form of physiological rather than mental retention. It was only through a corrective habit that we do not retain all impressions. He saw this persistence of image in the way a rotating piece of burning wood "exhibits a complete fiery circle to the eye". "Dr. R. Darwin seems to believe, that it is from habit only, and want of attention, that we do not see the remains of former impressions, or the musca volitantes, on all objects. Probably, this is an instance, in which the error of external sensation is corrected by experience, like the deceptions of perspective, which are undoubtedly strong in our childhood, and are only detected by repeated observation."

"'After having looked,' says Dr. Darwin, 'long at the meridian sun, in making some of the preceding experiments, till the disk faded into a pale blue, I frequently observed a bright blue spectrum of the sun in other objects all the next and the succeeding day, which constantly occurred when I attended to it, and frequently when I did not attend to it. When I closed and covered my eyes, this appeared of a dull yellow; and at other times mixed with the colours of other objects on which it was thrown.'

"It is scarcely necessary to mention the well-known experiment of giving a rotatory motion to a piece of burning wood, the effect of which is to exhibit a complete fiery circle to the eye, and he sees this process as akin to "the idle amusement of tracing landscapes, and pictures of various composition, in the discoloured spots of an old wall."[15]

In the paragraph that followed, Ferriar applied that principle that extends from the retained image of a bright light on the retina to the perception of images in confused impressions to explain such apparitions as the spectral army. He was not saying that what was seen was imagined, but that it was a physiological image reawakened on the retina by the stimulation of the new and imprecise image. "It is probably on the same principle, that we are to account for the appearances of armies marching, in desart and inaccessible places, which are sometimes beheld by the inhabitants of the vallies, in mountainous regions. The accidents of light and shade, and the interposition of partial fogs, or clouds, produce the same effect on the eye, as the discoloured patches of the wall; and the rolling of the mist adds motion to the spectral images."[16] If John Ferriar was thinking specifically of the spectral army on Souther Fell and there is every reason that that apparition would be foremost in his mind, his explanation was that Lancaster, Stricket and the others had seen clouds across the top of the fell and these clouds and the rolling of the mist re-awakened earlier images of armies marching that they already possessed. Ferriar did not explore the detail of the situation and it is easy to see flaws in the explanation, but it was one of the first possible references to the spectral army which would account for it as a mental or physiological rather than a specifically optical delusion.

John Ferriar saw a parallel process in the response various people had made to the Northern Lights. He may, in part, have been referring specifically to those reports of the Lord Derwentwater Lights from a century earlier. "In like manner, recollected images are attributed to the moving lights, in the splendid exhibitions of the Aurora Borealis. The Icelander beholds in them the spirits of his ancestors; and the vulgar discern encountering armies, and torrents of blood, in the lambent meteors of a winter-sky."[17]

The Brocken spectre was cited as a further example, but his explanation suggests that he was no longer thinking of the persistence or physical recollection of the image on the eyeball, but was now explaining how the workings of the external world may prompt the imagination in the perception of an apparition: "The humble diversion of seeing pictures in the fire, which occupies children of smaller growth in the nursery, is calculated on the same principles. In some cases, the imagination is assisted-by physical causes, in a very imposing manner, as in the instance of the Giant of the Broken, in Germany, the 'nursing mother' of ghosts. The giant was seen to occupy the summit of a mountain, at certain periods, to the inexpressible amazement of the inhabitants of the valley, and of travellers. After many years of alarm and wonder, a passenger, while he was contemplating the dreadful apparition, was obliged to raise his hand quickly to his head, to secure his hat from being carried away, by a gust of wind. The giant immediately performed a similar motion; when the traveller bowed, the giant bowed in return and after various experiments, it was ascertained, that the portentous appearance was nothing more than the shadow of the traveller, reflected from a dense white cloud, opposed to the sun."[18]

Doctor Ferriar became the popular reference point for tales of apparitions in succeeding years, so much so that when, in *Cranford*, Mrs Gaskell has Mrs Forrester whisper, in a room with candles snuffed, that ghosts would frighten her more than anything and she feels the full weight of Miss Pole's disapproval, we are told: "She looked at Miss Pole, as much as to say she had declared it, and would stand by it. Such a look was a challenge in itself. Miss Pole came down upon her with indigestion, spectral illusions, optical delusions, and a great deal out of Dr. Ferrier (sic) and Dr. Hibbert besides." [19]

The Dr. Hibbert invoked was an antiquarian, historian and medical doctor, and a close friend of Scott and Brewster. There is a story of Hibbert staying at Brewster's house and, despite his scepticism, being convinced there was an apparition before his very eyes as he prepared to retire for the night. The pale light which the rationalist doctor mistook for an apparition was the tassel of his night-cap which he had set alight. Scott urged him to incorporate papers he had given to the Edinburgh Philosophical Society on the medical basis of apparitions into a book. This book duly appeared in 1824 as *Sketches of the Philosophy of Apparitions or, An Attempt to Trace such Illusions to the Physical Causes*. Again James Hogg had his comments to make in the persona of the Ettrick Shepherd in one of the *Noctes Ambosianae* (Nights at Ambrose's Tavern), those wonderfully entertaining sketches which John Wilson contributed to *Blackwood's Magazine* under the guise of Christopher North:

"NORTH. By the way, James, that Ode to the Devil of yours makes me ask you, if you have seen Dr Hibbert's book on Apparitions?

"SHEPHERD. Ghosts? - no. Is't gude?

"NORTH. Excellent. The Doctor first gives a general view of the particular morbid affections with which the production of phantoms is often connected . . . Apparitions are likewise considered by him as nothing more than ideas, or the recollected images of the mind, which have been rendered more vivid than actual impressions.

"SHEPHERD. Does the Doctor daur to say that there are nae real ghosts? If sae, he needna come out to Ettrick. I've heard that failosophers say there is nae satisfactory evidence of the existence of flesh-and-blude men, (rax me ower the loaf, I want a shave,) but o' the existence o' ghosts and fairies I never heard before that the proof was counted defective. I've seen scores o' them, baith drunk and sober.

NORTH. Well, Hogg versus Hibbert. Sam very ingeniously points out that, in well-authenticated ghost-stories, of a supposed supernatural character, the ideas which are rendered so unduly intense, as to induce spectral illusions, may be traced to such phantastical agents of prior belief, as are incorporated in the various systems of superstition, which for ages possessed the minds of the vulgar."[20]

Isaac Newton had written about images which seemed to remain on the retina after gazing at the sun. Later serious discussion of apparitions and spectres in the eighteenth century had concerned itself with the idea that apparitions were images that presented themselves to the eye. John Ferriar had argued how the mind might be deceived by reactivated images, Erasmus Darwin had discussed a range of ocular spectra and Hibbert had pulled the issues together in a comprehensive discussion of apparitions. John Alderson and Scott's medical friend, Dr Abercrombie, had written on the way apparitions might be engendered by illness. However, it was David Brewster who first provided an overview of the physiological, psychological and physical nature of apparitions.

The chapter on optical phenomena in the *Letters on Natural Magic* is the only one that explores the way the senses can be deceived by nature. It brings together the whole range of apparent apparitions that had bemused the readers of popular literature and that had become part of the debate since M. Haue's article on the Brocken was popularised by Britton and Brayley and others.

Brewster surveyed natural wonders "which possess all the characters of supernatural phenomena" and which inspired terror. They included the phenomena which had been referred to recurrently in the popular press and had been connected with the spectral army of Souther Fell: the Spectre of the Brocken, the Fata Morgana of the Straits of Messina, the Spectre Ships which appeared in the air, and the other extraordinary mirages.

He briefly reviewed the mythology of the Brocken: "From the earliest periods of authentic history, the Brocken has been the seat of the marvellous. On its summits are still seen huge blocks of granite, called the Sorcerer's Chair and the Altar. A spring of pure water is known by the name of the Magic Fountain, and the anemone of the Brocken is distinguished by the title of the Sorcerer's Flower. These names are supposed to have originated in the rites of the great idol Cortho, whom the Saxons worshipped in secret on the summit of the Brocken, when Christianity was extending her benignant sway over the subjacent plains." Brewster then summarized M. Haue's account of the spectre, stressing the time, a quarter past four o'clock in the morning, and the atmospheric conditions – "a brisk west wind carried before it the transparent vapours, which had not yet been condensed into thick heavy clouds." He described and illustrated the process by which M. Haue determined that the colossal figure before him was a projection of himself and how, when joined by two companions, "Every movement that they made was imitated by the three figures, but the effect varied in its intensity, being sometimes weak and faint, and at other times strong and well defined."[21]

He explained the phenomenon and demystified it with a homely and personal example: "Phenomena perfectly analogous to the preceding, though seen under less imposing circumstances, have been often witnessed. When the spectator sees his own shadow opposite to the sun upon a mass of thin fleecy vapour passing near him, it not only imitates all his movements, but its head is distinctly encircled with a halo of light. The aerial figure is often not larger than life, its size and its apparent distance depending, as we shall afterwards see, upon particular causes. I have often seen a similar shadow when bathing in a bright summer's day in an extensive pool of deep water. When the fine mud deposited at the bottom of the pool is disturbed by the feet of the bather, so as to be disseminated through the mass of water in the direction of his shadow, his shadow is no longer a shapeless mass formed upon the bottom, but is a regular figure formed upon the floating particles of mud, and having the head surrounded with a halo, not only luminous, but consisting of distinct radiations."[22]

Without making any connection between the two, simply grouping them as "aerial spectres", Brewster then discussed the spectral army: "One of the most interesting accounts of aerial spectres with which we are acquainted has been given by Mr. James Clarke, in his *Survey of the Lakes of Cumberland*, and the accuracy of this account was confirmed by the attestations of two of the persons by whom the phenomena were first seen."[23] Brewster made no reference to Smith's version, which Scott, at least, would probably have been aware of from his reading of Hutchinson's *History of Cumberland*. He gave a slightly reduced, but mostly verbatim, version of Clarke's account omitting the dramatized dialogue and some of the sensationalist detail such as "They expected likewise to see prodigious grazes from the feet of these horses on the steep side of the mountain. And to find the man lying dead, as they were sure he ran so fast that he must kill himself." He added his own emphasis on the reliability of the witnesses: "These strange appearances, seen at the same time by two different persons in perfect health, could not fail to make a deep impression on their minds" and later he has Stricket "convinced that there could be no deception in the matter". However, he left out the reference to the auctioneer and, importantly Lancaster's question about the St John's Eve bonfire, and, in another detail that added credibility, following Britton and Brayley, he had Mr Lancaster's son "discover the aerial figures" before Stricket could point them out.

Brewster felt that such a potentially interesting phenomenon had not been subject to philosophical speculation: "These extraordinary sights were received not only with distrust but with absolute incredulity. They were not even honoured with a place in the records of natural phenomena, and the philosophers of the day were neither in possession of analogous facts, nor were they acquainted with those principles of atmospherical refraction upon which they depend. The strange phenomena, indeed, of the Fata Morgana, or the Castles of the Fairy Morgana, (the very comparison made by Smith more than eighty years before) had been long before observed, and had been described by Kircher in the seventeenth century, but they presented nothing so mysterious as the aerial troopers of Souterfell; and the general characters of the two phenomena were so unlike, that even a philosopher might have been excused for ascribing them to different causes."

There then follows an account of the Fata Morgana, giving details of atmospheric conditions and optical phenomena far more precisely than he had done in relation to Souther Fell. "This singular exhibition has been frequently seen in the Straits of Messina between Sicily and the coast of Italy, and whenever it takes place, the people, in a state of exultation, as if it were not only a pleasing but a lucky phenomenon, hurry down to the sea, exclaiming Morgana, Morgana. When the rays of the rising sun form an angle of 45° on the sea of Reggio, and when the surface of the water is perfectly unruffled either by the wind or the current, a spectator placed upon an eminence in the city, and having his back to the sun and his face to the sea, observes upon the surface of the water superb palaces with their balconies and windows, lofty towers, herds and flocks grazing in wooded valleys and fertile plains, armies of men on horseback and on foot, with multiplied fragments of buildings, such as columns, pilasters, and arches. These objects pass rapidly in succession along the surface of the sea during the brief period of their appearance. The various objects thus enumerated are pictures of palaces and buildings actually existing on shore, and the living objects are of course only seen when they happen to form a part of the general landscape.

"If at the time that these phenomena are visible the atmosphere is charged with vapour or dense exhalations, the same objects which are depicted upon the sea will be seen also in the air occupying a space which extends from the surface to the height of twenty-five feet. These images, however, are less distinctly delineated than the former.

"If the air is in such a state as to deposit dew, and is capable of forming the rainbow, the objects will be seen only on the surface of the sea, but they all appear fringed with red, yellow, and blue light as if they were seen through a prism."[24]

The account bears close comparison to Wordsworth's description of the faery palaces seen in the mirage of Lyulph's Tower on Ullswater.

Brewster then cited several instances of mirages reported by very reliable witnesses. "On Wednesday, the 26th July, 1798, about five o'clock in the afternoon, Mr. Latham, a Fellow of the Royal Society, then residing at Hastings . . . distinctly saw the cliffs extending for some leagues along the French coast, and they appeared as if they were only a few miles off." Latham and several experienced sailors present then "beheld at once Dungeness, Dover Cliffs, and the French coast all along from Calais, Boulogne, &c, to St. Vallery, and, as some of the fishermen affirmed, as far west as Dieppe . . . These curious phenomena continued "in the highest splendour" till past eight o'clock, although a black cloud had for some time totally obscured the face of the sun." At Ramsgate, on 6th August, 1806, a Dr.Vince of Cambridge saw Dover Castle as though it had been transported to stand before an adjacent hill.

He continued his classification of aerial visions with an inverted image that had been seen off the Cumbrian coast by a Mr. Huddart, a sea captain, and later a distinguished civil engineer, from Allonby. Earlier in the book, Brewster, in looking at the unreliability of the senses, had discussed Huddart's report of the case of a colour blind shoemaker, from Maryport called Harris, who was subject to this defect in a very remarkable degree. He seems to have been insensible to every colour, and to have been capable of recognizing only the two opposite tints of black and white. "His first suspicion of this defect arose when he was about four years old. Having by accident found in the street a child's stocking, he carried it to a neighbouring house to inquire for the owner: He observed the people call it a red stocking, though he did not understand why they gave it that denomination, as he himself thought it completely described by being called a stocking. The circumstance, however, remained in his memory, and, with other subsequent observations, led him to the knowledge of his defect. He observed also that, when young, other children could discern cherries on a tree by some pretended difference of colour, though he could only distinguish them from the leaves by their difference of size and shape. He observed also that, by means of this difference of colour, they could see the cherries at a greater distance than he could, though he could see other objects at as great a distance as they, that is, where the sight was not assisted by the colour."[25] Huddart had described the case to Joseph Priestley in 1777 and it was the subject of the first known account of colour blindness.

The inverted image off the Cumberland coast was seen in 1793. "Mr. Huddart, when residing at Allonby, in Cumberland, perceived the inverted image of a ship beneath the image," but Dr. Vince, who afterwards observed this phenomenon under a greater variety of forms, found that the ship which was here considered the real one, was only an erect image of the real ship, which was at the time beneath the horizon, and wholly invisible."

The most remarkable sightings of mirage ships had been made by Captain Scoresby in the icy seas to the west of Greenland in 1820. On one occasion he observed his father's ship, the Fame, as being close at hand when it was, in fact, seventeen miles over the horizon. The most extraordinary phenomenon of all occurred during a period of rapidly changing temperatures, when Scoresby attempted to sketch "the enchanted coast of Greenland". "The general telescopic appearance of the coast was that of an extensive ancient city abounding with the ruins of castles, obelisks, churches and monuments, with other large and conspicuous buildings. Some of the hills seemed to be surmounted by turrets, battlements, spires, and pinnacles; while others, subjected to one or two reflections, exhibited large masses of rock, apparently suspended in the air, at a considerable elevation above the actual termination of the mountains to which they referred. The whole exhibition was a grand phantasmagoria. Scarcely was any particular portion sketched before it changed its appearance, and assumed the form of an object totally different. It was perhaps alternately a castle, a cathedral, or an obelisk; then expanding horizontally, and coalescing with the adjoining hills, united the intermediate valleys, though some miles in width, by a bridge of a single arch, of the most magnificent appearance and extent. Notwithstanding these repeated changes, the various figures represented in the drawing had all the distinctness of reality; and not only the different strata, but also the veins of the rocks, with the wreaths of snow occupying ravines and fissures, formed sharp and distinct lines, and exhibited every appearance of the most perfect solidity."[26]

The experienced and respected traveller, Baron Humboldt, had reported mirages on several occasions of islands, fishing boats, hills and trees and even cows appearing as though floating or suspended in the air. Dr. A, P. Buchan while walking on the cliff about a mile to the east of Brighton on the morning of the 28th November, 1804 . . . saw . . . our own figures standing on the summit of the apparent opposite cliff, as well as the representation of the windmill near at hand. And the Reverend Mr. Hughes had observed that, "At the extremity of the vast shadow which Etna, projects across the island, appeared a perfect and distinct image of the mountain itself elevated above the horizon, and diminished as if viewed in a concave mirror."[27]

Having demonstrated the range and force of nature's illusions that must have led the credulous to look for supernatural explanations, David Brewster prepared to use science to dispel "the fears which her wonders must necessarily excite even in enlightened minds". "But when, in the midst of solitude, and in situations where the mind is undisturbed by sublunary cares, we see our own image delineated in the air, and mimicking in gigantic perspective the tiny movements of humanity; - when we see troops in military array performing their evolutions on the very face of an almost inaccessible precipice; - when in the eye of day a mountain seems to become transparent, and exhibits on one side of it a castle which we know to exist only on the other; - when distant objects, concealed by the roundness of the earth, and beyond the cognizance of the telescope, are actually transferred over the intervening convexity and presented in distinct and magnified outline to our accurate examination; - when such varied and striking phantasms are seen also by all around us, and therefore appear in the character of real phenomena of nature, our impressions of supernatural agency can only be removed by a distinct and satisfactory knowledge of the causes which gave them birth.

"It is only within the last forty years that science has brought these atmospherical spectres within the circle of her dominion; and not only are all their phenomena susceptible of distinct explanation, but we can even reproduce them on a small scale with the simplest elements of our optical apparatus."

At this point, the man who was too shy to preach a sermon, became very animated. He showed a boyish enthusiasm in constructing an optical apparatus, including a small model of a ship, to demonstrate refraction. "In order to convey a general idea of the causes of these phenomena, let A B C D, Fig. 35, be a glass trough filled with water, and let a small ship be placed at S. An eye situated about E, will see the topmast of the ship S directly through the plate of glass B D. Fix a convex lens a of short focus upon the plate of glass B D, and a little above a straight line S E joining the ship and the eye; and immediately above the convex lens a place a concave one b. The eye will now see through the convex lens an inverted image of the ship at S', and through the concave lens b, an erect image of the ship at S". . . But it will be asked, where are the lenses in nature to produce these effects? This question is easily answered." And David Brewster does provide an answer with a tin tube filled with water, cooled with ice at the sides to act like a concave lens, and heated to behave like a convex lens. "The very same effects are produced in the air, only a greater tract of air is necessary for showing the effect produced, by heating and cooling it unequally."

"Now it is easy to conceive how the changes of density which we can thus produce artificially may be produced in nature. If in serene weather the surface of the sea is much colder than the air of the atmosphere, as it frequently is, and as it was to a very great degree during the phenomena described by Mr. Scoresby, the air next the sea will gradually become colder and colder, by giving out its heat to the water; and the air immediately above will give out its heat to the cooler air immediately below it, so that the air from the surface of the sea, to a considerable height upwards, will gradually diminish in density, and therefore must produce the very phenomena we have described."

"The phenomenon of Dover Castle, seen on the Ramsgate side of the hill, was produced by the air being more dense near the ground, and above the sea, than at greater heights, and hence the rays proceeding from the castle reached the eye in curved lines, and the cause of its occupying its natural position on the hill, and not being seen in the air, was that the top of the hill itself, in consequence of being so near the castle, suffered the same change from the varying density of the air, and therefore the castle and the hill were equally elevated and retained their relative positions. The reason why the image of the castle and the hill appeared erect was that the rays from the top and bottom of the castle had not crossed before they reached Ramsgate; but as they met at Ramsgate, an eye at a greater distance from the castle, and in the path of the rays, would have seen the image inverted."[28]

The enthusiasm and perspicacity with which these explanations and others were offered made them appear totally convincing. However, when he dealt with the Souther Fell army, Sir David Brewster was content to explain the phenomenon as analogous to the other phenomena described. Surprisingly for an experimental scientist, he had no concern for the original quality of his evidence and he did not doubt the plausibility of his historical explanation. "The aerial troopers seen at Souterfell were produced by the very same process as the spectre of Dover Castle, having been brought by unequal refraction from one side of the hill to the other. It is not our business to discover how a troop of soldiers came to be performing their evolutions on the other side of Souterfell; but if there was then no road along which they could be marching, it is highly probable that they were troops exercising among the hills in secret previous to the breaking out of the Rebellion in 1745."[29]

Whereas all the other instances have precisely determined images that are subject to refraction, the supposition that there might be troops exercising among the hills does not bear close examination. Their appearance implies that they were Hanoverian troops and, with the Duke of Cumberland's army involved in war on the continent, there were insufficient troops in Britain a year prior to the Jacobite Rebellion to have refracted such a powerful display across the summit of Souther Fell.

Brewster accepted Clarke's account at its face value, read it with a tendency to underline its credibility, and, not having examined Smith's version, did not need to explain the coincidence of three appearances on midsummer's eve. His explanation is plausible, if the possibilities of refraction allowed people scattered among the various cottages, to view the image with the same conviction and as being in the same location, but, even from the physical point of view, the explanation is not probable. All the other cases of refraction concerned air that was above both land and water and would be subject to the effects of their very different thermal co-efficients.

That image of the third spectre joining the pair on the Brocken received a detailed analysis: "The spectre of the Brocken and other phenomena of the same kind have essentially a different origin from those which arise from unequal refraction. They are merely shadows of the observer projected on dense vapour or thin fleecy clouds, which have the power of reflecting much light. They are seen most frequently at sunrise, because it is at that time that the vapours and clouds necessary for their production are most likely to be generated; and they can be seen only when the sun is throwing his rays horizontally, because the shadow of the observer would otherwise be thrown either up in the air, or down upon the ground. If there are two persons looking at the phenomenon, as when M. Haue and the landlord saw it together, each observer will see his own image most distinctly, and the head will be more distinct than the rest of the figure, because the rays of the sun will be more copiously reflected at a perpendicular incidence; and as from this cause the light reflected from the vapour or cloud becomes fainter farther from the shadow, the appearance of a halo round the head of the observer is frequently visible. M. Haue mentions the extraordinary circumstance of the two spectres of him and the landlord being joined by a third figure, but he unfortunately does not inform us which of the two figures was doubled, for it is impossible that a person could have joined their party unobserved. It is very probable that the new spectre forms a natural addition to the group, as we have represented it in Fig. 30, and if this was the case, it could only have been produced by a duplication of one of the figures produced by unequal refraction."[30]

Sir David Brewster's little book rapidly became the talk of the nation and, if we are to judge by an article in the *Quarterly Review* on a novel translated from the Persian, the participants at Souther Fell had become household names. The anonymous reviewer wrote mischievously, questioning if happiness resulted from an advance in knowledge: "Sir David Brewster has, with 'impious hand,' attempted to destroy all the mysteries of our little planet by showing that magic is, in truth, nothing more than nature unexplained. We have the consolation of believing that the Sicilians, at least, have not yet read his book, and that they may go on for centuries to come in beholding, as supernatural wonders, the palaces, and towers, the green valleys with herds and flocks reposing in the shade, and the hosts of armed men on foot and on horseback, that sometimes suddenly appear to occupy the sea between them and the fair shores of Italy. We doubt if we should exchange for the cold philosophy of the Scotchman the feelings of astonishment and awe that must have excited the simple Cumberlander beyond himself, when he beheld with his corporeal eye the shadowy huntsman and his dog pursuing their wild chace of horses along Souterfell side; and still more when he, and all his neighbours too, saw countless troops of horsemen traversing the same perilous steeps. We venture to say that Daniel Stricket would not have been a whit the happier, if he had been told that these strange spectacles were referrible only to the refractory tricks of the atmosphere."[31]

No-one before David Brewster, the Scotchman of "the cold philosophy", had subjected the story of the spectral army to such a reasoned analysis, limited as it was. The range of phenomenon which Brewster discussed, Scoresby's ships, the fata morgana, the visions of Dover Castle, the spectral army and the Brocken spectre had been the commonplaces of popular discussion for up to thirty years. Commentators had been happy to talk about optical illusions or deceptio visi or refraction or atmospheric conditions, but they had been content to group dissimilar phenomenon together and had not attempted any degree of rigour in their explanation. David Brewster's analysis delighted his readers. He made science accessible and fun. Until he examined these phenomenon, with his Presbyterian zeal to explain away superstition, there was an unquestioning readiness to enjoy the mystery, to take pleasure in these things being inexplicable. Most educated men would not have believed in ghosts, but they would have accepted, like Scott, the existence of an immortal soul, and consequently believed in a spiritual world. There was still, perhaps, an emotional avoidance of denying the possibility of ghosts totally.

Brewster's resort to a physical explanation is interesting. The prime exemplar had been M. Haue's discovery on the Brocken that an image which had inspired fear for centuries, which was the cornerstone of German mythology, was simply his own responding shadow writ large upon the morning mist. John Ferriar had looked to explain ghosts as an image reanimated upon the retina. Otherwise individual reports of ghosts were understood as the result of inebriation or illness. The thinking of the time did not accommodate the ideas of group psychology, of mass deception and hallucination. If a phenomenon had been perceived by two people or more who were clearly of good faith, then it could only be accounted for by physical explanations. If honest people reported seeing the same thing, they must have seen the same thing. The only answer was to explain it as an optical illusion. David Brewster was dissecting Ossian. He was deconstructing the extravagant mythology of his father-in-law for nineteenth century scientific Edinburgh.

When, probably some years earlier, he edited the description of Cumberland in the *Edinburgh Encyclopedia*, David Brewster wrote or accepted the following note about the mountains in the Skiddaw massif: "On the margin of Bassenthwaite lake the roots of Skiddaw lie. This majestic mountain is nearly 3500 feet in perpendicular height above the level of the lake. The prospect from its summit is uncommonly varied and extensive. On one side the Irish Channel, on the other side the German Ocean, may be seen. On a clear day, the shipping in the Solway Frith, though at the distance of upwards of fifty miles, may be distinguished. On Bouscale Fell, to the north-east of Skiddaw, is a spacious lake of water so completely enclosed by a ridge of rocks that, during months in winter, the rays of the sun never reach its surface. On Souter fell, which is nearly 900 yards high, an extraordinary phenomena appeared towards the middle of the last century, which gave rise to much speculation, and "created no small degree of alarm and apprehension". Appearances of armed men, on foot and horseback. were seen. They moved in regular troops along the side of the fell, describing a kind of curvilinear path, their first and last appearance being bounded by the top of the mountain. From the description given of these phenomena, they seem to have been similar to the spectre of the Brocken, an aerial figure that appears among the Hartz mountains in Hanover, and were probably produced by the same cause. Saddleback, on the western side of Souter fell, seems to have been in a volcanic state; and a lake on the upper part of it, from the lava and burnt stones found in its neighbourhood, is conjectured to have been the crater. The views from the summit of Saddleback are very extensive; but it is scarcely possible to look down its sides without experiencing the most awful and shuddering sensations. The height of this mountain is 3324 feet."[32]

The legend of the spectral army of Souther Fell continued to play a disproportionate role in the public perception of Cumberland.

Chapter Nine:

James Hogg

The voluble James Hogg, shepherd and poet, was not quite the opinionated buffoon sensationalised in Christopher North's drunken nights in Ambrose's Tavern. He was a truly remarkable man whose innate intelligence and fierce egotism enabled him to bestride the huge intellectual chasm between the world of the illiterate penniless shepherd in Ettrick Forest and literary celebrity in Edinburgh and London. Born in the same year as Walter Scott, he had been a close friend since he helped in the collecting of Border ballads for *The Minstrelsy of the Scottish Borders* in 1802. His mother, a bearer of the folk tradition, according to her son, accused Scott of destroying the vigorous oral culture of the remote Borders: "They were made for singing an' no for reading; but ye hae broken the charm now, an' they'll never be sung mair. An' the worst thing of a', they're nouther right spell'd nor right setten down."[1]

Hogg was a citizen of enlightened Edinburgh. He'd "heard that failosophers say there is nae satisfactory evidence of the existence of flesh-and-blude men", but he also retained an almost tangible affinity with the supernatural, a peasant sense of another world. When he supposedly said, "O' the existence o' ghosts and fairies I never heard before that the proof was counted defective," he was drawing on the language and beliefs of the peasant and the logic of the enlightenment in a way that constantly challenged both enlightenment and superstition. His work, from his earliest folk ballads and his superb *The Queen's Wake* to the psychological complexity of *The Confessions of a Justified Sinner* subverted the cultured life of Edinburgh with the "uncouth" astuteness of a sophisticated "shepherd".

In 1833, two years before Wordsworth mourned his death, along with the deaths of Scott, Coleridge, Lamb, Crabbe and Mrs Hemans, in an *Extempore Effusion on the Death of James Hogg*, Hogg published *Nature's Magic Lantern* in *Chambers Edinburgh Journal*.[2] It appeared on 28th September in the eighty-eighth issue of the sixteen-page weekly alongside articles on subjects as diverse as the virtues of saving, the travels of Baron Humboldt, the ingenuity of bees and the sagacity of dogs and the life of Edward Gunn. Gunn was a bibulous, bearded transvestite who, for thirty years, ran Edinburgh's most successful painting academy for genteel young ladies. The miscellany, selling at three halfpence, was a popular success with a circulation of over eighty thousand copies.

James Hogg had dug up – he claimed he'd copied it in his note-book – Scott's earlier article from the *Edinburgh Annual Register* in 1812 where he had reprinted the article from the *Leeds Mercury* in which one farmer, thinking he had seen beasts in Havarah Park, was contradicted by his companion: "'Beasts!' cried Anthony, 'Lord bless us! they are not beasts, they are men!' - By this time the body was in motion, and the spectators discovered that it was an army of soldiers, dressed in a white military uniform, and that in the centre stood a personage of commanding aspect, clothed in scarlet." Scott had added, for the elucidation and amusement of his readers, Britton and Brayley's shortened version of James Clark's account of Souther Fell along with M. Haue's account of the Brocken spectre.

Walter Scott's reticence had allowed the narratives to speak for themselves, and left the mists of superstition to be dissipated by enlightened explanation. James Hogg, aged 63 with a young family and bankrupt yet again as a result of his usual careless ambition, was probably looking for cheap copy. Nonetheless, he made the story his own. The very title, *Nature's Magic Lantern*, borrowed a phrase from Scott and challenged Sir David Brewster. (He received his knighthood in 1832) He had not only explained away superstition through natural magic but had also demonstrated the (often duplicitous) working of the magic lantern. It also opposed the natural against the technological with the equivocal term "magic", standing both for the supernatural and the explicable, as the link. Hogg always had his feet in both camps.

The article begins by drawing us into a Border landscape where, above the dense fog, the hill tops are transformed into "golden islands in a sea of silver". It is an experience that has something of the magical about it, even though, initially, Hogg presented it as an objective experience, happening to the impersonal "one" of the Edinburgh drawing rooms and described with careful precision and with some sense of an optical explanation.

"It is well known, that, in warm summer mornings, the valleys among our mountains are generally filled with a dense white fog, so that, when the sun rises, the upper parts of the hills are all bathed in yellow sheen, looking like golden islands in a sea of silver. After one ascends through the mist to within a certain distance of the sunshine, a halo of glory is thrown round his head, something like a rainbow, but brighter and paler. It is upright or slanting, as the sun is lower or higher; but it uniformly attends one for a considerable space before he reaches the sunshine."

The tone switches, and we are with the barely literate Ettrick shepherd, who, at the age of seventeen or nineteen, had only just taught himself to read by fingering the Psalms. The year may have been either 1789, the year of Wordsworth's *An Evening Walk,* or 1791. The self-mythologizing Hogg proudly believed for many years that he had been born on the 25th January, 1772, the anniversary of the birth of Robert Burns. He was, parish records insist, baptised in Ettrick on 9th December, 1770. We are on the hill-side in the shepherd's world, signalled by the dialect words, and sharing the shepherd's superstition in the country that James Hogg had known intimately since his earliest childhood.

"One morning, at the time when I was about nineteen years of age, I was ascending a hillside towards the ewe-buchts, deeply absorbed in admiration of the halo around me, when suddenly my eyes fell upon a huge dark semblance of the human figure, which stood at a very small distance from me, and at first appeared to my affrighted imagination as the enemy of mankind. Without taking a moment to consider, I rushed from the spot, and never drew breath till I had got safe amongst the ewe-milkers. All that day, I felt very ill at ease; but next morning, being obliged to go past the same spot at the same hour, I resolved to exert, if possible, a little more courage, and put the phenomenon fairly to the proof. The fog was more dense than on the preceding morning, and when the sun arose, his brilliancy and fervour were more bright above. The lovely halo was thrown around me, and at length I reached the haunted spot without diverging a step from my usual little footpath; and at the very place there arose the same terrible apparition which had frightened me so much the morning before. It was a giant blackamoor, at least thirty feet high, and equally proportioned, and very near me. I was actually struck powerless with astonishment and terror. My first resolution was, if I could keep the power of my limbs, to run home and hide myself below the blankets, with the Bible beneath my head. But then again, I thought it was hard to let my master's 700 ewes go eild for fear of the de'il. In this perplexity (and I rather think I was crying) I took off my bonnet, and scratched my head bitterly with both hands; when, to my astonishment and delight, the de'il also took off his bonnet, and scratched his head with both hands - but in such a style: Oh, there's no man can describe it! His arms and his fingers were like trees and branches without the leaves. I laughed at him till I actually fell down upon the sward; the de'il also fell down and laughed at me. I then noted for the first time that he had two collie dogs at his foot, bigger than buffaloes. I arose, and made him a most graceful bow, which he returned at the same moment - but such a bow for awkwardness I never saw! It was as if the Tron Kirk steeple had bowed to me. I turned my cheek to the sun as well as I could, that I might see the de'il's profile properly defined in the cloud. It was capital! His nose was about half a yard long, and his face at least three yards; and then he was gaping and laughing so, that one would have thought he might have swallowed the biggest man in the country.

"It was quite a scene of enchantment. I could not leave it. On going five or six steps onward, it vanished; but, on returning to the same spot, there he stood, and I could cause him to make a fool of himself as much as I liked; but always as the sun rose higher, he grew shorter, so that, I think, could I have staid, he might have come into a respectable size of a de'il at the last."

No explanation is offered but the astonishing and terrifying apparition at the haunted spot shrinks "into a respectable size of a de'il". It is an occasion of enchantment, a time to revel in, not explain, the revelation, to be intoxicated by the response of that bowing, head-scratching monstrous figure "as if the Tron Kirk steeple had bowed to me". Hogg, in passing, has shaped an image in which literary Edinburgh is acknowledging his transformation of peasant superstition. He cannot recover the apparition in its full glory, nor will he ever, one suspects, "define it with a mathematical suirvey".

"I have seen this gigantic apparition several times since, but never half so well defined as that morning. It requires a certain kind of background which really I cannot describe; for, though I visited the place by day a hundred times, there was so little difference between the formation of that spot and the rest of the hill, that it is impossible to define it without taking a mathematical survey. The halo accompanies one always, but the gigantic apparition very seldom. I have seen it six or seven times in my life, always in a fog, and at sun-rising; but, saving these two times, never well defined, part being always light, and part dark.

"One-and-twenty years subsequent to this, I was delighted to read the following note, translated, I think, from a German paper, concerning the Bogle of the Broken, an aerial figure of the very same description with mine, which is occasionally seen on one particular spot among the Hartz Mountains, in Hanover. It was taken from the diary of a Mr. Hawe, and I kept a copy of it for the remembrance of auld lang syne. I shall transcribe a sentence or two from it here; and really it is so like mine, that one would almost be tempted to think the one was copied from the other."

Those one and twenty years would make James Hogg forty years old and see him, a failed farmer, seeking to make a literary reputation publishing his collection of ballads, *The Forest Minstrel*, and writing and publishing his own, controversial, periodical, *The Spy*. It wasn't until 1813, and the publication of *The Queen's Wake* that Hogg found fame and temporary fortune. It was at this time that Scott reprinted M. Haue's paper tgether with the accounts of the spectral armies at Havarah and Souther fell.

Who is copying whom? Is the precisely observant M.Hawe presenting the same vision as the emotional, imaginative shepherd? The spectre has become the alliterative Bogle of the Broken and is identical to Hogg's own aerial figure. James Hogg may never have seen his bogle in the Borders, but he is staking a prior claim to the apparition. He reprinted Haue's article (He spelled the name Hawe) and concluded with a comment on Haue's report of how, after he had been joined by the landlord of the Broken Inn, three and not just two spectres were to be seen: "I can easily account for the latter part of the phenomenon; for it could only be when the clouds of haze, or, as he calls them, 'thin transparent vapours,' were passing, that the shadows in the cloud could possibly be seen. But how there should have been three of them, and not either four, or only two, surpasses my comprehension altogether. It is quite out of nature; and I am obliged to doubt either Mr. Hawe's word or the accuracy of his optics. The matter did not pass David Brewster's comprehension for he had a ready explanation for the third figure, along with a diagram: 'It is very probable that the new spectre forms a natural addition to the group, as we have represented it in Fig. 30, and if this was the case, it could only have been produced by a duplication of one of the figures produced by unequal refraction'."

Hogg was not to be outdone. He recalled an incident when he was fifteen and as an old man he had constantly revisited the scene in order to find a physical explanation for the apparition of his two shadows, shadows that seem like a foreboding of two aspects of his own self, one the spruce master and the other "tall, dim and leaning backward", perhaps signifying that long peasant tradition that underpinned his character and his work. "Among the other strange sights which I have seen among the hills, I reckon one of the most curious to have been a double shadow of myself, at a moment when only the real sun was above the horizon. One morning, in April 1785, was walking on the Moor Brae of Berry Knowe, gathering the ewes, when, to my utter astonishment, I perceived that I had two shadows. I immediately looked to the east, where the sun had just risen above the horizon, expecting to see two suns. But no there was but one. There was not even one of those mock suns called by us weather-gaws. Yet there was I going to a certainty with two shadows - the one upright, and well defined, and the other tall, dim, and leaning backward, something like a very tall awkward servant waiting upon and walking behind a little spruce master. The tall one soon vanished, as I turned the hill into a glen called Carsen's Cleuch; but I never forgot the circumstance; and after I became an old man, I visited the very spot, as nearly as I could remember, again and again, thinking that the reflection of the sun from some pool or lake which I had not perceived, might have caused it; but there was no such thing.

"I never mentioned the circumstance to any living being before, save to Sir D. Brewster, who, of all men I ever met with, is the fondest of investigating every thing relating to natural phenomena: he pretended to account for it by some law of dioptrical refraction, which I did not understand."

The scientist can only pretend to account for the doubled shadow with an incomprehensible explanation. If this vision of the two figures should never have been mentioned to another person, Hogg's next account of an incredible apparition requires an insistent attestation on his part. That claim to be "on the word of an honest man" is offered with a novelist's complex irony.

"But what I am now going to relate will scarcely procure credit, though, on the word of an honest man, it is literally true. I once saw about two hundred natural apparitions at one time, and altogether. One fine summer morning, as I was coming along the Hawkshaw rigg of Black house, I perceived on the other side of Douglas Burn, in a little rich glen called Brakehope, a whole drove of Highland cattle, which I thought could not be fewer than ten scores. I saw them distinctly - I never saw any beasts more distinctly in my life. I saw the black ones, and the red ones, some with white faces, and four or five spotted ones. I saw three men driving them, and turning them quietly in at corners. They were on each side of the burn of Brakehope, and quite from the drove road. I was once thinking of going to them myself, but I wanted my breakfast, was very hungry, and had no charge of that part of the farm: so I hastened home, and sent off the shepherd who had charge of it, to drive the drove of cattle from his best land. His name was Robert Borthwick. He seized a staff in high chagrin at the drivers, and ran off; and Messrs. William and George Laidlaw both accompanied him, with good cudgels in their hands. They were both alive and well to testify the truth of my report: at least, when they went to Brakehope there were no cattle there, nor man, nor dogs, nor even sheep! There was not a living creature in the bottom of the glen where I had seen the drove, nor among the other strange sights which I have seen, the mark of a cow's hoof. I was of course laughed at as a dreamer and seer of visions; for, in fact, after inquiring at our neighbours, we found that there was not a drove of Highland cattle at that time in the district. I was neither a dreamer nor a seer of visions. I was in the highest health and spirits. It was between eight and nine o'clock on a fine summer morning of mingled clouds and sunshine. I was chanting a song to myself, or perhaps making one, when I first came in view of the drove. I was rather more than half a mile from it, but not three quarters of a mile; and as there never was a man had clearer sight than I had, I could not be mistaken in the appearance. In justification of myself, I must here copy two or three sentences from my note-book; but from whence taken, I do not know."

The story becomes an apologia for his visionary self. Every detail of Hogg's account is vivid and clear, "the black ones, and the red ones, some with white faces, and four or five spotted ones". Yet he had to accept the evidence of the facts and of the named shepherd, Robert Borthwick, and of his two maternal uncles, William and George Laidlaw, themselves the inheritors of the tradition. He accounts for the conventional explanations, he was dreaming, he was "in highest health and spirits", visibility was good, the cattle were just over half a mile away (though this appears a fair distance from which to see such detail). As he says, "There never was a man had clearer sight than I had, I could not be mistaken in the appearance."

The paragraphs that follow contain a verbatim account of the spectral army seen by the Turners, father and son in Havarah Park, and the account of the spectral army on Souther fell both in the versions transcribed by Walter Scott from the *Leeds Mercury* and Britton and Brayley's redaction of Clark's original account. The two accounts are separated by a short paragraph about a spectral fleet: "In addition to this, I may mention, that, during the last continental war, all the military and volunteers in Ireland were hurried to the north to defend the country against a spectre fleet, which had no existence in those seas." I have not been able to trace any other reference to this fleet and it may well be Hogg's invention.

He reproduced Clark's account with an insistence that he would not deviate from the original: "And I find likewise, in my note-book, the following extraordinary account, which I think was copied long ago from a book called A Guide to the Lakes of Cumberland. I was always so fond of those romantic and visionary subjects, that I have added thousands of lees to them, but in this I shall not deviate one word from the original writer's narrative." And he does not deviate except for a few slips of the pen, including calling Daniel Stricket, David. However, he does omit the sentence about the witnesses providing a signed attestation, ("The attestation is signed by Lancaster and Stricket, and dated the 21st of July, 1785.") which was the most significant sentence of all in ensuring the continuing interest in the spectral army. That sentence bridged the two worlds of the tale's imaginative presence and its credibility in the contemporary world. James Hogg looked for no such proof of the supernatural.

His own account of the highland cattle paralleled two aspects of Souther Fell. Like Wren and Stricket, he felt he would not be believed and, having seen the apparition, the witnesses went to the site to search for physical evidence and found nothing there.

He concluded: "It would therefore appear that my vision of a drove of Highland cattle, with their drivers, was not altogether an isolated instance of the same phenomena. It is quite evident that we must attribute these appearances to particular states of the atmosphere, and suppose them to be shadows of realities; the airy resemblance of scenes passing in distant parts of the country, and by some singular operation of natural causes thus expressively imaged on the acclivities of the mountains." This final acceptance of the scientific explanations provided by Sir David Brewster seems reluctant, if not dismissive.

James Hogg may have invented his apparitions, but they are presented with more convincing intensity than the demystifying explanation. Walter Scott quoted the story of the spectral army of Souther Fell almost as an antiquarian interested in justifying his poetic invention. David Brewster saw it as yet another case of superstition to be explained away by scientific knowledge. For James Hogg the bogle of the Broken and the spectral armies of Havarah and Souther Fell reinforced his own visionary heritage. He himself projected the two shadows, the defined spruce master and the faint long shadowy servant.

That dual personality, or persona, of the Ettrick Shepherd and the man of letters was both the product of his past and his own intentional adoption. It became a fixed public perception. When, aged forty, a failed farmer, he came to Edinburgh in 1810 to make some sort of niggardly living as a writer, he already had a minor reputation as a poet after the publication of *The Mountain Bard*. With characteristic self-believe, he wrote and published his own eight-page weekly. Hogg had the presumption to call this four-penny magazine *The Spy*, thereby comparing himself with the doyen of all magazines, *The Spectator*. Early issues and subscriptions promised well. Fine society may have found him lacking in taste and polish, but one patron, Robert Sym maintained that he was "a blockhead . . . (but) there is some 'smeddum' in him".[3] The indelicacy and vulgarity, however, was part cause of the magazine's failure. One early story, in particular, gave offence because of its country ways, the feckless shepherd hero daily "kissing Jessey below the plaid".[4] It purported to be a letter from the son of a Berwickshire farmer telling of his "instability of calling", of his failure, having been joiner, ploughman, fiddler, shepherd, grocer, farmer and soldier, to stick with any career. This picaresque tale was brought to a premature conclusion when the anonymous hero was "wind bound for three weeks" on the impoverished and backward district of Uig on the Hebridean island of Lewis, where he "could not have believed that such customs yet lingered on the shores of Britain".

Ten years later Oliver and Boyd published *Winter Evening Tales*. A much expanded version of this 'immoral' moralising analogue of Hogg's own life had become *The Renowned Adventures of Basil Lee*.[5] The military escapades in America now included a liaison with a good-hearted whore and the sojourn in the Hebrides had been extended to include supernatural material. The adventures concluded in benign penury in Edinburgh. The *Winter Evening Tales* were said to have been "collected among the cottagers of the South of Scotland" and their apparent artlessness hid a sophisticated subversion of conventional genres.

The wayward Basil Lee is fleeing from a newly independent America when his ship takes refuge in Loch Rog (Loch Roag) on the west coast of Lewis:

" I staid and sauntered about that island a month, and never in my life was in such a curious country, nor among so curious a people. They know all that is to happen by reason of a singular kind of divination called the second sight. They have power over the elements, and can stop the natural progress of them all save the tides. They are a people by themselves, neither Highlanders nor Lowlanders, at least those of Uig are, and have no communication with the rest of the world; but with the beings of another state of existence they have frequent intercourse. I at first laughed at their stories of hobgoblins, and water spirits, but after witnessing a scene that I am going to describe, I never disbelieved an item of any thing I heard afterwards, however far out of the course of nature it might be. I am now about to relate a story which will not be believed. I cannot help it. If it was any optical illusion, let those account for it who can. I shall relate what I saw as nearly as I can recollect, and it was not a scene to be easily forgotten."

As so often, James Hogg is equivocating. Earlier in the novella he had presented a scene in which a drunken rapscallion of an Irish soldier had doffed his breeches to wade what he thought was a broad river. His senses failed to tell him that it was only the moonlight casting a shadow across the road and that the sound of the rushing waters was merely the soughing of the wind in the trees. Later, Basil Lee had fallen passionately in love with an apparently unknown woman whom he failed to recognise as his lover of several years. Now he is asking us to accept the supernatural and fantastic and challenging those who would explain it away as an optical illusion.

"On the banks of this Loch Rog there stands a considerably large village, and above that the gentleman's house, who rents all the country around from Lord Seaforth, and lets it off again to numberless small tenants. Between his house and the village there lies a straight green lane, and above the house, on a rising ground, stand a great number of tall stones that have been raised in some early age, and appear at a distance like an army of tremendous giants. One day a party of seven from on board the Swallow was invited to dine with this gentleman. We went out a-shooting all the forenoon, and towards evening, on our return, we found all the family in the most dreadful alarm, on account of something that an old maiden lady had seen which they called Faileas More, (the Great Shadow), and which they alleged was the herald of terrible things, and the most dismal calamities. The villagers were likewise made acquainted with it, and they were running howling about in consternation."

The tall stones, now even taller since the embedding peat was removed in the nineteenth century, are the Calanish Stones. They are three to four thousand years old and are where Hogg placed them, in this remote Gaelic area rich in folklore. One legend has the stones erected by black giants; another suggests that "the shining one" walked along the avenue of stones at sunrise on a midsummer's day after the call of the cuckoo had been heard. "The Great Shadow" corresponds to "the second sight" among the islanders. This ability to see into the future had long been a topic of remark since Martin Martin's argument for it in *A Description of the Western Isles of Scotland* in 1703. However, there seems to be no direct written precedent for James Hogg's Faileas More or Great Shadow.

John Ferriar, in a paper *On Popular Illusions* read to Manchester Philosophical Society in 1790, which was discussed by both Scott and Brewster forty years later, offered a scientific perspective on Martin's report: "The visions are frightful, and uneasy to the Seer, who thinks himself unfortunate in possessing this faculty. His appearance to the spectators, during a vision, (for he alone perceives it) is, as described, something like that of a patient in catalepsy; he becomes immoveable, his eyes are fixed, and the eye-lids sometimes reverted . . . They do not always understand the meaning of what they see, and even when they form an absolute prediction, in consequence of former experience, they are treated with derision . . . it appears highly probable that the Seers are hypochondriacal persons. Their insular situation, their solitary employments, their oppressive poverty, added perhaps to the wild, uncultivated scenes of their country, are sufficient to produce a depraved state of body, and consequently of imagination, in those who are at all pre-disposed."[6]

Ferriar rationalised the idea of second sight that was found in the most remote corner of the kingdom, but it had been a force with some poetic potency throughout the eighteenth century, none more so than in that stanza from *The Castle Of Indolence* by James Thomson, which described a spectral army.

> As when a Shepherd of the Hebrid-Isles,
> Plac'd far amid the melancholy Main,
> (Whether it be lone Fancy him beguiles;
> Or that aerial Beings sometimes deign
> To stand, embodied, to our Senses plain)

Sees on the naked Hill, or Valley low,
The whilst in Ocean Phœbus dips his Wain,
A vast Assembly moving to and fro:
Then all at once in Air dissolves the wondrous Show.

Ferriar quoted the lines as the best description he knew of second sight.

In Hogg's tale, *Basil Lee*, the ne'er-do-well, travelled man of the world, listened intently to the story told by these isolated people: "The family consisted of an old man and his sister; a young man and his wife, and two children: the old man and the two ladies believed the matter throughout, but the young man pretended with us to laugh at it, though I could see he was deeply concerned at what he had heard. The vision was described to us in the following extraordinary manner.

"The Great Shadow never comes alone. The next morning after is M'Torquille Dhu's Visit. The loss of all the crops, and a grievous dearth in the island, invariably succeed to these. The apparitions rise sometimes in twelve, sometimes in three years, but always on the appearance of An Faileas More, Todhail Mac Torcill takes place next morning between day-break and the rising of the sun. A dark gigantic shade is seen stalking across the loch in the evening, which vanishes at a certain headland; and from that same place the next morning, at the same degree of lightness, a whole troop of ghosts arise, and with Mac Torcill Dhu (Black M'Torquille) at their head, walk in procession to the standing stones, and there hide themselves again in their ancient graves.

"As the one part of this story remained still to be proved, every one of us determined to watch, and see if there was any resemblance of such a thing. But the most extraordinary circumstance attending it was, that it could only be seen from the upper windows of that house, or from the same height in the air, a small space to the eastward of that; and that from no other point on the whole island had it ever been discovered that either of these visions had been seen.

"We testified some doubts that the morning might not prove clear, but the old man, and the old maiden lady, both assured us that it would be clear, as the morning of M'Torquille's Visit never was known to be otherwise. Some of us went to bed with our clothes on, but others sat up all night, and at an early hour we were all sitting at the windows, wearying for the break of day. The morning at length broke, and was perfectly clear and serene, as had been predicted. Every eye was strained toward the spot where the Great Shade had vanished, and at length the young gentleman of the house said, in a tone expressing great awe, 'Yonder they are now.' I could not discern any thing for the space of a few seconds, but at length, on looking very narrowly toward the spot, I thought I perceived something like a broad shadow on the shore; and on straining my sight a little more, it really did appear as if divided into small columns like the forms of men; It did not appear like a cloud, but rather like the shadow of a cloud; yet there was not the slightest cloud or vapour to be seen floating in the firmament. We lost sight of it for a very short space, and then beheld it again coming over the heath, above the rocks that overhung the shore. The vision was still very indistinct, but yet it had the appearance of a troop of warriors dressed in greenish tartans with a tinge of red. The headland where the apparition first arose, was distant from us about half a mile, - they appeared to be moving remarkably slow, yet notwithstanding of that, they were close upon us almost instantly. We were told that they would pass in array immediately before the windows, along the green lane between us and the back of the village; and seeing that they actually approached in that direction, Dr Scott, a rough, rash, intrepid fellow, proposed that we should fire at them. I objected to it, deeming that it was a trick, and that they were all fellow creatures; for we now saw them as distinctly as we could see any body of men in the gray of the morning. The young man however assuring us that it was nothing human that we saw, I agreed to the proposal; and as they passed in array immediately before the windows, we pointed all the eight loaded muskets directly at them, and fired on this mysterious troop all at once: but not one of them paused, or turned round his head. They all of them held on with the same solemn and ghostlike movement, still continuing in appearance to be walking very slow, yet some way they went over the ground with unaccountable celerity; and when they approached near to the group of tall obelisks, they rushed in amongst them, and we saw no more, save a reeling flicker of light that seemed to tremble through the stones for a moment.

"They appeared to be a troop of warriors, with plaids and helmets, each having a broad targe on his arm, and a long black lance in the other hand; and they were led on by a tall figure in black armour, that walked considerably a-head of the rest. Some of our people protested that they saw the bare skulls below the helmets, with empty eye sockets, and the nose and lips wanting; but I saw nothing like this. They appeared to me exactly like other men; but the truth is, that I never saw them very distinctly, for they were but a short time near us, and during that time, the smoke issuing from the muskets intervened, and, owing to the dead calm of the morning, made us see them much worse. All the people of the village were hid in groups within doors, and engaged in some rite which I did not witness, and cannot describe; but they took great umbrage at our audacity in firing at their unearthly visitors, and I believe there was not one among us, not even the regardless Dr Scott, who was not shocked at what had been done.

"I make no pretensions to account for this extraordinary phenomenon, but the singular circumstance of its being visible only from one point, and no other, makes it look like something that might be accounted for. I can well excuse any who do not believe it, for if I had not seen it with my own eyes, I never would have believed it. But of all things I ever beheld for wild sublimity, the march of that troop of apparitions excelled—not a day or a night hath yet passed over my head, on which I have not thought with wonder and awe on the Visit of M'Torquille."

There were numerous sources for that ghostly army. Hogg would have been aware of some of the Hebridean folklore after his visit to the Lewis in 1803, even though he met few people who could communicate adequately in English. Thomson perhaps provided the image, Ossian much of the atmosphere, but the marching in ranks and the distinct appearance may owe something to Clark's account of the spectral army, which we know that James Hogg had read and copied in the years between writing his tale of an inconstant Berwickshire farmer for *The Spy* and expanding it into *The Renowned Adventures of Basil Lee*. Hogg's vivid account, tempered by his suggestion that "its being visible only from one point, and no other, makes it look like something that might be accounted for", is illustrative of the divisions within his own personality and within the Romantic sensibility. It is the same duality that gave the story of the spectral army its staying power.

Basil Lee, who was a construct of Hogg, is now "in the country of the genii". "I grew like one half-crazed about spirits, and could think or speak about nothing else." That tension between the sublimity of enchantment and the banality of reason is articulated in Basil Lee's love for the mermaids. "Often when I saw the seals flouncing on the rocks at a distance, I painted them to myself as the most delicate and beautiful mermaids, but on coming near them, was always disappointed, and shocked at the ugly dog's heads that they set up to me; so that after all, I was obliged to give up my search after mermaids."

Basil Lee investigates the tale of Alexander M'Leod, who "had amorous dalliance with (a mermaid); but he soon fell sick and died, and when she came to the shore, and could no more find him, she cried one while, and sung another, in the most plaintive strains that ever were heard" and the story of "a water horse, a monster that inhabited an inland lake, of whom many frightful stories were told to me; but in my next attempt at an intercourse with the spirits that inhabit that dreary country, I had all the success that I could desire".

This "next attempt at an intercourse with the spirits" introduces one of the most deeply felt ghost stories of the nineteenth century and one that deserves to be better known. Lee visits "an old woman who lived in a lone sheiling, at the head of an arm of the sea, called Loch Kios, to whom a ghost paid a visit every night. I determined to see the place, and to tarry a night with the old woman, if possible. Accordingly, I travelled across the country by a wild and pathless rout, and came to her bothy at the fall of night, and going in, I sat down feigning to be very weary, and unable to move farther. We did not understand a word of each other's language, and consequently no conversation, save by signs, could pass between us. I found a miserable old shrivelled creature, rather neatly dressed for that country, but manifestly deranged somewhat in her intellects.

"Before I entered, I heard her singing some coronach or dirge, and when I went in, I found her endeavouring to mend an old mantle, and singing away in a wild unearthly croon; so intent was she on both, that she scarcely lifted her eyes from her work when I went toward her, and when she did, it was not to me that she looked, but to the hole in the roof, or to the door by which I entered. The sight affected me very much, and in all things that affect me I become deeply interested. I heard that she was speaking to herself of me; for I knew the sound of the word that meant Englishman, but it was not with any symptoms of fear or displeasure that she seemed to talk of me, but merely as a thing that, being before her eyes, her tongue mentioned as by rote.

"The story that prevailed of her was, that being left a widow with an only son, then a child at the breast, she nourished him; he became a man; and the love and affection that subsisted between them was of no ordinary nature, as might naturally be supposed. He was an amiable and enterprising young man; but going out to the fishing once with some associates to the Saint's Islands, he never returned, and there were suspicions that he had been foully murdered by his companions, the weather having been so mild that no accident could have been supposed to have happened at sea. There were besides many suspicious circumstances attending it, but no proof could be led. However, the woman hearing that she had lost her darling son, and only stay on earth, set no bounds to her grief, but raved and prayed, and called upon his name; conjuring him by every thing sacred to appear to her, and tell her if he was happy, and all that had befallen to him. These continued conjurations at length moved the dead to return. The spirit of her son appeared to her every night at midnight, and conversed with her about the most mysterious things - about things of life and death - the fates of kingdoms and of men; and of the world that is beyond the grave - she was happy in the communion, and abstracted from all things in this world beside.

"Such was the unearthly tale that was told in the country of this rueful old creature, and made me resolve to visit her before I left the island; but I could not procure a man in all the district of Uig to accompany me that could speak both languages; for except the minister and his wife, and one taxman and his family, there was not one in the district, which contained 3000 inhabitants, that could speak the English language, or were book learned. I procured a young lad to be my guide, named Malcolm Morison, but he having gathered something of my intentions before we left the banks of Loch Rog, would on no consideration accompany me into the cot, but left me as soon as we came in sight of it. I no sooner beheld the object of my curiosity, than I thought her crazy, and that the story might have arisen from her ravings. Still she was an interesting object to contemplate; and, resolving to do so for the night, I tried by signs to make her understand that I was a traveller fatigued with walking, and wished to repose myself in her cottage until next morning; but she regarded me no more than she would have done a strayed cat or dog that had come in to take shelter with her. There was one sentence which she often repeated, which I afterward understood to be of the following import, 'God shield the poor weary Saxon;' but I do not know how to spell it in Earse. I could likewise perceive, that for all the intentness with which she was mending the mantle, she was coming no speed, but was wasting cloth endeavouring to shape a piece suiting to the rent, which she was still making rather worse than better. It was quite visible that either she had no mind, or that it was engaged in something widely different from that at which her hands were employed.

"She did not offer me any victuals, nor did she take any herself, but sat shaping and sewing, and always between hands singing slow melancholy airs, having all the wildness of the native airs of that wild and primitive people. Those that she crooned were of a solemn and mournful cast, and seemed to affect her at times very deeply.

"Night came on, and still she gave herself no concern at all about me. She made no signs to me either to lie down and rest in the only couch the hovel contained, or to remain, or to go away. The fire sent forth a good deal of smoke, but neither light nor heat; at length, with much delay and fumbling, she put some white shreds of moss into a cruise of oil, and kindled it. This threw a feeble ray of light through the smoke, not much stronger than the light of a glow-worm, making darkness scarcely visible, if I may use the expression.

"The woman, who was seated on a dry sod at the side of the fire, not more than a foot from the ground, crossed her arms upon her knees, and, laying her head on them, fell fast asleep. I wrapt myself in my officer's cloak, and threw myself down on the moss couch, laying myself in such a position that I could watch all her motions as well as looks. About eleven o'clock she awoke, and sat for some time moaning like one about to expire; she then kneeled on the sod seat, and muttered some words, waving her withered arms, and stretching them upward, apparently performing some rite either of necromancy or devotion, which she concluded by uttering three or four feeble howls.

"When she was again seated, I watched her features and looks, and certainly never before saw any thing more unearthly. The haggard wildness of the features; the anxious and fearful way in which she looked about and about, as if looking for one that she missed away, made such an impression, on me, that my hairs stood all on end, a feeling that I never experienced before, for I had always been proof against superstitious terrors. But here I could not get the better of them, and wished myself any where else. The dim lamp, shining amidst smoke and darkness, made her features appear as if they had been a dull yellow, and she was altogether rather like a ghastly shade of something that had once been mortal than any thing connected with humanity.

"It was apparent from her looks that she expected some one to visit her, and I became firmly persuaded that I should see a ghost, and hear one speak. I was not afraid of any individual of my own species; for, though I had taken good care to conceal them from her, for fear of creating alarm, I had two loaded pistols and a short sword under my cloak; and as no one could enter without passing my couch, by a very narrow entrance, I was sure to distinguish who or what it was.

"I had quitted keeping my eyes upon the woman, and was watching the door, from which I thought I could distinguish voices. I watched still more intensely; but hearing that the sounds came from the other side, I moved my head slowly round, and saw, apparently, the corpse of her son sitting directly opposite to her. The figure was dressed in dead-clothes; that is, it was wrapt in a coarse white sheet, and had a napkin of the same colour round its head. This was raised up on the brow, as if thrust up recently with the hand, discovering the pale steadfast features, that neither moved eye-lid nor lip, though it spoke in an audible voice again and again. The face was not only pale, but there was a clear glazed whiteness upon it, on which the rays of the lamp falling, shewed a sight that could not be looked on without horror. The winding-sheet fell likewise aside at the knee, and I saw the bare feet and legs of the same bleached hue. The old woman's arms was stretched out towards the figure, and her face thrown upwards, the features meanwhile distorted as with ecstatic agony. My senses now became so bewildered, that I fell into a stupor, like a trance, without being able to move either hand or foot. I know not how long the apparition staid; for the next thing that I remember was being reluctantly wakened from my trance by a feeble cry, which I heard through my slumber repeated several times. I looked, and saw that the old miserable creature had fallen on her face, and was grasping, in feeble convulsions, the seat where the figure of her dead son had so lately reclined. My compassion overcame my terror; for she seemed on the last verge of life, or rather sliding helplessly from time's slippery precipice, after the thread of existence by which she hung had given way. I lifted her up, and found that all her sufferings were over - the joints were grown supple, and the cold damps of death had settled on her hands and brow. I carried her to the bed from which I had risen, and could scarcely believe that I carried a human body - it being not much heavier than a suit of clothes. After I had laid her down, I brought the lamp near, to see if there was any hope of renovation - she was living, but that was all, and with a resigned though ghastly smile, and a shaking of the head, she expired.

"I did not know what to do; for the night was dark as pitch; and I wist not where to fly, knowing the cot to be surrounded by precipitous shores, torrents, and winding bays of the sea; therefore all chance of escape, until day-light, was utterly impossible; so I resolved to trim the lamp, and keep my place, hoping it would not be long till day.

"I suppose that I sat about an hour in this dismal place, without moving or changing my attitude, with my brow leaning upon both my hands, and my eyes shut; when I was aroused by hearing a rustling in the bed where the body lay. On looking round, I perceived with horror that the corpse was sitting upright in the bed, shaking its head as it did in the agonies of death, and stretching out its hands towards the hearth. I thought the woman had been vivified, and looked steadily at the face; but I saw that it was the face of a corpse still; for the eye was white, being turned upward and fixed in the socket, the mouth was open, and all the other features immoveably fixed for ever. Seeing that it continued the same motion, I lifted the lamp, and looked fearfully round, and there beheld the figure I had so recently seen, sitting on the same seat, in the same attitude, only having its face turned toward the bed.

"I could stand this no longer, but fled stumbling out at the door, and ran straight forward. I soon found myself in the sea, and it being ebb tide, I fled along the shore like a deer pursued by the hounds. It was not long till the beach terminated, and I came to an abrupt precipice, washed by the sea. I climbed over a ridge on my hands and knees, and found that I was on a rocky point between two narrow friths, and farther progress impracticable.

"I had now no choice left me; so, wrapping myself in my cloak, I threw me down in a bush of heath, below an overhanging cliff, and gave up my whole mind to amazement at what I had witnessed. Astonished as I was, nature yielded to fatigue, and I fell into a sound sleep, from which I did not awake till about the rising of the sun. The scene all around me was frightfully wild and rugged, and I scarce could persuade myself that I was awake, thinking that I was still struggling with a dreadful dream. One would think this was a matter easily settled, but I remember well, it was not so with me that morning. I pulled heath, cut some parts of it off, and chewed them in my mouth; - rose, - walked about, and threw stones in the sea, and still had strong suspicions that I was in a dream. The adventures of the preceding night dawned on my recollection one by one, but these I regarded all as a dream for certain; and it may well be deemed not a little extraordinary, that to this day, if my oath were taken, I declare I could not tell whether I saw these things in a dream, or in reality. My own belief leaned to the former, but every circumstance rather tended to confirm the latter; else, how came I to be in the place where I was.

"I scrambled up among the rocks to the westward, and at length came to a small footpath which led from the head of the one bay to the other; and following that, it soon brought me to a straggling hamlet, called, I think, Battaline. Here I found a man that had been a soldier, and had a little broken English, and by his help I raised the inhabitants of the village; and, getting into a fishing-boat, we were soon at the cottage. There we found the body lying stretched, cold and stiff, exactly in the very place and the very position in which I laid it at first on the bed. The house was searched, and grievous to relate, there was no article either of meat, drink, or clothing in it, save the old mantle which I found her mending the evening before. It appeared to me on reflection, that it had been a settled matter between her and the spirit, that she was to yield up her frail life that night, and join his company; and that I had found her preparing for her change. The cloak she had meant for her winding-sheet, having nothing else; and by her little hymns and orgies she had been endeavouring to prepare her soul for the company among whom she knew she was so soon to be. There was a tint of spiritual sublimity in the whole matter.

"I have related this story exactly as I remember it. It is possible that the whole might have been a dream, and that I had walked off in my sleep; for I have sometimes been subjected to such vagaries, and have played wonderful pranks in my sleep; but I think the circumstance of the corpse being found in the very way in which I had laid it, or at least, supposed I had laid it, confirms it almost beyond a doubt, that I had looked upon the whole with my natural eyes. Or, perhaps part of it may have been real, and part of it a dream, for the whole, from the first, was so like a vision to me, that I can affirm nothing anent it."

We are left with a dream within the real within a vision within a fiction that may have retold a real event. There is always something unsettling, an epistemic rootlessness in Hogg's fiction and equally in his purportedly autobiographical writings.

James Hogg leaves the reader similarly unlocated in that most tantalising and disturbing of Gothic novels, *The Private Memoirs and Confessions of a Justified Sinner with a detail of curious traditionary facts, and other evidence, by the editor.*[vii] Hogg is not identified as the author.

The narrative is fractured between the editor's account and the document printed and completed in manuscript by the justified sinner, Robert Wringhim. The editorial matter includes a letter that James Hogg had published in *Blackwood's Magazine*, dated from Altrive Lake, 1st August, 1823, describing the suicide's grave and his exhumation. Appearing in the novel as 'himself', the Ettrick Shepherd, anxious about his market business, refused to show the editor the grave. As author, James Hogg introduced real people, including Scott's son-in-law, J.G. Lockhart, among the fictive, in a further dislocation of fictional space and, with authorial bravado, cast doubt on his own truthfulness. The editor writes: "I took that opportunity to pay a visit to my townsman and fellow collegian, Mr. L t (Lockhart) of C d, advocate. I mentioned to him Hogg's letter, asking him if the statement was founded at all on truth. His answer was, 'I suppose so. For my part I never doubted the thing, having been told that there has been a deal of talking about it up in the Forest for some time past. But, God knows! Hogg has imposed as ingenious lies on the public ere now.'"

Character is also fractured with the reader left uncertain as to the physical, psychological or supernatural being of the unidentified Gil Martin and unsure of the actions of Robert Wringhim; and the laws of the physical world seem fractured with inadequately explained apparitions: George Colwan freed for a time from the "pertinacious" attentions of the figure of his brother, Robert Wringhim, was about early in Edinburgh. "One morning, chancing to awaken very early, he arose to make an excursion to the top of Arthur's Seat, to breathe the breeze of the dawning, and see the sun arise out of the eastern ocean. The morning was calm and serene; and as he walked down the south back of the Canongate, toward the Palace, the haze was so close around him that he could not see the houses on the opposite side of the way. As he passed the lord-commissioner's house, the guards were in attendance, who cautioned him not to go by the Palace, as all the gates would be shut and guarded for an hour to come, on which he went by the back of St. Anthony's gardens, and found his way into that little romantic glade adjoining to the Saint's chapel and well. He was still involved in a blue haze, like a dense smoke, but yet in the midst of it the respiration was the most refreshing and delicious. The grass and the flowers were loaden with dew; and, on taking off his hat to wipe his forehead, he perceived that the black glossy fur of which his chaperon was wrought, was all covered with a tissue of the most delicate silver - a fairy web, composed of little spheres, so minute that no eye could discern any one of them; yet there they were shining in lovely millions. Afraid of defacing so beautiful and so delicate a garnish, he replaced his hat with the greatest caution, and went on his way light of heart.

"As he approached the swire at the head of the dell, - that little delightful verge from which in one moment the eastern limits and shores of Lothian arise on the view, - as he approached it, I say, and a little space from the height, he beheld, to his astonishment, a bright halo in the cloud of haze, that rose in a semi-circle over his head like a pale rainbow. He was struck motionless at the view of the lovely vision; for it so chanced that he had never seen the same appearance before, though common at early morn. But he soon perceived the cause of the phenomenon, and that it proceeded from the rays of the sun from a pure unclouded morning sky striking upon this dense vapour which refracted them. But the better all the works of nature are understood, the more they will be ever admired. That was a scene that would have entranced the man of science with delight, but which the uninitiated and sordid man would have regarded less than the mole rearing up his hill in silence and in darkness.

George did admire this halo of glory, which still grew wider, and less defined, as he approached the surface of the cloud. But, to his utter amazement and supreme delight, he found, on reaching the top of Arthur's Seat, that this sublunary rainbow, this terrestrial glory, was spread in its most vivid hues beneath his feet. Still he could not perceive the body of the sun, although the light behind him was dazzling; but the cloud of haze lying dense in that deep dell that separates the hill from the rocks of Salisbury, and the dull shadow of the hill mingling with that cloud, made the dell a pit of darkness. On that shadowy cloud was the lovely rainbow formed, spreading itself on a horizontal plain, and having a slight and brilliant shade of all the colours of the heavenly bow, but all of them paler and less defined. But this terrestrial phenomenon of the early morn cannot be better delineated than by the name given of it by the shepherd boys, 'The little wee ghost of the rainbow.'

"Such was the description of the morning, and the wild shades of the hill, that George gave to his father and Mr. Adam Gordon that same day on which he had witnessed them; and it is necessary that the reader should comprehend something of their nature, to understand what follows.

"He seated himself on the pinnacle of the rocky precipice, a little within the top of the hill to the westward, and, with a light and buoyant heart, viewed the beauties of the morning, and inhaled its salubrious breeze. 'Here,' thought he, 'I can converse with nature without disturbance, and without being intruded on by any appalling or obnoxious visitor.' The idea of his brother's dark and malevolent looks coming at that moment across his mind, he turned his eyes instinctively to the right, to the point where that unwelcome guest was wont to make his appearance. Gracious Heaven! What an apparition was there presented to his view! He saw, delineated in the cloud, the shoulders, arms, and features of a human being of the most dreadful aspect. The face was the face of his brother, but dilated to twenty times the natural size. Its dark eyes gleamed on him through the mist, while every furrow of its hideous brow frowned deep as the ravines on the brow of the hill. George started, and his hair stood up in bristles as he gazed on this horrible monster. He saw every feature, and every line of the face, distinctly, as it gazed on him with an intensity that was hardly brookable. Its eyes were fixed on him, in the same manner as those of some carnivorous animal fixed on its prey; and yet there was fear and trembling, in these unearthly features, as plainly depicted as murderous malice. The giant apparition seemed sometimes to be cowering down as in terror, so that nothing but its brow and eyes were seen; still these never turned one moment from their object—again it rose imperceptibly up, and began to approach with great caution; and as it neared, the dimensions of its form lessened, still continuing, however, far above the natural size.

"George conceived it to be a spirit. He could conceive it to be nothing else; and he took it for some horrid demon by which he was haunted, that had assumed the features of his brother in every lineament, but in taking on itself the human form, had miscalculated dreadfully on the size, and presented itself thus to him in a blown-up, dilated frame of embodied air, exhaled from the caverns of death or the regions of devouring fire. He was farther confirmed in the belief that it was a malignant spirit, on perceiving that it approached him across the front of a precipice, where there was not footing for thing of mortal frame. Still, what with terror and astonishment, he continued rivetted to the spot, till it approached, as he deemed, to within two yards of him; and then, perceiving that it was setting itself to make a violent spring on him, he started to his feet and fled distractedly in the opposite direction, keeping his eye cast behind him lest he had been seized in that dangerous place. But the very first bolt that he made in his flight he came in contact with a real body of flesh and blood, and that with such violence that both went down among some scragged rocks, and George rolled over the other. The being called out 'Murder;' and, rising, fled precipitately. George then perceived that it was his brother; and, being confounded between the shadow and the substance, he knew not what he was doing or what he had done; and there being only one natural way of retreat from the brink of the rock, he likewise arose and pursued the affrighted culprit with all his speed towards the top of the hill."

George, whilst observing them with minuteness and precision, was entranced by the sparkling droplets on his hat which he romantically described as "fairy spheres". He was struck motionless at the lovely vision of the rainbow, but was ready to explain it scientifically and even claim, anachronistically, in a post-enlightenment sentiment that "the better all the works of nature are understood, the more they will be ever admired". As the rainbow appeared even more delicate and intensely beautiful, despite having suggested that such things delighted the scientist and not the sordid man, he reclaimed the vision for the unenlightened man: "This terrestrial phenomenon of the early morn cannot be better delineated than by the name given of it by the shepherd boys, 'The little wee ghost of the rainbow.'"

He turned, and saw, being placed between the sun and his own projected shadow on the clouds, a Brocken spectre which, at his own imaginative suggesting, appeared to be in the monstrous form of his brother. It is no longer an explicable phenomenon, but a demon, a malignant spirit, "exhaled from the caverns of death or the regions of devouring fire" to be met "with terror and astonishment". The "bogle of the Brocken" retains the power to terrify and astonish beyond the reach of scientific explanation.

Hogg, perhaps uniquely among the writers of the Romantic period, contained within himself both the scientific perspective of the rational man and the imaginative perceptions of the pre-literate. In his encounters with phenomenon he does not give priority to the scientific over the preliterate. The cattle in the Border hills, the army in the Hebrides and the monstrous figure on Arthur's Mount in the very city of the Enlightenment, are possessed of an imaginative power that overrides all rational or scientific considerations. The farm-workers and farmers who saw the spectral army on Souther Fell found that their pre-literate perceptions were suborned by the rationalist George Smith, who, at least acknowledged that there was something inexplicable in their vision, and by the literate James Clarke who sought to make their perceptions into a marketable commodity.

Chapter Ten:

Allan Cunningham

Allan Cunningham first met James Hogg in 1806. Hogg, with "bare-feet and ragged trousers" "was herding my master's ewes on the great hill of Queensberry, in Nithsdale," and Cunningham was "a dark ungainly youth of about eighteen, with a boardly frame for his age, and strongly marked manly features—the very model of Burns, and exactly such a man. Had they been of the same age, it would not have been easy to distinguish the one from the other". Allan Cunningham, who was, in fact twenty-one at the time, had been born in 1784 on a farm just across the River Nith from Ellisland where Burns lived from 1788 to 1792. He claimed to remember – he must have been five at the time – Robert Burns reciting Tam O'Shanter seated at their kitchen table.

James Hogg was initially wary of meeting the two men. He "was afraid" (with good reason, since he had fathered two illegitimate children that year) "they were come to look after me with an accusation regarding some of the lasses". However, after James introduced his "younger brother Allan, the greatest admirer that you have on earth, and himself a young aspiring poet of some promise" and they had shared a bottle together, their friendship was assured. Hogg described that memorable afternoon: "I had a small bothy upon the hill, in which I took my breakfast and dinner on wet days, and rested myself. It was so small, that we had to walk in on all fours; and when we were in, we could not get up our heads any way, but in a sitting posture. It was exactly my own length, and, on the one side, I had a bed of rushes, which served likewise as a seat; on this we all three sat down, and there we spent the whole afternoon, - and, I am sure, a happier group of three never met on the hill of Queensberry. Allan brightened up prodigiously after he got into the dark bothy, repeating all his early pieces of poetry, and part of his brother's, to me. The two brothers partook heartily, and without reserve, of my scrip and bottle of sweet milk, and the elder Mr Cunningham had a strong bottle with him - I have forgot whether it was brandy or rum, but I remember it was excessively good, and helped to keep up our spirits to a late hour. Thus began at that bothy in the wilderness a friendship, and a mutual attachment between two aspiring Scottish peasants, over which the shadow of a cloud has never yet passed."[1]

Allan had been apprenticed as a stone-mason to his forty-year-old brother James and his poetic aspirations were confined to his little leisure time. A year after their meeting, which Hogg mythologized into a line of bardic descent, Allan Cunningham published a few verses in a magazine called *Literary Recollections* under the punning pseudonym of Hidallan, one of Ossian's many heroes. In 1809, he assisted Cromek in his collection of traditional poetry in Nithsdale. Robert Hartley Cromek, himself the son of a stonemason, was an entrepreneurial publisher from London who sensed that there was money in Scottish poetry. He wanted to follow up his *Reliques of Robert Burns, consisting chiefly of original letters, poems, and critical observations on Scottish songs* with more of the same kind culled from the countryside where Burns had lived. A fortuitous meeting with Allan Cunningham led to the publication of *Remains of Nithsdale and Galloway song, with historical and traditional notices relative to the manners and customs of the peasantry*. The young poet, following James MacPherson and Thomas Chatterton, offered his own compositions as the traditional songs of the area. The willingly deceived Cromek was enabled to present his collection of peasant poetry to the world and Allan Cunningham to publish, albeit anonymously, his own songs and poems together with his thoughts on his native verse and traditions. Hogg claimed not to have been deceived: "When Cromek's 'Nithsdale and Galloway Relics' came to my hand, I at once discerned the strains of my friend, and I cannot describe with what sensations of delight I first heard Mr Morrison read the 'Mermaid of Galloway,' while at every verse I kept naming the author. . . I continued my asseverations to all my intimate friends, that Allan Cunningham was the author of all that was beautiful in the work . . . When I went to Sir Walter Scott, (then Mr Scott,) I found him decidedly of the same opinion as myself; and he said he wished to God we had that valuable and original young man fairly out of Cromek's hands again." Scott, in a later letter, described the brash and cheating Cromek as "a perfect Brain-sucker".[2]

Allan Cunningham placed himself in Cromek's hands. He went to live in London in 1810 and sought to earn his living with his pen as a parliamentary reporter. He married in 1811 a certain Jean Walker, a servant girl, whom he had celebrated as *The Lovely Lass of Preston Mill*:

> Her naked feet amang the grass,
> Seemed like twa dew-gemmed lilies fair;
> Her brows shone comely 'mang her locks,
> Black curling owre her shouthers bare:
> Her cheeks were rich wi' bloomy youth;
> Her lips were like a honey well,
> An' heaven seemed looking through her een,
> The lovely lass of Preston Mill.[3]

The entrepreneurial ballad collector either had little ear for poetry or he seems to have been willingly duped by Allan Cunningham's freshly-minted traditional verse.

Cromek introduced him to Francis Leggatt Chantrey, who was then enjoying the greatest of artistic and financial success carving busts of George the Third and Nelson and other heroic figures and members of the aristocracy. In 1814, perhaps through a degree of personal affinity, Cunningham became Chantrey's secretary and workshop manager. Throughout succeeding years he enjoyed personal contact with many of the country's leading figures, as Chantrey's vivid and penetrating sculptures were carved only after he knew his sitters. Chantrey insisted that Walter Scott "should breakfast with me, always before his sittings, and never come along alone, nor bring more than three friends at once, and that they should all be good talkers".[4] It was at this time that "Allan said that he was so piqued by Cromek's manner of receiving some of his own songs which he took to him, that he composed the ballads he had been employed by Cromek to collect, and these actually form the greatest part of the Nithsdale and Galloway songs. On hearing this, Sir Walter courteously replies, 'I always suspected this, Mr Cunningham; they are far too good to be old.'"[5]

Working intimately in Pimlico with a man who was described as the greatest sculptor of his age, Allan Cunningham found himself at the heart of London's society, artistic, cultural and aristocratic. Robert Southey, for instance, wrote a verse epistle to him from Keswick in 1828, after he'd returned from the noisome city:

> And therefore, in that loathed metropolis,
> Time measured out to me some golden hours.
> They were not leaden-footed while the clay
> Beneath the patient touch of Chantrey's hand
> Grew to the semblance of my lineaments.
> Lit up in memory's landscape, like green spots
> Of sunshine, are the mornings, when, in talk
> With him, and thee, and Bedford, (my true friend
> Of forty years,) I saw the work proceed,
> Subject the while myself to no restraint,
> But pleasurably in frank discourse engaged;[6]

He earned his living at Chantrey's and wrote in the evenings. Cunningham had been writing stories based on folk traditions for *Blackwood's* Magazine, "a series of tales under the title of *Recollections of Mark Macrabin, the Cameronian*, which for humour, and glowing description of Scottish manners, sectarian feeling, and superstitions, are inimitable".[7] He then became one of the remarkable group of writers who were brought together by the unfortunate John Scott to produce the *London Magazine*. From the first issue in 1820 there was a sense that they were rivals to the successful Edinburgh magazines, *The Review*, *The Quarterly* and *Blackwood's*. The rivalry extended to the mistaken shooting of Scott in a duel as a result of a quarrel with Blackwood's editor, Lockhart. The *London Magazine*, however, appears to have been a generous and convivial operation. "The contributors met once a month over an excellent dinner, given by the firm; and consulted and talked on literary matters together. . . . Allan Cunningham, a stalwart man, was generally there; very Scotch in aspect, but ready to do a good turn to any one. His talk was not too abundant, although he was a voluminous writer of prose . . His face shone at these festivities."[8] Other authors who dined regularly were Charles Lamb, Thomas Wainwright (the poisoner), Thomas Hood, J. F. Cary, John Keats and John Clare, Walter Savage Landor and occasionally William Hazlitt and Thomas de Quincey, whose *Confessions of an English Opium Eater*, like Lamb's *Essays of Elia*, first appeared in the magazine.

Cunningham's *Traditional Tales of the English and Scottish Peasantry* offered direct competition to the regional stories of Hogg, Galt and others that were appearing in the Edinburgh magazines. His tales fitted well in the metropolitan magazine which took a romantic interest in folk literature as was demonstrated by their enthusiastic, but paternalistic, support for the Northamptonshire peasant poet, John Clare. Ten of the twelve supernatural stories were set on either side of the Solway, four in Nithsdale, and six in Cumberland. Even though Cunningham does not seem to have lived in Cumberland, they were dated as being written in, the possibly fictitious, "Lammerlea, Cumberland". These tales were published, in 1822, in book form by the *London Magazine*'s owners, Taylor and Hessey, who were also responsible for works by Keats, Clare, Coleridge, Lamb, Hazlitt, Cary, Carlyle, de Quincey and Landor.

Although so closely involved with London's literary elite, Allan Cunningham found himself caught between two worlds. He was still the working stone-mason from Scotland. One of his most famous songs, highly praised by Scott and Hogg was

> It's hame, and it's hame, hame fain wad I be,
> An' it's hame, hame, hame, to my ain countree!
> When the flower is i' the bud and the leaf is on the tree,
> The lark shall sing me hame in my ain countree;
> It's hame, and it's hame, hame fain wad I be,
> An' it's hame, hame, hame, to my ain countree![9]

The cultured, metropolitan "Honest Allan" expressed a similar ardent longing for a romanticised folk past in the preface to the *Traditional Tales*: "In former times, and within my own remembrance, old men wandered from house to house, chanting ballads, reciting portions of the old romances, and curious stories of real or fictitious adventure." Oral culture, as James Hogg's mother insisted, retreated before the written word, in a rapidly changing society: "The attachment of our peasantry to the recital or chant of chivalrous ballads or superstitious legends, has abated by the diffusion of printed knowledge. The oral wisdom, the unwritten sallies of wit and humour, the lyric compositions and legendary histories, have begun to vanish like all unrecorded things." He saw himself as "more the collector and embellisher, than the creator of these tales; and such as are not immediately copied from recitation are founded upon traditions or stories prevalent in the north" and sentimentally he felt that "These tales and legends, rude and imperfect as they are, have sweetened for me many an hour of remission from daily labour, and, by the light of my evening fire, have given me a pleasure which the kindness or the severity of criticism can scarcely enlarge or lessen."[10] The urban, urbane Allan Cunningham needed to excuse the pleasure he took in the peasant tradition in which he had been raised.

The principal story in the collection, and the one which concerns us, is *The Selbys of Cumberland*.[11] The story is set during the Jacobite Rebellion of 1715, and transposes the legend of the spectral army to that earlier date.

The narrator is a gentleman farmer who recalls an incident in his youth. Lost and fatigued with fox hunting he encountered an old lady heedlessly running her fingers through her once-beautiful hair while she chanted an old ballad beneath a "large and doddered tree of green holly, on the top of which sat a raven, grey-backed and bald-headed from extreme age, looking down intently on something which it thought worthy of watching beneath". She had "a look of lady-like stateliness" and was dressed in the manner "common seventy or eighty years ago". The ballad told of how the Selbys had fought and how

> All in a nook of bloody ground
> That lady sat by a bleeding knight,
> And strove with her fingers to staunch the wound:
> Her locks, like sun-beams when summer's in pride,
> She pluck'd and plac'd on his wounded side.

Eleanor Selby turns away from the two green ridges that lie beneath the holly and takes the narrator to Fremett Ha'. "a large old-fashioned house, constructed of rough and undressed stones, such as are found in abundance on the northern uplands, and roofed with a heavy coating of heath, near an ell in thickness,—the whole secured with bands of wood and ropes of flax".

Eleanor Selby, the last of her line, was welcomed into the old home and, under the ministrations of a fair Cumberland milkmaid, began to relax her aristocratic hauteur and "proceeded to relate some of the adventures she had witnessed in the time of her youth. These she poured out in a very singular manner, unconscious, apparently, at times, of the presence of others, and often addressing herself to the individuals whom her narrative recalled to life, as if they stood life-like and breathing before her.

"When I was young, like thee, Maude Rode, a marvel happened, which amazed many: it is, and will be, a lasting tale, and a wonder; for it came even as a vision, and I beheld it with these eyes. In those days . . . Rumours of rebellions and invasions were as frequent as the winds on our heaths; and each day brought a darker and more varied tale of risings in the east, and risings in the west; for the king abroad, and for the king at home . . . Those who still loved the ancient church were dreaded by those who loved the new; . . . Thus, hot discussion and sore dispute divided the people of this land.

"It happened on a fine summer evening, that I stopped at the dwelling of David Forester, of Wilton hall, along with young Walter Selby of Glamora, to refresh myself after the chase on the banks of Derwentwater. The mountain air was mild and balmy, and the lofty and rugged outline of Soutrafell appeared on a canopied back ground of sky so pure, so blue, and so still, that the earth and heaven seemed blended together. Eagles were visible, perched among the star-light, on the peaks of the rocks; ravens roosted at a vast distance below; and where the greensward joined the acclivity of rock and stone, the flocks lay in undisturbed repose, with their fleeces shining in dew, and reflected in a broad deep lake at the bottom, so pure and so motionless, that it seemed a sea of glass. The living, or rather human portion of the picture, partook of the same silent and austere character, for inanimate nature often lends a softness or a sternness to man; the meditative melancholy of the mountain, and the companionable garrulity of the vale, have not escaped proverbial observation. I had alighted from my horse, and, seated on a little green hillock before the house, which the imagination of our mountaineers had not failed to people at times with fairies and elves—tasted some of the shepherds' curds and cream, the readiest and the sweetest beverage which rustic hospitality supplies. Walter Selby had seated himself at my feet, and behind me stood the proprietor of Wilton-hall and his wife, awaiting my wishes with that ready and respectful frankness, which those of birth and ancestry always obtain among our mountain peasantry. A number of domestics, shepherds and maidens, stood at a distance, as much for the purpose of listening to our conversation, as from the desire to encumber us with their assistance in recommencing our journey.

"'Young lady,' said David Forester, 'have you heard tidings of note from the north or from the south? The Selbys are an ancient and renowned race, and in days of old held rule from sunny Carlisle to the vale of Keswick—a day's flight for a hawk. They are now lordless and landless; but the day may soon come, when to thee I shall go hat in hand to beg a boon, and find thee lady of thy lands again, and the noble house of Lanercost risen anew from its briers and desolation.'

Eleanor understood clearly the reference to the Stuart cause. A peddler arrived, "His horse, loaded with heavy panniers, came foremost, anxious for a resting, place; and behind came the owner, a middle-aged man, tall and robust, with hair as black as the raven, curled close beneath a very broad bonnet, and in his hand one of those measuring rods of root grown oak, piked with iron at the under end, and mounted with brass at the upper, which seemed alike adapted for defending or measuring his property." He was questioned as to his knowledge of the times and answered enigmatically. "'But, do you think,' said I, 'that the people will continue to prefer the cold blood of the man who keeps the chair, to the warm kindly English blood o' him that's far away?'— 'Ay, ay,' quoth he, 'nae doubt, nae doubt, when we wou'd drink ditch-water rather than red wine.'"

He sang a song whose allegory was transparent to any Stuart sympathisers:

> The Cuckoo is a princely bird,
> And we will wait awhile,
> And welcome him with shout and song,
> In the morn of green April;

We 'll lay our thighs o'er our good steeds,
And gird our claymores on,
And chase away the hooded crows
That croak around the throne.

Then taking Eleanor aside, he spoke to her: 'This cross and rosary,' - and he held in his hand these devotional symbols, carved of dark wood, and slightly ornamented with gold, - 'are of no common wood - a princess has sat under the shadow of its bough, and seen her kingdom won and lost - and may the fair one, who will now wear it, warm it in her bosom, till she sees a kingdom long lost - won as boldly, and as bravely, as ever the swords of the Selbys won their land!'

"Walter Selby, who all this while— though then a hot and forward youth —had remained mute, addressed me in a whisper. 'Fair Eleanor—mine own giddy cousin—this pedlar—this dispenser of rosaries, made of Queen Mary's yew tree—he, whom the churls call Simon Packpin, is no seeker of profit from vulgar merchandise—I'll wager a kiss of thine own ruddy lips against one of mine, that he carries swords made of good Ripon steel, and pistols of good Swedish iron, in yon horse-pack of his—wilt thou pledge a kiss on this wager, my gentle cousin? And instead of a brain stored with plans for passing an English yard for a Scottish ell, and making pieces of homespun plaiding seem costly works from the looms of Arras or even of Leeds, it is furnished with more perilous stuff, pretty Eleanor —and no man can tell us better how many of the Scottish cavaliers have their feet ready for the stirrup, and on what day they will call on the Selbys to mount and strike for their ancient lord and their lost inheritance.' Something of this matter had been passing in my own mind, but the temper of the Selbys ever required more to be repressed than encouraged—and so I endeavoured to manage thee, poor Walter Selby!" She sighed while she named the name of him who had guided and gladdened her youth, and in a tone low and almost inaudible, she addressed herself to the image which her affections had thus charmed into life, — 'I saw thee, thou last and thou bravest of all the Selbys, with thy banner spread, thy sword bright, and thy long golden locks waving on thy shoulders, when the barriers of Preston were lost and won, and the gallant laird of Ashiesteel[12] fought like a brother by thy side—O, that this last bright picture were all I remembered of thee! But can the heart of woman, though her head be gray, forget that she saw those long locks which made the dames sigh, waving, soiled and bloody, on the gates of Carlisle. There is much done in this world must be answered for in the next, and this cruel and remorseless deed is one.' She looked while she spoke as if her wild and agitated fancy had given motion to the picture which she drew of her lover—her face changed, and her eyes, from beneath their moist and depressed lids, became fixed and frozen, like stars in a winter night. This passed away with a smothered groan and a moving of her hand over her bosom: she again resumed her narrative. "'Truly,' said I, 'my froward cousin, thou art the best soldier our poor prince could peril his cause with—thou canst make a pedlar churl into a deep plodding politician, capable of overturning a throne; and his pack, filled with shreds of lace and remnants of ribbon, into a magazine of weapons fit for furnishing an army. What will thy most wise head make of these dubious sibyl verses, which this mysterious politician of thine has been doling out for thy especial instruction?' 'By the rood, my witty Eleanor,' said Walter Selby, 'I shall win a battle, and wed thee in revenge for this. But thinkest thou not, that the box which has endowed that round white neck of thine with a cross and rosary of gold and wood still more precious, may not contain things equally curious and strange? Some golden information this pedlar—since pedlar thou wilt have him—carries in his looks—I wish I could find the way to extract it.' The stranger, as if guessing by our looks and our whispers what was passing between us, proceeded to instruct us in his own singular way—he described the excellent temper of his Sheffield whittles, praised the curious qualities of his spectacles, which might enable the wearer to see distant events—and after soothing over some lines of a psalm or hymn, common to the presbyterians, he proceeded to chant the following ballad, of which I regret the loss of several verses

Thy sword's rusty, Howard—hot Dacre, art thou
So cool when the war-horse is bounding?
Come Percy, come thou, like a Percy of yore,
When the trumpet of England is sounding:
And come, gallant Selby—thy name is a name,
While a soldier has soul, and a minstrel has flame.

And come too, ye names that are nameless—come mount,
And win ye a name in proud story:
A thousand long years at the sock and the share
Are not worth one moment of glory.
Come arm ye, and mount ye, and make the helms ring
Of the Whigs, as ye strike for your country and king!

"The whole household of Wilton-hall, including Walter Selby and myself, had gradually gathered around this merchant minstrel, whose voice, from an ordinary chant, had arisen, as we became interested, into a tone of deep and martial melody. Nor was it the voice alone of the stranger that became changed—his face, which at the commencement of the ballad had a grave and a dubious expression, brightened up with enthusiasm —his frame grew erect, and his eyes gleamed with that fierce light, which has been observed in the eyes of the English soldiers on the eve of battle. 'What thinkest thou, pretty Eleanor, of our merchant now?' said Walter Selby: —'I should like to have such a form on my right hand when I try to empty the saddles of the southern horse of some of the boldest Whigs.' - 'And I'll pledge thee, young gentleman,' said the pedlar, - raising his voice at once from the provincial drawl and obscurity of lowland Scotch into the purest English, - ' any vow thou askest of me, to ride on which hand thou wilt - and be to thee as a friend and a brother, when the battle is at the hottest - and so I give thee my hand on't.' - 'I touch no hand,' said Walter Selby, 'and I vow no vow either - I am a Selby, and the Selbys -' 'The Selbys,' said the stranger, in a tone, slow and deliberate,' are an ancient and a noble race - but this is no time, young gentleman, to scruple precedence of blood. In the fields where I have ridden, noble deeds have been achieved by common hands - while the gentle and the far descended have sat apart nor soiled their swords. - I neither say I am of a race churlish nor noble - but my sword is as sharp as other men's, and might do thee a friendly deed were it nigh thee in danger.' - ' Now God help us,' said the dame of Wilton-hall, 'what will old England become! - here's young Wat Selby debating lineage and blood with a packman churl: - in good truth, if I had but one drop of gentle blood in my veins, I would wrap him up in his own plaid, and beat him to death with his ell wand - which I'll warrant is a full thumb-breadth short of measure.' I stood looking on Walter Selby and on the stranger -

the former standing aloof with a look of haughty determination - and the latter, with an aspect of calm and intrepid resolution, enduring the scoff of the hot-headed youth, and the scorn of the vulgar matron.

"It might be now about nine o'clock - the air was balmy and mute, the sky blue and unclouded, and the moon, yet unrisen, had sent as much of her light before her as served, with the innumerable stars, to lighten the earth from the summit of the mountains to the deepest vales. I never looked upon a more lovely night, and gladly turned my face from the idle disputants to the green mountain-side, upon which that forerunner gleam which precedes the moon had begun to scatter its light. While I continued gazing, there appeared a sight on Soutra-fell side - strange, ominous, and obscure to many, at that time, but which was soon after explained in desolation and in blood. I saw all at once a body of horsemen coming swiftly down the steep and impassable side of the mountain - where no earthly horse ever rode. They amounted to many hundreds, and trooped onwards in succession - their helmets gleaming, and their drawn swords shining amid the starlight. On beholding this vision, I uttered a faint scream, and Walter Selby, who was always less or more than other men, shouted till the mountain echoed. 'Saw ever man so gallant a sight? A thousand steeds and riders on the perpendicular side of old Soutra - see where they gallop along a linn, where I could hardly fly a hawk! O for a horse with so sure and so swift a foot as these, that I might match me with this elfin chivalry! My wanton brown, which can bound across the Derwent like a bird, with me on its back, is but a pack-horse to one of these.' Alarm was visible in every face around - for we all knew what the apparition foreboded—a lost battle, and a ruined cause. I heard my father say that the like sight appeared on Helvellyn side, before the battle of Marston-moor - with this remarkable difference - the leader wore on his head the semblance of a royal crown, whereas the leaders of the troop whom I beheld wore only earl's coronets.

'"Now his right hand protect us!' said the dame of Wilton-hall. 'What are we doomed to endure? - what will follow this?' – 'Misery to many,' answered the pedlar, 'and sudden and early death to some who are present.' 'Cease thy croak, thou northern raven!' said Walter Selby - 'if they are phantoms, let them pass - what care we for men of mist? - and if they are flesh and bone, as I guess by their bearing they must surely be -

they are good gallant soldiers of our good king, and thus do I bid them welcome with my bugle.' He winded his horn till the mountain echoed far and wide - the spectre horsemen, distant nearly a quarter of a mile, seemed to halt - and the youth had his horn again at his lips to renew the note, when he was interrupted by the pedlar, who, laying his hand on the instrument, said, 'Young gentleman, be wise, and be ruled - yon vision is sent for man's instruction - not for his scoff and his scorn.' - The shadowy troop now advanced, and passed toward the south at the distance of an hundred yards. I looked on them as they went, and I imagined I knew the forms of many living men - doomed speedily to perish in the battle-field, or on the scaffold. I saw the flower of the Jacobite chivalry - the Maxwells, the Gordons, the Boyds, the Drummonds, the Ogilvys, the Camerons, the Scotts, the Foresters, and the Selbys. The havoc which happened among these noble names it is needless to relate - it is written in tale - related in ballad - sung in song - and deeper still it is written in family feeling and national sympathy. A supernatural light accompanied this pageant, and rendered perfectly visible horse and man: - in the rear I saw a form that made me shudder - a form still present to my eye, and impressed upon my heart - old and sorrow-worn as it is - as vividly as in early youth. I saw the shape of Walter Selby - his short cloak, his scarlet dress - his hat and feather - his sword by his side - and that smiling glance in his deep dark eye which was never there but for me, and which I could know among the looks of a thousand thousand. As he came, he laid his bridle on his horse's neck, and leaned aside, and took at me a long, long look. The youth himself, full of life and gladness beside me, seemed to discover the resemblance between the spectre rider and himself, and it was only by throwing myself in his bosom, that I hindered him from addressing the apparition. How long I remained insensible in his arms I know not, but when I recovered, I found myself pressed to the youth's bosom - and a gentleman with several armed attendants standing beside me - all showing by their looks the deep interest they took in my fate."

Before dame Eleanor Selby had concluded her account of the Spectre Horsemen of Soutra-fell, the sun had set - and the twilight, warm, silent, and dewy, had succeeded - that pleasant time between light and dark, in which domestic labour finds a brief remission. The shepherd, returned from hill or moor, spread out his hose - moistened in morass or rivulet - before the hearth fire, which glimmered far and wide, and taking his accustomed seat, sat mute and motionless as a figure of stone. The cows came lowing homewards from the pasture-hills; others feeding out of cribs filled with rich moist clover, yielded their milk into a score of pails; while the ewes, folded on the sheltered side of the remote glen, submitted their udders, not without the frequent butt and bleat, to the pressure of maidens' hands. Pastoral verse has not many finer pictures than what it borrows from the shepherd returning from the hill, and the shepherdess from the fold - the former with his pipe and dogs, and the latter with her pail of reeking milk, each singing with a hearty country freedom of voice, and in their own peculiar way, the loves and the joys of a pastoral life. The home of Randal Rode presented a scene of rough plenty, and abounded in pastoral wealth; the head of the house associated with his domestics, and maintained that authority over their words and conduct which belonged to simpler times; and something of the rustic dignity of the master was observable in his men. His daughter Maude busied herself among the maidens with a meekness and a diligence which had more of the matron than is commonly found in so young a dame. All this escaped not the notice of her old and capricious kinswoman Eleanor Selby but scenes of homely and domestic joy seemed alien to her heart. The intrusion too of the churlish name of Rode among the martial Selbys, never failed to darken the picture which she would have enjoyed had this rustic alloy mixed with the precious metal of any other house. It was her chief delight, since all the males of her name, had perished, to chant ballads in their praise, and relate their deeds from the time of the Norman invasion down to their ruin in the last rebellion. Many snatches of these chivalrous, ballads are still current on the Border - the debateable land of song as well as of the sword - where minstrels sought their themes, and entered, harp in hand, into rivalry - a kind of contest which the sword, the critic's weapon of those days, was often drawn to decide. Much of this stirring and heroic border-life mingles with the traditionary tales of Eleanor Selby. Her narratives contain, occasionally, a vivid presentment of character and action. I shall endeavour to preserve something of this, and retain, at the same time, their dramatic cast, while I prune and condense the whole, to render them more acceptable to the impatience of modern readers. She thus pursued her story.

"I am now to tell a tale I have related a thousand times to the noble and the low - it is presented to me in my dreams, for the memory of spilt blood clings to a young mind - and the life's blood of Walter Selby was no common blood to me. The vision of the spectre horsemen, in which human fate was darkly shadowed forth, passed away - and departed too, I am afraid, from the thoughts of those to whom it came as a signal and a warning - as a cloud passes from the face of the summer-moon. Seated on horseback, with Walter Selby at my bridle-rein, and before and behind me upwards of a score of armed cavaliers, I had proceeded along the mountain side about a mile, when a horn was winded at a small distance in our front.2

Inevitably, (to considerably telescope the latter part of the story) as the spectral army had portended, Eleanor and Walter rode on to Preston with an increasing band of Jacobites. The invested the streets of the town, but were betrayed by their commanders and Walter Selby was fatally wounded in a skirmish with Colonel Preston's dragoons.

Eleanor, Thomas Scott and others "recommenced our journey to the north, with sorrowful hearts, and diminished numbers. I rode by the side of the litter, which, alas! became a bier, ere we reached the green hills of Cumberland. We halted in a lonely glen; a grave was prepared; and there, without priest, prayer, or requiem, was all that I loved of man consigned to a sylvan grave."

The story did not end there: "But, alas! the form of the lovely and the brave was not permitted to sink silently into dust - it was plucked out of its lonely and obscure grave - displayed on a gibbet, and the head, separated from the body, was placed on the gate of Carlisle. All day I sat looking, in sadness and tears, on this sorrowful sight, and all night I wandered wild and distracted about, conjuring all men who passed by to win me but one tress of the long bright hair of Walter Selby. Even the rude sentinels were moved by my grief, but no one dared to do a deed so daring and so perilous.

"I remember it well - it was on a wild and stormy night - the rain fell fast - the thunder rocked the walls, and the lightnings flashing far and wide showed the castle's shattered towers, and the river Eden rolling deep in flood. I wrapped my robe about me, and approached the gate. The sentinels, obeying the storm, had sought shelter in the turrets, and no living soul seemed abroad but my own unhappy self. I gazed up to the gate where, alas! I had often gazed, and I thought I beheld a human form - a flash of lightning passed, and I saw it was a living being - it descended and approached me, motioning me back with its hand. I retired in awe, and still the figure followed. I turned suddenly round and said, 'Whether thou comest for evil or for good, farther shall I not go till I know thy errand.'

"'Fair and unhappy lady,' said a voice which I had often heard before, 'I have come, not without peril, from a distant place; for I heard the story of your daily and nightly sorrowings, and I vowed I would not leave a relique of the noble and the brave to gladden the eyes of vulgar men, and feast the fowls of heaven. Here, take this tress of thy lover's hair, and mourn over it as thou wilt - men shall look on the morrow for the golden locks of Walter Selby waving on Carlisle gate, and when they see nothing there they shall know that the faithful and the valiant are never without friends. His body has been won, and his head removed, and his dust shall mingle with the knightly and the far descended, even as I vowed when we laid him in his early grave.' With these words Sir Thomas Scott departed, and I placed the ringlet in my bosom, from which it shall never be separated."

Such was the story of Eleanor Selby. In a latter day some unknown Scottish minstrel heard the uncertain and varying tradition, and, with a minstrel's licence, wove it into verse, suppressing the name of Selby and giving the whole a colour and character most vehemently Scottish.

A northern lady is made to sing the following rude and simple lament:

CARLISLE YETTS.

White was the rose in my love's hat,
While he rowed me in his lowland plaidy,
His heart was true as death in love,
His hand was ay in battle ready;
His lang lang hair in yellow hanks
Waved o'er his cheeks sae sweet and ruddy,
But now it waves o'er Carlisle yetts,
In dripping ringlets soiled and bloody.

When I came first through fair Carlisle
Ne'er was a town sae gladsome seeming,
The white rose flaunted o'er the wall,
The thistled pennons far were streaming.
When I came next through fair Carlisle
0! sad, sad seemed the town and eerie,
The old men sobbed, and grey dames wept,
O! lady, come ye to seek your dearie?
I tarried on a heathery hill,
My tresses to my cheeks were frozen,
And far adown the midnight wind
I heard the din of battle closing.
The grey day dawned, where 'mang the snow
Lay many a young and gallant fellow,
But the sun came visiting in vain
Two lovely een tween locks of yellow.

There's a tress of soiled and yellow hair
Close in my bosom I am keeping,
Oh! I have done with delight and love,
So welcome want, and woe, and weeping.
Woe, woe upon that cruel heart,
Woe, woe, upon that hand so bloody,
That lordless leaves my true love's hall,
And makes me wail a virgin widow."

Allan Cunningham, like Scott, was inventing a tradition. The landscape - "the lofty and rugged outline of Soutrafell appeared on a canopied back ground of sky" - is that of a painter, imprecise in time, the eagles were "perched among the starlight" and inaccurate in pictorial precision, the flocks were "reflected in a broad deep lake at the bottom, so pure and so motionless, that it seemed a sea of glass". Cunningham's Soutrafell is not the Souther Fell of William Lancaster and Daniel Stricket. In his Cumberland the native inhabitants, "the mountaineers", still imagine a world "peopled with fairies and elves" and they maintain a proper deference towards their aristocratic betters. In James Clark's country the farm servant had become an auctioneer.

The name *Soutrafell* was probably, and typically, Cunningham's coinage. *The Place Names of Cumberland* gives no authority for the form. It does cite *Souterfel* from *The Calendar of Inquisitions post mortem* in 1323 and *Souterfell in Grysedale* which was recorded in *The Gaol Delivery Rolls* nearly twenty years later. Otherwise the only authority offered is *Souther Fell* which is the way the name appeared on Donald's *Map of Cumberland in* 1783.[13] *Souther* is a Northern dialect word for *cobbler* derived from the Old English *sutere*, but there is no explanation of why this term should be applied to this mountain. R.S. Ferguson suggested that the name might derive from "the fertility of its sheep pastures. . . . from Old Norse *saudar,* sheep, and would therefore be the same name as *Saudfjeld* in Norway, and *SaudaFell* in Iceland, those names being in the singular number, and ours in the plural. This etymology is confirmed by the character of the mountain, which is peculiarly favourable for sheep pastures."[14]

The Selbys' spectral army when it appears, after sunset, just before the moon rises, is "strange, ominous, and obscure to many, at that time". That apparition of the army with its glittering helmets and shining swords, the flower of Jacobite chivalry, is glorious to Walter Selby, the projection of all that seemed finest in Scottish history and tradition. It was also, as Eleanor Selby realised, disastrous for Scotland, to be "explained in desolation and in blood". Walter Selby answered the call "with that smiling glance in his deep dark eye which was never there but for me", with a passion akin to love. The vision became a cruel and inevitable reality as Eleanor recovered from her faint to see the gentleman and several armed attendants standing above her and then she accompanied the ill-fated army as it marched towards Preston.

Cunningham's description of the spectral army marching towards the observer is remarkably similar to Hogg's tartan clad army in the Hebrides. Both must have been aware of the respective folklore in Cumberland and Lewis. Cunningham is almost certain to have read *The Renowned Adventures of Basil Lee*, which had been published two years before his story appeared in the London Magazine.

Seventy-five years after Culloden and Cumberland's butchery in the Highlands, Scotland had come to terms with the disaster of the Jacobites.

The glorious, intelligent flowering of enlightenment Edinburgh and the literary assimilation of its folk past in Ossian and Burns and Scott and Hogg reached its incredible apogee when a bloated George IV paraded in Edinburgh in a tartan kilt in 1822. In his use of the story of the spectral army, Allan Cunningham acknowledged the glorious futility of a once heroic ambition. His Jacobite aristocrats were proud, romantic, impetuous, but they were doomed to be hung on Carlisle Yetts and buried beneath green mounds in lonely hills. The present belonged to the world of the gentleman farmer, the lost hunter, who could stumble occasionally among the desolate hills and find pleasure in the stories of a glorious and tragic past.

The London Speculum felt the story offered a different kind of pleasure: "Does any good soul want a tale of wonder and terror? The London has an assortment of staple articles, from Lammerlea, Cumberland, which out-Lewis Lewis, and throw Mrs. Radcliff herself into the shade".[15] The story of Eleanor Selby proved very popular. In the manner of the times within a year or two of its first publication, the *Monthly Review* and The *Leeds Correspondent: a Literary, Mathematical and Philosophical Miscellany* availed themselves of the free copy by reprinting a part of the Tale of the Selbys and in the United States the full story was to be found in *The Portfolio* in Philadelphia and in *The New York Literary Gazette and American Atheneum*. In 1826, *The Spectre Horse-men of Soutra-Fell or The Fall of the House of Selby: A Cumberland Tradition* was reprinted in a volume extravagantly titled *Legends of terror! And tales of the wonderful and wild; with original historical illustrations and elegant engravings on wood.* The elegant engraving on wood shows a cavalier Walter Selby astounded as ghostly soldiers ride by beneath the standard of the skull and cross-bones.

Cunningham's biographer, David Hogg speaks of him having "a strong regard for the belief in the 'fairy Folk' as it enabled him to exercise his luxuriant fancy at will. The following anecdote is told of him on the subject. "'Do you believe in fairies, Mac?' he said to a Celtic acquaintance one day in the course of conversation. 'Deet, I'm no ferry shure,' was the characteristically cautious reply of the mountaineer; 'but do you pelieve in them your nainsel, Mister Kinnikun?' 'I once did,' said the burly poet, 'and would to God I could do still! For the woodland and the moor have lost for me a great portion of their romance, since my faith in their existence has departed.' He then quoted the following lines from Campbell's *Address to the Rainbow*: -

'When Science from Creation's face
Enchantment's veil withdraws;
What lovely visions yield their place
To cold material laws!'"[16]

Allan Cunningham, like so many writers of the Romantic Age, felt as though the world of romance had been lost and that he was left with a shallower world of nostalgic fancy. He could suspend his educated disbelief, but unlike James Hogg, he did not insist in co-existing in both worlds at the same time. A brief, ironic footnote at the end of the story demonstrates how clearly his work was a literary construct and not the product of someone who really believed in the stories of the folk. That note reads: "The attested account of this extraordinary vision, as we find it in the pages of several travellers, differs little from the narrative of Eleanor Selby; it is signed by two peasants, Daniel Stricket and William Lancaster, who with about twenty-four other persons witnessed this spectral procession for several hours. Several learned men have written many wise pages, to prove that all this was either real or imaginary - a conclusion to which many will probably be able to come without the aid of learning."[17]

Harriet Martineau, in her condescending manner, was particularly taken with Allan Cunningham as he seemed to represent something of the coming man: "It was quite a sight to see stalwart Allan and his stalwart wife enter a drawing room, and to see how his fine face and head towered above others in expression as much as in altitude. His simple sense and cheerful humour rendered his conversation as lively as that of a wit; and his literary knowledge and taste gave it refinement enough to suit any society . . . Allan Cunningham was one of the hard handed order, privileged to know the realities of practical life, while also a man of letters and a poet, exempt from the deficiencies and foibles of mere literary life. Thus, while a workman, a student and a poet, he was above all a man; and thorough manliness was his dominant characteristic."[18]

"Honest Allan" may have remained one of "the hard handed order", but he had long abandoned the peasant's understanding of the supernatural, if, indeed, he had ever held it. The story of the spectral army came from another country and he had received it not from the mouths of the people but from reading James Clarke's account or one of the later versions. The story was not "copied from recitation", but was very artistically adapted from a story that, at best, might be claimed "as prevalent in the north".

One of the most curious responses to Allan Cunningham's tale was a poem that appeared one month later in *The Lonsdale Magazine and Provincial Repository*. The magazine, published initially in Kirkby Lonsdale and then in Kendal and into the second year of its three year existence, was one of the many that flourished at that time. The August issue included a lengthy article on Dallam Tower with a steel engraving of the same; a rambling, folksy *Letter from the Lakes*, one of a series by the editor, John Briggs; A Sketch of an Angling Expedition in the River Lowther; An Essay on Clothing by the Philosopher; comments on the news by Centinel; a lengthy article by the editor on the indifferent response to the coronation that was observed throughout the locality; a description of an ingenious invention known as The Marine Velocipede; and numerous letters and poetic pieces from correspondents. One such poetic piece was *Soutra Fell: A Visionary Tale of the Scotch Rebellion*. It was signed N.S. and dated from Wensleydale, 21st July, 1821. It was either an immediate response to Allan Cunningham's story or else, by remarkable co-incidence drew on the same intermediary source. The Editor, employing the term *Soutrafell,* provided the following introduction which offered a spectacle of the troops making ever more remarkable evolutions on impossible terrain and managed to see the vision of the spectral army as both optical illusion and a prophecy of Culloden. "Immediately before the last Scottish rebellion, a wonderful phenomenon appeared on the side of Soutrafell, which much astonished the rustics of the vale. On a part of the hill so steep that no human foot could tread, were seen troops, advancing and retreating, horse and foot soldiers performing different military evolutions. The apparition made its appearance just before sunset; and the consternation of the whole country was indescribable. – It was, however, discovered afterwards, to have been the rebels exercising on the western coast of Scotland, whose movements had been reflected by some fine transparent vapour, similar to the Fata Morgana. An intelligent correspondent has finely illustrated this optical illusion in conformity with the popular belief of the lake villagers: - that it really was a presentiment of the Scottish rebellion; and that the horrors of the final battle were depicted in a prophetic manner. – With this explanation, we are confident that the following poem will be read with a degree of interest, by our well informed readers, which ordinary articles are incapable of exciting."[19] The "lake villagers" suggests that the editor did not know the topography of the area. He also seems to have held a despairing view of his other articles.

The part of the 200 line poem that directly concerns us runs as set out below. The underlining indicates words and phrases borrowed almost verbatim from Cunningham's original. Except for some expansion to accommodate the rhyme, this first part of the poem follows the story almost point by point as it is told by Eleanor Selby. Eleanor Selby is not named and her character and presence do not emerge from the poem.

While yet I <u>gazed on Soutra's fell,</u>
A sight <u>appeared</u> (I live and tell!),
<u>Strange, ominous, and yet obscure</u>.
But fate has wrought the vision sure;
Too soon <u>explained</u>, it bodes no good,
But <u>desolation</u> marks, and <u>blood</u>.
<u>I saw at once</u> in full career
Equestrian troops dire-armed appear,
Descending swift the <u>mountain's steep</u>
<u>No earthly steed</u> could footstep keep;
<u>Yet many hundreds</u> were their might.
The glitt'ring <u>stars</u> revealed the sight -
Lightnings, forbidding to conceal,
Burst, 'midst drawn swords and helmets' steel.
On me when burst their dreadful gleam
Faint my sunk soul emits <u>a scream;</u>
<u>And Walter Selby</u> thus began -
<u>(Walter still less, or more than man)</u>
<u>Shouting till every echo</u> round
The mountain nymphs appalled resound:

"Saw ever man such gallant sight?
A thousand steeds on Soutra's height,
Its fierce descent - in martial pride
A thousand riders stem its side.
With managed pride and daring front !
What mortal force shall bide their brunt?
See how they gallop down yon rock! -
What mortal eye can bear the shock? -
The roe of Soutra's lightest bound
Shrinks from the delvy deep profound,
Where not the falcon strains her flight
Above the eagled eyrey's height?
0, for a steed so sure and swift
That might me with these horsemen lift -
These airy knights! My wanton brown,
Famed far and wide for fleet renown.
That darts o'er Derwent like a bird.
Matched with such palfrey and its lord
With wonder froze, its progress slow,
Would think the Derwent ceased to flow.
Ne'er gossamer in summer race
So swift, so sylphy held the chace.
Alarm in every village dwells,
For we all know what this foretells -
A battle lost, a ruined cause.
I heard my father say there was
Then seen on dread Ilelvellyn's side
An armed host like this to ride:
Yet difference marked — beneath a crown
The eye of royalty there frowns;
A regal glaive, like mailed Mars,
That streams a meteor thro' the wars.
Points at their head to Marston Moor,
Soon to be drenched with British gore.
On those whose standard now unfurls.
Menace the coronets of earls;

The wode weird sisters waft each count.
And thanes ride wild at their surmount.
"Now Heav'n's right hand protect us!" cried
The dame that shares stern Wilton's pride;
(Once bride of Grey, for beauty famed.
And oft for boast of lineage named;
But now her blood, by age grown cold,
Yet tumult's in her mortal mould;)
"What evils shall I yet sustain!
Portentous scene — terrific train!
What follows these?" with instant breath
The pedlar cries; "misfortune — death;
To many, misery — death, to some -
Some who are present, sure will come
Death sudden, early - "
"Cease thy croak.
Thou northern raven,"Walter spoke;
"If they are phantoms, let them pass -
For men of mist what care e'er was
In constant souls; if flesh and bone,
(Such by their bearing are alone
This gallant band) as 1 believe.
As such I greet them and receive,
Good gallant soldiers for our King -
For them shall then the welkin ring."
No sooner said, but seized his horn;
Around the mountain echoes borne
Resounds the bugle far and wide.
The spectred steedmen then descried
A mile's full quarter, seem'd to halt;
The youth again, with lips at fault,
Seized mad the ill-directed horn;
His hand the pedlar seized with scorn;
"Unhallowed, dare not thus deride
What heaven's all pregnant powers confide,
For man's instruction is this vision sent;"

(With that the bugle from his hand he rent);
"Young gentleman, be wise, be ruled:"
The lost musician stood in silence school 'd.
The shadowy troops, with sword and lance.
And martial pride elate, advance;
Within a hundred yards they seem;
Terrific now their hauberks gleam -
As dazzling more than mortal sight.
Yet 'midst my trance of wild affright,
I marked them, as along they went.
And living forms as such they meant,
I then imagined that I knew
Of many men in dreadful hue -
Death's pale discolour — doomed the ghost to yield,
Instance exact to perish in the field,
Or in cold blood to wait their doom -
The scaffold's fate — without a tomb;
Pride of the Stuart's strength, nor unallied.
In blood, that Brunswick's happier host defied;
The Maxwells, Boyds, Drummonds, and Gordons famed,
Scots, Ogilvies, Camerons, Foresters, high named!

From this point on the poem departs from the original story and expands Eleanor Selby's premonition of Walter's mortal wounding at Preston into a pre-vision of a gory battle-scene taking place during the forty-five and not the 1715 Jacobite Rebellion. Selby's noble death is imagined in bloody mode:

And, as his faint companions fell, he stood
Erect in arms, and drenched in hostile blood;
At last his prowess sunk - a falchion keen
Light' on his helm, and burst the warrior's screen;
Then, as he fell, a visage too well known
Burst on my view, with death's stern front though prone,
'Twas Selby's self - his dread eidolon's form,
Like Brutus threatened in Philippi's storm,
Selby looked thunderstruck with wild amaze,
But mortal eye could not abide the gaze.

He sunk, forestalled the agonies of death.
And on the ground suspended was his breath;
His horn then sounds the melody of woe.
Some few sad notes that reach the issue's flow.
E'er the seer's hand had checked his purpose bold;
Such notes the furies whilsom did unfold,
When Plato gave to Proserpine his hand.
And Love stood awed, nor dared his force withstand
The tyrant's force - we wait all frenzied o'er.
And Selby yet alive, as dead, deplore.

Worse was to follow as noble houses were destroyed and the Highlands were ravaged:

Feelings of family perpetual burn,
And tears incessant fill the nation's urn.
Such was the scene ere dire Culloden's plain
The northern ravens glutted with the slain;

Civil war soon "spends its savage rage" and reason returns:

- but nobler thoughts evince,
Convinced by reason they salute their Prince,
Convinced, revere the majesty of laws.

The poem concludes with a firm admonition against rebellion.

Then check this brutal rage, while yet there's power.
While yet the monster's something to devour;
While not by treason borne, to ruin hurled.
Stands in its frame the firm majestic world.

I do not know whether Allan Cunningham was flattered by the imitation.

The poem resurfaced in Wilson Armistead's *Tales and Legends of the Lakes*. When Armistead first published this book in 1850 he did so under the mysterious pseudonym Lorenzo Tuvar.. Armistead was from Leeds, an enthusiastic Quaker and senior partner in the family business of mustard manufacturing and oil crushing. He published widely against slavery and his brief obituary described him as an "indefatigable correspondent on behalf of the oppressed".[20] He had "culled" his twenty-seven tales and legends "during visits to those nooks hallowed by poetry, or consecrated by history, which a frequent residence in this locality has afforded him the opportunity of exploring".[21] Fortunately, his excessively flowery text is broken up with numerous ill-assorted and frequently unacknowledged borrowings.

His account of *The Spectre Army: A Weird Tale of Soutra Fell*[xxii] reprinted a disjointed version of George Smith's account in Hutchinson confused with Wordsworth's lines from *An Evening Walk*, and then added a little speculation of his own on the optics of the case: "As instances have frequently occurred in which the forms and action of human beings have been pictured in the clouds, or in vapour, it seems highly probable, on a consideration of all the circumstances of the case, that certain vapours must have hovered round the mountain when these appearances were observed. It is also possible that these vapours may have been impressed with the shadowy forms which seemed to 'imitate humanity,' by a particular operation of the sun's rays, united with some singular, but unknown, refractive combination then taking place in the atmosphere." He then opined that: "These optical illusions, occurring on Soutra Fell, form a subject peculiarly adapted for 'the poet's pen' and are finely illustrated in the following poem." N.S's poem followed in its entirety to be succeeded by James Clarke's words on Mr Wren's apparition, which are attributed to *Clarke's Wonders of the World*. Armistead concluded by quoting M. Haue on the Brocken spectre which he again claimed to have retrieved from *Clarke's Wonders of the World*.

Armistead, recklessly mixing his metaphors, considered that: "A part of the land so famous for beauty and for song, . . ., is one peculiarly favourable to the lovers of old legends; its atmosphere is one in which fancy most delights to soar and to hover, and it contains a mine of materials for romance yet almost untouched."

Allan Cunningham's sophisticated fabrication of a peasant's tradition had travelled a long way. A story which domesticated the tragedy of Scotland's history now served to add "romance" to a land where the tourist finds "hidden, placid, silver lakes, embosomed in the most delicious, fairyland valleys". Armistead was probably very much a man of his time and many a sentimental Victorian might have shared his acceptance of the necessity of commercial progress: "We can even look with complacency upon a railroad, though it intersect, with its prosaic line, the woodlands where we first met the poetry of life – though the very hawthorn, beneath which we breathed our vows of eternal fidelity to her who now lies nightly in our bosom, has been rooted up to prepare a path for it."[23] In his well-intentioned way, Wilson Armistead, lover of the Lakes and collector of folk tales, felt nostalgic about the romantic past.

Chapter Eleven:

John Charles Bristow

N.S. was not the only person in the Lake District to harbour poetic yearnings. John Charles Bristow aspired to cultivate the muse. He sought to do for Ullswater what Walter Scott had done for Loch Katrine: to immortalize the waters in verse and make their shores the haunt of tourists. He declared his ambition boldly as he opened his preface to *Ullsmere: A Poem*. "Yet none of our ancient Poets have noticed their distant beauties. They still remain unsung and unconsecrated in classic story. One of the Scottish Lakes has lately been more fortunate. Yet, who ever heard of Loch Katrine till the Minstrel peopled its lonely isle with phantoms of valour and of beauty?

And sweetly o'er the Lake was heard his strain
"Mix'd with the sounding harp."[1]

Unfortunately, Bristow lacked Scott's poetic ability.

He did, however, live in a house that was peculiarly sympathetic to the muse. In 1819, the artist William Green of Ambleside had been enchanted by the property: "Near the foot of Ulls Water, a quarter of a mile from the inn at Powley Bridge, stands Ewesmere. It was built by Thomas Clarkson, Esq., whose publications on the slave trade are well known. Ewesmere was purchased by the Earl of Lonsdale from Mr. Clarkson. It commands a view of the lower reach of the lake, which, on all hands, rich and splendid in its woods, inclosures, and scatterings of trees, is additionally valuable from its beautifully embayed shores. Hallin Fell from no situation displays so fine a line as from Ewesmere, and the mountains of Martindale and Glenridden, (amongst which, Place Fell and Helvellen rise high above the rest), by their aerial receding, give to this scene an uncommon degree of interest; and observed under the effects of a thin celestial azure, it will appear like enchantment, rather than reality."[2]

Bristow quoted Green's adulatory words in the notes to his poem. He had purchased Eusemere Hill in 1824 from the Earl of Lonsdale who had bought it twenty years earlier when Clarkson left to reinvigorate the anti-slavery campaign. This prosperous gentleman, whose father had been a civil servant in Bengal, caused the house to be "much enlarged and beautified",[3] felled and planted trees to improve the prospect and was noted for keeping "a Sloop on the Lake",[4] a sure indication of his affluence.

Thomas Clarkson had built a modest house on the thirty-five acre property in 1796 when he married Catherine Buck, and, when, after years of vigorous campaigning, he chose to retire to a secluded life in order to write a book on Quakerism. Catherine, in the days when she lived in Bury St. Edmunds, had been a friend of Dorothy Wordsworth and a strong friendship and mutual admiration developed between the Clarksons and the Wordsworths. Dorothy stayed at Eusemere for three weeks in the winter of 1801 and three years later, on June 4th, 1804, she wrote to Catherine of her feelings about the house: "I have always felt at Eusemere, when I have entered one of the rooms without thinking what was to be seen – particularly when I had been there only a short time – that there was some thing unearthly in the prospect. So it seemed the last time. I was entirely occupied in the thought of you, and past times, when I went into the drawing room; and, indeed, I think that I never before saw any sight that was so purely, so *heavenly* beautiful."[5]

Another time, William Wordsworth had arrived at Eusemere late on Wednesday, 14th April, 1802, and he and Dorothy made a delayed departure for home the following day: "It was a threatening, misty morning, but mild. We set off after dinner from Eusemere. Mrs Clarkson went a short way with us, but turned back. The wind was furious, and we thought we must have returned. We first rested in the large boat-house, then under a furze bush opposite Mr Clarkson's. Saw the plough going in the field. The wind seized our breath. The Lake was rough. There was a boat by itself floating in the middle of the bay below Water Millock. We rested again in Water Millock Lane. The hawthorns are black and green, the birches, here and there, greenish, but there is yet more of purple to be seen on the twigs. We got over into a field to avoid some cows – people working. A few primroses by the roadside – woodsorrel flower, the anemone, scentless violets, strawberries, and that starry yellow flower which Mrs C. calls pilewort. When we were in the woods beyond Gowbarrow Park we saw a few daffodils close to the waterside. We fancied that the lake had floated the seeds ashore, and that the little colony had so sprung up. But as we went along there were more and yet more; and, at last, under the boughs of the trees, we saw that there was a long belt of them along the shore, and the breadth of a country turnpike road. I never saw daffodils so beautiful. They grew among the mossy stones as on a pillow for weariness; and the rest tossed and reeled and danced, and seemed as if they verily laughed with the wind that blew upon them over the lake; they looked so gay, ever glancing, ever changing. The wind blew directly over the lake to them. There was here and there a little knot, and a few stragglers a few yards higher up; but they were so few as not to disturb the simplicity, unity, and life of that busy highway."[6]

Dorothy Wordsworth's descriptions are fertile with that precise, individual detail, which William felt to be the essence of his poetry. A page of her observant notation is worth far more than all of the two hundred and fifty pages of Bristow's six ambitious cantos:

> In glowing Summer and in Winter hoar
> How much I love to tread my charming shore
> Unwearied, mutt'ring my wild fancies o'er and o'er!
> There when the earliest primrose 'gins to peep,
> And from the rippled bosom of the deep
> At the first spring-fly when the trout is seen to leap:[7]

The lines that concern us occur half way through the poem after the stag has been driven into the lake and has petitioned for its life; after the hermit has blessed the union of the rustic beauty and the heir to the land; before the walking party has been lost in the mists on Fairfield and before they have partaken of a picnic on the sloop in the middle of Ullswater; and after and before the infinite scenic pleasures of Ullswater have been celebrated, and its shores have been peopled with oreads, dryads and nymphs readily transported from the warmer shores of ancient Greece; and after due obeisance has been paid to Lord Lyulph and other local gentry. Lyulph's Tower, which can be seen from Eusemere Hill, is a centrepiece of the poem, and Bristow quotes the passage from Wordsworth's *Guide* concerning the mist and the apparently visionary appearance of a fairy palace reflected in the waters. Prompted by Wordsworth, the incautious Bristow created a faery world in which his avid imagination wove complex tales among the bare hills and over the cold waters. And, then, at the conclusion of the poem, with one wave of his poetic wand, he dismissed the beguiling vision:

> Lo! with the Castle, Chapel, Banquet-hall,
> The Knights, the Dames, the Minstrels, vanish all!
> All where the little mimic Towers arise
> That charm afar th' approaching Traveller's eyes.

In the third canto, "The Vision: Part III: The Capture i: Matterdale" he described the final stages of a day-long medieval tournament: "The sports protracted to the setting sun". Then, as Lord Lyulph sat down at table, there was a disturbance:

> Where, scarcely seated, when they start aghast,
> To hear its roaring voice the helm-wind raise,
> And at the Beacon, too, all in a blaze,
> That seems to kindle at the furious blast —
> And when a horseman, rushing through the crowd,
> Approach'd Lord Lyulph, and exclaimed aloud, -
> "Arm, arm, Lord Lyulph, arm, and speed, this hour,
> With all your force, if you would save your Tower,
> 'Gainst which Lord Ronald marches, of his clan so proud!"[8]

Lord Lyulph is more than ready to rise to the challenge:

> "I 'll halt him in that march, th' audacious Scot!"
> Lord Lyulph in his ire, indignant, cried,
> "And humble to the dust, I ween, his pride!
> And oh! let not the feats, Phorne, be forgot,
> Which on this glorious day thou hast achieved:
> The time is come, or I am much deceived,
> When I will settle this long Border strife,
> And see this vaunting Chieftain of his life
> Or of his vain aspiring hopes at length bereav'd!

The beacons are fired as an alarm and to call his supporters together,

much like the fiery cross in *The Lady of the Lake.* Our poet invokes the military prowess of these parts calling on the memory of Pendragon and Penrith, Brougham and Dacre to enhance his theme.
He thinks of:

> Th' appalling apparitions now of days by-gone: -
> Such as could sway the English Baron Old,
> Or Castle of Otranto scarce less dread,

And then, he recalls Anne Radcliffe's imaginative horrors as she traversed the wild lands beyond Greystoke Castle:

> Or the Enchantress who such terrors spread
> The Mysteries of Udolpho to unfold; —
> Or such as o'er the fancy may prevail
> Close on the moorish tract of Matterdale, —
> The Weird Sisters on the blasted heath,
> The solemn greeting of the great Macbeth, —
> The Voices that pronounc'd the awful "Hail! hail! hail!

J.C. Bristow raises up a spectral figure in the moonlight, along with all the cluttered ragbag of gothic fantasy: a dreary desert, freezing blood, a glooming and fiend-like figure and a meteor, which may well be an echo of George Smith's attempt at a scientific explanation. Bristow's notes suggest he was acquainted with Hutchinson, as well as Nicolson and Burn, Clarke, Green and Wordsworth.

> As there, the ominous rising moon between,
> Forth stalking to his fancy, as it stood
> (Enough indeed to freeze its poet's blood!)
> The Spectre of the dreary desert scene
> Upon his darken'd volume seem'd to cast
> Its shadow, as its glooming figure pass'd —
> With fiend-like glances that like meteors glow
> Beneath its low'ring brow, — and locks of snow
> Uplifted with its mantle, in the whistling blast!

That fiend-like spectre is no other than the spirit of Border strife that troubled these areas in former times and had so recently been embodied in the form of Bonnie Prince Charlie.

> The same malignant Spirit from the North,
> That e'er across the fated Border led

The forces, which such desolation spread,
Upon the South with fury to pour forth:
The same, that moves the troops round Souter Fell,
Beneath the influence of such potent spell,
"Careering there so fast along its side,
Where mortal horseman ne'er" indeed "might ride,"
The visions of which many at each time could tell: —
The visions, on midsummer's glowing eve,
With which, from Blakehills and from Wilton Hill,
That Spirit could so many gazers fill, —
Twice, at the very self-same hour could weave —
Erst, the approaching foray to portray,
Could put the charging squadrons in array —
The same, "far on the future battle-heath,"
That, like a vulture, snuff'd the ranks of death —

The blast which o'er that desert 'gan to howl,
And fiercer, on the mountain-tops so high,
Lit up the blazing signals in the sky,
On which the heavens cast their deepest scowl: —
When, at its beck'ning, issued from a den
An ambush'd armed band of plaided men,
Who, as in haste they strode across the wild
And through an opening 'twixt the hills defiled,
Following their phantom leader, disappear'd again

As quickly. In your absence to surprise
Your stronghold, as your evil spirit led,
Who, in the Druid, on such errand sped, —
Presiding o'er your happier destinies,
Lo ! then the guardian genius of your race,
Lord Lyulph, in its emblem o'er that place,
Seem'd hovering in the brilliant twinkling star,
With thy "jagg'd summit, Saddleback," afar,
There, where from Holy Land th' illustrious name
Of Acre bearing (as we may areed

Upon the page of venerable Bede),
Transmitted from that realm of pious fame,
For his achievements by the valiant knight,
First of the race, to its distinguish'd site, —
There cloister, well as castle, to mine eye,
Shake off the dust of hoar antiquity,
In feudal glory and monastic splendour bright.

And so the verse continues with smoke and mirrors being substituted for simple narration and a general sense of Lord Ronald's attack embodying all the Scottish depredations across the Border and the English defence comprising all the stalwart Christian forces from Lord Dacre on to Lord Lyulph and, no doubt, his descendant, the Duke of Norfolk, whose mystical folly, which was visible from Eusemire Hill, had served to inspire our poet's song.

Contrived and confused as these stanzas might be, they are an interesting presentation of the mental furniture of a well-to-do, articulate, aspiring, literate country gentleman of the time.

Seventy years after Walpole published T*he Castle of Otranto* and forty years after Ann Radcliffe and Monk Lewis terrified their readers, the Gothic is still a potent force. The spectral army is no longer a unsettling narrative requiring explanation or a folk belief that disturbed the rational order of the educated bourgeoisie. It has become another fiction alongside Shakespeare's witches and the imaginings of Walpole, Radcliffe and Scott.

In the notes, the full account of the spectral army is quoted verbatim from Clarke's *Survey*, including James Clarke's brief speculations on its cause. Bristow's imaginative machinery has the troops being moved around Souther Fell by the "malignant Spirit of the North". He borrows Scott's words from *The Lady of the Lake* and has the troops "careering" rather than marching and, with the inclusion of a confirmatory, emphatic foot, he contrives to change Scott's tetrameter into an iambic pentameter:

"Where mortal horsemen ne'er" indeed "might ride."

The Spirit has deluded the visions of the many gazers from Blakehills and Wilton Hill, and, even though, "midsummer's glowing eve" may have been a contributory factor the vision of "the charging squadrons" has been raised "the approaching foray to portray." It has become a portent of the Jacobite invasion.

The whole passage is steeped in the literature of the Gothic. In addition to the quotations from Scott's *The Lady of the Lake* – the mortal horsemen and the hermit's ominous "future battle heath" and the obvious invocation of Shakespeare's *Macbeth*, (a key Gothic text, which had drawn on Highland legend and folklore well before James Macpherson and Walter Scott) there are acknowledged and unacknowledged quotes from several other revealing sources. "Moorish tract" had been used by Boswell in describing the landscape of Skye[9] in *The Journal of a Tour to the Hebrides* in which Johnson denounced the authenticity of Ossian as "as gross an imposition as ever the world was troubled with". Forty years later, in *Guy Mannering*, Scott described the Waste of Cumberland, the area beyond Gilsland, as "a moorish tract";[10] and the phrase was illustrated by Copley Fielding in Scott's *Collected Works*.

Ossian himself is there, of course. James Macpherson in one of his earliest poems, *Fingal*, wrote of the appearance of spirits in words which Hugh Blair characterized as "full of that awful and solemn sublimity"[11] and Bristow has availed himself of a phrase from the poem to lend added atmosphere: "Like the darkened moon he retired, in the midst of the whistling blast".[12] The phrase, "the whistling blast" was not original to Ossian, but Macpherson used it several times and made it his own.

Bristow's most interesting borrowing in this process, whereby an author absorbs and reflects the patterns of thought and feeling current in his day, was from the poetry of the melancholic William Collins. "Brew the stormful day" comes from *An Ode on the Popular Superstitions of the Highlands of Scotland* which Collins had addressed to a friend, John Home, before his return to the Highlands. The poem was written within five years of the Jacobite Rebellion, when Collins had already written his *Ode on Duty*, "How sleep the Brave/ Who sink to rest", and also an *Ode to Mercy,* which questioned the treatment of the Scottish captives. Opposing itself to the prevailing anti-Scottish sentiment of the day, *Popular Superstitions* urged Home to look to the lore and legend of his native country for poetic themes. Home knew the young James Macpherson and it was on his instigation that Macpherson published the first of the Ossian poems in 1762. Collins's poem was not printed in his lifetime, but lay in manuscript until it was rediscovered and published in

The frontispiece to Ulsmere.
The view of Ullswater from Ewesmere

1788, when it exercised a significant influence on the eighteen-year old Wordsworth, amongst many others.[13]

Ulsmere received two admonitory reviews. *Fraser's Magazine* softened its criticism with admiration for the elegance of the volume and the attractiveness of the frontispiece: "An elegant book we say; and it would not be giving much praise to the work, were we to say, an elegant poem also - something more than elegance being needed by readers of verse now-a-days. The Spenserian stanza, however, is used with some effect; though the writer has much to learn in its management, and, we are afraid, is somewhat deficient in poetic spirit. An engraving by Starling, from a picture by William Westall, embellishes the volume by way of frontispiece; and, were it not for the previous labours of Wilson and Wordsworth, it might altogether form an acceptable present. As it is, it seems not only o'er heavy in itself, but, on account of extrinsic circumstances, wearisome as a thrice told tale."[14] *The Metropolitan* was more severe in its strictures: "We have here a highly and gracefully decorated waxen image of poetry with the form, the colour, and all the splendid accessories, but the life and the spirit are not . . . it is a work of that pleasant mediocrity that hundreds of the present day could equal, thousands would praise, but few read through without feeling the utmost weariness. . . . Oreads, Dryads, and Naiads, are not graceful upon the shores of an English lake; and the author appeals so frequently to the Muses that it would seem that he has but little influence with those very shy personages. Then to the mixture of the decidedly familiar with the attempted sublime we strongly object, because the familiarity appears a little vulgar, and the sublime has unfortunately taken its next step into the ridiculous. The anonymous author has not succeeded in 'drinking deep at the Pierian spring', we would, therefore, recommend him to try to get a draught of the pure liquid of the Ullswater, suppress his present poem, and then begin again - and, in his next attempt, not marry 'in immortal verse' obsolete English with modern Latin, nor jumble 'Thamis' 'eftsoones,' 'sithens,' and 'ogres,' together. We would not have the author despair; let him make another essay, for he has already written some pretty lines, and with a little more practice, he may make, to use his own language, 'his chums in Cheapside stare.' "[15]

Unabashed, Bristow appears to have taken "a little more practice" because in 1848 there appeared a six volume edition of his *Poetical Works* and in 1851 *The Publishers' circular and general record of British and foreign Literature* carried the following announcement: "THE POETICAL WORKS of JOHN CHARLES BRISTOW, Esq. With Illustrations by WILLIAM WESTALL, A.R.A. Containing Travels, Dramas, Tales, and Miscellaneous Poems. 5 vols, post 8vo. 30s. cloth. Samuel Hodgson, Wimpole Street; and all Booksellers."[16] Like *Ullsmere* both sets were probably vanity publications – there are no other titles attributed to Samuel Hodgson of Wimpole Street and no listing of him as a publisher.[17] A brief notice in *The International Magazine of Literature, Art and Science* seems to promise little success: "NEW POET, John Charles Bristow, of whom no one ever heard before, has come out in London with five thick volumes of his 'Works'."[18]

The brief statistics of Bristow's life are found in the memorial plaque on the north wall of the chancel in Barton Church: "To the memory of Sophia Anne eldest daughter of John Richardson Esqre of Calcutta who was born Feb: 10th 1793 married to John Charles Bristow Esqre March 30th 1812 and died November 16th 1836 leaving five sons and seven daughters with their father to lament the irreparable loss of her who in life fulfilled every duty of Christian Faith and Charity. Also John Charles

Bristow Esqre husband of the above who died 18th of September 1856 aged 72 and whose mortal remains opposite this tablet and in the Chancel of this Church are deposited."

The local newspapers have preserved one brief, sensational incident, worthy of his gothic fancy. While our musing poet gazed romantically over the waters of his beloved lake from his study window, a real-life romance was taking place on his doorstep. "On Friday last, Lieutenant LEESON, nephew to Lord MILLTOWN, and the youngest son of the late Hon. Mr. LEESON, of the Thorn, near Penrith, Cumberland, who is on leave of absence from his regiment, which is in the East Indies, eloped to Gretna Green, with Miss. Laura Bristow, a daughter of John Charles Bristow, Esq., of Eusemere-hill, Ullswater, Westmoreland, and over whose head 16 summers have scarcely flown.

"It appears that this young and gallant officer had laid his plans for the accomplishment of the siege of Eusemere-hill with great skill. Wednesday week was the day in which he intended to have stormed the works, but the garrison having doubtless, been apprised of his intentions, manned the walls so well all that day and night, that the besieger thought it right not to commence operations at that time. Next morning, however, the besieged, thinking all safe, made a sortie, and set sail up the lake of Ullswater to Patterdale, taking the young lady with them. "The besieger was not aware of this, and the besieged had nearly made a safe retreat into the garrison again, but one of the gallant officer's sharpshooters lay concealed among the brushwood, who seized the fair prize, and away she was taken to her betrothed, who was waiting at a short distance with a coach and four, and off the officer went with his booty. Pursuit was in vain; the fugitives soon passed over the six and twenty miles to Gretna Green, were married, and, it is said they contemplate a speedy embarkation for India; but, it is expected that a reconciliation with her family will first take place, for that which is passed cannot be recalled."[19] Here, indeed, with its aristocratic connection, was a romance worthy of the pen of John Charles Bristow.

Bristow's feelings about the landscape were probably representative of his class, education and times, but it was William Wordsworth's poem, prompted by those blustery daffodils on the shores of Ullswater, that made Ullswater as popular as Loch Katrine.

Chapter Twelve:

White, Gresley and Soane

John Pagen White, who spent his adult life as a surgeon in Liverpool, was another Lakeland enthusiast and amateur poet. His *Lays and Legends of English Lakeland with Copious Notes,* which was published in 1873, had been prepared by his sister after his death in 1868. She apologised for the notes which "may by some be thought unnecessarily long, and in many instances they undoubtedly are very discursive", but commended the book as having occupied "for years the leisure hours of a busy professional life".[1]

Pagen White viewed Lakeland historically, seeing it as long the abode of warfare and feuding "conducted with a rancour and cruelty which spared neither age or sex". It was a place where, in conformity with the racial stereotypes of the time, he felt "the dwellers in the unsettled districts lying along the English and Scottish borders, being originally derived from the same Celtic stock, had been gradually and progressively influenced as a race by the admixture of Saxon and Danish blood into the population; and although much of the Celtic character was thereby lost, they seem to have retained in their mountains and forests much of the spirit, and many of the laws and manners, of the ancient Britons". If the past had been characterised by violence and a rich culture, the Lakeland he knew was untroubled, the home of peace and prosperity. "The mountains look down upon a peaceful domain, the valleys, everywhere the abode of quiet and security, yield their rich pasturage to the herds, or their corn-fields redden, though coyly, to the harvest; and the population, much of it rooted in the soil, and attached by hereditary ties to the same plots of ancestral ground in many instances for six or seven hundred years, is independent, prosperous, and happy."[2]

He, the dedicated surgeon in industrial Liverpool, characterized himself as a border raider shaping tales and superstitions to the needs of his pen, but doing them no harm in the process: "And if in a spirit somewhat more akin to the moss-trooping Borderer of an earlier time, an occasional intruder has scoured the vales in search of their traditions; and in the pursuit of these has ransacked their annals, plundered their guides, and levied a sort of black-mail upon even casual and anonymous contributors to their history; it may in some degree extenuate the offence to remember that such literary free-booting makes no one poorer for what it takes away; and that the opima spolia (the plundered weaponry) of the adventurer are only so much gathered to be distributed again. More especially to the Notes which constitute so large a portion of the present Volume may this remark be applied. Scenery long outlasts all traditional and historical associations. To revive these among their ancient haunts, and to awaken yet another interest in this land of beauty, has been the aim and end of this modern raid into the valleys of the North, and the regions that own the sovereignty of the 'mighty Helvellyn'." John Pagen White in his lays certainly behaved like a Border reiver taking what he wanted and using it in any way he saw fit. Those "discursive . . . unnecessarily long" notes were a different matter. The book remains a useful, if unreliable, source of the folklore of the Lake District.

He was born in Whitehaven in 1812 and was apprenticed as a surgeon in Liverpool when he was sixteen. Ten years later he became a member of the College of Surgeons, and after a further thirty years of medical practice in Liverpool, "where he was "greatly valued in his professional, esteemed in his social, and beloved in his more intimate and domestic relations", he became a fellow of the college. He hoped "to acquire such a modest competency as might enable him to settle down in retirement amid the scenery and the people he loved so well. This object was all but obtained when an affection of the throat, fatally aggravated by exposure, incurred in the over-anxious discharge of a professional duty, brought his useful and (to many) invaluable life to a close on the 27th of September, 1868."[3]

Pagen White allowed himself considerable freedom with the contents of his poeticising, and, although the long notes attached to his versifications indicate a respect for his original material, his powers of invention allowed little room for authenticity. The story of the spectral army was used by White in a nicely turned ballad on Sir Lancelot Threlkeld. The poem incorporated some details of the historical life of the hero together with aspects of the story of Sir Henry Clifford brought up as a shepherd boy on Carrock Fell. White meshed the fourteenth century Wordsworth had used in *Song at the Feast of Brougham Castle* with the eighteenth century reports made by George Smith and James Clarke.

In this treatment, the noble Sir Lancelot, step-father to the shepherd lord, became an Arthurian figure returning to save his people and riding with his army across the sides of Souther Fell. The exiled shepherd lord was summoned by the new king to take up his aristocratic and military duties and, at his departure, Clifford, who was reputed to have learnt astronomy, if not astrology, on the Northern Fells, prophesied to the aged knight:

"If ever a Knight might revisit this earth — . . ."
Said the Clifford — "When troubles and wars have birth.
Thou never shalt fail from Threlkeld's hearth!"

The old knight and the young lord parted on Souther Fell, and, shortly afterwards, Sir Lancelot died. At some unspecified time in the future, the widows in Threlkeld Hall were aware of the ghostly presence of the knight and the farmers and peasants told them how they had seen him in charge of a spectral army on the side of Souther Fell. This is the poem:

SIR LANCELOT THRELKELD.

The widows were sitting in Threlkeld Hall;
The corn stood green on Midsummer-day;
Their little grand-children were tossing the ball;
And the farmers leaned over the garden wall;
And the widows were spinning the eve away.

They busily talk'd of the days long gone,

While the corn stood green on Midsummer-day;
How old Sir Lancelot's armour had shone
On the panels of oak by the broad hearth-stone,
Where the widows sat spinning that eve away.

For, Threlkeld Hall of his mansions three —
Where the corn stood green on Midsummer-day —
Was his noblest house; and a stately tree
Was the good old Knight, and of high degree;
And a braver rode never in battle array.

Now peaceful farmers think of their corn —
The corn so green on Midsummer-day —
Where once, at the blast of Sir Lancelot's horn,
His horsemen all mustered, his banner was borne;
And he went like a Chief in his pride to the fray.

And there the good Clifford, the Shepherd-Lord,
When the corn stood green on Midsummer-day,
Sat, humbly clad, at Sir Lancelot's board;
And tended the flocks, while rusted his sword
In the hall where the widows were spinning away;

Till the new King called him back to his own —
When the corn stood green on Midsummer-day —
To his honours and name of high renown;
When Sir Lancelot old and feeble had grown;
From his rude shepherd-life called Lord Clifford away.

And sad was that morrow in Threlkeld Hall —
And the corn was green on that Midsummer-day —
When the Clifford stood ready to part from all;
And his shepherd's staff was hung up on the wall,
In that room where the widows sat spinning away.

And Sir Lancelot mounted, and called his men —

While the corn stood green on Midsummer-day —
And he gazed on Lord Clifford again and again;
And Sir Lancelot rode with him over the plain;
And at length with strong effort his silence gave way.

"I am old," Sir Lancelot said; "and I know —
When the corn stands green on Midsummer-day —
There will wars arise, and I shall be low,
Who ever was ready to arm and go!" —
For he loved the war tramp and the martial array.

"If ever a Knight might revisit this earth —
While the corn stands green on Midsummer-day" —
Said the Clifford — "When troubles and wars have birth.
Thou never shalt fail from Threlkeld's hearth!"
From that hearth where the widows were spinning away.

And so, along Souter-fell side they press'd —
While the corn stood green on Midsummer-day, —
And then they parted — to east and to west —
And Sir Lancelot came and was laid to his rest.
Said the widows there spinning the eve away.

And the Shepherd had power in unwritten lore:
The corn stands green on Midsummer-day:
And although the Knight's coffin his banner hangs o'er,
Sir Lancelot yet can tread this floor;
Said the widows there spinning the eve away. —

Thus gossip'd the widows in Threlkeld Hall,
While the corn stood green on Midsummer-day:
When the sound of a footstep was heard to fall,
And an arm'd shadow pass'd over the wall —
Of a Knight with his plume and in martial array.

With a growl the fierce dogs slunk behind the huge chair,

While the corn stood green on that Midsummer- day;
And the widows stopt spinning; and each was aware
Of a tread to the porch, and Sir Lancelot there —
And a stir as of horsemen all riding away.

They turned their dim eyes to the lattice to gaze —
While the corn stood green on Midsummer-day —
But before their old limbs they could feebly raise,
The horsemen and horses were far on the ways —
From the Hall, where the widows were spinning away.

And far along Souter-fell side they strode,
While the com stood green on that Midsummer-day.
And the brave old Knight on his charger rode,
As he wont to ride from his old abode.
With his sword by his side and in martial array.

Like a chief he galloped before and behind —
While the corn stood green on Midsummer-day —
To the marshalled ranks he waved, and signed;
And his banner streamed out on the evening wind,
As they rode along Souter-fell side away.

And to many an eye was revealed the sight.
While the corn stood green that Midsummer-day;
As Sir Lancelot Threlkeld the ancient Knight
With all his horsemen went over the height:
O'er the steep mountain summit went riding away.

And then as the twilight closed over the dell —
Where the corn stood green that Midsummer-day —
Came the farmers and peasants all flocking to tell
How Sir Lancelot's troop had gone over the fell!
And the widows sat listening, and spinning away.

And the widows looked mournfully round the old hall;

And the corn stood green on Midsummer-day;
"He is come at the good Lord Clifford's call!
He is up for the King, with his warriors all!" —
Said the widows there spinning the eve away.

"There is evil to happen, and war is at hand —
Where the corn stands green this Midsummer-day —
Or rebels are plotting to waste the land;
Or he never would come with his armed band" —
Said the widows there spinning the eve away.

"Our old men sleep in the grave. They cease:
While the corn stands green on Midsummer-day —
They rest, though troubles on earth increase;
And soon may Sir Lancelot's soul have peace!"
Sighed the widows while spinning the eve away.

" But this was the Promise the Shepherd-Lord —
When the corn stood green that Midsummer-day —
Gave, parting from Threlkeld's hearth and board,
To the brave old Knight — and he keeps his word!"
Said the widows all putting their spinning away.[4]

In White's hands the spectral army has been displaced over three centuries to the time of Henry VII (and one day since it is seen on Midsummer Day rather than the evening before) and the vision is given to the widows of Threlkeld Hall, which lay at the foot of Blencathra and out of sight of Souther Fell. Today, what little remains of the medieval hall has been incorporated into a farmhouse that sits on the edge of Keswick Golf Course.

At the climax of his poem White retained and strengthened one of the most striking images of the original accounts, those officers, who, in George Smith's words, "would quit rank, and seem to stand in a fronting posture, as if he was observing and regulating the order of their march, or taking account of their numbers, and, after some time, appeared to return full gallop to the station he had left, which they never failed to do as often as they quitted their lines; and the figure that did so was generally one of the middlemost men in the rank."

> And the brave old Knight on his charger rode,
> As he wont to ride from his old abode.
> With his sword by his side and in martial array.
> Like a chief he galloped before and behind — . . .
> To the marshalled ranks he waved, and signed;
> And his banner streamed out on the evening wind,

That streaming banner is part of the Gothic vision Wordsworth rejected.

Pagen White's extensive notes[5] tell the story of the Clifford family from the days of the conquest. After his father, John, the black-faced Clifford, had been killed when the Yorkists triumphed at the Battle of Towton in 1461, the seven-year-old Henry Clifford sought refuge with a shepherd family in Yorkshire. His mother married Lancelot Threlkeld even though he was a Yorkist. Henry's identity was discovered and he was moved for his safety to the Cumberland fells north of Threlkeld. His fortunes and those of the House of Clifford were restored in 1485 with the Lancaster victory at Bosworth Field.

William Wordsworth in *The Waggoner* gave a succinct account of Clifford's story:

> And see beyond that hamlet small,
> The ruined towers of Threlkeld Hall,
> Lurking in a double shade.
> By trees and lingering twilight made!
> There at Blencathara's rugged feet,
> Sir Lancelot gave a safe retreat
> To noble Clifford; from annoy
> Concealed the persecuted boy.
> Well pleased in rustic garb to feed
> His flock, and pipe on shepherd's reed,
> Among this multitude of hills,
> Crags, woodlands, waterfalls, and rills.[6]

Wordsworth saw Clifford as an exemplar of the moral worth of a natural education. Hartley Coleridge, in a remarkably impassioned plea on behalf of peasant values, defended the quality of Clifford's education:

"It is asserted that at the period of his restoration he was almost wholly illiterate. Very probably he was so; but it does not follow that he was *ignorant*. He might know many things well worth knowing, without being able to write his name. He might learn a great deal of Astronomy by patient observation. He might know where each native flower of the hills was grown, what real qualities it possessed, and what occult powers the fancy, the fears, or the wishes of men had ascribed to it. The haunts, habits, and instincts of animals, the notes of birds, and their wondrous architecture, were to him instead of books; but above all, he learned to know something of what man is, in that condition to which the greater number of men are born, and to know himself better than he could have done in his hereditary sphere."[7]

Pagen White, who romantically made raids on Border lore, transformed this visionary philosophy into a rural nostalgia which he garnished with a touch of the occult: "The Shepherd Lord, came forth upon the world with a mind in advance of the age, a spirit of knowledge, of goodness, and of light, such as was rarely seen in that time of ignorance and superstition; averse to courtly pomp, delighting himself chiefly in country pursuits, in re-pairing his castles, and in learned intercourse with such literate persons as he could find. He was the wisest of his race, and falling upon more peaceful times, was enabled to indulge in the studies and thoughtful dispositions which his early misfortunes had induced and cultured. Throughout a long life he remained one, whose precious example, though it had but few imitators, and even exposed him to be regarded with dread, as dealing in the occult sciences, and leagued with beings that mortal man ought not to know, was nevertheless so far appreciated by his less enlightened countrymen, that his image was always linked in their memories and affections with whatever was great and ennobling, and caused him to be recorded to this, our day, by the endearing appellation of the 'Good Lord Clifford'."[8]

The notes on the spectral army, extensive and detailed as they are, subtly distort the story and the landscape so as to render the story a superstitious folly and clearly explain it as the consequence of mirages. White suggested that a tradition "had long been current in the neighbourhood" and paraphrased Smith's remarks to colour in a picture of "superstitious fear and wonder". The unnamed Smith became only one of many who purposely went to examine the witnesses and he did so, it appears, as a contributor to Hutchinson's *History,* which was published almost fifty years after his visit.

"About three miles from Threlkeld, the ancient home of Sir Lancelot Threlkeld and his noble step-son, stands as the eastern barrier of the Blencathra group of mountains, that part of it which is known as Souter Fell; whose irregular and precipitous summit, everywhere difficult of access, rises to a height of about 2,500 feet. It is on the south of Bowscale Fell, leaning westward from the Hesketh and Carlisle road, by which its eastern base is skirted. This mountain is celebrated in local history as having several times been the scene of those singular aerial phenomena known as mirages. A tradition of a spectral army having been seen marching over these mountains had long been current in the neighbourhood, and this remarkable exhibition was actually witnessed in the years 1735, 1737, and 1745, by several independent parties of the dalesmen; and, as may well be supposed, excited much attention in the north of England, and long formed a subject of superstitious fear and wonder in the surrounding district. A sight so strange as that of the whole side of the mountain appearing covered with troops, both infantry and cavalry, who after going through regular military evolutions for more than an hour, defiled off in good order, and disappeared over a precipitous ridge on the summit, was sure to be the subject of much speculation and enquiry. Many persons at a distance hearing of the phenomenon, proceeded to the places where it was witnessed, purposely to examine the spectators who asserted the fact, and who continued positive in their assertions as to the appearances. Amongst others, one of the contributors to Hutchinson's *History of Cumberland* went to inquire into the subject; and the following is the account of the information he obtained, given in his own words."

Smith's full account followed ending with his conclusion as to the fantastical nature of the phenomenon: "This whole story has so much the air of a romance, that it seemed fitter for Amadis dc Gaul, or Glenvilles System of Witches, than the repository of the learned; but as the country was full of it, I only give it verbatim from the original relation of a people, that could have no end in imposing upon their fellow-creatures, and are of good repute in the place where they live." Pagen White did not include

Smith's reasoning as to the difficulties of providing a physical, in his case, meteoric, explanation.

He then printed James Clarke's account at a similar length and commended him as "the intelligent author of *The Survey of the Lakes*". Sir David Brewster was also introduced and allowed to pronounce authoritatively on the subject. White then provided a contemporary consensus on the matter, without venturing into any of the contradictions or implausibilities in the account: "The accepted explanation of this appearance now is, that on the evenings in question, the rebel Scotch troops were performing their military evolutions on the west coast of Scotland, and that by some peculiar refraction of the atmosphere their movements were reflected on this mountain." He supported this assertion by citing an impressive list of other reports of spectral armies, as though the military element was a necessary rather than an incidental part of the optical illusion: "Phenomena similar to these were seen near Stockton-on-the-Forest, in Yorkshire, in 1792; in Harrogate, on June 28th, 1812; and near St. Neot's, in Huntingdonshire, in 1820. Tradition also records the tramp of armies over Helvellyn, on the eve of the battle of Marston Moor. To these may be added the appearance of the Spectre of the Brocken in the Hartz Mountains; and an instance mentioned by Hutchinson, that in the spring of the year 1707, early on a serene still morning, two persons who were walking from one village to another in Leicestershire, observed a like appearance of an army marching along, till, going behind a great hill, it disappeared. The forms of pikes and carbines were distinguishable, the march was not entirely in one direction, but was at first like the junction of two armies, and the meeting of generals.

"Aerial phenomena of a like nature are recorded by Livy, Josephus, and Suetonius; and a passage in Sacred History seems to refer to a similar circumstance. See Judges ix. 36."

He then hinted at a metaphysical explanation whose reference to the much later wars with France and America seems anachronistic: "Many in this country considered these appearances as ominous of the great waste of blood spilt by Britain in her wars with America and France." And then, to conclude with a fitting poetic resonance, he quoted Casca's famous words from Julius Caesar about prodigies being "portentous things".

In White's hands the spectral army has become a curious legend, the idle amusement of an evening after work, a local colour to add to the charm of a landscape he was forced to love from a distance.

The *Lays and Legends of English Lakeland* consisted of some three dozen poems, including one called *Threlkeld Tarn or Truth from the Deep* that celebrated the stars to be seen in the depths of Scales Tarn, and another that painted *Lord Derwentwater's Lights* in spectacular Technicolor:

> Through all the arches of the sky
> The Northern Lights streamed broad and high.
> Wide o'er the realm their shields of light
> Flung reddening tumults on the night.
>
> Then dalesmen hoar and matrons old
> Look'd out in fear from farm and fold:
> Look'd out o'er Derwent, mere and isle,
> On Skiddaw's mounds, Blencathra's pile.
>
> They saw the vast ensanguined scroll
> Across the stars the streamers roll:
> The Derwent stain'd with crimson dyes:
> And portents wandering through the skies.
>
> And prophet-like the bodings came —
> "The good Earl dies the death of fame;
> For him the Prince that came in vain,
> A King, to enjoy his own again." —[9]

John Pagen White was confident enough to have sent copies of his poetry to Wordsworth in 1833 for his critical approbation. He was rewarded with a short polite note in Dora Wordsworth's hand acknowledging receipt and thanking him for his kind words.[10]

The Pall Mall Gazette was a little more discerning in its criticism: "The poems are written for the most part in the ballad style. Some of them have the ring of Scott's versification, a good many recall Wordsworth, and all are more noticeable for good taste and refined feeling than for originality . . . but the writer does not appear to have possessed any of the higher gifts of the poet. . . the information thus supplied (in the notes) is always readable and sometimes very curious."[11]

The Rev. William Gresley, like John Pagen White, chose to retell the story of the spectral army anachronistically. His novel, *Coniston Hall*, the third of a well-received trilogy, was set at the time of Lord Derwentwater's involvement in the Jacobite rising of 1715. The earlier novels, *The Forest of Arden* and *The Siege of Lichfield* were historical adventures, written "to illustrate the three principal epochs of modern English History". The first was "devoted to the Reformation of the Sixteenth Century" and the second to the Great Rebellion.[12] Coniston Hall though it dealt with a later period was to illustrate the consequences of the Revolution of 1688 when the Catholic James II was replaced by the protestant William of Orange. Gresley, writing a book that might well be seen as a romantic thriller of his day, intended "to exhibit the tone of feeling, and the disorders in Church and State, to which that measure gave rise".

The young hero Edward Dalton and his lover Clara – their love was first awakened when he saved her from falling masonry as the spirited girl attempted to scale a ruined tower at Furness Abbey – were standing at the foot of Lodore Falls. He spoke: "'You know, dear Clara, or have you guessed, that I may at any time be summoned to duties which I cannot decline, and obliged to leave these delightful scenes, which, believe me, never appeared so lovely before I visited them with you?'

"Clara looked earnestly at her cousin: 'I feared it was so; you are, then, determined to encounter this great peril. But I am sure you will act according to the dictates of your conscience. I know not whether I ought to endeavour to dissuade you.'

Thus the moral dimensions of the novel are set – the hero will dutifully pursue the wrong cause through loyalty to his king, but will finally win love and happiness after defeat, when he vows loyalty to George I and thereby the Anglican Church.

Before that Edward Dalton found himself trapped on Lord's Island in Derwentwater, where Lady Derwentwater fearfully awaited the outcome of the rebellion:

"The party re-assembled at supper-time in the old hall of the mansion, which looked gloomy enough, especially for so small a party. The storm still beat violently against the windows, and the rain pattered down the wide chimney. The only additional guest was the priest residing in the mansion, who blessed the meal, and took Lord Derwentwater's place in doing the honours of the table.

"A good deal of embarrassment was felt by most of the party. Lady Derwentwater, with all her efforts to appear calm, could not prevent her mind continually reverting to her husband's danger; Edward's thoughts wandered to the approaching crisis; Clara watched his anxious looks with fond alarm and sadness; George was light-hearted and gay, as usual, but even *his* spirits insensibly sank under the general gloom.

"'I have heard a strange story, which is commonly reported in the country,' said the priest, after the domestics had retired.

"'Pray tell us what it is,' said Lady Derwentwater, glad to find some subject of interest; and the rest of the party looked anxiously for information.

"'The story is shortly told,' said the priest. 'It appears that certain persons of the country were gathered at a small village on the road from hence to Penrith. It was late in the evening of yesterday, when the sun had nearly finished his course. The village of which I speak is at the foot of a long high range of hills, or moorland, called Soutra Fell; or, rather, at such a distance from the base, that the broad heathery back of the hill itself could easily be taken in with the eye. At the time I mention, just before the setting of the sun, loud noises were heard, as of artillery; and the persons whom I have spoken of distinctly saw, in the distance, troops of horsemen, with helmets gleaming and swords glancing; they climbed the steep hill-side in regular array, where horse's hoofs had never trod before, and on the top they met another host advancing to oppose them. The two armies, with their respective leaders, were seen to charge each other several times, sometimes one side prevailed and sometimes the other, until at last a mist enveloped the hill, and they were lost to sight. So convinced were the spectators of the reality of what they had seen, that several of them ascended the hill as soon as the morning sun had dawned, but, when they arrived at the supposed scene of action, not a trace could they find of the contending parties; not a drop of blood stained the ground: no, not even the marks of a horse's hoofs were discoverable.

Nor have any tidings been received of troops being in the neighbourhood up to this time.'

"''Tis a strange story, indeed,' said Edward, after a pause. 'I think I have heard of such spectral armies having been seen on former occasions, and if I remember right, at the time of some battle which has taken place elsewhere. There are instances even in ancient history of the intelligence of battles being known at places far distant, long before any messenger could have passed."

"'It reminds one,' said the priest, 'of Micaiah's vision in Holy Writ, which appears to have been an instance of what they call in the north country the second-sight. "I saw all Israel scattered upon the hills as sheep that have no shepherd; and the LORD said, These have no master; let them return every man to his home in peace." In this case the vision was prophetic. Such visions are, in truth, usually supposed to portend approaching strife. Strange coincidences have certainly sometimes occurred. I have heard that a troop of phantom horsemen was seen coursing over the heights of Helvellyn the day before the fatal battle of Marston Moor: the leader of that band had on his head a king's crown; those that appeared at Soutra, as I have been informed, had earls' coronets.'

"Lady Derwentwater, who had listened with deep attention, turned pale at this intelligence; and Clara was evidently much impressed with the narrative.

"'May not these men of the mist,' said George, 'have been a mere optical delusion arising from some natural phenomenon?'

"'It is possible,' said the priest; and a pause ensued.

"George's suggestion, however, did not at all fall in with the prevailing sentiments of the party, who were clearly of opinion that the vision was supernatural and ominous. In fact, they had their private reasons for knowing that the events which such appearances were supposed to foreshow were far from being unlikely to be realised. It may be supposed that this incident, though it interested the party, and furnished a topic of conversation, did not tend to raise their spirits. When the interest had subsided, they fell into a greater gloom than ever, and Lady Derwentwater rose to depart, taking Clara with her. Edward whispered in Clara's ear as she left the room:

"'Do not be surprised, if I should be gone tomorrow early without seeing you.'

"Clara looked inquiringly and sorrowfully, but did not make any remark—too well guessing the import of his words."

For the purposes of the novel, we are on Allan Cunningham's "Soutra Fell" and two armies clash in indecisive skirmishes. The fictionalised whole bears little resemblance save for the spectral armies, the location and the odd phrase from the originals, but we do have Cunningham's "earls' coronets" and we are presented with the tension between the scientific explanation and the mist-hidden prophetic possibilities of the story. We also have the Helvellyn/Marston Moor story, which, again, may derive from Allan Cunningham. The anonymous "Romish" priest offered scriptural parallels for the vision being portentous of approaching strife, but he saw no specific prophecy and he even equivocated on whether it might be a coincidence. George's suggestion of an "optical delusion" would have been very improbable in the year 1715. The chapter, titled *The Spectre Army*, has, as an epigraph, Wordsworth's lines from *An Evening Walk* where he rejected gothic stories.

Edward escaped from an impossible window by hauling up a rope with a fishing line and using it for his descent to a waiting rowing boat. Beneath the moonlit "spectral stones" of the Druid's stone circle he was met by Lord Derwentwater and, pledging his loyalty, his fate was sealed.

Coniston Hall was sufficiently popular for Murray's *Handbook* to refer to it in 1880. But popular success was not William Gresley's intention in writing his dozen or so novels as well as his numerous theological books and pamphlets. He was a leading member of the Tractarian Movement, committed to a High Anglican position within the Church of England. The novel was published in 1846, the year after John Henry Newman was received into the Roman Catholic Church. Gresley stated his ecclesiological position stridently in the concluding chapter of his novel. His politics grew out of his theology. A nation must submit "to those whom GOD has placed over them". The so-called "Glorious Revolution" was a source of schism within the nation. Democracy was a turning away from the authority of the church and against the will of God. Gresley was opposed to Dissent and Popery. *Coniston Hall* is a theological tract. However, the story of the spectral army, even though it was placed in the mouth of a catholic priest, was not used to make any theological point, but merely to add local colour to what now seems a rather stiff old-fashioned novel.

Altogether racier, but equally of its time, was *The Last Ball*[13] by the rebellious George Soane. The story of the spectral army makes a brief appearance in this salacious melodrama by the 55 year old Soane. Born in 1789, George was the younger son of the industrious, dedicated and difficult knight, Sir John Soane. He must frequently have despaired of this charming, ne'er-do-well. George fathered a child by his wife's sister. Always short of money, he was imprisoned for debt on several occasions and, at the age of twenty-five, he was found guilty of fraud. His father was a distinguished architect and the creator of the omnivorous and idiosyncratic museum in Lincoln's Inn Fields that still bears his name. George likened it to a mausoleum. The rift between father and son was completed one year later in 1826, when George, anonymously, damned his father's architectural style. Sir John felt the open conflict and the harsh criticism were like "death blows" to his sick wife.

Disinherited, George was forced to earn his living with his pen. He was a lively, entertaining and versatile writer producing everything from the *Frolics of Puck* to the *Life of the Duke of Wellington*.

The Last Ball is such a melodramatic melodrama that it worth giving a brief summary of its racy plot. The notoriously profligate lords Rochester and Buckingham are competing for the virtue of Marie de los Dolores, a wealthy, young and voluptuous Andalusian widow. Rochester, disguised as the necromancer Alexander Bendo, is about to persuade Maria "to peep into old Time's show-box", when she is abducted by Buckingham and taken to his country mansion. She is locked in the bedroom, "A sort pf Paphian temple, where Chastity herself might have turned renegade and worshipped at the shrine of passion." From there she is rescued by the sooty Jacob Snee, familiarly known as Cherry-nob, who comes down the chimney, and George Wilmot, Earl of Rochester, who comes up a ladder.

Maria's unrequited lover, "the moody and passion-stricken" Alfred Trevanion, challenges Buckingham to a duel and is injured. Maria rejects him. She can only care for him as a brother. At the ball, the mother desperately pleads his desperate case. As Maria de los Dolores dances the fandango, her rejected lover shoots himself below the balcony.

Maria seeks repose in the Isle of Wight. Cherry-nob persuades her to explore a cave where she is saved from a gang of ruffians by the handsome Mervyn, "a model of manly beauty", who is wounded. She is warned of his duplicity by the Jewess Rachael, who is disguised as a gypsy, but she falls in love with him: "And mine is yours," murmured the Andalusian, sinking in the ecstasy of joy upon his bosom."

At the very moment of their marriage, just as the marble bust of Alfred crashes to the ground, Mervyn rejects her, reveals that he is Julian Trevanion and that he has acted out of revenge for the death of his mother and brother.

However, Julian truly loves her, but she spurns his pleas. Invited to a last ball, Maria prepares to wear a poisoned mask and thereby deforming her features into "charred wood", she hopes to take revenge on her besotted lover. Julian hurries Maria to a bridal altar. At the moment when he would receive her bridal kiss she threatens to remove her mask and force him to endure her deformity. Fortunately, the Jewess has switched the poisoned mask for one of innocent silk. The penitent Rochester, on his death-bed, has sent a message that puts everything to rights and they live happily ever after.

It was not the sort of story to issue from the pen of the pious William Gresley.

The spectral apparition, a funeral procession in this case, appeared immediately after the duel. Cherry-nob had forced Charles Sedley, the rake and poet, to yield, Trevanion was bleeding from several wounds and Buckingham had just come round from being beaten unconscious by Cherry-nob. Through the heavy mist, they heard the blast of a trumpet followed by the sound of a funeral bell.[14]

"'If this cursed mist would only lift for a moment,' said Buckingham, 'that one might see what was going on—it's safer trusting to the eyes than the ears.'

"The words had scarcely escaped his lips when the beams of the rising sun burst through the fog, and mingled with it, presenting, for a moderate space, a field of the palest amber, the edges of which passed off again by gradual shadowings into the common grey vapour. Through this semi-transparent medium, as through a veil, they saw, to their great astonishment, a funeral creeping along with all the usual trappings and accompaniments of that melancholy ceremonial when it belongs either to the rich or noble. But if this were a strange sight for such a time and place, it was rendered yet more extraordinary by the circumstances that attended it; the men and horses,— some more visible, and others, less so—loomed out gigantically from the fog, and, stranger still, appeared to move in air at a few paces above the ground, phenomena, which might, perhaps, be referred to natural causes, but for which the knowledge of the beholders supplied them with no satisfactory solution.

"'Is this real?' cried Sedley —'or have we all drunk of the inebriating waters of the Erigone—or eaten of the honey that they say makes people mad?'

"'Faith, I know not whether I am drunk or dreaming,' replied the Duke — 'or if I am myself, or any other person; but thus much I can safely swear to—the whole business passes my comprehension.'

"'Whether real, or only an illusion,' said Alfred doubtfully, 'it is not without a precedent. I have heard the Yorkshire peasant tell how he saw, at even-tide, a cavalcade on foot and on horseback passing over the highest ridge of Souter Fell, yet, when he had climbed the mountain, not a blade of grass was turned —not a vestige was left of all the heavy array he had seen marching over it.'

"'His eyes must have fooled him,' replied Buckingham, 'as ours, perhaps, are just now fooling us.'

"Trevanion shook his head—

"'That may hardly be; the same thing was soon after witnessed by scores of the country people, with some slight differences only in the number and actions of the shadowy array. The spectres, or whatever else they might be, marched on five abreast, with colours waving in the wind, but their spears showing like so many dark lines, instead of reflecting the sunbeams, though just then the setting luminary glowed strongly upon the mountain. To complete the illusion, if illusion it were, a horseman would ever and anon start out from his place in the ranks, give, as it seemed, some necessary orders and then gallop back to his station. As it grew later, the airy figures appeared more regardless of discipline, and had less the appearance of a martial host than of people riding to a market.

But still the march went on with no diminution of the numbers, till at length darkness fell upon the mountain top, and shut it from the view of those below.'"

The spectral army has been imported rather awkwardly, - Sedley's extravagant classicism "have we all drunk of the inebriating waters of the Erigone?" - the whole business passing Buckingham's comprehension – and then Alfred's philosophic "It is not without a precedent". Even though topographically displaced, it is there with all its specific details from Clarke, Smith and Wordsworth (the banners streaming and the light of the setting sun). And it is being used to lend credibility to the author's fantastic device of a spectral funeral procession. The apparition, which appears without any prior indication and is not referred to later in the novel, is used as a portent of Alfred's death: "'He's a doomed man!' exclaimed Sedley, . . . 'This same shadowy procession, that came no one knows whence, and has gone no one knows whither, betokens a violent, if not an early, death to some of us, and who bids so fair to realize the omen as he who made it his own by being the first to run after it?'"

Before Sedley makes his prognostication Alfred has rushed into the dispersing mist only for them to find him "lying senseless at the foot of a blighted oak, whose rotting trunk and leafless branches seemed to hold out a melancholy warning". There was a black mark across his forehead. "A low growl of thunder, which a superstitious fancy might easily have construed into a ratification of the doom thus rashly pronounced; the wind, too . . . suddenly veered round, without the slightest warning, to the North, blowing in such short, furious gusts, that it was hardly possible to stand up against it. This was quickly followed by a still more singular phenomenon. At about half a mile from them, or somewhat less, the dust and even gravel were suddenly swept from the loose soil, and carried up into the air by a whirlwind, the mass continuing to increase, till, in height, it reached above the tallest trees. For a time this immense column remained stationary, revolving only on itself with great rapidity, but then smoke began to mingle with the dust, and fire to dart from it, now in a single flash, and now again, like several bright arrows, shot simultaneously from it into the earth." The windspout ripped up a mountain and an oak.

"'By St. George and his dragon!' exclaimed the Duke, 'but this transcends! I laughed, as a wise man might, at the tales they used to tell of the storm in Rutland, a few years since, and now we have its very copy. - Passion o' my heart, though, we are forgetting our invalid all the while — how goes it with him, man?'

George Soane is using the popular folk lore of the time – Souther Fell and the windspout in Rutland – to justify his pointless pyrotechnics.

Three years before it added colour to Edward Gresley's religious propaganda, the apparent phenomenon of Souther Fell, which had caused George Smith to question his rationalist assumptions, was being used to add credibility to melodramatic fustian.

Chapter Thirteen:

Harriet Martineau

Harriet Martineau left us at the beginning of this book with the equivocal permission: "And now the tourist may proceed, - looking for ghosts, if he pleases, on Souther Fell."[1]

She does not appear to have been the sort of person to encourage idle interest in ghost stories and yet her energetic and enthusiastic guide was the first to present the story at any length. The story must have been widely known and any traveller keen enough to write a book would have scanned the pages of *The Beauties of England*, even if he had not waded through Hutchinson's *History of Cumberland* or sought out Clarke's *Survey of the Lakes*.

Souther Fell and all of the Northern Fells, except Skiddaw and Latrigg, were largely ignored. Blencathra, or Saddleback as it was usually referred to in the eighteenth and nineteenth centuries, received little attention from the tourists making their way to Keswick. The melancholic Thomas Gray only paused to empathize with Blencathra's melancholy appearance when, on October 2nd, 1769, he "passed through Penradoch and Threlcot at the foot of Saddleback, whose furrowed sides were gilt by the noonday sun, whilst its brow appeared of a sad purple from the shadow of the clouds as they sailed slowly by it."[2]

During the next ten years, Father Thomas West, who guided the aesthetic tourist to the best viewing stations, only looked towards Saddleback as he walked down from his seventh select station on Latrigg: "In the course of the descent, remark Threlkeld-pike, browned with storms, and rent by a dreadful wedge-like rock, that tends to the centre. There are many pastoral cots, and rural seats, scattered round the cultivated skirts of this side of the mountains of Skiddaw and Saddle-back, sweetly placed, and picturesque. The northern side is less hospitable, being more precipitous, and much concealed in shade."[3]

The Rev. William Gilpin, always indefatigable in the pursuit of the picturesque, noted in his analytic way the view of Saddleback and Skiddaw as he investigated "a pathless desert over the mountains" to Watermillock and Ullswater. "The side next us was composed of Skiddaw. - Threlkate fell, a part of which is called Saddle-back and Grisedale-fell. As we rode nearer the northern limit of this chain, Skiddaw, which is by much the highest mountain, appeared in perspective, the least. Behind these mountains arise, in order, Mosedale-fell—Carric— and Caudbeck— the tops of which we sometimes saw, from the higher grounds, peering, in their blue attire, over the concave parts of the browner mountains, which stood nearer the eye.

"Between us, and this circular chain, which occupied the whole horizon on the left; was spread a very extensive vale; stretching from side to side hardly less than seven or eight miles; and in length winding out of sight. It affords little beauty, except what arises from the gradations of distance: but it suggests an idea of greatness; which space, and grand boundaries, however unadorned, will always suggest."[4] On his refined aesthetic scale, the distinctive lines of Saddleback counted for very little: "Mountains therefore rising in regular, mathematical lines, or in whimsical, grotesque shapes, are displeasing. Thus . . . and a mountain in Cumberland, which from its peculiar appearance in some situations, takes the name of *Saddle-back,* all form disagreeable lines. And thus many of the pointed summits of the *Alps* are objects rather of singularity, than of beauty. Such forms also as suggest the idea of lumpish *heaviness* are disgusting — round, swelling forms, without any break to disincumber them of their weight."[5] I fear that Grisedale Fell, that is Souther fell, probably suffered from "lumpish heaviness".

James Clarke, even though he gratuitously mocked Thomas Gray, – "His tender and delicate muse, delighted to sport in sunny vales" – does not appear to have climbed Saddleback himself since he reported the ascent of a certain Mr Crosfeild. Crosfeild had speculated about the formation of Scales Tarn: "I was for some time of the opinion that it had been formed by water spouts frequently breaking on the top of the mountain; but when I reflected that water could hardly be powerful enough to excavate solid rocks in so wonderful a manner, I . . . begun to imagine that no agent of nature, except fire, could produce such an astonishing effect." Crosfeild set out to explore the mountain at "eight in the morning, without any companion but my dog and my fowling-piece". "The road leads obliquely along the side of Souther-Fell, which may be reckoned the first landing place: here the ground is composed of loose fragments of stone intermixed with detached lumps of quartz and killas." When he reached Scales Tarn, he found the "first chasm, though by far the least formidable . . . inconceivably horrid. . . . after a steep and painful ascent of about a mile I came to the brink of the other gulfs. Here a point of the mountain juts out like a bastion between two of these horrid abysses. I stood upon this, (though my head turned giddy I could not go to the extremity of it, and had on each side a gulf about two hundred yards wide, and at least eight hundred deep!"

Crosfeild climbed on to the summit where he had "the most beautiful view of the countryside for many miles around" and then descended to the tarn: "It is surrounded by rocks, except an opening towards the East, where they have been evidently broken down. Standing near this opening I discharged my gun, when the echo was inconceivable: it resembled a peal of thunder bursting over my head, and was so prodigiously loud and fierce, that my dog (though a staunch pointer) crept trembling behind me." He noted the position of the prodigious rocks – "Evident marks of some dreadful convulsion!" and concluded "that this mountain has been formerly in a volcanic state, and that this Tairn has been the mouth or crater of the mountain."[6]

A gentleman interested in making "natural, oeconomical and literary observations" reached the opposite conclusion when he climbed the mountain on 20th August, 1791: "SADDLEBACK figures in the scenery of this Vale, a frightfully broken mountain on one side, and pretty smooth on the other. On its top are hideous chasms of near a thousand yards deep! and near it a lake or tarn (as the country people call a small lake) that seems the mouth of an extinguished volcano. Many vitrified substances found on this mountain make this conjecture not improbable, though I must confess I think *water* rather than *fire* has been the agent concerned in the formation of these mountains."[7] The gentleman was one Adam Walker, a natural philosopher from Patterdale. He had very decided views of how the tourist trade and agricultural and economic change were bringing London manners to the innocent fells: "Solitude and peace reign here undisturbed, except by the rattling Tourist, who excites envy and false ideas of happiness among the peaceful inhabitants; for now it ceases to excite laughter or contempt when the ruddy lass forgets her dialect, and appears at church in a tall bonnet fluttering with ribbands."

William Hutchinson, who was a solicitor from Barnard Castle, did not climb Saddleback when he made his two excursions in 1772 and 1773. In his *History of Cumberland* published twenty years later, just before he reprinted George Smith's article on the Caudbec Fells and the phenomenon on Souter Fell, he wrote of a party who had visited Scales Tarn in 1793. They began their ascent on Scales Fell. The account given by one of them runs thus: "When we had ascended about a mile, one of our party on looking round was so astonished with the different appearance of objects in the valley so far beneath us, that he declined proceeding. We had not gone much farther when another was taken ill, and wished to loose blood and return. I was almost ready to give up my project, which I should have done with great reluctance, as the day was remarkably favourable, and exhibited every scene to the greatest advantage. Mr. Clement (the conductor) assured us, if we proceeded a little way, we should find a resting place, where the second defaulter might recover the effects of the journey. After labouring another half hour we gained the margin of an immense cavity, in the side of the mountain, the bottom of which formed a wide bason, and was filled with water, that from our station looked black, though smooth as glass, covering the space of many acres. It is said to be so deep that the sun never shines upon it, and that the reflection of the stars may be seen therein at noonday, but this was a curiosity we did not enjoy." The same correspondent also wrote of being on the summit of Saddleback at four o'clock of a summer morning: "The sun was rising; the air was calm and serene, and I enjoyed the view of the magnificent scenery around me for near an hour. So many writers have given descriptions of their passage, and the scenery around Skiddaw, that I forbear adding thereto; but must repeat that Saddleback, in respect to curiosity, will afford the traveller more satisfaction."[8]

Thomas Wilkinson, that keenest and most venturesome of mountaineers, rejoiced in the "rugged Blencathra". "I seek for no authorities; but it occurs to me while writing, that our ancestors, when they gave this magnificent mountain its name, might think the name appropriate for a mountain with cataracts." However, with five companions, one blind and another lame, this Quaker farmer found himself on an ill-conceived venture. At the summit he "attempted a description of the fearful precipices beneath us; but it was the *first* thing I repented of that day, - when I saw him fall on the ground with dizziness, and cling to the earth, and scream out, with the apprehension of tumbling down the rocks into the abyss below." They breakfasted on Blencathra at eight o'clock and "spread their table-cloth" for lunch as they contemplated the view from Skiddaw. Later in a tiring day, anxious for more food, the party split into two in the valley between the two mountains and Wilkinson led a party of three back over Blencathra. "He that did the greatest wonders was he that reascended the mountain with his crutch and staff. Indeed, this was in fact ascending three mountains in one day: and from this extraordinary exertion he did not shrink. But having attained the summit of the mountain, he sunk to the ground. He trembled, and his speech failed him. The sun was set, and a cold wind rose from the north. He had perspired much through excessive exertion; and though perhaps he was once the most animated of us all in conversation, he could not now make answers to an enquiry. Our third companion now left us, and hurried down the mountain for help. With aching heart I hung over my poor friend. I sometimes lay down upon him to keep him warm; sometimes got him on my back and bore him where the descent was rugged; and sometimes dragged him down by the feet, where I met with a green slope. Perhaps anguish of mind, and the hope of saving life, aided my exertions; for by the time our other companion arrived with assistance, refreshment, and a horse, I believe I had got him a third part of the way down the mountain. Proper attention, refreshment, and rest, in a little while restored him."[9]

Wilkinson, a long-time friend of Wordsworth, lived about ten miles from Blencathra in an idiosyncratic house at Yanwath. His description of a distant thunderstorm over the mountain hints at an association of the view, which would have included Souther Fell, with military matters: "It was on a perfectly still afternoon in the fore-part of summer, when I looked towards this magnificent mountain. The firmament was of a pale orange, and there appeared something dreadful going on in that direction: daggers of fire seemed shaken by unseen hands towards the horizon, and one almost imagined the sharp sound of encountering weapons. The sky became dark; and by and by, thunder announced the conflict of the elements."[10]

Like Ann Radcliffe many tourists had found the approach to Saddleback uninspiring. John Housman, originally a gardener at Corby Castle near Carlisle, had supplied Hutchinson with topographical notes and knew the area well. In 1800, he wrote that "Leaving Penruddock we cross a dreary moor of considerable extent, and descend through the peaceful vales of Grisdale and Threlkeld, having Saddleback on the right, and, on the left, a heavy dull mountain branching from huge Helvellin, whose top is seen rearing into the airy regions." Surprisingly, even though he reprints Hutchinson's awestruck account of John Graves and Thomas Clement and others climbing Saddleback with one walker overcome by the height and another asking to be bled, Housman appears to have hurried on to the scenic delights of St John's in the Vale. [11]

Wordsworth was equally unoved by Blencathra's appeal. In his *A Guide through the Lakes in the north of England*, conforming to his "principal wish to furnish a Guide or Companion for the Minds of Persons of taste, and feeling for Landscape, who might be inclined to explore the District of the Lakes with that degree of attention to which its beauty may fairly lay claim", he only had time to view "the jagged summit of Saddleback" from the distance of Dalemain with Dacre Castle in the foreground.[12] However, when his *Guide* had been expanded by his publisher Hudson in 1843, the mountain was given a little more attention, even though the words may have been added by the editor: "Saddleback is, in the opinion of some tourists, more worthy of a visit than Skiddaw. 'Derwent Water,' says Dr. Southey, 'as seen from the top of Saddleback, is one of the finest mountain scenes in the country'." [13]

Robert Southey, who had little time for the new breed of "Tourists who are annually brought to this Land of Lakes by what have now become the migratory habits of the opulent classes," was keen to recommend

Blencathra to those with time and interest. In contrast to the horrid terror experienced by many of his predecessors, he finds Scales Tarn a place of sociable delight: "A wild spot it is as ever was chosen by a cheerful party where to rest, and take their merry repast upon a summer's day. The green mountain, the dark pool, the crag under which it lies, and the little stream which steals from it, are the only objects; the gentle voice of that stream the only sound, unless a kite be wheeling above, or a sheep bleats on the fell side. A silent, solitary place; and such solitude heightens social enjoyment, as much as it conduces to lonely meditation." On the heights, he found: "In looking down these ravines from the brow you have a sense of perfect security; there is not even an appearance of danger; and yet, if the whole depth below were one precipice, the effect could not be grander." Southey's "friend, William Westall, . . . with the eye of a painter, and the feeling of a poet, burst into an exclamation of delight and wonder" at the view toward Derwentwater. Southey was enthusiastic about the romantic interest of the area, the story of the shepherd lord, which Wordsworth had used, and the other associations with the Cliffords, but, being somewhat less credulous than George Smith, he was equally ready to dismiss much of the folklore that had grown up about Blencathra: "Absurd accounts have been published both of the place itself, and the difficulty of reaching it . . The Tarn has been said to be so deep that the reflection of the stars may be seen in it at noon day, and that the sun never shines on it. One of these assertions is as fabulous as the other, and the Tarn, like all our Tarns, is shallow."[14]

Jonathan Otley, clockmaker, self-taught and distinguished geologist, and meteorologist from Keswick, wrote a conscientiously *Concise Description of the English Lakes and Adjacent Mountains* in which he briefly described in order the lakes, tarns, rivers, waterfalls, mountains, crags and antiquities and then offered general directions to tourists and comparatively detailed accounts of the geology and meteorology of the Lake District. The final sixteen pages of his 141 page book were reserved for two of his hobby-horses on which he had much of interest to say: *The Floating Island in Derwentwater* and *The Black Lead Mine in Borrowdale.*[15]

The guide, which included his own map of the Lakes, issued in 1818, was published by the author and printed in Kirkby Lonsdale. It appeared in eight editions between 1825 and 1849 when it had expanded to become *The Descriptive Guide to the English Lakes*. Otley died in 1856 at the age of 90 still busily occupying his small cottage "up t'steps" in Packhorse Court, Keswick.[16]

In the early editions the account of Saddleback is typically succinct and precise in its observations. There is no room for exclamations of horror. "SADDLEBACK - being at a greater distance from the station at Keswick than Skiddaw, of somewhat inferior elevation, and the ascent not quite so easy - is seldom visited by strangers. It is better situated than Skiddaw for a view towards the south, and also of the neighbourhood of Lowther and Penrith; but the western view is greatly intercepted. It has been called Threlkeld Fell, and sometimes Blencrater, or Blenk-arthur; and it is from its form, as seen from the vicinity of Penrith, that it has received the name of Saddleback. Its height is 2787 feet, and its rock is a primitive clay slate, similar to that of Skiddaw. In walking along the ridge it is worth while to notice, how the southern side is formed into a series of deep ravines and rocky projections; while to the north, it descends in a smooth grassy slope. And deeply below a rocky precipice on its eastern end, a small tarn is singularly placed."[17] By the eighth and final edition of 1850 he has added that, "On two occasions, in 1743-4, the aerial phenomenon called mirage was observed on a portion of the mountain called Souther-Fell or Souterfell: the lover of the marvellous will find ample detail of the circumstances in 'Clarke's Survey of the Lakes'."[18]

William Green, the artist, accompanied Otley on an expedition up Blencathra when they boldly attempted the vertiginous rocks of Sharp Edge. "We had not gone far, before we were aware that our journey would be attended with perils; the passage gradually grew narrower, and the declivity on each hand, awfully precipitous. From walking erect, we were reduced to the necessity either of bestriding the ridge, or of moving on one of its sides with our hands lying over the top, as a security against tumbling into the tarn, on the left, or into a frightful gulley on the right, both of immense depth."[19]

However, Green, who, in 1819, had produced his own *New Tourist's Guide to the Lakes* in two volumes, proved himself equally intrepid in pursuing "some most extraordinary aerial phenomena". He gave a summary of George Smith's version of events and then added a few comments drawing on his local knowledge and research. Green was born in 1760 in Manchester. In 1795 he published *Picturesque Views of the North of England and Wales*. At the age of forty, he married a sixteen-year-old barmaid and settled in Ambleside. There is just the slightest possibility that he might have known Stricket and some of the other witnesses and even James Clarke, but, unlike almost all the other commentators, he would have known people who had known them. "All enquiries on the subject are in corroboration of the reality of the vision; those on the west of the Hesket road, were generally not more than a mile from the scene of action, but from the High Nest five miles from Souter Fell, it was noticed by an aunt of Mr. John Allison, of Rosthwaite in Borrowdale. Daniel Stricket was well known in Keswick, and always spoke of the appearance in a positive and assured manner, and Mr. Clark in his Survey of the Lakes, to leave no doubt on his readers mind got his description attested in the following words by Stricket and Lancaster. "We whose names are hereunto subscribed declare the above account to be true, and that we saw the phenomenon as here related." As witness our hands this 21st day of February 1785". William Green, however, did not trouble himself with the discrepancies between Smith's and Clarke's accounts. Finally, in his usual direct and honest way, William Green confessed his enthusiasm for such phenomenon: "The writer would joyfully have witnessed such scenes; and even to have interrogated the favoured parties, would have furnished to him the means of considerable gratification. Though not abounding in credulity, he is well convinced that the presentations must have been of a very extraordinary nature."[20]

Thomas and Edward Gilks, the authors of the cheery, fanciful *Sylvan's Pictorial Handbook*, had the strength to climb Saddleback by Southey's route in 1847. They observed the Glenderamakin winding round Souter Fell, but their imagination is confined to memories of Walter Scott's *Bridal of Triermain*.[21]

Black's *Guide* was one of the most successful of all guides. It appeared from 1841 to 1929 in various guises including the *Economical*, the *Shilling* and the *Picturesque*. Earlier guides and handbooks and tours had been comparatively amateur. They had been written by ladies or gentlemen telling of their pleasures and experiences and offering a little advice, or by local enthusiasts such as Clarke, Housman, Otley or Green and were often self-published or produced in collaboration with a local bookseller. Black's Guides were different. A and C Black, based in Edinburgh had already published guides to Edinburgh, the Highlands and Scotland and Travelling Maps of England and Ireland and their books had a more commercial feel, with detailed information on travel and on accommodation and with adverts at the back. They were meeting the needs of the new middle class travellers. Directions were comprehensive – it recommended three ways up Saddleback – and the tone was bright and informative. There was room for popular literary associations, but folklore only received a dismissive shrug: "The path is by the side of a dashing stream, which flows from Threlkeld Tarn, the greatest depth of which is not more than twenty feet. Exaggerating travellers have described this tarn as an abyss of waters upon which the sun never shines, and wherein the stars of heaven may be seen at noonday."[22]

Murray's *Handbooks* were the English *Baedekers*. Compact, solid and produced in durable red bindings, they were intended to provide a pocket volume for the English traveller on the Continent. The *Handbook on Cumberland, Westmorland and the English Lakes* did not appear until 1867, but it spoke with a succinct authority: "Descriptive writing has in general been avoided; to indicate what is best worth seeing, and how it may be best seen, ought to be the principal aim of a Handbook". The anonymous editor, a long-time resident of the Lake District, found that "the peculiar form of Blencathra, its deep gorges and stern precipices, make the ascent one of much interest and some little excitement. The sides are scarred by ravines, and strewn with debris, the effects of waterspouts breaking upon what was once the smooth grassy side of the mountain." The *Handbook* records the legends of Sir Lancelot Threlkeld and Henry Clifford, the "frightful inundation" in St John's in the Vale, the noon-time stars in Scales Tarn, the immortal fish in Bowscale and the spectral army of Souther Fell: "A singular and well-attested atmospheric phenomenon was observed on Saddleback in the last century. On Midsummer Eve, 1745, it appeared covered with troops who defiled over it for more than an hour, and disappeared in a crevice near the summit. The explanation of the phenomenon was that on the evening in question some mounted partizans of the Stuarts were exercising on the western coast, and their movements were refracted by some peculiar condition of the atmosphere upon the summit of Saddleback. There is a tradition of a spectral army, probably originating in some similar cause, having been seen marching over Helvellyn on the eve of the battle of Marston Moor:

> " Anon appears a brave, a gorgeous show
> Of horsemen—shadows moving to and fro;
> At intervals imperial banners stream,
> And now the van reflects the solar beam;
> While silent stands the admiring crowd below,
> Silent the visionary warriors go,
> Winding in ordered pomp their upward way,
> Till the last banner of their long array
> Has disappeared, and every trace is fled
> Of splendour—save the mountain's lofty head
> Tipped with eve's latest gleam of burning red."—*Wordsworth.*[xxiii]

The army has been transposed to Saddleback and is seen on just one evening; the explanation is cobbled together from Brewster and that brief note in *The Lonsdale Magazine* and Wordsworth's lines from *An Evening Walk* are misapplied to a legend of troops from the Civil War being seen on Helvellyn. The spectral army of Marston Moor has entered the ghostly lore alongside other tales of phantom armies. The earliest reference to it is Allan Cunningham's tale of Dame Eleanor Selby which first appeared in *The London Magazine* in 1821 and was reprinted many times afterwards. Cunningham may well have invented the story as he was a master of the creation of folk tales and ballads, but he could just as readily have known the story, probably from an oral source. It is only referred to by Harriet Martineau, before Murray's editor misapplies it. However, the whole story of the Souther Fell apparitions is now condensed into the one sighting, and, as "a singular and well-attested atmospheric phenomenon" has been neatly rationalised without the contradictions and questions that disturbed George Smith.

Otherwise, throughout the array of handbooks and pedestrian tours and guides to picturesque scenery and all the other publications excited by the discovery of the Lakes, by first the gentleman traveller, by locals like Green and Otley and then those opulent middle classes, there was very little mention of Saddleback and only the rare glancing reference to

Souther Fell. The area was off the main tourist routes or the tourists hurried through having been told there was nothing of interest. Travelling from Penrith to Keswick, they found the country dull and uninviting and chose to push on to St John's in the Vale. "A Cambridge Man" writing in 1850 summed up the general view of the area: "A good road – but for a long time a very dull one – of eighteen miles connects the two towns . . . And for one climber who reaches the summit of Saddleback there are probably a hundred that reach that of Skiddaw."[24]

One of the few mentions of the spectral army in all the tourist literature between Britton and Brayley's disproportionately extensive account and the terse reference in the later editions of Otley's *Guide* fifty years later is in a curious little book. Published in 1822, *The History and Topography of Cumberland, with biographical sketches, &c., &c., &c.* is a small duodecimo, a sharp commercial publication by G. & W. B. Whittaker of Ave Marie Court in London, a volume in *Pinnock's County Histories*. The 14 page catalogue appended to the 68 page book suggests the range of William Pinnock's interests from new and improved globes and atlases to square, cabinet, grand and cottage pianofortes and the latest in new and popular music. The series sold at one shilling per volume and offered "a compendious account of its History and Topography, its Antiquities, natural and artificial curiosities, local peculiarities, Commerce, Manufactures, &c.; comprising also the Biography of its most eminent persons; and every local information to be met with in larger statistical works; and embellished by a neat and correct Travelling Map."

From its first page to its last, from "What is the situation of Cumberland?" to "Who was Thomas Tickell?" the book is written in a series of questions and answers. Its clipped manner and easy way with facts and opinions reveals metropolitan attitudes more clearly than many extended comments:

"Q. What primitive race of men inhabits these wilds?

A. A species of shepherd inhabits these secluded scenes, called by the inhabitants the Estatesmen. His riches consist in his paternal meads and his numerous flocks; in the midst of these he lives a calm, inoffensive life, and exercises a degree of primitive hospitality, not now to be found among the busy and populous haunts of men."

"Q. What celebrated mountain is near?

A. Three miles to the north of Keswick is the majestic Skiddaw, rising more than 3,500 feet above the level of the lake of Bassenthwaite, which lies at its foot. The ascent is difficult and intricate, but the frequent views of the surrounding country which present themselves from occasional openings, the romantic scenes of precipices and torrents which occur on the way, and the glorious prospect which astonishes and delights the eye on reaching the summit, banish all sensations of fear and fatigue, and enwrap the soul in enthusiastic admiration.

Q. Is there not another celebrated mountain here?

A. Yes; about three miles to the east of Skiddaw is Saddleback, so called from its shape resembling a saddle. Its height is little less than that of Skiddaw, and it appears to have been originally a volcano, of which the crater now forms a lake called Threlkeld Tarn. Lava and burnt stones have been found on its borders.

Q. What other celebrated mountain may be noticed here?

A. Souter Fell, to the east of Saddleback, which is upwards of 2,500 feet in height. About the middle of the last century a phenomenon took place here, which greatly alarmed numbers who witnessed it. Several troops of horsemen appeared to ride along the side of the mountain, where it was impracticable for horsemen to pass; and, this continued at intervals for upwards of two hours.

Q. What explanation can be given of this phenomenon?

A. As this was about the time of the rebellion, it is supposed that this extraordinary appearance originated from real troops passing at some distance, whose figures were reflected by the vapours on the mountain side. Something of the same nature had been witnessed before."[25]

William Pinnock, or his anonymous scribbler, had probably cobbled the book together from works he had to hand, especially *The Beauties of England*. This was a cheap "educational" guide for the general public and it probably circulated far more widely than the tasteful guides of the period.

Works of reference such as Parson and White's *Directory* of 1829 are typically brief, distorting and dismissive: "Souter Fell, a lofty, rocky eminence on which several distant observers, on three different nights in 1735, 1737, and 1745, saw grand exhibitions of ignis fatuus, representing marching armies, with horses, carriages, &c. ominous, 'twas said, of war and rebellion."[26]

The person who breathed new life into the story of the spectral army on Souther Fell was Harriet Martineau. "Harriet Martineau! Of all appalling things!" is how the good lady is first announced as a walk-on part in Hugh Walpole's *Rogue Herries Chronicle.* Judith Paris "recognised that she was exceedingly wise, immensely learned, and possibly the greatest woman now alive in England, but Judith did not care for so much learning. She had never herself had much education, she was not a Positivist, she detested the thought of mesmerism, and she envied the way in which Miss Martineau milked her own cows and ploughed her own fields. Moreover, Miss Martineau never ceased to talk – about Comte, about America, about her marvellous Cure, about her weak heart, about her pigs and cows, about her novels , . . about Mr Atkinson, about her *Guide to the Lakes.* Miss Martineau spoke of the Lakes as though they were her own creation and would not have existed had it not been for her. She patronised the Lakes. In addition, Harriet was all for women taking man's place."[27] When she actually appears, she does not disappoint: " 'Is it a woman or a man,' an old lady once said of her to William Howitt, 'or what sort of animal is it?' Said I to myself; there she came – stride, stride, stride – great heavy shoes, stout leather leggings on, and a knapsack on her back – they say she mows her own grass, and digs her own cabbages and taturs!' " The catty remarks are redeemed by a final assessment of her character: "She was as good-hearted and free of meanness as she was egoistic and free of sensitiveness. . . . Her heart was warm and kind and it was not her fault that she knew such a terrible deal about so many different things."[28]

The scene is Walpole's invention. Harriet Martineau was not capable of striding around the Lakes after the *Guide* had been published. In 1855, at the age of 53, she had been diagnosed with a heart disease that threatened her imminent death. She immediately set about putting her affairs in order with an ease and acceptance that surprised her religious friends. In her *Autobiography*, which became the occupation of those supposed last months, she wrote with a calm serenity of her time as she approached death: "I may, in short, take a free and lavish holiday before I go."[29] But ardent philosophical reformer as she was, she was still equally determined to continue to argue the case for a better, more rational world.

In 1853 she had translated and abridged Auguste Comte's *Cours de philosophie positive*, a self-imposed task that she saw as a great pleasure. Comte's Positivist Philosophy illuminated her thinking on the progress man made through superstition to theology and then to rationalism. It also confirmed her belief in necessarianism, a form of social determinism that she had derived from her Unitarian background. This had prompted that positive assertiveness that lectured the workers of Ambleside on sanitary conditions, but also built cottages and improved social conditions and established a model farm of two acres. It was the same drive that had made her such a resonant political voice.

She had spent the most vigorous ten years of her often vigorous life in Ambleside. Coming to this small, squalid town had been like a rebirth. The 1830s had seen her become a public celebrity almost overnight after the publication of the twenty three tales that were *Illustrations of Political Economy.* She capitalised on her fame to become a strong voice speaking on behalf of economic freedom and the role of women. In particular she campaigned for the abolition of slavery, most notably during a two year tour in the United States from 1834 to 1836. Her strenuous activities as a political journalist and author – her moralistic novel *Deerbrook* was published in 1839 – came to a sudden end with illness. She was suffering from a prolapsed uterus, probably as a result of an ovarian cyst.[30]

"On the sofa where I stretched myself after my drive to Tynemouth, on 16th March, 1840, I lay for nearly five years, till obedience to a newly discovered law of nature raised me up, and sent me forth into the world again, for another ten years of strenuous work and almost undisturbed peace and enjoyment of mind and heart"[31] The "newly discovered law of nature" was Mesmerism and the cure was administered by Henry George Atkinson, who became something of a philosophical mentor to Harriet. In 1845 she built The Knoll, the house that she designed herself, and which she came to feel to be an emblem of the fulfilled, industrious life. "And my own ideal of an innocent and happy life was a house of my own among poor improvable neighbours, with young servants whom I might train and attach to myself; with pure air, a garden, leisure, solitude at command, and freedom to work in peace and quietness. When to all this could be added fine natural scenery, the temptation was such as London could not rival."[32]

Waiting to settle into her new house, she looked about her with her customary thoroughness and gusto: "I set myself to learn the Lake District which was still a terra incognita veiled in bright mists before my mind's eye. And by the close of the year from the purchase of my field, I knew every lake (I think) but two, and almost every mountain pass . . . Of these joyous labours" (that is, mastering subjects of study) "none has been sweeter than that of my first recovered health, when Lakeland became gradually disclosed before my explorations, till it lay before me, map-like, as if seen from a mountain top."[33]

However, she claimed to have been reluctant to write the *Guide*. "I had before promised, most unwillingly, and merely for neighbourly reasons, to write a *Guide to Windermere and the neighbourhood*."[34] She was writing six leaders a week for the *Daily News* in addition to her usual literary commitments, but she was readily susceptible and flattered by the request. The *Guide to Windermere, with tours to the neighbouring lakes and other interesting places* appeared in 1854. The 103 "foolscap octavo" pages with six engravings and a folding map could be purchased at the price of one shilling in paper covers or 1/6 in "neat cloth".[35]

It must have been just after publication that John Garnett, her enterprising local publisher from Windermere, approached his eminent author a second time: "When I fancied I was going to do what I pleased till I left home in July 1854, the proprietor of the *Windermere Guide* made an irresistible appeal to me to do the whole district, under the form of a *Complete Guide to the Lakes*. Still in hope that leisure would come at last and feeling that I should enjoy it more from having omitted no duty, I gave up my holiday evenings now. I made the tour of the district once more with a delightful party of friends – reviving impressions and noting facts and then came home, resigned to work "double tides" for the remaining weeks before my summer absence – dining early after my morning's work, and writing topography in the evenings. I received much aid in the collection of materials from the publisher and from the accomplished artist, Mr Lynsey Aspland who illustrated the volume: and I finished my work, and went forth on a series of visits, which were to occupy the tourist season – my house being let at that time. I little imagined, when I left my own gate, that the ease and light-hearted pleasure of my life, - I might almost say, my life itself, - were left behind me, - that I was going to meet sorrow, sickness, and death."[36]

It was to be another twenty years of continuing, useful activity before she died. However, in 1855, she felt death was close and faced it with cheerful equanimity. She had been raised in the Unitarian Church and grown increasingly at odds with established religion. She told the devout Charlotte Bronte that she "was an atheist in the vulgar sense – that of rejecting the popular theology – but not in the philosophical sense, of denying a First Cause".[37] She increasingly, but still with agnostic caution, rejected the idea of a life after death: "So ignorant as I am of what is possible in nature, I do not deny the possibility of a life after death: and if I believed the desire for it to be as universal as I once thought it, I should look on so universal a tendency as some presumption of a continuous life."[38] She looked to science as her only guide in life: "It seems to us, even now, . . . the rarest thing in the world to find any one who has the remotest conception of the indispensablesness of science as the only source of, not only enlightenment, but wisdom, goodness, and happiness."[39] And she could be scathing – remember those "great heavy shoes" - about any suggestion of a world of the spirits: "If any such students (of table rapping) should think fit to summon me when I am gone hence, they will get a visit from – not me – but the ghosts of their own thoughts: . . . I do not attempt to offer any explanation of that curious class of phenomena, but I do confidently deny that we can be justified in believing that Bacon, Washington and other wise men are the speakers of the trash that "spiritual circles" report as their revelations."[40]

The *Guide* was eminently practical. She'd got to know the Lakes in her business-like way. She'd entertained numerous guests at the Knoll, which she thought of as "My Knoll position and house together – the prettiest dwelling in the valley; - airy, gay, and sunny within and without."[41] And Garnett, wily publisher that he was, both flattered Harriet by placing a vignette of her treasured house on the title page and endorsed his product with the strongest and most personal brand of all. Her gratitude, the gratitude of an author of international repute, to Garnett, a small town printer, is unduly effusive. "With what pride and pleasure I have looked over the accessories and embellishments with which by his (the publisher's) zeal and spirit, and by the admirable cooperation he has been so fortunate to secure, my humble work is elevated to a quality of real importance."

Norman Nicholson was scathing about her *Guide*: "But after nearly ten years in the Lakes her view of them was as scrappy, as superficial, as that of a week-end visitor."[42] The guide had been undertaken as a holiday task by someone with "stout leather leggings on, and a knapsack on her back" and the guidance resonated with a healthy outdoor morality: "Nothing can be more refreshing than bathing in the lakes or the mountain streams and pools; and it may be perfectly safe, if ordinary precautions are taken."

Miss Martineau is keenly aware of the tourists' needs. For instance, in taking the long walk to Castle Head from Keswick, the tourist is advised to take the "interesting path that winds up through the woods" to obtain the best view for those "who cannot undertake more arduous ascents . . . The southern view is the special glory of this station." The view is enumerated and the final advice is considerate of the social pleasures to be derived, but also contains a veiled caution: "The best time for enjoying this walk is early morning – for those who do not object to dewy paths. It is a favourite place for pic-nics which are sometimes got up on a large scale; and it is the resort of all strangers."

And in so far as it is appropriate for a tourist guide she is observant of the economic and social conditions of the ordinary people. She makes a plea for public baths in Ambleside on the back of the inadequate provision for the tourist; remarks on the neglected homesteads in Langdale; notes the bloomeries in Furness and provides up-to-date statistics of iron-ore production and intelligent comments on mineralogy; she finds the woodcutters huts picturesque, but you feel her real sympathies lie with the dalesmen who "have no regard for the picturesque, and never hesitate to sacrifice it when it can be replaced by the useful". As a laissez-faire economist she was an advocate of change and progress. The Lakeland statesman that Wordsworth sought to preserve had become "unable to keep his children at home; and they went to the manufacturing towns, leaving home yet more cheerless . . . Having reached this pass, it is clearly best that it should go on till the primitive population, having . . . kept its ignorance and grossness, shall have given place to a new set of inhabitants better skilled in agriculture, and in every way more up to the times." She continued in justifying her unsentimental view of progress:

"We have no fear of injury, moral and economical, from the great recent change, — the introduction of railways . . . nowhere is drunkenness a more prevalent and desperate curse than in the Lake District. . . . Under the old seclusion, the material comfort of the inhabitants had long been dwindling; and their best chance of recovery is clearly in the widest possible intercourse with classes which, parallel in social rank, are more intelligent and better informed than themselves."[43]

Yet, despite this view, her favourite character might well have been an old shepherd on Fairfield: "There is an aged man in the district, however, who hears more than this, and sees more than people would, perhaps, imagine. An old shepherd has the charge of four rain-guages which are set up on four ridges, — desolate, misty spots, sometimes below and often above the clouds. He visits each once a month, notes down what these guages record; and when the tall old man, with his staff, passes out of sight into the cloud, or among the cresting rocks, it is a striking thought that science has set up a tabernacle in these wildernesses, and found a priest among the shepherds. That old man has seen and heard wonderful things: has trod upon rainbows, and been waited upon by a dim retinue of spectral mists. He has seen the hail and the lightnings go forth as from under his hand; and has stood in the sunshine, listening to the thunder growling and the tempest bursting beneath his feet. He well knows the silence of the hills, and all the solemn ways in which that silence is broken. The stranger, however, coming hither on a calm summer-day, may well fancy that a silence like this can never be broken."[44] That strained fantasy of the rational picturesque, the Wordsworthian shepherd that is both priest and scientist, experiencing nature's poeticized mysteries epitomizes the extent to which Harriet Martineau was manufacturing her subject rather uncomfortably from the relaxed holiday urgings of a modern scientific mind. She was someone who saw the world about her, often with analytic precision. Her understandings were predetermined. Her senses were not open and receptive – "a mind that watches and receives" - and in Harriet Martineau's case they were seriously limited by her deafness and her deficient senses of taste and smell. It is tempting to think that image of the shepherd recording the rainfall "waited upon by his dim retinue of spectral mists" is the scientific equivalent of Wordswoth's dismissal of the "Strange apparitions mocked the shepherd's sight".

The *Guide* was a holiday task and, in her regular three hours in the evening of a busy day, she was writing to interest and entertain the middle class tourist. And thus, amid the social and aesthetic commentary, she found place for many tantalising, teasing tales of folklore and the supernatural. She was quite happy to evoke the midnight Crier of Claife and then leave its truth an open question: "Whatever may be said about the repute of ghosts in our day, it is certain that this particular story is not dead." She delighted in the image of the haunted mansion at Armboth on Thirlmere: "Lights are seen there at night, the people say; and the bells ring; and just as the bells all set off ringing, a large dog is seen swimming across the lake. The plates and dishes clatter; and the table is spread by unseen hands. That is the preparation for the ghostly wedding feast of a murdered bride, who comes up from her watery bed m the lake to keep her terrible nuptials. There is really something remarkable, and like witchery, about the house. On a bright moonlight night, the spectator who looks towards it from a distance of two or three miles, sees the light reflected from its windows into the lake; and, when a slight fog gives a reddish hue to the light, the whole might easily be taken for an illumination of a great mansion. And this mansion seems to vanish as you approach, - being no mansion, but a small house lying in a nook, and overshadowed by a hill."[45]

When she described Castlerigg Stone Circle she seems to have given way to a fantasy more worthy of Hollywood than a guidebook written by an atheist renowned for her moral seriousness: "The old legend about the last human sacrifice of the Druids may belong to any of the monuments of that age in the district; and it is probably claimed for them all. According to that old story; when some people settled in a clearing of the woods, beside a river, somewhere to the south of the district, the priests took up their station further north, among the mountains, where there were plenty of stones fit and ready for their temple. After a time, a fever laid waste the lower settlement; and the oracle demanded a sacrifice to appease the divine wrath. The lot fell on a young girl who was betrothed; and, on an appointed day, she was conveyed, with all the ceremonies, to the temple. A small hut of wicker-work, like a large bee-hive, was found set up on the western side of the temple. The girl was led into the circle, and placed in the midst, while the dedication proceeded. We are even told that she was adorned with an oak garland, and held mistletoe in her hand. The whole population was looking on from a distance: but it must have been within reasonable reach, as every one was required to contribute a stick to the fire. The wretched lover saw all from afar; and he daringly resolved, - let the god be as wrathful as he pleased, - not to contribute so much as a twig to the burning of his beloved. She was seen to enter the door, which was next the circle; and then the priest closed it up, and heaped dry leaves and sticks that were brought all round the hut. The arch-druid meantime was procuring fire from two pieces of wood. He succeeded, and set the pile in a blaze. In this moment of desperation, the lover saw every mountain round give forth a great cataract; and all the floods gushed to the temple as to a centre, and made an island of the little hut, - returning when they had extinguished the fire. The victim came forth, with not a hair singed, and not a leaf of her garland withered.

The arch-druid, skilled to interpret thunder, seems to have understood in this case the voice of waters; for he announced that, henceforth, the god would have no more human sacrifices."[46]

The "old legend" is in the worst tradition of tourist hokum. By a sleight of hand Miss Martineau claimed the authority of tradition and the freedom to attach the tale to any of the monuments in the district. The veracity of the legend is assured by the circumstantial detail and the reasoned, perspicacious telling. We are in the hands of a highly skilled story-teller. The legend seems to have no foundation. One version of it where "the devoted Ella is happily restored to the arms of the over-joyed Mudor" appeared in Wilson Armistead's *Tales and Legends of the Lake Counties*[xlvii] published under a pseudonym Lothar five years before the guide. Armistead, who came from Leeds, was an enthusiastic supporter of the anti-slavery movement and Harriet Martineau must have been aware of him, even if she did not know this reputedly retiring man personally. It is probable that Armistead – he is happy to give no sources - plagiarised his "legend", which was told with a certain extravagantly romantic elan, that is taken directly, without acknowledgment, from a story written some thirty years earlier, by John Briggs, the editor of the *Lonsdale Magazine*.[48] Briggs, who came from Kirkby Stephen, set his tale, a purported foundation myth for the Brigantine tribe, in Caer Werid, the Green City, the Brigantine name for their settlement near Lancaster, and the sacrifice took place at an unidentified temple further north. Armistead behaved in the same cavalier way when he reprinted his account of Soutra Fell borrowing a poetic rendering of Allan Cunningham's fiction that had appeared in *The Lonsdale Magazine*.

The clue to why an historian of considerable repute should repeat such humbug lies in the religious framework in which she sets her tale. The story demonstrates one step in the progress from superstition to rationalism. The god had declared that there will be no more human sacrifices. The terms employed, such as temple, priest and divine sacrifice, present pagan religion as analogous to the Christian church. The religion of the Druids is barbaric, but the religion of her own day is not totally from such pagan practices.

Miss Martineau concluded her account of Castlerigg with a shorter anecdote. In her matronly, heavy footed manner she began, "Any resident who is sufficiently familiar with the country people to get them to speak their minds fully," and outlined the story that the Druid stones cannot be counted correctly and that a treasure is buried under the larger one. She then developed an extended simile that may apply just to the stone in question: "Nobody wants to undermine the stone, to get rid of the tradition: so our neighbours are like the Arabs at Petra, who have been shooting with sling, bow, and matchlock, for a thousand years, at the urn where they are sure Pharaoh's treasure is, — in its niche in the rock temple. For a thousand years they have failed to bring it down, and are determined that no European shall. And no European would dismantle the temple to disabuse the Arabs; and so the tradition and the urn stand untouched. So may it be for ages to come with Long Meg, and the giant of eight tons weight that presides over the Keswick circle!"

On the other hand, the stone with the supposed treasure and the urn may be analogies of the Christian religion and the failure to obtain the treasure by the obvious means is akin to our failure to dismantle religion by rational means. And that willing of the preservation of an old tradition with its affirmative exclamation mark is stridently ironic. A tourist guide is as powerful place for rationalist propaganda as a leader column in a national newspaper.

She hoped for the same kind of progress in "the middle of that far-famed Borrowdale of which so many tales are told". There was the story of the man who tried to dowse burning lime with water; the man who needed his scholar son to remove his feet from his new-fangled stirrups; the people who kept adding a course to the wall to retain the cuckoos and keep eternal spring in the valley; the scholar who concluded that a mule was a peacock; and there were the men of Borrowdale transporting their valuable wadd to London, who let off their blunderbusses at a mocking clock for saying cuckoo. She concluded that: "This cannot last much longer, - judging by the new houses – abodes of gentry, - built or building in Borrowdale. The wrath must presently turn to a laugh in the humblest chimney-corner in the dale."[49]

She then had the traveller ascend Watendlath, "the most primitive dale" in the Lakes, and observe the incredible strength and athleticism of the slate-carriers on Honister, before descending to Buttermere. She made no mention of the innocent maid of Buttermere and her notorious abductor, but simply described the views and pleasant excursions. There is a succinct account of the shepherd lord when she passes through Threlkeld and Scott was acknowledged as we're taken to St John's in the Vale, but these accounts are concise and cursory. We are told: "The ascent of Skiddaw is easy, even for ladies, who have only to sit their ponies to find themselves at the top, after a ride of six miles". Nevertheless, before surveying the circumambient view, we are given a stern warning of the dangers of making even "the mild ascent of green Skiddaw" without a guide.[50]

Harriet Martineau recommended the tourist to ascend Saddleback via the toll gate at Scales. He should then cross a piece of open ground to "a gate which opens upon the hill path, leading on the breast of Souther Fell. For nearly a mile a wall is followed in an easterly direction; then turn to the left into the depression where the infant stream Glenderamakin runs." The proposed route barely touches on the southern edge of Souther fell before descending to the stream. Today's walkers generally follow a path well above on the southern side of the river. The tourist has not passed over Souther fell.

The account begins with two key words in the Martineau vocabulary: "Souther fell is the very home of superstition and romance". In 1833 she had written a long and forceful review of *The Letters on*

Demonology. She had been scathing about Walter Scott's failure, drawing back when he might have demonstrated the superstition at the heart of all religion. "What an opportunity has he lost of illustrating a dark region of life! The subject of supernatural appearances has for ages been treated poetically, and of late, medically and philosophically. Sir Walter Scott, by uniting the philosophy and the poetry as we expected he would, might have produced a work of singular interest and beauty, instead of doing what in him lay to set back the world which he has such mighty power to roll onward. This is the more mischievous as it is certain that very gross superstition not only lurks among the ignorant classes of society, but is countenanced by some who ought to know better."[51]

There was no place for believing in superstition in Harriet Martineau's rational pantheon, although there was room for romance, for the aesthetics of superstition. "As long as superstitions are linked with truth, as long as they preserve any thing of the character of allegory, they must be permanent. The Grecian mythology, ancient as it is, is not worn out; but it remains, not as a system of superstition, but as a reservoir of beauty whence the imagination may draw refreshment, perhaps for ever." And such beauty is not confined to the superstitions of the ancients: "As far as the superstitions of our country subserve the same purpose, let them abide; but not as superstitions."[52]

The question becomes one of tone. In her account of the spectral army was Harriet Martineau retelling an interesting and attractive romance or was she, by demonstrating its credibility, perpetuating a superstition? "The ghosts" – the word is printed in a jittery gothic typeface – "appeared in myriads"; "The multitude was beyond imagination"; "There was nothing vaporous or indistinct about the appearance of these spectres". The language she chose served to underline the credibility of the story. She was casual with detail in a way which increased the authenticity of the sightings. Slack phrasing multiplied the number of witnesses: "Presenting the same appearances to twenty-six chosen witnesses and to all the inhabitants of all the cottages within view of the mountain". In place of the twenty six neighbours who "affirm" the sighting in Smith's account and the two principle witnesses, Lancaster and Stricket, who, forty years on, sign an attestation for James Clarke, Harriet Martineau stated of the twenty six who saw the phenomenon:

"The witnesses attested the whole story on oath before a magistrate;" and, without justification from the original texts, she suggested the extent to which the story was seen as a portent among the population of the neighbourhood: "and fearful were the expectations held by the whole country side about the coming events of the Scotch rebellion".

The story of the spectral army maintained its credibility among the credulous over succeeding years, because unlike other reported sightings, which were seen by individuals or by pairs of witnesses, the Souther Fell army was seen by a large number of witnesses. When Clarke presented his claim to a signed attestation, he gave the story a peculiar authority. When Harriet Martineau, perhaps with the intention of making a good story better, claimed that twenty six witnesses "attested the whole story on oath before a magistrate", she gave the spectral army an authority that was probably greater than any other secular ghost in history.

A Guide to the English Lakes, with its sub-text of demonstrating both the beauty and the obsolescence and credulity of superstition, may have subverted its own best intentions. More than forty years later that arch spiritualist and charlatan C. W. Leadbeater was quoting Harriet Martineau verbatim and at length as he demonstrated the "prevision of clairvoyance".

In Charles Webster Leadbeater we are dealing with a very special and peculiar intelligence. He began life in Stockport as the son of a railway clerk in 1854, and ended it as the leader of the Liberal Catholic Church in Australia. He is still highly respected by those who respect occult and spiritual and theosophist matters. On his journey, he became a disciple of Madame Blavatsky, a leading theosophist, the soul companion of Annie Besant, a disgraced pederast, and a promulgator of the theory of astral projection.

He believed that though the ordinary man's perception was limited by his physical body, the higher man could see beyond the limits of the physical world to perceive the past, the complete present and the future.

His writings – and he wrote voluminously – are pseudo-scientific and deceptively reasonable. The intellectual sleight of hand can be seen clearly in the introductory chapter of *Clairvoyance*: "Clairvoyance, like so many other things in nature, is mainly a question of vibrations, and is in fact nothing but an extension of powers which we are all using every day of our lives. We are living all the while surrounded by a vast sea of mingled air and ether . . . and it is chiefly by means of vibrations in that vast sea of matter that impressions reach us from the outside. This much we all know, but it may perhaps never have occurred to many of us that the number of these vibrations to which we are capable of responding is in reality quite infinitesimal. . . . But besides and beyond all this we know that man possesses an astral and a mental body, each of which can in process of time be aroused into activity, and will respond in turn to the vibrations of the matter of its own plane, thus opening up before the Ego, as he learns to function through these vehicles, two entirely new and far wider worlds of knowledge and power . . . It is not then difficult for us to grasp the possibility of a steady and progressive extension of our senses . . . When we come to deal with the astral senses themselves the methods of working are very different. . . . Every order of physical matter has its corresponding order of astral matter in constant association with it . . . we can no longer speak of separate senses such as sight and hearing, but rather have to postulate one general sense which responds so fully to the vibrations reaching it that when any object comes within its cognition it at once comprehends it fully, and as it were sees it, hears it, feels it, and knows all there is to know about it by the one instantaneous operation."[53]

That long extract demonstrates how specious thought can erect an intellectual structure that attracted many eminent people of the time. We move from a caricature of theories of perception through an analogy of atomic theory to a justification of fourth dimensions and astral modes of being.

Leadbeater's use of Harriet Martineau's account of the spectral army occurs as he expounds a peculiarly difficult concept: "Even if, in a dim sort of way, we feel ourselves able to grasp the idea that the whole of the past may be simultaneously and actively present in a sufficiently exalted consciousness, we are confronted by a far greater difficulty when we endeavour to realize how all the future may also be comprehended in that consciousness."[54]

An intellectual encounter with Charles Leadbeater would probably have been a bruising experience. He allows little room for disagreement: "There may still be some people who deny the possibility of prevision, but such denial simply shows their ignorance of the evidence on the subject." And yet some of his ideas are not so far removed from, for instance, Harriet Martineau's idea of necessarianism and the various ideas of predestination espoused by people as diverse as the Calvinists and the Unitarians. "There is no doubt whatever that, just as what is happening now is the result of causes set in motion in the past, so what will happen in the future will be the result of causes already in operation. Even down here we can calculate that if certain actions are performed certain results will follow."

Leadbeater developed his idea of prevision by drawing on examples from the past beginning with Martin Martin and his reports on second sight in the Hebrides from two centuries before: "It is best known to us as a not infrequent possession of the Scottish Highlanders, though it is by no means confined to them. Occasional instances of it have appeared in almost every nation, but it has always been commonest among mountaineers and men of lonely life. With us in England it is often spoken of as though it were the exclusive appanage of the Celtic race . . . It has a ghastly symbolism which is all its own—a symbolism of shrouds and corpse-candles, and other funereal horrors. In some cases it appears to be to a certain extent dependent on locality, for it is stated that inhabitants of the Isle of Skye who possess the faculty often lose it when they leave the island, even though it be only to cross to the mainland. The gift of such sight is sometimes hereditary in a family for generations, but this is not an invariable rule, for it often appears sporadically in one member of a family otherwise free from its lugubrious influence."[55]

Mrs Crowe's *The Night-side of Nature* and Dr. F. G. Lee's *Glimpses of the Supernatural* lend him stories of prevision when a Glasgow doctor had anticipated being charged by a bull and a lonely spinster had been prepared for a man with a bludgeon. As well as a mother of his acquaintance who had foreseen her sick child's need for an operation, Leadbeater also cited the case of the Cornish tin-miner who dreamt of the assassination of the Chancellor of the Exchequer, Spencer Perceval, and did nothing to avert the tragedy. He found it difficult to explain how the astral forces had acted so ineffectually.

He then moved on to discuss the "comparatively rare" "variety of clairvoyance in time" involving spectral armies and flocks of animals: "I refer to the cases in which spectral armies or phantom flocks of animals have been seen. In *The Night Side of Nature* we have accounts of several such visions. We are there told how at Havarah Park, near Ripley, a body of soldiers in white uniform, amounting to several hundreds, was seen by reputable people to go through various evolutions and then vanish; and how some years earlier a similar visionary army was seen in the neighbourhood of Inverness by a respectable farmer and his son.

"A phenomenon of the same sort was observed in the earlier part of this century at Paderborn in Westphalia, and seen by at least thirty people; but as, some years later, a review of twenty thousand men was held on the very same spot, it was concluded that the vision must have been some sort of second-sight—a faculty not uncommon in the district.[56]

Such spectral hosts, however, are sometimes seen where an army of ordinary men could by no possibility have marched, either before or after. One of the most remarkable accounts of such apparitions is given by Miss Harriet Martineau, in her description of The English Lakes. She writes as follows:"[57] Harriet Martineau's full account was reprinted verbatim, before Leadbeater offered his observations.

"Now in these cases, as so often happens in the investigation of occult phenomena, there are several possible causes, any one of which would be quite adequate to the production of the observed occurrences, but in the absence of fuller information it is hardly feasible to do more than guess as to which of these possible causes were in operation in any particular instance.

"The explanation usually suggested (whenever the whole story is not ridiculed as a falsehood) is that what is seen is a reflection by mirage of the movements of a real body of troops, taking place at a considerable distance. I have myself seen the ordinary mirage on several occasions, and know something therefore of its wonderful powers of deception; but it seems to me that we should need some entirely new variety of mirage, quite different from that at present known to science, to account for these tales of phantom armies, some of which pass the spectator within a few yards.

"First of all, they may be, as apparently in the Westphalian case above mentioned, simply instances of prevision on a gigantic scale—by whom arranged, and for what purpose, it is not easy to divine. Again, they may often belong to the past instead of the future, and be in fact the reflection of scenes from the âkâshic records—though here again the reason and method of such reflection is not obvious.

"There are plenty of tribes of nature-spirits perfectly capable, if for any reason they wished to do so, of producing such appearances by their wonderful power of glamour and such action would be quite in keeping with their delight in mystifying and impressing human beings. Or it may even sometimes be kindly intended by them as a warning to their friends of events that they know to be about to take place. It seems as though some explanation along these lines would be the most reasonable method of accounting for the extraordinary series of phenomena described by Miss Martineau—that is, if the stories told to her can be relied upon.

"Another possibility is that in some cases what have been taken for soldiers were simply the nature-spirits themselves going through some of the ordered evolutions in which they take so much delight, though it must be admitted that these are rarely of a character which could be mistaken for military manœuvres except by the most ignorant.

"The flocks of animals are probably in most instances mere records, but there are cases where they, like the "wild huntsmen" of German story, belong to an entirely different class of phenomena, which is altogether outside of our present subject. Students of the occult will be familiar with the fact that the circumstances surrounding any scene of intense terror or passion, such as an exceptionally horrible murder, are liable to be occasionally reproduced in a form which it needs a very slight development of psychic faculty to be able to see and it has sometimes happened that various animals formed part of such surroundings, and consequently they also are periodically reproduced by the action of the guilty conscience of the murderer (see Manual V., p. 83).

"Probably whatever foundation of fact underlies the various stories of spectral horsemen and hunting-troops may generally be referred to this category. This is also the explanation, evidently, of some of the visions of ghostly armies, such as that remarkable re-enactment of the battle of Edgehill which seems to have taken place at intervals for some months after the date of the real struggle, as testified by a justice of the peace, a clergyman, and other eye-witnesses, in a curious contemporary pamphlet entitled Prodigious Noises of War and Battle, at Edgehill, near Keinton, in Northamptonshire. According to the pamphlet this case was investigated at the time by some officers of the army, who clearly recognized many of the phantom figures that they saw. This looks decidedly like an instance of the terrible power of man's unrestrained passions to reproduce themselves, and to cause in some strange way a kind of materialization of their record."

Fortunately, Harriet Martineau did not live to read Charles Webster Leadbetter on *Clairvoyance*.

It would have made Miss Martineau smash her ear-trumpet.

The Knoll, Harriet Martineau's home in Ambleside as it appeared on the title-page of her Guide,

Chapter Fourteen:

Comclusion

Harriet Martineau was adamant in her opinion: "A ghost is no more an objective reality than I am the image of myself in the glass." With one heavy-handed joke she demolished the book that provided Leadbeater's evidence: "In our friend Mrs. Crowe's very interesting and ingenious book, "The Night Side of Nature," she sets out with the assumption that Mind is a spiritual entity, separate from the body; and in consequence, a pervading fallacy is introduced into her reasoning, and it becomes but the ghost of reasoning."[1]

Catherine Crowe was a remarkable woman in her own right. She separated from her military husband in her forties and had the courage, living among the literary elite of Edinburgh, to make her own way in the world as a novelist and writer, arguing forcefully for the rights of women. She was ten years older than the century when she published *The Night Side of Nature, or, Ghosts and Ghost Seers* in 1848, that year of uncertainty and revolutions. Taking her cue from German philosophy and works on dreams and the supernatural, she wrote about hauntings, apparitions, premonitions and revelations that came from somnambulism and hypnotism. The popular but rational way in which she presented evidence of the irrational, of the spiritual side of nature, caught the mood of the time and, within six years, the book went into sixteen editions. It was hugely influential. It stimulated Charles Baudelaire towards his understanding of "Correspondences" and much late nineteenth century spiritualist and theosophical writing treated the work as a source text.

Amidst her *Miscellaneous Phenomena*, she considered the cases of spectral armies, only to question the all-too-easy scientific explanation of them: "Neither can we consider the numerous instances of armies seen in the air to be apparitions; and yet these phenomena are so well established, that they have been accounted for by supposing them to be atmospherical reflections of armies elsewhere, in actual motion." In the rather slipshod way that she argued her case, she raised what she saw as a problematic issue: "But how are we to account for the visionary troops which are not seen in the air, but on the very ground on which the seers themselves stand?" She cited the case of the hundreds of soldiers making their evolutions in Havarah Park in 1812, naively stressing the reliability of the witnesses and dismissing possible explanations: "They were both men of excellent character and unimpeachable veracity, insomuch that nobody who knew them doubted that they actually saw what they described, or, at all events, believed that they did. It is to be observed also, that the ground is not swampy, nor subject to any exhalations."

She did not mention the apparition on Souther Fell, but she did describe in great detail a report of a very similar occurrence a few years later, when memories of 'Butcher' Cumberland's troops were still painfully fresh in the Highlands: "About the year 1750, a visionary army of the same description was seen in the neighbourhood of Inverness, by a respectable farmer, of Glenary, and his son. The number of troops was very great, and they had not the slightest doubt that they were otherwise than substantial forms of flesh and blood. They counted at least sixteen pairs of columns, and had abundance of time to observe every particular. The front ranks marched seven abreast, and were accompanied by a good many women and children, who were carrying tin cans and other implements of cookery. The men were clothed in red, and their arms shone brightly in the sun. In the midst of them was an animal, a deer or a horse, they could not distinguish which, that they were driving furiously forward with their bayonets. The younger of the two men observed to the other, that every now and then, the rear ranks were obliged to run to overtake the van; and the elder one, who had been a soldier, remarked that that was always the case, and recommended him, if he ever served, to try and march in the front. There was only one mounted officer; he rode a grey dragoon horse, and wore a gold-laced hat, and blue Hussar cloak, with wide open sleeves lined with red. The two spectators observed him so particularly, that they said afterwards, they should recognize him anywhere. They were, however, afraid of being ill-treated, or forced to go along with the troops, whom they concluded had come from Ireland, and landed at Kyntyre; and whilst they were climbing over a dyke to get out of their way, the whole thing vanished." The parallels, with the breaking of the column to catch up, are striking although perhaps little more so than we might expect from any contemporary description of an army marching.

Mrs Crowe also cited a very recent case, one that Leadbeater had quoted, that had happened within a dozen years of her writing, and for which she had both human and animal witnesses: "Some years since, a phenomenon of the same sort was observed at Paderborn, in Westphalia, and seen by at least thirty persons, as well as by horses and dogs, as was discovered by the demeanour of these animals, In October, 1836, on the very same spot, there was a review of twenty thousand men; and the people then concluded, that the former vision was a *second sight.*

"A similar circumstance occurred in Stockton Forest, some years ago; and there are many recorded elsewhere; one especially, in the year 1686, near Lanark, where, for several afternoons, in the months of June and July there were seen, by numerous spectators, companies of men in arms, marching in order by the banks of the Clyde, and other companies meeting them, &c. &c.; added to which, there were showers of bonnets, hats, guns, swords, &c, which the seers described with the greatest exactness. All who were present could not see these things, and Walker relates, that one gentleman, particularly, was turning the thing into ridicule, calling the seers 'Damned witches and warlocks, with the second sight!' boasting that 'The devil a thing he could see!' when he suddenly exclaimed, with fear and trembling, that he now saw it all; and entreated those who did not see, to say nothing—a change that may be easily accounted for, be the phenomena of what nature it may, by supposing him to have touched one of the seers, when the faculty would be communicated like a shock of electricity."[2]

The stories were reported with an easy credulity and, probably read with an equal enthusiasm. Mrs Crowe's work satisfied a need to believe in supernatural phenomenon. People wanted a more tangible sense of a life after death than was offered by orthodox religion in a society that was about to undergo the intellectual revolution brought about by the work of Charles Darwin. It also made her a laughing stock. In 1854, Catherine Crowe, may have been subject to a mental aberration. She denied the incident, and claimed to have sought rest and recuperation in a hydropathic resort. However, Charles Dickens, who did so much to fashion our modern sensitivity to the fictional ghost, was merciless in his letters: "Mrs Crowe has gone stark mad – and stark naked – on the spirit-rapping imposition. She was found t'other day in the street, clothed only in her chastity, a pocket-handkerchief and a visiting card. She had been informed, it appeared, by the spirits, that if she went out in that trim she would be invisible. She is now in a mad-house and, I fear, hopelessly insane."[3]

Thirty years later, Moncure Daniel Conway, a distinguished American, exiled in Britain, preaching a liberal, if not a secular, universal theology, offered a sceptical and rationalist view of Souther Fell's spectral army: "What was seen on this strongly-authenticated occasion? Was anything seen? None can tell. It is open to us to believe that there may have been some play of mirage. As there are purely aerial echoes, so are their aerial reflectors for the eye. On the other hand, the vision so nearly resembles the spectral processions which have passed through the mythology of the world, that we can never be sure that it was not the troop of King Arthur emerging from Avallon to announce the approaching strife. A few fleecy, strangely shaped clouds, chasing each-other along the hillside in the evening's dusk would have amply sufficed to create the latter vision, and the danger of the time would have supplied all the second-sight required to reveal it to considerable numbers. In questions of this kind a very small circumstance – a phrase, a name, perhaps – may turn the balance of probabilities. Thus it may be noted that, in the instance just related, the vision was seen on the steep side of Souter Fell. Fell means a hill or steep rock, as in Drachenfels. But as to Souter, although as Mr Robert Ferguson says, the word may originally have meant sheep, it is found in Scotland used as 'shoemaker' in connection with fabulous giants of that region. Sir Thomas Urquhart, in the seventeenth century, relates it as the tradition of the two promontories of Cromarty, called 'Soutars', that they were the work-stools of two giants who supplied their comrades with shoes and buskins. Possessing but one set of implements, they used to fling these to each other across the opening of the firth, where the promontories are only two miles apart. In process of time the name Soutar, shoemaker, was bequeathed by the craftsmen to their stools. It is not improbable that the name gradually connected itself with other places bearing traditions connecting them with the fabulous race, and that in this way the Soutar Fell, from meaning in earlier times much the same as Giant's Hill, preserved even in 1743-44 enough of the earlier uncanny associations to awaken the awe of Borderers in a time of rebellion. The vision may therefore have been seen by light which had journeyed all the way from the mythologic heavens of ancient India: substantially subjective – such stuff as dreams and dreamers are made of - no doubt there were outer clouds, shapes and afterglows enough, even in the absence of any fata morgana, to supply canvas and pigment to the cunning artist that hides in the eye."[4]

Moncure Conway was the first commentator to place the imagination at the heart of any explanation of the spectral army. His book on *Demonology and Devil-lore* was another of those vade-mecums that comprised numerous mythologies, that sought, like Scott and Brewster, to eradicate superstition by exposing it to the light of reason. Conway was a greater iconoclast and he roamed widely through all religions and all regions, and, unlike his two predecessors, he was prepared to challenge the superstitions of the Christian religion. He sensed, even though he had little idea of the geography and was fairly cavalier in his abridgement of Clarke's account, that the story was prompted by a physical event as insubstantial as a fleecy cloud, but that it fed on the tensions of the time and grew in a soil that was rich in "earlier uncanny associations". Nevertheless, the inventive and imaginative translator of Rabelais, Sir Thomas Urquhart, must have been a peculiarly unreliable source. Conway may have been exercising his speculative imagination when he made an etymological connection between Cromarty and Cumberland and suggested that there might have been some imaginative association between the Soutars of Cromarty and Souther Fell.

However, his etymology agrees with modern scholarly interpretations and may hint at older, forgotten legends that might once have been associated with the fell and might well be part of a shared Celtic folk-lore. Earlier writers had explained the spectral army in meteorological or optical terms or, by not questioning the story itself or the terms within which it was couched, they had accepted, seriously or ludically, the metaphysical pre-suppositions of words such as 'spectral', 'ghostly' or 'phantom'.

A modern explanation should employ the model suggested by Conway of identifying a physical stimulus consistent with the evidence, such as it is, and demonstrate the complexities of contemporaneous and inherited individual and group psychology that caused the story to emerge in the form that it did.

George Smith was convinced that the people were speaking in good faith, that "they apprehended they saw such appearances", and he was aware that imagination might have played a role in attributing significance to a vapour, "No doubt fancy will extend to miraculous heights in persons disposed to indulge it". However, he felt that if there was a physical explanation, his "lambent agitated meteor", he was faced with three difficulties. Two related to the agreed specificity of the report: that is how the meteor or vapour might indicate the regular movement of the officer who left the column and then returned to it; and how the vapour could remain consistent over time so as to represent the reported five columns. The hardest of the three to explain, however, was that, if the supposed appearances were the consequence of a natural phenomenon, why was it that the apparition returned at the same time, St. John's Eve, in the three years, 1735, 1737 and 1745.

The answer, surprisingly, was provided by James Clarke. The one atmospheric vapour that might consistently return on St John's Eve, and return only in the pattern indicated, was the smoke from the bonfires built by the shepherds who had gathered in the fells for their celebration of the summer solstice. In recounting his story some forty years after the event, William Lancaster chose to recall and James Clarke chose to record Lancaster's initial response in his exchange with the excited Stricket: "He went into the house, and informed Mr. Lancaster he had something curious to shew him, Mr. Lancaster asked what it was, adding, "I suppose some bonfire," (for it was then, and still is a custom, for the shepherds, on the evening before St John's day, to light bonfires, and vie with each other in having the largest.)" In 1841, R.T. Hampson in *Medii Aevi*

Kalendarium, a curious book that investigated the dates, charters and customs of the Middle Ages, made the perceptive comment: "Connected with, and in all probability resulting from, the fires on St. John's eve, is a remarkable and extraordinary phenomenon, which was twice witnessed on the mountain called Soutra Fell, or Southerfell, in Westmoreland. Many of the prodigies related by our ancient historians, whose credulity led them to look upon all strange effects, of which they could not perceive the cause, as miraculous portents, may, like the apparitions on Soutra Fell, admit of natural explanations."[5]

It would be surprising if the well-travelled and canny James Clarke had not appreciated the implication of the exchange, and registered an accustomed scepticism to Stricket's apparitions on the part of Lancaster. It is possible that the dismissive interrogation was Clarke's own invention. Introducing his unparalleled and improbable account, he wrote: "I cannot help relating it, and then my readers must judge for themselves." Sensing, perhaps, that the smoke was the origin of the phenomenon, it would have been in character for Clarke to promote the story, so consistent with the lively, popular anecdotes in his *Survey*, but leave the clue for the amusement of his less gullible readers.

The shepherds from the Skiddaw fells met until recent times to return stray sheep and they naturally turned the meetings into something of a festivity. Such gatherings on Midsummer Eve had a long history. The shepherds in the early part of the eighteenth century were probably among the most conservative in the maintenance of their folk traditions and their gatherings may have partaken of the myths of the Beltane fire, which was very widespread particularly in the north of the country. Thomas Pennant, having been "tossed violently with what is called a bottom wind", on Derwentwater, commented, on his visit to "the Elysium of the north", that: "Till of late years the superstition of the bel-tin was kept up in these parts; and in this rural sacrifice it was customary for the performers to bring with them boughs of the mountain ash."[6] William Hutchinson found it worth noting, thereby indicating that the custom had been largely abandoned by 1794, that in the then remote parish of Cumwhitton, to the east of Carlisle, which was dominated by "a druidical temple . . . in the middle of a dark and dreary waste", "They hold the wake, on the eve of St John, with lighting fires, dancing, &c, the old bel-teing."[7] Jonathan

Boucher, the supplier of those few lines of biography of George Smith, in an ambitious *Glossary of Archaic and Provincial Words*, a supplement to Johnson's *Dictionary*, contended that the Beltane was not, specifically, the Baal-fire, but a bon or bone-fire, and recalled some observations he had made as a boy: "Being a Northern man, and having myself oftentimes seen in the county of Cumberland, *bone-fires* literally made of *bones,* - collected from motives either of frugality or of convenience, or both, from the carcases of the animals that had died in or around the village during the preceding year."[8]

St John's Eve, marking the summer solstice, had been celebrated with the lighting of fires since the earliest times. Nineteenth century antiquarians assumed a continuous tradition going back to the Persians and the Zoroastrians. Jeremiah Sullivan from Kendal would have it that: "The Midsummer rejoicings are most generally known under the name of bone-fires, being so called from the custom of burning bones on that night . . . together with sports, which were kept up in some places till midnight, in others till cockcrow . . . According to the general opinion of the old writers, the bonefires were intended to drive away dragons and evil spirits by their offensive smell. Stow thinks that a great fire purges the "infection of the air;" but another author declares that "dragons hate nothyng more than the stenche of brennynge bones."[9] The learned but disorganised John Brand of Gateshead, one of the great collectors of folklore, quoted a disturbingly unreliable source on the Irish mythology of Midsummer bonfires: "The author of the Comical Pilgrim's Pilgrimage into Ireland, 1723, p. 92, says: "On the vigil of St, John the Baptist's Nativity, they make bonfires, and run along the streets and fields with wisps of straw blazing on long poles to purify the air, which they think infectious, by believing all the devils, spirits, ghosts, and hobgoblins fly abroad this night to hurt mankind. Farthermore, it is their dull theology to affirm the souls of all people leave their bodies on the eve of this feast, and take their ramble to that very place, where, by land or sea, a final separation shall divorce them for evermore in this world."[10]

The people of the area around Souther Fell, like those throughout most of Cumberland would have drawn on a long and complex heritage of folklore and mythology. Place names in the immediate vicinity indicate overlays of settlement. Blencathra includes the Welsh element 'blaen' for 'hill' and 'cathera' may be the Welsh 'cadair' or 'chair'. An eighteenth century form appears as 'Blenk Arthur; suggesting a folk etymology related to the medieval legends that associated Arthur with Inglewood Forest and Carlisle. This association was strengthened with the publication of Bishop Percy's *Reliques* and Scott's *Bridal of Triermain*. Moncure Conway's suggestion "the troop of King Arthur emerging from Avallon" was not just facetious. Blencathra's once popular alternative English name of 'Saddleback' was first recorded by Thomas Gray and is found on the maps by Thomas Donald and James Clarke. 'Souther Fell' is probably Norse. 'Carrock Fell' combines Celtic and Norse elements. 'Grisdale' is Old Norse for 'valley of the pigs' and 'Mungrisdale' may indicate an early association with the Northumbrian St. Kentigern, although there is no pre-Reformation evidence for such a connection. 'Mosedale' is Norse.[11]

Insofar as any observations might be made, the earlier Celtic inhabitants were replaced on the better agricultural land by the Angles and Northumbrians. The Norse settlement in the ninth and tenth centuries was of people who had first settled in Ireland. These people tended to occupy new ground, hence there is a clear pattern of Norse names in the more remote areas.

One intriguing possibility in the racial and folkloric mix in the area is supplied by the development of mining in the Caldbeck Fells. An ancient rhyme indicates that the rich deposits were well-known:

> "Caldbeck and Caldbeck fells
> Are worth all England else."

It wasn't until the sixteenth century that mining on any scale returned to the Northern Fells. In 1564 Daniel Hechstetter led a team of mining engineers financed by the Hans Langnauer Company of Augsburg to mine for copper in Borrowdale and the Newlands Valley. Within a year or two, the German miners were also exploiting the fells south of Caldbeck, where the steep-sided ghylls exposed quartz veins in the rock giving possible access to both copper and lead. The miners came from Keswick and opened up over twenty-four workings in the area. Although they were financed by the house in Augsburg, the miners themselves came from the Harz Mountains and from mining areas in Austria. They had names like Martin Andere, Hans Hellensteiner, Benedikt Efflender, Bernhard

Fetchenbach and Jobst Stoltz. We still have the names of two hundred or so of those miners from the days of Queen Elizabeth and of those, about two thirds have German names. Many brought their wives and families over and others stayed in the area and married local girls.[12] Somewhat nearer to Souther Fell were the significantly named Dutchman's Moss on the side of Carrock, reopened in 1692 by Doctor Edward Wright, and Brandy Gill, a mile west of Mosedale, which was probably mined before 1700. George Smith describes it as "long since worn out". A Joseph Hechstetter is recorded as negotiating a lease with Sir John Lowther in 1664 for a mine high up on the side of Gategill on the Threlkeld side of Blencathra.

The name Stricket is not on any of the lists of workers. It is a name found in Germany and the Netherlands, but, even though it is an extremely uncommon English surname, William Green refers to a Stricket Dodd, a hill near St John's Vale. The name is no longer known by farmers in the area and is not mentioned in *The Place-Names of Cumberland.* Whether or not Daniel Stricket was of German descent, it is probable that memories of the folklore of the Harz mountains were retained by the German miners among the Caldbeck Fells and equally probable, since they worked alongside English workers and inter-married and made their homes in Cumberland, that traces of such lore were known to the farmers and shepherds who lived in and around the fells.

Just as there might have been a residual awareness of the Brocken spectre, memories of Celtic, Irish and Norse mythology might well have persisted in the more remote parts of the fells. Midsummer's eve is one of the most significant of all days in the mythological calendar, rich with stories in all cultures. It is a time when we might expect country people to feel a particular awareness and openness to suggestion. The figures of the Brocken, the myth that may have persisted in Ireland that "all the devils, spirits, ghosts, and hobgoblins fly abroad this night to hurt mankind", and the image of figures leaping through fires may well have lain dormant in the small community of peasants who lived beneath Southerfell. Mrs Crowe's account of a spectral army near Inverness in 1750 and James Thomson's immediately contemporary lines about apparitions in the Hebrides show how such perceptions remained part of the mind-set of the times.

There is one further folk memory that may be even more pertinent. Harriet Martineau over a century later wrote of the aurora borealis being known in the North as 'Lord Derwentwater's Lights'. At the time Mary, Countess Cowper, had confided to her diary about the agitation in London: "The town full of lies of what was seen in the air last night. Papers printed and sold that two armies were seen to fight in the air, that two men with flaming swords were seen to fight over Lincom's-inn-fields. The mob that went to Mr. Linet's burial last night said they saw two men in the sky fight without heads." Tales of armies fighting in the sky and much else were equally prevalent in the north. This quite exceptional aurora borealis must have lived long in the folk memory and continued to be associated with Lord Derwentwater and the Jacobites. The lands in the Mungrisdale area were under the Lordship of the Duke of Norfolk, whose family had been strong supporters of William of Orange during the Glorious Revolution even though they were the most senior Catholic family in England, and the people may not have felt that strong sympathy for the Derwentwaters that was probable in their lands around Keswick. The first sighting on Souther Fell was within twenty, and the last within thirty, years of Lord Derwentwater's execution and the association of mysterious lights in the sky with the Jacobite Insurrection of 1715 must have been particularly strong during those years.

The people of the area were perhaps not the illiterate and credulous peasants characterised by later London commentators. George Smith's map shows perhaps 16 dwellings in the area at the foot of Southerfell, although a group of eight of them are difficult to account for unless they represent the village of Scales. James Clarke only showed four dwellings north of the road, Blakehills, Blakebeck, Lowside and Southerfell, although his map does not extend as far as Wiltonhill.

The area was a poor one, but not without education. Hutchinson was scandalised at "the meagre support of the clergyman" before he benefited from Queen Anne's Bounty: "Animadversions are unnecessary on the disproportions of church revenues, when the poor curate here laboured in the holy vineyard for 6l. 0s, 9d, a year with the scanty contingent payments of the churchings."[13] Those churchings consisted of twenty tenements in Mungrisdale itself, seven in Murrey, four in Bousgill, seven houses in Mosedale, four in Gill and four in Swineside – a total of only forty-six in a widespread area. Hutchinson also told the story of Joseph Sowerby, born in the hamlet of Murrey in 1721, for a short time a pupil of George Smith, who, merited the following obituary from Dr. James Bradley of Oxford: "Cut off at the age of twenty-eight a genius that wanted only time to have ripened into that of a second Newton".[14] The Quaker Meeting House at Mosedale, which was established in 1702, and other meeting houses in this area to the east of the fells, testify to a strong tradition of education and intellectual independence in the area. Clarke, in a rather superior manner, talked of "This country, like every other where cultivation has been lately introduced, abounds in the aniles fabulae of fairies, ghosts, and apparitions". Nevertheless, these were people who would have known their Bible and may well have read Josephus and Milton.

We are dealing with a small community of able, independent-minded people, distant from the highways of the wider world, but far from totally isolated. The long history of mining in the area suggests a continuing commerce. The lands were part of the estate of one of the great landholders in the country who maintained his castle in the same parish. Mungrisdale was a remote but not isolated community.

The process by which the story grew is interesting. If we assume the account as presented by Smith is as he received it from William Lancaster, then we have the development of the story as it was understood by one of the principle participants. Smith's account is the way William Lancaster wanted it explained. The first sighting was by a servant, who provided a distinct and specific picture, but, since his story was not corroborated – there is no mention of it being questioned or contradicted – "he was discredited and laughed at".

William Lancaster's first sight two years later was of something he saw as perfectly normal, that was of "several gentlemen . . . following their horses at a distance, as if they had been hunting". (The area was, and is, prime hunting territory, the home of Joe Bowman and the lands beneath Saddleback provided the setting for one of Anthony Trollope's finest hunting scenes, in *Lady Anna*.) It was only ten minutes later that he looked again and saw the men "mounted and a vast army following, five in rank, crowding over at the same place where the servant said he had saw them two years before". The family were called "who all agreed in the same opinion". It was when the family were watching that the further detail was added of "some of the five would quit rank, and stand in a fronting posture". The larger group also observed how the orderly march "grew more regardless of discipline and rather had the appearance of people riding from a market". They all continued to perceive this level of detail even as the light faded.

It was eight years later that the next sighting occurred, eight years in a farming household where the details of the incredible sight were discussed, developed and confirmed into a precise and consistent story. The story was told with what we might assume were the usual anecdotal expansions and assertive precisions to the wider community, the people in Wiltonhill and Southerfellside. These were people who were unlikely to question the reality of what had supposedly been seen, but ones who were primed by folklore, legend and literature, as well as the accepted understandings of earlier times, to believe in its possibility. It was not surprising that they should "all affirm they saw the same appearance", having been very thoroughly prepared as to what they might expect. The last comment that "it did appear to be less real" suggests that the strong set of communally pre-conceived ideas gradually weakened as the apparition was observed. Smith's final sentence, "for some of the company were so affected with it, as, in the morning, to climb the mountain, through an idle expectation of finding horse shoes after so numerous an army; but saw not the vestige or print of a foot," seems to suggest that they believed in the physical reality of what they thought they had seen.

The witnesses were all looking into the setting sun above Southerfell on a clear night. If we follow Smith's account the shepherd's bonfire must have been located to the north, possibly on the Tongue or on the easternmost part of Bowscale Fell, for the smoke to blow along Souther Fell from north to south. This would explain the irregularity of the sightings over the years since the prevailing wind was from the west. Clarke's version, with the army marching northwards from Knott at the southern end of the fell, would suggest a fire at that end, possibly on Knott itself. The Land Revenue Records from 1589 refer to a 'Brunte Knott' or 'burnt hill', which may well indicate a hill used regularly for such bonfires.[15] If the fire had included bones and the carcases of dead animals the smoke would have been particularly thick and acrid. The actual description of the apparition in all cases has aspects that would correspond to smoke from a bonfire. The servant's distinct bodies of troops implies a break in the continuous flow of the smoke. Lancaster's later sighting of a few gentleman and horses that developed into a vast army suggests the first clouds of smoke growing and becoming a thickening flow and the 1745 reference to people riding from market might indicate the spreading out and breaking up of the regular flow of smoke.

Smith's version of events, if taken at face value, is consistent with the story of the spectral army being a case of mass suggestion to an unsophisticated community, already well acquainted with the mythology, folklore and Biblical, and possibly secular, literature of spectres and spectral armies. They would have been a community that knew little of the ideas of the Enlightenment, but still thought in the manner of Joseph Glanvil and his predecessors and understood ghosts as part of a theological cosmogony. Their visions were actuated by gazing into the setting sun at the smoke from shepherd's bonfires on an evening when their minds would have been particularly sensitised to such phenomenon and in a period of national unease which in their understandings was closely connected with the images in the sky which they called 'Lord Derwentwater's Lights'.

George Smith cannot have been the neutral transmitter of a story told by an unsophisticated farmer to the intellectual and enlightened readers of *The Gentleman's Magazine.* The story he heard was already two years old and had already "made so much noise in the world". He would certainly have clarified and shaped the story, 'purified the dialect' and rendered the whole in a rational and sequential order. In so doing he would have added further form and credibility to that which had already developed as a result of public inquisition.

However, George Smith may have acted as a government agent. He may have sought to change a story from a remote area that seemed to portend further unrest and insurrection to a society still traumatized by rebellion, a story, which the authorities feared would prompt and strengthen further unrest and rebellion. Smith would have changed that story into one that spoke of government order and power, a story of a strong and well-disciplined Hanoverian army. If the latter was the case, then much or most of the story, other than the initial concept, could well have been his creation.

For many reasons James Clarke's account must be regarded as highly suspect. William Bell, writing of *Shakespeare's Puck and his Folklore,* in 1844, reprinted Clarke's account verbatim, albeit as a footnote, even though he irritably discounted the whole story: "When we, however, find that Clarke's careful attestation of an event happening in 1744 is made by the parties for the first time in 1785; that these parties were illiterate and credulous peasants; and that the document is evidently drawn up by the author in his own language, with motives and consequences which a peasant could neither have suggested nor understood, we may fairly be allowed to receive the narrative with considerable drawbacks; and as the memorable rebellion by the Jacobites occurred in the following few months – the great rebellion of 1745, which disturbed the north, and gave Britain its last experience of the horrors of war upon her own soil – we may almost be permitted to believe, that in the interval of forty-one years, a story may have grown up in the imagination of the narrators, founded upon some under-current of prevalent superstition: this belief, the haze of so large an interval of time and frequent repetition of what ought to have occurred according to the subsequent events, may have so deeply imprinted a fiction on the mind of the narrators, that they could, no doubt, have conscientiously given an oath as to its truth and occurrence."[16]

James Clarke met the two witnesses forty years after the event by arrangement. In those forty years, the spectral army of Souther Fell had been sufficiently notorious to be the standard fare of at least one sensationalist national magazine and Stricket and Lancaster must have retold the story many, many times. Green's comments suggest that Daniel Stricket had become something of a local celebrity speaking of the "appearance in a positive and assured manner". William Green was able to accept the ridiculous claim that the spectral army was noticed "from the High Nest five miles from Souter Fell, . . . by an aunt of Mr. John Allison, of Rosthwaite in Borrowdale". That claim must have been part of the gossip over the forty years before Clarke received his attestations. James Clarke also wrote of "many concurrent testimonies" and yet he gave an account that is different in almost every detail from George

Smith's. Clarke's is a sophisticated, abridged retelling that employs an embedded narrative and uses dramatic devices to add credibility. The signed attestation is the neat confirmatory conclusion to "a phenomenon that perhaps can scarcely be paralleled by history, or reconciled to probability".

George Smith had some acquaintance with the area. He had lived within twelve miles of Carlisle, at Boothby near Brampton and at Wigton, and he may have lived at Unthank near Hutton in the Forest for a short time when he taught Joseph Sowerby. Yet his account of the country is that of a stranger, of the scientist and antiquarian, observing and notating, compiling lists of the rocks and the flora, and noting the scenery he sees according to a predetermined system, using terms such as "turbinated trough". When he departed from this ordered tabulation, he sought the security of classical mythology to provide him with his reference points. He exaggerated the more rounded hills of the Northern Fells into "insuperable precipices and towering peaks" and he found landscapes of a "more romantic air". He may have been employing the language of the Burkean sublime, but he was a learned surveyor describing the landscape and not seeking to discover a re-affirming emotional charge in the scenery before him. When he encountered the story of the spectral army, he discounted it, except, being, perhaps too readily impressed with the quality of his witnesses, for the listed anomalies which he could not explain.

James Clarke, even though he too was a surveyor, was very different. He was describing scenery he knew well and seeking to project those aspects of his favoured county that he thought would interest the intended purchaser, the new breed of tourist. Even though he dedicated his book to the Prince of Wales, he was not the same class as Smith and self-educated, lacked his urbane education. When he told the story of the spectral army, it was to relish its curiosity, to feel himself touched by the magic of romance. It was not a problem that challenged his assumptions about the world, but one to which he could provide a facile resolution.

William Hutchinson recorded something very different. He was barely a presence, drawing on the work of others, always quoted at length, to create a composite but unsystematic mosaic of understandings of the county. Everything was there, the genealogies and history, the folklore and the husbandry, the antiquities and the industry, but there were no views of the landscape.

Seeing the mountains of her novels for the first time, having a mind stocked with the painted imaginings of Salvator Rosa and Gaspard Dughet, Anne Radcliffe paid little or no attention to the particularity of place, but looked for the hills to correspond to her pre-conceived Gothic perceptions.

Britton and Brayley may not even have seen the landscape, simply transcribing other texts in their cramped London office and readily using analogous phenomena as ready copy, but it was their work that laid the foundation and set the terms for the discussion of the spectral army from a scientific and romantic perspective for the next quarter of a century or more.

William and Dorothy Wordsworth and Coleridge did see the landscape. Wordsworth rejoiced in freeing himself from the restricting poeticisms of a previous generation and seeing things individually and freshly. The spectral army was dismissed as the false perceptions of an old shepherd and used as the symbol of the rejected, but once tempting gothic self-projection. Dorothy simply took a delight in everything she saw, the world was constantly renewed before her eyes. Coleridge took a physical pleasure in the landscape itself, losing himself on Saddleback, relishing his own exertions and feeling himself one with the rocks and streams. It was when abstracting himself that the images derived from the physical world became the tools of his thought, they lent him the metaphors to understand the world.

For Walter Scott the landscape and history, which he understood in grand generalized particularities, was the vast backdrop on which his imagination played like some grandly orchestrated aurora borealis. His relish of the richness of humanity is seen in his enthusiastic collecting of border folklore and antiquities as well as the crowded canvases of his fiction. The spectral army was another example of folk belief, absorbed into the vast mental repository that supplied the plots, the characters and the local colour for his poetry and novels. The note uncritically reprinting James Clarke's text gave credibility to his poetic imaginings. More than anyone else, it was Scott who confirmed the developing taste for a Romantic landscape. The Highlands of Scotland, the rolling hills of the

Borders and the people of another time and place offered an escapist vision of a passionate life to the multitudes who found themselves part of a rapidly developing industrialised and urban culture.

James Hogg participated in the story, relived it and made it his own. The landscape was the place where he worked throughout his life, a failing farmer to the very end. His portrayal of the countryside is always complete with mists and rain and sunlight and beasta and men. With James Hogg, the story itself had the possibility of actuality. It could be inhabited by his imagination, an imagination that, fiercely intelligent as it was, never allowed itself to be encumbered by the restraints of reason.

Allan Cunningham, having lived the life of a working man and absorbed the same tradition as James Hogg, retained the dignity of his upbringing, but, removed from his past, recreated it in respectful detail for an audience that was nostalgic for a pre-industrial past, an audience that felt itself to be both superior to that past, but also felt a sense of unidentified loss. His meticulously observed details of peasant life and his honest respect for character were balanced by the freedom with which he felt he could deploy and recreate the folk tradition.

Sir David Brewster came from the same community, but he expressed little sensitivity for the landscape. The peculiar situation of the spectral army was irrelevant to his explanation. He was concerned with the optical possibilities and had little sense of the possible part played by the land or the people in the production of the phenomenon.

For J.C. Bristow, Ulsmere reflected his egotistic personality, just as the waters of Ullsmere reflected the expanding grandeur of his lakeside mansion. The newly affluent from the cities and the empire were building their mansions on the shores of Windermere and the Lakes were becoming the cultivated projection of an industrialised society. Bristow was acquisitive and lived in order to display his acquisitions. He sailed his sloop on the lake and he pillaged English poetry. The story of the spectral army, unexamined, was simply yet another object in his over ornate parlour.

A generation later, John Pagen White and Wilson Armistead, one a surgeon in Liverpool and the other a businessman in Leeds, were recreating a fictional Lakeland past to add lustre to the pretty landscape they loved. Armistead's thorn bush of treasured romantic memory was a nostalgic, sentimental reminiscence. Any sense of the countryside as James Hogg experienced it was lost in the urban smog of memory. William Gresley, with his high church didacticism, and George Soane, of the risque melodramas, used landscape like a painted backdrop in the theatre, to lend colour and emotion to the action they placed before our eyes.

Harriet Martineau's Lake District was a place to be known and explored. There were places to visit, paths to be walked, observations to be made and facts to be noted. Father West's stations became views to be taken. The landscape was there to be consumed. If she wished to describe a view, she drew on the words of her predecessors, otherwise she restricted herself to practical directions and the occasional piece of advice as to the best spot for a picnic or the place to hire a pony or catch a train. The process of organizing the tourist, mapping out how he might securely obtain the maximum amount of aesthetic pleasure that began with Thomas West, was completed by Harriet Martineau with her well-informed packages of Lakeland experience awaiting the eager visitor. Black's and Murray's Guides provided even neater, tighter, more convenient packages.

The story of the spectral army of Souther Fell was part of this process whereby the individual and particular lost these qualities and became a commodity, a useful package with a set of significances, to be traded from book to book, losing its original identity and being shaped to the requirements of different times and places, meeting the needs of new audiences in changing cultures.

The story had been reprinted and repeated as fantasy and fiction and scientific fact in newspapers and magazines and journals and novels and poems throughout Britain, Europe and America. Scott's poetry had swept across Europe and was translated, usually with the notes, into Russian, Polish, French, German, Spanish, Italian and most of the other European languages. "Daniello Stricket", for instance, was to be found in *Collezione sei romanzi storici e poetici di Walter Scott.* Sir David Brewster's *Letters on Natural* Magic found many imitators and plagiarists. So influential was the work that the published response to his accessible and popular science seemed, within a decade, to cover all subjects from *An Introduction to Meteorology* by David Purdie Thomson, *A Treatise on Mathematical and Physical Geography* by John Lee Comstock and *A*

System of Geography: Popular and Scientific by James Bell, *An Essay Towards a Science of Consciousness* by J L Murphy and *The Wonders of Nature and Providence Displayed* by Joseph Priest. Brewster's version of the spectral army was in the *Dublin Review* in 1837 and the *Young Men's Magazine* two years later. In Germany, the *Briefe uber der Naturaliche Magie* found its content repeated in *Das Meer, seine Bewohner und seine Wunder* and Marbach's *Populares Physikalische Lexicon.* James Hogg and Allan Cunningham's stories and articles were reprinted throughout the next twenty years in papers and journals in Britain and the United States. They were to be read throughout the English-speaking world.

The story told by one man about what he had seen one evening on the fells was now available to millions throughout the world. In the process it had been utterly transformed. In 1735, England was entering the modern age. The responses to the aurora borealis in 1716 revealed how one hierarchical and diverse society had within itself totally contradictory understandings. Edmund Halley used the objective language of science, but also resorted to dramatic metaphor, to describe and explain the amazing lights which the fearful tenants of Lord Derwentwater's Dilston Hall saw as armies and rivers running with blood. George Smith, when he interpreted the story which William Lancaster had told him, may well have purged it of its emotion and superstition in his retelling. For a man of science notating the landscape, there was no possibility of an apparition being the direct intervention of the deity. The people of Blakehills and Wiltonhill, despite Smith claiming that he gave the story verbatim, may have understood things very differently. The antiquarian would have found the story curious, but it perplexed natural philosopher because it could not be explained by the physical laws that he used to explain the universe. The Hanoverian politician may have found the original story dangerous and acted accordingly.

Forty years later, in a society ready to be excited by fictions of ghosts, James Clarke offered his much-changed version of the story with a degree of sceptical playfulness or commercial acuity. It was intriguing. It belonged to an unimproved country where the old beliefs still persisted and had no place in the modern world, but yet there had been so many witnesses and thee were those two undeniable attestations.

Britton and Brayley were the casual participants in a more scientific age. M. Haue's account of the Brocken spectre was entertaining in itself and seemed to offer an explanation to so many phenomenon. The stories of ghosts were, as the spectres in Ann Radcliffe's novels, always subject to rational explication. Physical science and not psychology had the answers. Otherwise, they were a part of the folklore of a pre-modern past which was there to be collected and marvelled at. It was part of that process that enabled nineteenth century society to see itself as the end and aim of a progressive history. David Brewster was part of that process, when he demonstrated in *Murray's Family Library* to everyone who could read, how superstition grew out of the deception of priests and the failure to appreciate the laws of science. Allan Cunningham and James Hogg, in particular, felt a tension between the imaginative force of earlier beliefs and the way that reason and science had placed them at a distance and their fiction took energy from this tension.

By the mid century, William Lancaster's story had become the plaything of popular novelists and a curio for tourist guides and such, despite C.W.Leadbeater and his ilk, it has remained.

The story of the spectral army of Souther Fell has come a long way from that first Midsummer evening when an unnamed farm servant had been dazzled by a smoky sunset.

Notes

Chapter One: Chinese Whispers

[1] Martineau, Harriet: A Complete Guide to the English Lakes, 1855. pp.141-3.
[2] Smith, Colin: *Mungrisdale Heritage Trails.* 2008
[3] Walker, Tony: *The Ghostly Guide to the Lake District.* 2000
[4] Findler, Gerald: *Legends of the Lake Counties.* 1967
[5] Findler, Gerald: *Ghosts of the Lake Counties.* 1975
[6] Griffin, A.H.: In Mountain Lakeland. 1963. pp.154-6
[7] Wainwright, Alfred: *A Pictorial Guide to the Lakeland Fells: Book Five: The Northern Fells.* 1961
[8] Carruthers, Frank: *Lore of the Lake Country.* 1965
[9] Brooks, J.A. *Ghosts and Legends of the Lake District.* 1988
[10] Nicholson, Norman: *The Lakers.* 1955

Chapter Two: The Original Accounts

[1] (Smith, George): *A Journey to the Caudebec Fells with a Map and Description of the Same* in *The Gentleman's Magazine*, November, 1747.
[2] Clarke, James: *A Survey of the Lakes.* 1787
[3] Information from Susan Dench of Carlisle Records Office, quoted by McCue and Gauld, 2005.
[4] Glanvil, Joseph: Sadducismus trimphatus. Fourth edition. 1726 p.4
[5] The Royal Society: Philosophical Transactions. Vol. 47-1752□ - p. 3

Chapter Three: Smith and Clarke

[1] Smith, George: *A Journey to Caudebec Fells* in *The Gentleman's Magazine, November, 1747.*
[2] Carruthers, Frank: *Lore of the Lake Country.*
[3] Smith, George in *The Gentleman's Magazine, XVII* 1747, August p.384
[4] Boucher, Jonathan: Biographia Cumbriensis in Hutchinsom: History of Cumberland, 1795.
[5] These articles were attributed to Smith by Emily Lorraine de Montluzin, who takes the later date for his death, in *Topographical, Antiquarian, Astronomical, and Meteorological Contributions by George Smith of Wigton* in the *Gentleman's Magazine*, 1735-59." *ANQ* 14, no. 2 (Spring 2001): 5-12.
[6] Smith, George in Gentleman's Magazine XVII 1747 p.525
[7] Boucher, Jonathan: *Biographia Cumbriensis* in Hutchinson: *History of Cumberland.* 1795
[8] Nichol, John: *Illustrations of the Literary History of the Eighteenth Century*
[9] Information from Denis Perriam.
[10] Thomlinson, T. in Gentleman's Magazine Vol 26 1755 p.431.
[11] Bicknell, Peter.
[12] *The European Magazine and London Review* 1st July, 1799.
[13] Hodge, Edmund W., Enjoying the Lakes. Oliver and Boyd, 1957. p.65 With thanks to Professor Heather Glen of Cambridge University.
[14] Marginalia in the copy of Clarke's *Survey* in Barrow Public Library.
[15] *The Cumberland Pacquet,* 28th February, 1809,
[16] Boucher, Jonathan: *Biographia Cumbriensis* in Hutchinson: *History of Cumberland.* 1795 Vol I pp334-8)
[17] The Critical Review: or Annals of literature, Vol. 68, 1789

Chapter Four: The Jacobites

[1] The Gentleman's Magazine, Vol XV 1746. January p.30-32. Signed G.S. and dated.

[2] McCarthy, Michael Robin, Summerson, H.R.T. and Annis, R.T.: Carlisle Castle. 1990. p 213 .

[3] The Gentleman's Magazine, Vol. 16 (*1746)*:pp. 233-235.. A:. "A Letter to a friend, containing an account of the march of the rebels into England, a description of the castle of Carlisle, and a dissertation on the old Roman wall . . . by G. Smith."

[4] CRO D/Hud 8/49/3/5 Informants against George Smith. For commentary on the case see Perriam, D. George Smith: 18th century double agent?. Cumberland News. 4th April, 1996.

[5] Roberts, John Leonard: The Jacobite Wars: Scotland and the Military Campaigns of 1715 and 1745.

[6] The Gentleman's Magazine, Vol XVI, 1746 p.300

[7] Tomasson, Katherine: The Jacobite General. 1958 p74-5

[8] McCarthy, Michael Robin, Summerson, H.R.T. and Annis, R.T.: Carlisle Castle. 1990 p.218

[9] Mounsey, George Gill: Carlisle in !745: An Authentic Account of the Occupation of Carlisle in 1745 by Prince Charles Edward Stewart. Steel, Carlisle. 1846. p.149

[10] Now the Port Road Business Park.

[11] Mounsey, George Gill: Carlisle in !745: An Authentic Account of the Occupation of Carlisle in 1745 by Prince Charles Edward Stewart. Steel, Carlisle. 1846. p.150

[12] PRO MPQ 17(1)

[13] PRO MPI 300 (1) and (2)

[14] C498 Jackson Collection, Carlisle Library.

[15] The Gentleman's Magazine, XVI 1746, July p.358

[16] The Gentleman's Magazine, XVII 1747, August p.384

[17] Sopwith, T.: An Account of the Mining Districts of Alston Moor, weardale and Teesdale etc. Davidson, Alnwick 1833 p14

[18] The Gentleman's Magazine, XVII 1747, October. p522

[19] Amy Lax, Robert Maxwell The Seathwaite Connection. *Annual Archaeological Review 1998-99*

[20] The Gentleman's Magazine, XXI 1751, January. P51=53

[21] Otley, Jonathan: The Concise Guide to the Lakes. 1820 p.177

[22] Speck, W.A.: The Butcher: The Duke of Cumberland and the Suppression of the 45. Welsh Academic Press, 1995. p.98.

[23] Jarvis, Rupert C.: The Jacobite Risings of 1715 and 1745. 1954. p.46.

[24] British Library E.85.(41.)

[25] British Library E.86.(23.)

[26] McCue, Peter A. and Gauld, Alan, Edgehill and Souter Fell: A Critical Examination of Two English 'Phantom Army' Cases in *Journal of the Society for Psychical Research*. Vol.69,2.No.879 April 2005 pp78-94.

[27] Quoted by Raymond, J. (ed.) Making the News: An Anthology of the Newsbooks of Revolutionary England 1641-1660. Windrush Press.

[28] See Symonds, E.M. The Diary of John Greene (1635-57) English Historical Review 43, 1928, pp385-394. P.391.

[29] The Five Strange Wonders in the North and West of England. 1659, p.5.

[30] *Diary of Mary Countess Cowper* (Murray, 1864), under the date of March 6, 1716.

[31] Howitt: Visits to Remarkable Places 1845
[32] Child, Francis James: The English and Scottish Ballads vol IV. Dover 1965. p116.
[33] Hogg, James: The Jacobite Relics of Scotland. 1821. p.270
[34] Darwin, Erasmus: the Botanic Garden. 1825 p.203
[35] Apocrypha: Maccabbees,ii 5 2-4
[36] Josephus, Flavius trans William Whiston: The Antiquities of the Jews.1732.V p.103
[37] Shakespeare, William: Julius Caesar. II 2.19-24
[38] Milton, John: Paradise Lost Bk II lines 534 –9
[39] Thomson, James: The Castle of Indolence. 1747. I:xxxi

Chapter Five: Ann Radcliffe and Britton & Brayley
[1] *The London Evening Post:* 29th December, 1764
[2] Plumptre, James: *The Lakers: A Comic Opera.* 1795 p.17
[3] Coleridge, Samuel Taylor: in *The Critical Review XI* Aug 1794 p 364
[4] Radcliffe, Ann: A Journey made in the Summer of 1794 through Holland and the Western Frontier of Germany with a Return down the Rhine to which are added Observations made during a Tour of the Lakes of Lancashire, Westmorland and Cumberland. 1795 pp.438-442
[5] Hyde, Matthew and Pevsner, Nikolaus: The Buildings of England: Cumberland, Westmorland and Furness. 2010. p.287.
[6] Britton, John and Brayley, Edward Wedloke: *The Beauties of England and Wales, or, Delineations, topographical Vol. III Cornwall, Cumberland and Derbyshire.* 1802 pp 58-62

Chapter Six: William and Dorothy Wordsworth and Coleridge.
[1] The Notebooks of Samuel Taylor Coleridge edited Kathleen Coburn Vol I 1794-1804 entry 258
[2] de Quincey, Thomas: Confessions of an English Opium Eater. 1850 p.231. footnote.
[3] R A Foakes: Coleridge on Shakespeare: The Text of the Lectures 1811-12, 2005 p. 102
[4] de Quincey, Thomas: Confessions of an English Opium Eater. 1850 pp.231-4.
[5] Wordsworth, Dorothy. Letters
[6] Wordsworth Guide 1822 122
[7] Curtis, Jared: The Fenwick Notes of William Wordsworth. P.146.
[8] Wordsworth Guide 1822 126
[9] Moorman, Mary: William Wordsworth: A Biography: The Early Years 1770 - 1803. Oxford. 1957 p.61
[10]Johnston, Kenneth R.: The Hidden Wordsworth: Poet, Lover, Rebel, Spy. Norton. 1998. p108
[11]Johnston, Kenneth R.: The Hidden Wordsworth: Poet, Lover, Rebel, Spy. Norton. 1998. p.108
[12]The Vale of Easthwaite ll211-214 in Landon, Carol, and Curtis, Jared, edited: Wordsworth, William: Early Poems and Fragments, 1785-1797. Cornell. 1997
[13]The Vale of Easthwaite ll.211-214 in Landon, Carol, and Curtis, Jared, edited: Wordsworth, William: Early Poems and Fragments, 1785-1797. Cornell. 1997 p.551 Affinitive Piece III
[14]The Vale of Easthwaite ll2-214 in Landon, Carol, and Curtis, Jared, edited: Wordswoth, William: Early Poems and Fragments, 1785-1797. 1997 p.551

[15] The Prelude Book VII Text of 1850 ll. 626-34
[16] Owen, W.J.B. "A Second –Sight Procession" in Wordsworth's London. *Notes and Queries*. February, 1969 pp49-50
[17] Prelude 1805 Book VII ll
[18] Williams, Raymond: The Country and the City, 1975. p.159.
[19] de Selincourt – Darbishire, p. 533
[20] Wordsworth, William: Michael .
[21] Caldbeck Falls is a good two miles from Hesket Newmarket.
[22] Wordsworth, Dorothy. Edited E De Selincourt: Journals of Dorothy Wordsworth. Volume One, 1952. p.193.
[23] Britton and Brayley. Beauties of England and Wales: Vol iv: Cumberland . 1893 p.175.
[24] Wordsworth, Dorothy. Edited E De Selincourt: Journals of Dorothy Wordsworth. Volume One. 1952. p193.
[25] The Notebooks of Samuel Taylor Coleridge edited Kathleen Coburn Vol I 1794-1804 entry 793
[27] The Notebooks of Samuel Taylor Coleridge edited Kathleen Coburn Vol I 1794-1804 entry 795
[28] The Notebooks of Samuel Taylor Coleridge edited Kathleen Coburn Vol I 1794-1804 entry 795
[29] Coleridge, Samuel Taylor; edited Foakes, R.A. Lectures on Literature 1808-1819. Vol II. 1987 p.208

Chapter Seven: Sir Walter Scott

[1] The Edinburgh Review: Vol. 16, 1810. p.263
[2] Scott, Walter: The Lady of the Lake. Ballantyne, 1810. pp. 105-6, Canto III:IV
[3] Scott, Walter: The Lady of the Lake. Ballantyne, 1810. pp. 105-6, Canto III:VII
[4] Scott, Walter: The Lady of the Lake. Ballantyne, 1810. pp. 347
[5] Scott, Sir Walterr: The Life of Napoleon Bonaparte, Emperor of the French. Vol 3. 1827. p.332
[6] The Edinburgh Annual Register, 1812. 1814. p.125
[7] Scott, Sir Walter: The Antiquary. 1816. Vol. I. p.192
[8] Scott, Sir Walter: Waverley Novels. 1832. Vol. V. p.240
[9] Dorson, Richard: History of British Folklore. 1968. p.12
[10] Scott, Sir Walter: Letters on Demonology and Witchcraft addressed to J.G.Lockhart, Esq. 1830 Second edition catalogue p.4
[11] Scott, Sir Walter: Letters on Demonology and Witchcraft addressed to J.G.Lockhart, Esq. 1830 pp. 3-7
[12] Scott, Sir Walter: The Novels of Ernest Theodore Hoffmann in *The Foreign Quarterly Review*, July, 1827.
[13] Scott, Sir Walter: Letters on Demonology and Witchcraft addressed to J.G.Lockhart, Esq. 1830. p37
[14] Scott, Sir Walter: Letters on Demonology and Witchcraft addressed to J.G.Lockhart, Esq. 1830. p35
[15] Scott, Sir Walter: Letters on Demonology and Witchcraft addressed to J.G.Lockhart, Esq. 1830. p.390.
[16] Scott, Sir Walter: The Bridal of Triermain, or The Vale of St John. 1813. p.210.

Chapter Eight: Sir David Brewster anf the Scientists

[1] Brewster, Sir David: Letters on Natural Magic: addressed to Sir Walter Scott, Bart. 1832. p.2

[2] Hogg, James: Sir David Brewster, K.B. in Fraser's Magazine Vol 6. 1832. p.416
[3] Pratt, Josiah; Macaulay Zachary: The Christian Observer. Vol. 17. p.437.
[4] Brewster, Sir David: Memoirs of the Life, Writings and Discoveries of Sir Isaac Newton. Vol II. 1855. p.375
[5] Gordon, Margaret Maria: The Home Life of Sir David Brewster. 1870 p. 72
[6] Brewster, Sir David: Letters on Natural Magic: addressed to Sir Walter Scott, Bart. 1832. p.6
[7] Brewster, Sir David: Letters on Natural Magic: addressed to Sir Walter Scott, Bart. 1832 p.350
[8] Defoe, Daniel: The History and Reality of Apparitions in Chalmers, George: the Novels and Miscellaneous Works of Daniel Defoe. 1840. p.151
[9] Defoe, Daniel: The History and Reality of Apparitions in Chalmers, George: the Novels and Miscellaneous Works of Daniel Defoe. 1840. p.391.
[10] Boswell, Jammes: The Life of Samuel Johnson, LL.D. 1791 p.384.
[11] Ferriar, John: An Essay Towards a Theory of Apparitions. 1813 p.ix.
[12] Ferriar, John: An Essay Towards a Theory of Apparitions. 1813 p.15.
[13] Ferriar, John: An Essay Towards a Theory of Apparitions. 1813 p.16.
[14] Ferriar, John: An Essay Towards a Theory of Apparitions. 1813 p.17.
[15] Ferriar, John: An Essay Towards a Theory of Apparitions. 1813 p.18
[16] Ferriar, John: An Essay Towards a Theory of Apparitions. 1813 p.20
[17] Ferriar, John: An Essay Towards a Theory of Apparitions. 1813 p.20
[18] Ferriar, John: An Essay Towards a Theory of Apparitions. 1813 p.23
[19] Gaskell, Elizabeth: Cranford. 1853. p.205.
[20] Blackwood's Magazine. Vol.17. 1825. p.370.
[21] Brewster, Sir David: Letters on Natural Magic: addressed to Sir Walter Scott, Bart. 1832. p.128
[22] Brewster, Sir David: Letters on Natural Magic: addressed to Sir Walter Scott, Bart. 1832. p.131
[23] Brewster, Sir David: Letters on Natural Magic: addressed to Sir Walter Scott, Bart. 1832. p.131
[24] Brewster, Sir David: Letters on Natural Magic: addressed to Sir Walter Scott, Bart. 1832. p.135
[25] Brewster, Sir David: Letters on Natural Magic: addressed to Sir Walter Scott, Bart. 1832. p.29
[26] Brewster, Sir David: Letters on Natural Magic: addressed to Sir Walter Scott, Bart. 1832. p. 144
[27] Brewster, Sir David: Letters on Natural Magic: addressed to Sir Walter Scott, Bart. 1832. p. 146
[28] Brewster, Sir David: Letters on Natural Magic: addressed to Sir Walter Scott, Bart. 1832. p. 152
[29] Brewster, Sir David: Letters on Natural Magic: addressed to Sir Walter Scott, Bart. 1832. p. 152
[30] Brewster, Sir David: Letters on Natural Magic: addressed to Sir Walter Scott, Bart. 1832. p. 154
[31] The Quarterly Review. 1833 p.507
[32] Brewster, D. editor. The Edinburgh Encyclopaedia. 1830 p. 492

Chapter Nine: James Hogg

[1] Hogg, James: The Domestic Manners and Private Life of Sir Walter Scott. 1834. p.61
[2] Hogg, James: Nature's Magic Lantern: *Chambers Edinburgh Journal.* 28th Sept. 1833.

[3] Hogg, James. Altrive Tales. 1834. p. cxlvii
[4] Hogg, James: The Spy. 1810. p.43
[5] Hogg, James. The Renowned Adventures of Basil Lee in Winter Evening Tales. 1820
[6] Ferriar, John: Of Popular Illusions and Particularly of Medical Demonology in Memoirs and Proceedings of the Manchester Philosophical Society. 1790. Vol. 3 p.33.
[7] (Hogg, James): The Private Memoirs and Confessions of a Justified Sinner. 1824

Chapter Ten: Allan Cunningham
[1] Hogg, James: Altrive Tales. 1832. cxxxvi
[2] H. J. C. Grierson, Letters of Sir Walter Scott, 1932, 2.409
[3] Cromek, R.H.: remains of Nithsdale and Galloway Song. 1810. p.38
[4] Lockhart, J.G. Memoirs of the Life of Scott. 1837 Vol 2 p.756.
[5] Mrs Fletcher Autobiography 1876 p130
[6] Southey, Robert: The Poetical Works. 1829. p.724.
[7] Hogg, David. Life of Allan Cunningham. P.176
[8] Cornwall, Barry. Memoir of Charles Lamb.
[9] Cunningham, Allan: Poems and Songs. 1847. p.25.
[10] Cunningham, Allan: Traditional Tales of the English and Scottish Peasantry. Vol. I.1822. Preface.
[11] Cunningham, Allan: Traditional Tales of the English and Scottish Peasantry. Vol.I. 1822. pp. 49-148.
[12] Ashiestiel was the home of Sir Walter Scott from 1804 to 1812 when he moved to Abbotsford.
[13] Armstrong, A.M. et al: the Place Names of Cumberland. CUP. 1971. pp. 227 & 493
[14] Ferguson, R.S.: The Northmen in Cumberland and Westmorland. Longman. 1856 p.81
[15] The literary speculum: Volume 1 - p. 241. 1821
[16] Hogg, David. Life of Allan Cunningham. P234.
[17] The London Magazine, 1822. p.622
[18] Martineau, Harriet: Autobiography p.277
[19] Briggs, John: The Lonsdale Magazine. Vol II Issue 8 August 1821. p.313.
[20] Death of Mr. Wilson Armistead, of Leeds. The Leeds Mercury, Thursday, February 20, 1868: Issue 9315.
[21] Armistead, Wilson: Tales and Legends of the English Lakes. Simpkin, Marshall. 1891. p.viii
[22] Armistead, Wilson: Tales and Legends of the English Lakes. Simpkin, Marshall. 1891. p.160-173.
[23] Armistead, Wilson: Tales and Legends of the English Lakes. Simpkin, Marshall. 1891. p.viii

Chapter Eleven: John Charles Bristow
[1] Bristow, J.C.: Ullsmere: A Poem . Samuel Hodgson. 1832. Preface.
[2] Green, William, of Ambleside: The Tourist's New Guide containing a description of the Lakes. 1819. Vol.I p.357
[3] Phillips, John: Black's Picturesque Guide to the English Lakes. 1868. p.150.
[4] Allison's Northern Touriost's Guide to the Lakes of Cumberland, 1832. p.18
[5] Selincourt, Ernest de, editor: The Early Letters of William and Dorothy Wordsworth. 1935. p.394

[6] E.de Selincourt: The Journals of Dorothy Wordsworth. Vol.I 1952. pp. 131-2
[7] Bristow: John Charles: Ullsmere: A Poem. Stanley Hodgson. 1832 p.xiii
[8] Bristow: John Charles: Ullsmere: A Poem. Stanley Hodgson. 1832 p. 134
[9] Boswell, James: The Journal of a Tour to the Hebrides, with Samuel Johnson, LL.D. 1785. p.173
[10] Blair, Hugh: A Critical Dissertation on the Poems of Ossian. 1763. p.35
[11] MacPherson, James: Fingal: Together with several other poems. 1762. p.23
[12] Wu, Duncan: Wordsworth's Poets. 2006.
[13] Fraser's Magazine, Vol. II. 1835. p.728.
[14] The Metropolitan. 1835. p.43
[15] The Publishers' circular and general record etc. Vol. 14. 1851. p.viii
[16] Exeter Working Papers in British Book Trade History; 0
[17] The International Magazine of Literature, Art, and Science. Vol 2, 1-4. 1851. p.304
[18] Carlisle Patriot. 19 July 1844

Chapter Twelve: White, Gresley and Soane.

[1] White, John Pagen: Lays and Legends of the English Lake Country. John Russell Smith and C&G Coward. Carlisle. 1873. p. v
[2] White, John Pagen: Lays and Legends of the English Lake Country. John Russell Smith and C&G Coward. Carlisle. 1873. pp. viii-xiii.
[3] Gilpin, Sidney, editor: The Songs and Ballads of Cumberland and the Lake Country. 1874. p.94
[4] White, John Pagen: Lays and Legends of the English Lake Country. John Russell Smith and C&G Coward. Carlisle. 1873. pp. 44-49
[5] White, John Pagen: Lays and Legends of the English Lake Country. John Russell Smith and C&G Coward. Carlisle. 1873. p. 50-66
[6] Reed, Henry, editor: The Complete Poetical Works of Willaim Wordsworth. 1851. p.160
[7] Coleridge, Hartley: Biographia Borealis: or Lives of Distinguished Northerns. 1833. p.250
[8] White, John Pagen: Lays and Legends of the English Lake Country. John Russell Smith and C&G Coward. Carlisle. 1873. P 58.
[9] White, John Pagen: Lays and Legends of the English Lake Country. John Russell Smith and C&G Coward. Carlisle. 1873. pp. 110-123
[10] Selincourt, Ernest de, Editor: The Letters of William and Dorothy Wordsworth: 1967. p.617 no. 763
[11] The Pall Mall Gazette Monday, October 27, 1873; Issue 2714
[12] Gresley, William: Coniston Hall. 1846.
[13] Soane, George: The Last Ball and Other Stories. 1843
[14] Soane, George: The Last Ball and Other Stories. 1843 pp. 103-110

Chapter Thirteen: Harriet Martineau

[1] Martineau, Harriet. A Guide to the English Lakes. Garnett. 1855 pp 262-5
[2] Gray, Thomas: The Poems of Mr. Gray. 1775. p. 354
[3] West, Thomas: A guide to the lakes, in Cumberland, Westmorland, and Lancashire: ... 1789. p.108
[4] Gilpin, Willian: Observations on several parts of England. 1808. Vol I p.89
[5] Gilpin, William: Observations, relative chiefly to picturesque beauty,. 1786. p.85
[6] Clark, James. A Survey of the Lakes. p.60-61.
[7] A Gentleman: A tour from London to the lakes: 1792 p.88.

[8] Hutchinson, W: History of the County of Cumberland. 1794. Vol I p.423-5
[9] Wilkinson, Thomas: Tours to the British mountains: 1824. p.192
[10] Wilkinson, Thomas: . Tours to the British mountains: 1824. p.192
[11] Housman, John: A descriptive tour, and guide to the lakes, caves, mountains, and ... - 1800. p.83.
[12] Wordsworth, William: A Guide to the Lakes. 1835 p.xix
[13] Hudson, John: A complete guide to the Lakes. 1843. p.77
[14] Southey, Robert: Colloquies of Sir Thomas More, Vol II. 1829. p.147.
[15] See Otley, Jonathan: 1819: Account of the Floating Island in Derwent Lake, Keswick: Manchester Literary and Philosophical Society: series 2 vol.3: p.64 Otley, Jonathan: 1819: Account of the Black Lead Mine in Borrowdale: Manchester Literary and Philosophical Society: series 2 vol.3: p.168
[16] Smith, Tom Fletcher:9 Jonathan Otley. Bookcase. 2005.
[17] Otley, Jonathan: A Concise Description of the English Lakes. Second ed. 1825 p.48
[18] Otley, Jonathan. A Descriptive Guide to the English Lakes. Keswick. 1850 p.56
[19] Green, William: The tourist's new guide to the Lakes. 1819. Vol. 2 . p.465
[20] Green, William: The Tourist's New Guide to the Lakes. 1819. Vol.2. Pp. 449-50
[21] Sylvan's Pictorial handbook to the English Lakes. 1847 p.182
[22] Phillips, John: Black's Picturesque Guide to the English Lakes. 1853. p.163
[23] Handbook for Westmorland, Cumberland, and the Lakes:John Murray. 1869 p.134
[24] A Guide to the English Lake District intended principally for the use of Pedestrians by a Cambridge Man. 1850 pp 61 & 72
[25] Pinnock, W. A: The History and Topography of Cumberland, with biographical sketches, pp 54-55
[26] Parson, William, and White, William: A History, Directory and Gazetteer of Cumberland and Westmorland. 1829.
[27] Walpole, Hugh. The Fortress. 1938. p.591
[28] Martineau, Harriet, ed.Chapman, Maria Weston. Autobiography.1877. Vol II p113
[29] Webb, R.K. Harriet Martineau. DNB
[30] Martineau, Harriet, ed.Chapman, Maria Weston. Autobiography.1877. Vol I p.443
[31] Martineau, Harriet, ed.Chapman, Maria Weston. Autobiography.1877. Vol I p.498
[32] Martineau, Harriet, ed.Chapman, Maria Weston. Autobiography.1877. Vol I p.513
[34] Bicknell, Peter: The Picturesque Scenery of the Lake District. 1752-1855. 1990. p.179.
[35] Martineau, Harriet, ed.Chapman, Maria Weston. Autobiography.1877. Vol II p.96-96.
[36] Martineau, Harriet, ed.Chapman, Maria Weston. Autobiography.1877. Vol II p.42.
[37] Martineau, Harriet, ed.Chapman, Maria Weston. Autobiography.1877. Vol I p.543.
[38] Martineau, Harriet, ed.Chapman, Maria Weston. Autobiography.1877. Vol II p.26.
[39] Martineau, Harriet, ed.Chapman, Maria Weston. Autobiography.1877. Vol I p.516.

[40] Martineau, Harriet, ed.Chapman, Maria Weston. Autobiography.1877. Vol I p.500
[41] Nicholson, Norman: The Lakers. 1955. p.200
[42] Martineau, Harriet. A Guide to the English Lakes. Garnett. 1855 p.190
[43] Martineau, Harriet. A Guide to the English Lakes. Garnett. 1855 p.162
[44] Martineau, Harriet. A Guide to the English Lakes. Garnett. 1855 p.174
[45] Martineau, Harriet. A Guide to the English Lakes. Garnett. 1855 p. 258
[46] Armistead, Wilson: Tales and Legends of the Lake Counties. *1855* pp.102-110
[47] The Remains of John Briggs. 1825. p.272
[48] Martineau, Harriet. A Guide to the English Lakes. Garnett. 1855 p. 245
[49] Martineau, Harriet. A Guide to the English Lakes. Garnett. 1855 p. 260
[50] Martineau, Harriet: Miscellanies 2. 1836 p.113
[51] Martineau, Harriet: Miscellanies 2. 1836 p.114
[52] Leadbetter, C.W.: Clairvoyance. 1899. pp.8-9
[53] Leadbetter, C.W.: Clairvoyance. 1899. p.131
[54] Leadbetter, C.W.: Clairvoyance. 1899. p.141
[55] Leadbetter, C.W.: Clairvoyance. 1899. p.155
[56] Leadbetter, C.W.: Clairvoyance. 1899. p.156

Chapter Fourteen: Conclusion

[1] Atkinson, Henry George, and Martineau, Harriet: Letters on the Laws of Man's Nature and Development. 1851 p.142
[2] Crowe, Catherine: The Night Side of Nature, or, Ghosts and Ghost Seers. 1848. Vol II pp.323-5
[3] Dickens a letter to the Revd. James White, dated 7 March 1854 [Storey pp.285-6]
[4] Conway, Moncure Daniel: Demonology and Devil Lore. vol ii 1879 pp.242-4
[5] Hampson, R.T.: Medii Aevi Kalendarium. 1841. Vol.I p.310.
[6] Hutchinson, William: History of the County of Cumberland. 1794. Vol II p.162.
[7] Hutchinson, William: History of the County of Cumberland. 1794. Vol I p.177.
[8] Boucher, Jonathan: Glossary of Archaic and Provincial Words. 1833. Vol 2: Banefire
[9] Sullivan, Jeremiah: Cumberland and Westmorland, Ancient and Modern: People, Dialect, Superstitions and Customs. 1857. pp.150-1
[10] Brand, John: Observations on the Popular Antiquities of Great Britain, 1777. New edition, 1855. Vol.I. pp305-7
[11] Armstrong, Mawer et al: The Place Names of Cumberland. 1971. p.226.
[12] Tyler, Ian: Roughton Gill and the Mines of the Caldbeck Fells. Pp 15-16. 299-303.
[13] Hutchinson, William: The History of the County of Cumberland. 1794. Vol.I. p.417.
[14] Hutchinson, William: The History of the County of Cumberland. 1794. Vol.I. p.407. footnote..
[15] Armstrong, Mawer et al: The Place Names of Cumberland. 1971. p.226.
[16] Bell, William: Shakespeare's Puck and his Folkslore. 1844. Vol.II. pp.144-6

Select Bibliography

The bibliography lists only those books that are significant in the story of the spectral army of Souther Fell. Many of the other books used are referred to in the notes.

Armistead, Wilson: Tales and Legends of the English Lakes. 1891
Brewster, D. editor. The Edinburgh Encyclopaedia. 1830
Brewster, Sir David: Letters on Natural Magic: addressed to Sir Walter Scott, Bart. 1832.
Briggs, John: The Lonsdale Magazine. Vol II 1821.
Bristow, J.C.: Ullsmere: A Poem . Samuel Hodgson. 1832.
Britton and Brayley. Beauties of England and Wales: Vol iv: Cumberland 1804
Britton, John & Brayley, Edward Wedlake: The Beauties of England and Wales, Vol. III Cornwall, Cumberland and Derbyshire. 1802
Clarke, James: A Survey of the Lakes. 1787
Coleridge, Samuel Taylor: The Notebooks ed. K Coburn.
Coleridge, Samuel Taylor; ed.Foakes, R.A. Lectures on Literature 1808-1819. 1987
Crowe, Catherine: The Night Side of Nature, or, Ghosts and Ghost Seers. 1848
Conway, Moncure Daniel: Demonology and Devil Lore. 1879
Cunningham, Allan: Poems and Songs. 1847..
Cunningham, Allan: Traditional Tales of the English and Scottish Peasantry.1822.
Curtis, Jared: The Fenwick Notes of William Wordsworth.
de Quincey, Thomas: Confessions of an English Opium Eater. 1850.
Ferriar, John: An Essay Towards a Theory of Apparitions. 1813
Green, William, of Ambleside: The Tourist's New Guide containing a description of the Lakes. 1819.
Gresley, William: Coniston Hall. 1846.
Hampson, R.T.: Medii Aevi Kalendarium. 1841.
Hogg, David. Life of Allan Cunningham.
Hogg, James. Altrive Tales. 1834.
Hogg, James. The Renowned Adventures of Basil Lee, in Winter Evening Tales. 1820
Hogg, James: Nature's Magic Lantern, in Chambers Edinburgh Journal. 28th September, 1833.
Hogg, James: The Domestic Manners and Private Life of Sir Walter Scott. 1834.
Hogg, James: The Jacobite Relics of Scotland. 1821.
Hogg, James: The Private Memoirs and Confessions of a Justified Sinner. 1824
Hogg, James: The Spy. 1810.
Hutchinson, William: History of Cumberland. 1794
Jarvis, Rupert C.: The Jacobite Risings of 1715 and 1745. 1954.
Leadbetter, C.W.: Clairvoyance. 1899.
Martineau, Harriet, ed.Chapman, Maria Weston. Autobiography.1877.
Martineau, Harriet: A Complete Guide to the English Lakes, Garnett. 1855.
McCarthy, Michael Robin, Summerson, H.R.T. and Annis, R.T.: Carlisle Castle. 1990
McCue, Peter A. and Gauld, Alan, Edgehill and Souter Fell: A Critical Examination of Two English 'Phantom Army' Cases, in Journal of the Society for Psychical Research. Vol.69,2.No.879 April 2005 pp.78-94..

Mounsey, George Gill: Carlisle in !745: An Authentic Account of the Occupation of Carlisle in 1745 by Prince Charles Edward Stewart. Steel, Carlisle. 1846.
Nicholson, Norman: The Lakers. 1955
Otley, Jonathan: The Concise Guide to the Lakes. 1820
Radcliffe, Ann: A Journey made in the Summer of 1794 through Holland and the Western Frontier of Germany with a Return down the Rhine to which are added Observations made during a Tour of the Lakes of Lancashire, Westmorland and Cumberland. 1795
Scott, Sir Walter: Letters on Demonology and Witchcraft addressed to J.G.Lockhart, Esq. 1830
Scott, Sir Walter: The Antiquary. 1816.
Scott, Sir Walter: The Bridal of Triermain, or The Vale of St John. 1813.
Scott, Walter: The Lady of the Lake. Ballantyne, 1810.
Smith, George: A Journey to the Caudebec Fells with a Map and Description of the Same in The Gentleman's Magazine, November, 1747.
Soane, George: The Last Ball and Other Stories. 1843
Sullivan, Jeremiah: Cumberland and Westmorland, Ancient and Modern: People, Dialect, Superstitions and Customs. 1857.
The Edinburgh Annual Register, 1812. 1814.
The Gentleman's Magazine, Vol. 16 (1746):pp. 233-235.. A:. "A Letter to a friend, containing an account of the march of the rebels into England, a description of the castle of Carlisle, and a dissertation on the old Roman wall . . . by G. Smith."
The Vale of Esthwaite ll211-214 in Landon, Carol, and Curtis, Jared, edited: Wordsworth, William: Early Poems and Fragments, 1785-1797. Cornell. 1997
Tyler, Ian: Roughton Gill and the Mines of the Caldbeck Fells.
Wainwright, Alfred: A Pictorial Guide to the Lakeland Fells: Book Five: The Northern Fells. 1961
White, John Pagen: Lays and Legends of the English Lake Country. 1873.
Wordsworth, Dorothy. Ed. E De Selincourt: Journals of Dorothy Wordsworth. 1952.
Wordsworth, Dorothy. Letters
Wordsworth, William: A Guide to the Lakes. 1835

INDEX

Achtermannshohe: 100,
Alderson, John: 149,
Allonby: 158
Alston: 84Amadis of Gaul: 31, 76
Ambleside 7, 260, 266, 269
Anderson, Robert: 52,
Antiquary, The: 137,
Apocrypha: 86
Arderon, William: 34,
Armboth: 271
Arminian Magazine: 90
Armistead, Wilson: 217-219, 272, 299
Arthur, King: 233, 285, 290
Aspland, Lynsey: 267
Atkinson, Henry George: 266
Aubrey, john: 128
Augsburg: 290
Aurora Borealis: 83-84, 152, 292, 301
Bannerdale: 123, 126, 128
Basil Lee: 175-187, 209
Bassenthwaite: 29, 165, 264
Baudelaire, Charles: 282
Bell, William: 296
Beltane Fire: 288
Besant, Annie: 276
Bible, The: 292
Black's Guide: 260, 300
Blackwood's Magazine: 153, 187, 195
Blake Hills Farm: 10, 22, 23, 52, 97, 115, 292
Blavatsky, Madame: 276
Blencathra/ Saddleback: 9, 91, 92, 101, 121, 123, 143, 165, 252, 254, 255, 257, 259, 261, 264, 290
Blencogo: 43,
Boothby: 44, 58, 62, 297
Borrowdale: 92, 274, 290
Boucher, rev. Jonathan: 42-3, 289
Bousgill: 292
Bowman, Joe: 293
Bowscale Fell: 294
Bowscale Tarn: 47, 96, 121, 126, 127, 143, 261
Brampton: 64, 297
Brand, John: 139, 289
Brandy Gill: 291
Brewster, Sir David: 33, 144 – 166, 167, 172, 286, 298, 300, 302
Briggs, John: 212, 272
Bristow, John Charles: 220-230, 298
Bristow, Laura: 229-230
Britton, John, and Brayley, Edward Wedlake: 95-102, 103, 104, 122, 130, 136, 154, 156, 167, 173, 252, 263, 298, 302
Brocken spectre: 11, 99-102, 103-108, 136, 142, 152, 154, 162, 164, 165, 171, 191, 218, 302
Brocken: 104, 137, 155
Bronte, Charlotte: 268
Brooks, A.: 14,
Brunte Knott: 28, 294
Buckingham, Duke of: 247-248
Burns, Robert: 168, 192, 193, 210
Buttermere: 274
Byron, Lord George: 141.
Caldbeck Fells: 18, 38, 45, 73, 96, 253, 290
Caldbeck: 122
Caldew, River: 46, 122, 127
Campbell, Thomas: 211
Carlisle Yetts: 208
Carlisle: 44, 59-77, 288
Carrock: 96, 121, 123, 126, 127, 128, 233, 253, 290, 291
Carruthers, Frank: 14, 39,
Castlerigg: 84, 271-273
Cave, Edward: 40
Cervantes: 31
Chamber's Edinburgh Journal: 167
Chantrey, Francis Leggatt: 194-195
Claife: 271
Clare, John: 196
Clarke, James: 10, 13, 15, 23-32, 35-37, 48-56, 90, 95, 96, 98, 116, 118, 128, 130, 133, 136, 156,162,212, 218, 224, 241, 253, 259, 260,286, 287, 288, 290, 292, 293, 296, 297, 301
Clarke, Rev. C.C.: 15, 218, 276
Clarkson, Thomas: 220-221.
Clifford, Lord Robert: 121, 233, 238-239, 261
Clifton, Battle of: 66,
Cockermouth: 46,
Coleridge, Hartley: 238
Coleridge, Samuel Taylor: 103-107, 108-9, 113, 123-129, 142, 150, 298
Coleridge, Sara: 103

Collins, William: 227
Comte, Auguste: 266
Confessions of a Justified Sinner: 187-188
Conway, Moncur Daniel: 285-287, 290
Cope, Sir John:
Cowper, Countess Mary: 83, 292
Cromek, Robert Hartley: 193, 194
Crosfeild, mr.: 244
Cross Fell: 38, 73,
Crosthwaite, Peter: 53, 54,
Crowe, Mrs. Catherine: 276, 282-6, 291
Culloden: 16, 133, 209, 212
Cumberland Pacquet: 54, 55,
Cumberland, Duke of ('Butcher'): 58, 69, 71, 162, 209, 283
Cumwhitton: 288
Cunningham, Allan: 192-212, 218, 262, 298, 300, 302
Dacre Castle: 257
Dalemain: 257
Darwin, Charles: 285
Darwin, Erasmus: 86, 150-151
Davy, Humphrey: 123
De Quincey, Thomas: 17, 107-108, 196
Defoe, Daniel: 148
Derwentwater, James Radclyffe, Earl of: 73, 84-85, 292, 301
Derwentwater: 48, 90, 243, 257, 288
Derwentwater's Lights, Lord: 83-83, 152, 242, 292, 295, 301
Desagulier, John Theophilus: 39, 42, 85
Dickens, Charles: 285
Donald, Thomas: 52, 102, 290
Dorson, Richard: 139,
Dover Castle: 161-162
Dughet, Gaspard: 91, 93, 296
Edgehill: 16, 77-81, 280
Edinburgh Annual Register: 134-135, 167
Edinburgh Encyclopaedia: 144, 165
Edinburgh Review: 130
Elcho, Lord: 76,
Esthwaite, vale of: 114-117
Evening Walk, An: 117
Ewesmere: 220
Fairfield: 270
Fata Morgana: 9, 106, 155-157, 164, 213
Ferguson, Robert: 285
Ferriar, John: 149-153, 177,
Findler, Gerald: 10-12
Fontenoy, Battle of: 58, 69
Fraser's Magazine: 228
Garnett, John: 267
Gaskell, Mrs: 153
Gentleman's Magazine, The: 10, 15, 18, 23, 39, 40, 58, 72, 73, 295
George I, King: 83, 243
Gilks, Thomas and Edward: 260
Gilpin, Rev. Willaim: 253
Glamis castle: 141
Glanvil, Joseph: 31-33, 76, 140-141, 147
Glenary: 283
Glenderamackin: 12, 21, 128, 260, 274
Glover, Jonathan: 112
Goethe:, Johann Wolfgang von: 104, 133
Goslar: 108-110
Gottingen: 102
Grasmere, Lake: 113
Gray, Thomas: 55, 252, 253, 293
Green, William of Ambleside: 220, 224, 259, 260, 262, 291, 296
Gresley, William: 243-247, 251, 300
Gretna: 68,
Greystoke Castle: 91, 93, 94, 112,
Griffin Inn: 49, 115
Griffin, A.H.: 11,
Grisdale: 46, 128, 257, 290
Hadrian's Wall: 72
Halley, Edmund: 40, 83, 85, 301
Hallin Fell: 220
Hampson, R.T.: 288
Harraby: 64, 143
Harz, Hartz Mountains: 99, 108, 137, 165, 241, 290-291
Haue, M.: 99, 136, 154, 163, 164, 170, 302
Havarah Park: 135, 137, 167, 173, 241, 277, 283
Haygarth, John: 102
Hebrides: 87, 209, 277, 291
Hechstetter, Daniel: 290
Hechstetter, Jospeh: 391
Heinrichshohe: 100,
Helvellyn: 16, 93, 143, 221, 232, 241, 262
Herodotus: 129
Hesket Newmarket: 122, 123
Hibbert, Dr. John: 153, 154
Highgate: 128
Hogg, David: 210
Hogg, James: 144, 153, 166-191, 192, 193, 196, 209, 210, 211, 298, 300, 301, 302
Housman, John: 257, 260
Huddart, Mr.: 158
Humboldt, Baron von: 159
Hutchinson, William: 15, 17, 18, 42, 95, 96, 124, 156, 218, 240, 242, 252, 255, 257, 297
Hutton Moor: 92,

Inverness: 283, 291
Jackson, A: 135
Jacobites: 57-77, 162, 197, 209, 216, 292
Jedburgh: 144,
Johnson, Dr. Samuel: 40, 148, 227
Jordan, M.: 102
Josephus, Flavius: 86, 241, 293
Katrine, Loch: 131, 220, 230
Keinton 77-81, 280
Kendal: 91, 212, 289
Keswick: 92, 195, 252, 259, 269, 290
Kirkby Lonsdale: 212, 258
Kirkby Stephen: 272
Knott: 28, 98, 294
Ku Klux Klan: 131
Lakers, The: A Comic Opera: 90
Lanark: 284
Lancaster, William: 7, 10, 15, 16, 18, 21, 22, 26, 27, 29, 57, 77, 86, 97, 133, 156, 174, 211, 260, 287, 288, 293, 295, 296, 302
Landseer, Edwin: 130
Langdale: 269
Latrigg: 252
Lavater: 149
Leadbeater, C.W.: 276-281, 282, 284, 302
Lee, Dr.F.G.: 276
Leeds: 135, 167, 217, 299
Leyberthwaite: 92
Liverpool: 232, 299
Locke, John: 113
Lockhart, J.G.: 195
London Magazine: 195, 209, 262
Long Meg: 39,
Longtown: 60
Lonsdale Magazine: 9, 15, 212, 262, 272
Lonsdale, earl of: 220-221
Lorrain, Claude: 91
Lyulph's Tower: 111-113, 157, 223, 226
MacPherson, Juliet: 146
Mapp, Walter: 15,
Marshall, Samuel: 77-81
Marston Moor: 16, 143, 262
Martin, Martin: 177, 277
Martineau, Harriet: 7-9, 211, 252, 265-276, 277, 278, 279, 281, 282, 292
Maryport: 158
Mendellsohn, Felix: 130
Mendelssohn, Fanny: 130.
Meyer, M. 149
Mill, John Stuart: 7,
Milton, John: 87, 293
Mosedale: 15, 38, 46, 121, 126, 127, 252, 290, 293
Mounsey, Thomas: 69
Mousthwaite Col: 12-13
Mungo, St (Kentigern): 126
Mungrisdaale: 10, 124, 292
Murray, Lord George: 67,
Murray's Family Library: 139, 144, 302
Murray's Handbook: 261, 300
Murrey: 292-293
N.S. 212, 218
Napoleon: 133-134, 138
Naworth Castle: 44, 60
Newlands: 290
Newton, Sir Isaac: 39, 145, 150, 154
Nichol, John: 43,
Nicholson, Norman: 16-17, 134, 269,
Norfolk, Duke of: 75, 91, 112, 226, 292
Ossian (James MacPherson): 16, 133, 146, 164, 193, 227
Otley, Jonathan: 74, 258, 260, 262
Paderborn: 277, 284
Pall Mall Gazette: 242
Parson and White's Directory: 264
Pasaunias: 129
Pennant, Thomas: 288
Penrith: 50, 67, 91, 115, 143
Perceval, Spencer: 276
Percy, Bishop Thomas: 290
Petra: 273
Pinnock, William: 263
Plumptre, James: 90
Prelude, The: 118-120
Prestonpaans: 58,
Priestley, Joseph: 158
Radcliffe, Ann: 90-95, 112, 150, 210, 224, 226, 257, 298, 302
Ravenglass: 72,
Rhealt:
Ritson, Isaac: 55, 124
Robinson: John: 48,
Rochester, George Wilmot, Earl of: 247-250
Rosa, Salvator: 91, 93, 298
Rossini, Giacomo: 130
Saddleback: See Blencathra. 9, 11, 12
Scales (Threlkeld) tarn: 101, 125, 143, 242, 253, 255, 258, 261
Schubert, Franz: 130
Scoresby, Captain William: 159
Scot, Thomas: 61,
Scott, John: 195
Scott, Sir Walter: 33, 91, 130-143, 144, 146, 147, 148, 150, 157, 167, 173, 174,

196, 210, 220, 226, 227, 242, 260, 274, 275, 286, 298, 300
Selby's of Cumberland: 197-208, 211, 213-
Shakespeare, William: 87, 92, 227
Shap: 91
Skiddaw: 101, 102, 123, 128, 165, 252, 259, 264
Smith, Colin: 10,
Smith, George: 10, 15, 18-23, 28-32, 35, 37-47, 54, 57-77, 85, 124, 127, 143, 156, 218, 224, 237, 239, 240, 251, 258, 259, 262, 287, 291, 292, 293, 295, 297, 301
Smythe, F.S.: 15
Soane, George: 247-251, 300
Soane, Sir John: 247
Somnambulist, The: 111-115
Song at the Feast of Brougham Castle: 121, 233
Soutars: 285
Southerfell-side: 22, 27, 28, 292, 294
Southey, Robert: 143, 195, 257
Sowerby, Joseph: 293, 297
St John's, Vale of: 92, 143, 257, 261, 263, 274, 291
Stanwix: 60, 71
Stockton Forest: 136, 241, 284
Stricket, Daniel: 15, 16, 25, 27, 28, 29, 77, 86, 97, 133, 156, 164, 174, 211, 260, 287, 288, 291, 293, 296, 300
Stuart, Prince Charles Edward: 17, 44, 58-77, 224
Stulkeley, William: 95
Suetonius: 241
Sullivan, Jeremiah: 289
Swan Inn: 49, 115
Swinsted / Swinside: 39, 44, 127
Tennent, William: 62
Thomson, James: 87, 177, 291
Threlkeld Hall: 233
Threlkeld, Sir Lancelot: 233-237, 238, 261
Threlkeld: 93, 240, 257, 274
Tickell, Thomas: 263
Todd, Isaak: 124, 126
Tomlinson, T.: 44,
Tongue, the: 126, 294
Trollope, Anthony: 293
Turner, M: 135,
Tynemouth: 266
Uig: 175
Ullswater: 48, 109, 111, 143, 157, 220, 253, 298
Unthank: 297
Urquhart, Sir Thomas: 285
Vince, Dr,: 158
Wadd Mines: 38, 73-4
Wade, General: 64
Wainwright, Alfred: 12-14,
Walker, Jean: 194
Walker, Tony: 10.
Walpole, Hugh: 265-6
Wasdale, Thomas: 61,
Watendlath: 274
Watermillock: 48, 221, 253
West, Thomas: 54, 252, 300
Westall, William: 258
Whiston, William: 85, 86,
White Swan: 49,
White, John Pagen: 231- 243, 299
Whitehaven: 69, 232
Wigton: 39, 43, 297
Wilkinson, Thomas: 256
Wilson, John (Christopher North): 153
Wiltonhill: 8, 10, 22, 97, 292, 294
Windermere: 48, 267, 298
Wonderful Magazine: 88
Wood, William: 77-81
Wordsworth, Dora: 242
Wordsworth, Dorothy: 104, 108-111, 121-123, 221-3, 298
Wordsworth, William: 7, 17, 104, 108-123, 143, 157, 168, 218, 221, 223, 228, 230, 238, 242, 256, 257, 258, 262, 269, 298
Wren, Mr of Wiltonhill: 9, 10, 25, 27, 29, 97, 174
Yanwath: 256

Sarah Losh
and
Wreay
Church
Stephen Matthews